CONCEPTS AND CHALLENGES

THE HUMAN BODY

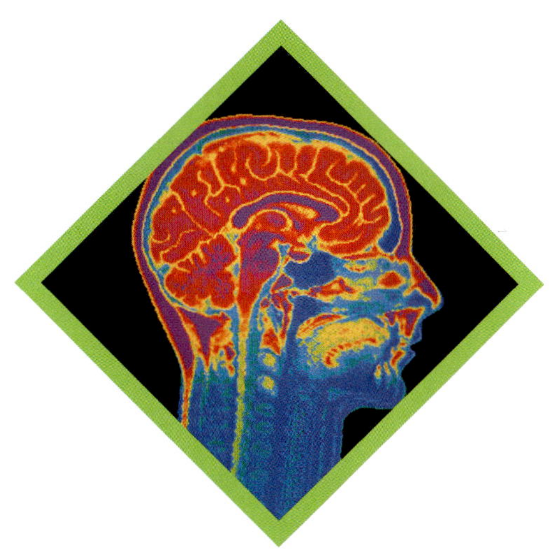

Leonard Bernstein ◆ Martin Schachter ◆ Alan Winkler ◆ Stanley Wolfe

Stanley Wolfe
Project Coordinator

GLOBE FEARON
Pearson Learning Group

Acknowledgments

Science Consultant
Dr. Richard Lowell
Ramapo College of New Jersey
Mahwah, NJ

Laboratory Consultants
Sean Devine
Science Teacher
Ridge High School
Basking Ridge, NJ

Vincent R. Dionisio
Science Teacher
Clifton High School
Clifton, NJ

Reading Consultant
Sharon Cook
Consultant
Leadership in Literacy

Internet Consultant
Janet M. Gaudino
Science Teacher
Montgomery Middle School
Skillman, NJ

ESL/ELL Consultant
Elizabeth Jimenez
Consultant
Pomona, CA

Content Reviewers
Dr. Vincent Adamo, M.D.
(pp. 32–33, 80–81, 104–105, 146–147, 170–171)
Parsippany, NJ

Ivan Dmochowski (pp. 58–59)
Helen Hay Whitney Postdoctoral Scholar
California Institute of Technology
Pasadena, CA

Rusty Lansford (Chs. 3, 5, & 6)
Senior Scientist
Division of Biology
California Institute of Technology
Pasadena, CA

Terry Moran (pp. 22–23)
Moran Research Service
Harvard, MA

Alyssa Perz-Edwards, Ph.D. (Chs. 2 & 7)
Lecturer
Duke University
Durham, NC

Xanthia Samaropoulos, M.S., M.S. (Chs. 1 & 4)
Lab Assistant Professor, Dept. of Biology
Georgetown University
Washington, DC

Teacher Reviewers
Jennifer L. Salmon
Belleville Middle School
Belleville, NJ

Robert L. Fincham
Keithley Middle School
Tacoma, WA

About the Cover: Humans are complex organisms with sophisticated organ systems that all work together. To run the race, the athletes on the cover will use their respiratory, circulatory, and nervous systems, among others. The smaller photograph is a false-color MRI image of a healthy human brain. The brain controls all of the activities of a body's organ systems.

ISBN: 0-13-024206-3

Printed in the United States of America

3 4 5 6 7 8 9 10   06 05

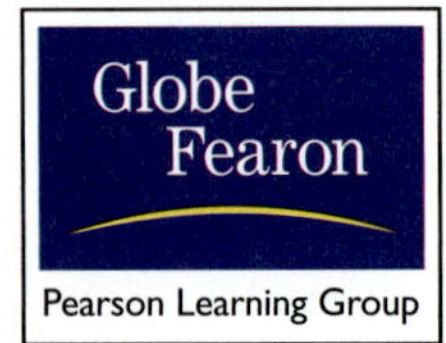

1-800-321-3106
www.pearsonlearning.com

Contents

Scientific Skills and Investigations Handbooks

Handbook A: What are scientific skills? . . . 1

Handbook B: How do you conduct a scientific investigation? . . . 9

Chapter 1 Support and Movement . . . **15**

1-1 What are tissues? . . . 16

1-2 What are organs and organ systems? . . . 18

1-3 What is the skeletal system? . . . 20

1-4 What are bones? . . . 22

1-5 How do joints work? . . . 24

1-6 What is the muscular system? . . . 26

LAB ACTIVITY: Modeling Muscle Movement . . . 28

1-7 What are the kinds of muscles? . . . 30

THE Big IDEA Integrating Technology: How are sports injuries treated? . . . 32

Chapter Summary and Challenges . . . 34

Chapter 2 Digestion and Nutrition . . . **37**

2-1 What are nutrients? . . . 38

2-2 Why are proteins important? . . . 40

2-3 Why are vitamins important? . . . 42

2-4 Why are minerals important? . . . 44

LAB ACTIVITY: Testing Foods for Nutrients . . . 46

2-5 What is a balanced diet? . . . 48

2-6 What is the digestive system? . . . 50

2-7 What is digestion? . . . 52

2-8 What happens to food in the stomach? . . . 54

2-9 What happens to food in the small intestine? . . . 56

THE Big IDEA Integrating Chemistry: What chemical reactions take place during digestion? . . . 58

2-10 How do living things get energy? . . . 60

Chapter Summary and Challenges . . . 62

Chapter 3 Transport in the Body 65

3-1 What is the circulatory system? 66
3-2 What are the parts of the heart? 68
3-3 What are blood vessels? 70
3-4 What is blood? 72
LAB ACTIVITY: Observing Blood Cells 74
3-5 What happens to blood as it circulates? 76
3-6 What is heart disease? 78
THE Big IDEA Integrating Health Technology: How is technology used to treat cardiovascular disease? 80
Chapter Summary and Challenges 82

Chapter 4 Respiration and Excretion 85

4-1 What is the respiratory system? 86
4-2 What are breathing and respiration? 88
LAB ACTIVITY: Modeling Breathing 90
4-3 What happens to air before it reaches the lungs? 92
4-4 How does oxygen get into the blood? 94
4-5 How does tobacco affect the body? 96
4-6 What is the excretory system? 98
4-7 How do the kidneys work? 100
4-8 How does the skin remove wastes? 102
THE Big IDEA Integrating Health: What happens when the body overheats? 104
Chapter Summary and Challenges 106

Chapter 5 Fighting Disease 109

5-1 How does the body fight disease? 110
5-2 What is immunity? 112
5-3 What are some bacterial diseases? 114
LAB ACTIVITY: Determining the Effectiveness of Antiseptics 116
5-4 What are some viral diseases? 118
5-5 What are noninfectious diseases? 120
THE Big IDEA Integrating History: How has disease affected us over time? 122
Chapter Summary and Challenges 124

Chapter 6 Control and Regulation 127

6-1 What is the nervous system? 128
6-2 What are the parts of the brain? 130
6-3 What are reflexes? 132
6-4 What are sense organs? 134
LAB ACTIVITY: Identifying Taste Receptors 136
6-5 How do you see? 138
6-6 How do you hear? 140
6-7 What is the endocrine system? 142
6-8 What are hormones? 144
THE Big IDEA Integrating Art: How do we respond to artistic expression? 146
6-9 How do some drugs affect the body? 148
6-10 How does alcohol affect the body? 150
Chapter Summary and Challenges 152

Chapter 7 Reproduction and Development 155

7-1 What are the parts of the female reproductive system? 156
7-2 What are the parts of the male reproductive system? 158
7-3 What is the menstrual cycle? 160
7-4 How does fertilization take place? 162
7-5 How does a human embryo develop? 164
LAB ACTIVITY: Graphing Changes in Fetal Development 166
7-6 What are the stages of human development? 168
THE Big IDEA Integrating Technology: How has technology improved life at various stages? 170
Chapter Summary and Challenges 172

Appendices

Appendix A: Metric System 175
Appendix B: Science Terms 176
Glossary 177
Index 182
Photo Credits 186

Features

Hands-On Activity

Handbook: Making Observations 2
Handbook: Organizing Living Things 3
Handbook: Calculating Area and Volume 6
Handbook: Reading a Thermometer 7
Handbook: Carrying Out an Experiment 12
1-5 Observing Joint Movements 25
2-1 Testing for Starch 39
2-6 Modeling Peristalsis 51
2-10 Calculating Calories 61
3-3 Measuring Pulse Rate 71
4-2 Exercise and Breathing Rate 89
4-4 Analyzing Exhaled Air 95
6-1 Modeling Touch Receptors 129
6-5 Analyzing Optical Illusions 139

How Do They Know That?

2-3 Vitamin K and Blood 43
2-8 Dr. William Beaumont (1785–1853) 55
3-1 Blood Transfusions 67
5-2 Edward Jenner's Discovery of Vaccinations 113
6-8 Treating Diabetes with Insulin 145
7-3 Graafian Follicles 161

Integrating the Sciences

2-2 Physical Science: Peptide Bonds 41
2-4 Earth Science: Minerals from Earth 45
3-5 Physical Science: Iron in Hemoglobin 77
6-3 Engineering: Treating Spinal Injuries with Bionics 133
6-6 Physical Science: Pitch and Frequency 141
7-4 Physical Science: Chemicals Involved in Fertilization 163

People in Science

1-7 Physical Therapist 31
2-7 Dental Hygienist 53
3-6 Cardiologist 79
4-1 Respiratory Therapist 87

Real-Life Science

1-2 Organ Transplants 19
1-6 Exercise and Muscles 27
2-5 Cholesterol 49
4-3 Protecting the Respiratory System 93
4-5 Effects of Smoking on the Human Body 97
6-7 Emergency Gland 143
6-10 Breathalyzers 151
7-2 Sexually Transmitted Diseases 159

Science and Technology

1-1 Testing Mummy DNA 17
1-4 Bone Marrow Transplants 23
3-2 Heart Valve Replacement 69
4-6 Using Sound to Break Apart Kidney Stones 99
4-7 Dialysis 101
5-4 Treatments for AIDS 119
5-5 Parkinson's Disease Research 121
6-2 Taking Pictures of the Brain 131
7-1 Treatment of Ovarian Cysts 157

INVESTIGATE

1-3 Examining Bone Structure 20
2-8 Modeling Digestion 54
2-9 Modeling Fat Digestion 56
4-3 Modeling Filtering Hairs 92
4-8 Observing Evaporation and Cooling 102
6-3 Observing Reactions 132

Web InfoSearch

1-2 Plant Organs 19
1-5 Arthritis 25
1-6 Anabolic Steroids 27
2-4 Calcium 45
2-9 Appendix 57
3-2 Artificial Hearts 67
3-3 High Blood Pressure 71
3-4 Artificial Blood 73
3-6 Pacemakers 79
5-4 Virus Mutations 119
6-4 Braille 135
6-6 Hearing in Animals 141
6-9 DARE 149
7-6 Speech Development 169

What are scientific skills?

People are naturally curious. They want to understand the world around them. They want to understand what makes flowers grow and how their own bodies work. The field of science would probably not exist if it were not for human curiosity about the natural world.

People also want to be able to make good guesses about the future. They want to know when it will rain again and which nutrients in soil grow the best crops.

Scientists use many skills to explore the world and gather information about it. These skills are called science process skills. Another name for them is science inquiry skills.

Science process skills allow you to think like a scientist. They help you identify problems and answer questions. Sometimes they help you solve problems. More often, they provide some possible answers and lead to more questions. In this book, you will use a variety of science process skills to understand the facts and theories in life science. Science process skills are not only used in science. You compare prices when you shop and you observe what happens to foods when you cook them. You predict what the weather will be by looking at the sky. In fact, science process skills are really everyday life skills that have been adapted for problem solving in science.

1 **NAME:** What is the name for the skills scientists use to solve problems?

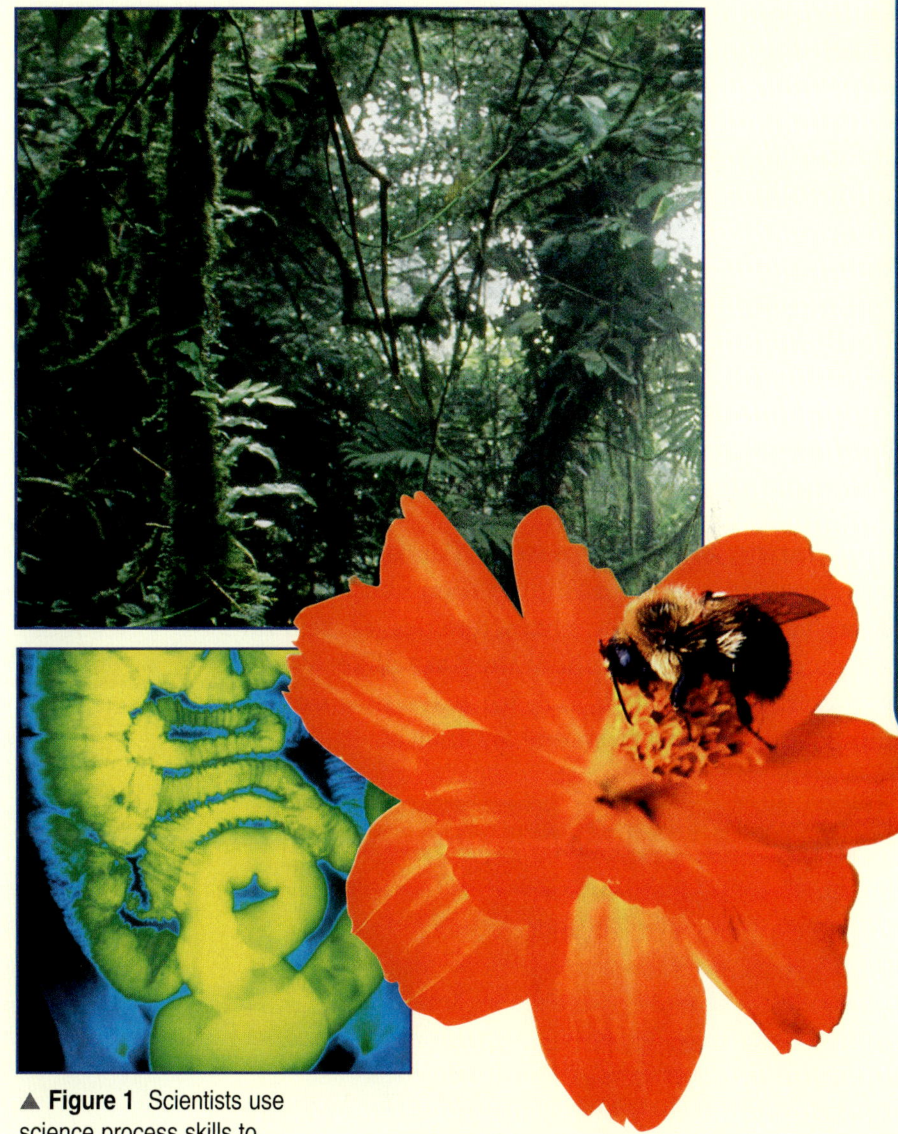

▲ **Figure 1** Scientists use science process skills to understand what makes trees grow, what attracts bees to flowers, and how the human digestive system works.

Contents

1 Observing and Comparing
2 Classifying Data
3 Modeling and Simulating
4 Measuring
5 Analyzing Data and Communicating Results
6 Making Predictions

1 Observing and Comparing

Making Observations An important part of solving any problem is observing, or using your senses to find out what is going on around you. The five senses are sight, hearing, touch, smell, and taste. When you look at the petals on a flower or touch the hard shell of a hermit crab, you are observing. When you observe, you pay close attention to everything that happens around you.

Scientists observe the world in ways that other scientists can repeat. This is a goal of scientific observation. It is expected that when a scientist has made an observation, other people will be able to make the same observation.

 **LIST:** What are the five senses?

Comparing and Contrasting Part of observing is comparing and contrasting. When you compare data, you observe the characteristics of several things or events to see how they are alike. When you contrast data, you look for ways that similar things are different from one another.

▲ **Figure 2** Crocodiles and alligators are alike in many ways. They also have many differences.

3 **COMPARE/CONTRAST:** How are a crocodile and an alligator similar? How are they different?

Using Tools to Observe Sometimes an object is too small to see with your eyes alone. You need a special tool to help you make observations. One tool that life scientists use to observe things is a microscope. A microscope magnifies, or makes objects appear larger than they actually are.

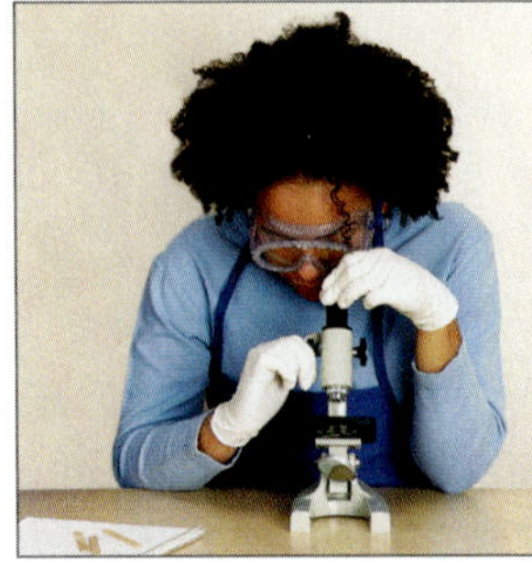

▲ **Figure 3** Scientists use microscopes to observe very small objects.

4 **INFER:** What are some things that scientists might need a microscope to see?

MAKING OBSERVATIONS

You and a partner will need 2 shoeboxes with lids, 2 rubber bands, and several small objects.

1. Place several small objects into the shoebox. Do not let your partner see what you put into the shoebox.
2. Cover the shoebox with the lid. Put a rubber band around the shoebox to keep the lid on.
3. Exchange shoeboxes with your partner.
4. Gently shake, turn, and rattle the shoebox.
5. Try to describe what is in the shoebox without opening it. Write your descriptions on a sheet of paper.

Practicing Your Skills

6. **IDENTIFY:** What science process skill did you use?
7. **IDENTIFY:** Which of your senses was most important to you?
8. **ANALYZE:** Direct observation is seeing something with your eyes or hearing it with your ears. Indirect observation involves using a model or past experience to make a guess about something. Which kind of observation did you use?

2 Classifying Data

Key Term

data: information you collect when you observe something

Collecting and Classifying Data The information you collect when you observe something is called **data.** The data from an experiment or from observations you have made are first recorded, or written down. Then, they are classified.

When you classify data, you group things together based on how they are alike. This information often comes from making comparisons as you observe. You may classify by size, shape, color, use, or any other important feature. Classifying data helps you recognize and understand the relationships between things. Classification makes studying large groups of things easier. For example, life scientists use classification to organize the different types of living things.

5 **EXPLAIN:** How can you classify data?

Hands-On Activity
ORGANIZING LIVING THINGS

You will need 15 index cards with photographs of living things taped to them.

1. Look at the pictures on the index cards. Classify the photographs into two categories, *Plants* and *Animals*.
2. Look at the pictures you classified as *Plants*. Choose a general characteristic, such as if they have flowers or not. Divide the plants into two groups based on that specific characteristic.
3. Repeat Step 2 for the pictures you classified as *Animals*.
4. Divide these four groups into smaller groups.

Practicing Your Skills

5. **ANALYZE:** How did you classify the pictures?
6. **EXPLAIN:** Why is a classification system useful?

3 Modeling and Simulating

Key Terms

model: tool scientists use to represent an object or process

simulation: computer model that usually shows a process

Modeling Sometimes things are too small to see with your eyes alone. Other times, an object is too large to see. You may need a model to help you examine the object. A **model** is a good way to show what a very small or a very large object looks like. A model can have more details than what may be seen with just your eyes. It can be used to represent a process or an object that is hard to explain with words. A model can be a three-dimensional picture, a drawing, a computer image, or a diagram.

6 **DEFINE:** What is a model?

Simulating A **simulation** is a kind of model that shows a process. It is often done using a computer. You can use a simulation to predict the outcome of an experiment. Scientists use simulations to study everything from the insides of a frog to the development of an embryo.

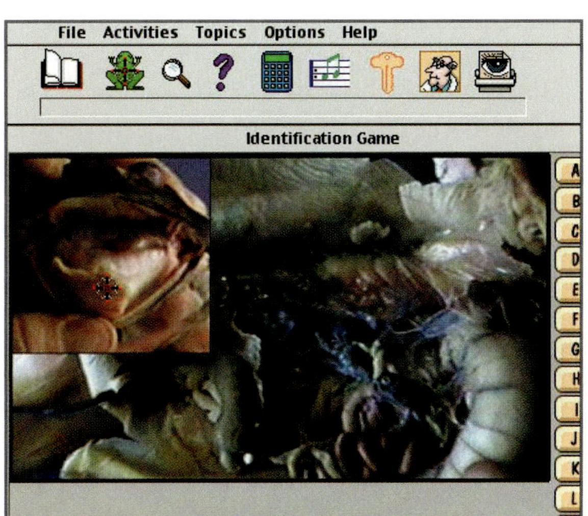

▲ **Figure 4** Some schools use a computer simulation program instead of dissecting a preserved frog.

7 **DEFINE:** What is a simulation?

4 Measuring

Key Terms

unit: amount used to measure something

meter: basic unit of length or distance

mass: amount of matter in something

gram: basic unit of mass

volume: amount of space an object takes up

liter: basic unit of liquid volume

meniscus: curve at the surface of a liquid in a thin tube

temperature: measure of the amount of heat energy something contains

Two Systems of Measurement When you measure, you compare an unknown value with a known value using standard units. A **unit** is an amount used to measure something. The metric system is an international system of measurement. Examples of metric units are the gram, the kilometer, and the liter. In the United States, the English system and the metric system are both used. Examples of units in the English system are the pound, the foot, and the gallon.

There is also a more modern form of the metric system called SI. The letters *SI* stand for the French words *Système International.* Many of the units in the SI are the same as those in the metric system.

The metric and SI systems are both based on units of 10. This makes them easy to use. Each unit in these systems is ten times greater than the one before it. To show a change in the size of a unit, you add a prefix to the unit. The prefix tells you whether the unit is larger or smaller. For example, a centimeter is ten times bigger than a millimeter.

PREFIXES AND THEIR MEANINGS	
kilo-	one thousand (1,000)
hecto-	one hundred (100)
deca-	ten (10)
deci-	one-tenth (1/10)
centi-	one-hundredth (1/100)
milli-	one-thousandth (1/1,000)

◀ **Figure 5**

8 IDENTIFY: What are two measurement systems?

Units of Length Length is the distance from one point to another. In the metric system, the basic unit of length or distance is the **meter.** A meter is about the length from a doorknob to the floor. Longer distances, such as the distances between cities, are measured in kilometers. A kilometer is 1,000 meters. Centimeters and millimeters measure shorter distances. A centimeter is 1/100 of a meter. A millimeter is 1/1,000 of a meter. Figure 6 compares common units of length. It also shows the abbreviation for each unit.

SI/METRIC UNITS OF LENGTH	
1,000 millimeters (mm)	1 meter (m)
100 centimeters (cm)	1 meter
10 decimeters (dm)	1 meter
10 millimeters	1 centimeter
1,000 meters	1 kilometer (km)

▲ **Figure 6**

Length can be measured with a meter stick. A meter stick is 1 m long and is divided into 100 equal lengths by numbered lines. The distance between each of these lines is equal to 1 cm. Each centimeter is divided into ten equal parts. Each one of these parts is equal to 1 mm.

▲ **Figure 7** A meter stick is divided into centimeters and millimeters.

9 CALCULATE: How many centimeters are there in 3 m?

Measuring Area Do you know how people find the area of the floor of a room? They measure the length and the width of the room. Then, they multiply the two numbers. You can find the area of any rectangle by multiplying its length by its width. Area is expressed in square units, such as square meters (m^2) or square centimeters (cm^2).

Area = length × width

5 cm | 50 cm^2 | 10 cm

◀ **Figure 8** The area of a rectangle equals length times width.

10 **CALCULATE:** What is the area of a rectangle 2 cm × 3 cm?

Mass and Weight The amount of matter in something is its **mass.** The basic metric unit of mass is called a **gram (g).** A paper clip has about 1 g of mass. Mass is measured with an instrument called a balance. A balance works like a seesaw. It compares an unknown mass with a known mass.

One kind of balance that is commonly used to measure mass is a triple-beam balance. A triple-beam balance has a pan. The object being measured is placed on the pan. The balance also has three beams. Weights, called riders, are moved along each beam until the object on the pan is balanced. Each rider gives a reading in grams. The mass of the object is equal to the total readings of all three riders.

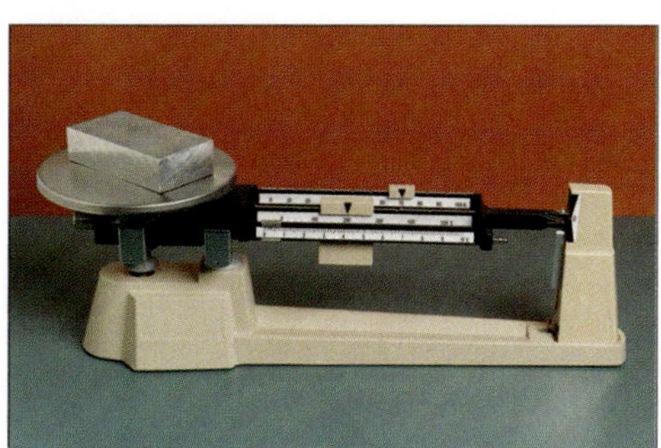

◀ **Figure 9** A triple-beam balance

Mass and weight are related; however, they are not the same. The weight of an object is a measure of Earth's pull of gravity between Earth and that object. Gravity is the force that pulls objects toward the center of Earth. The strength of the pull of gravity between two objects depends on the distance between the objects and how much mass they each contain. So, the weight changes as its distance from the center of Earth changes.

11 **IDENTIFY:** What instrument is used to measure mass?

Volume The amount of space an object takes up is its **volume.** You can measure the volume of liquids and solids. Liquid volume is usually measured in **liters.** Soft drinks in the United States often come in 2-liter bottles.

A graduated cylinder is used to measure liquid volume. Graduated cylinders are calibrated, or marked off, at regular intervals. Look at Figure 10. It shows a graduated cylinder. On this graduated cylinder, each small line is equal to 0.05 mL. The longer lines mark off every 0.25 mL up to 5.00 mL. However, every graduated cylinder is not calibrated in this manner. They come in different sizes up to 2,000 mL, with different calibrations.

Always read the measurement at eye level. If you are using a glass graduated cylinder, you will need to read the mark on the graduated cylinder closest to the bottom of the meniscus. A **meniscus** is the curve at the surface of a liquid in a thin tube. A plastic graduated cylinder does not show a meniscus.

5.00
4.75
4.50
4.25
4.00
3.75
3.50
3.25
3.00
2.75
2.50
2.25
2.00

▲ **Figure 10** This glass graduated cylinder shows a meniscus.

The volume of solid objects is often measured in cubic centimeters. One cubic centimeter is the same as 1 milliliter (mL).

Look at Figure 11. Each side of the cube is 1 cm long. The volume of the cube is 1 cubic centimeter (cm^3). Now, look at the drawing of the box in Figure 12. Its length is 3 cm. Its width is 2 cm. Its height is 2 cm. The volume of the box can be found by multiplying length by width by height. In this case, volume equals $3 \times 2 \times 2$. Therefore, the volume of the box in Figure 12 is 12 cm^3.

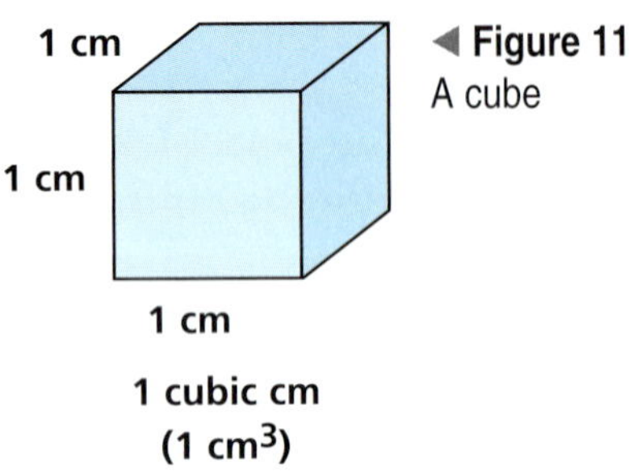

◀ **Figure 11**
A cube

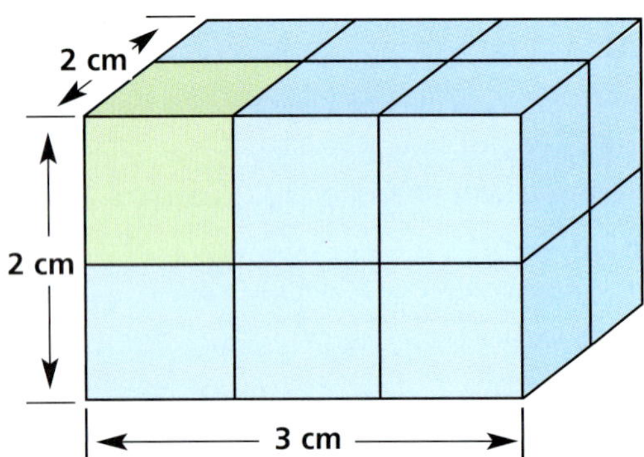

▲ **Figure 12** The volume of a box equals length by width by height.

$$V = l \times w \times h$$

If you have a box that is 10 cm on each side, its volume would be 1,000 cm^3. A liter is the same as 1,000 cm^3. One liter of liquid will fill the box exactly.

12 **CALCULATE:** How many milliliters of water would fill a 12-cm^3 box?

CALCULATING AREA AND VOLUME

You will need 3 boxes of different sizes, paper, and a metric ruler.

1. Measure the length, width, and height of each box in centimeters. Record each measurement in your notes.
2. Calculate the volume of each box. Record each volume in your notes.
3. Find the surface area of each box. Record each area in your notes.

Practicing Your Skills

4. **ANALYZE:** Which of the three boxes has the largest volume?
5. **CALCULATE:** How many milliliters of liquid would fill each box?
6. **ANALYZE:** What is the surface area of the largest box?

Temperature **Temperature** is a measure of the amount of heat energy something contains. An instrument that measures temperature is called a thermometer.

Most thermometers are glass tubes. At the bottom of the tube is a wider part, called the bulb. The bulb is filled with liquid. Liquids that are often used include mercury, colored alcohol, or colored water. When heat is added, the liquid expands, or gets larger. It rises in the glass tube. When heat is taken away, the liquid contracts, or gets smaller. The liquid falls in the tube. On the side of the tube is a series of marks. You read the temperature by looking at the mark on the tube where the liquid stops.

Temperature can be measured on three different scales. These scales are the Fahrenheit (F) scale, the Celsius (C) scale, and the Kelvin (K) scale. The Fahrenheit scale is part of the English system of measurement. The Celsius scale is usually used in science. Almost all scientists, even in the United States, use the Celsius scale. Each unit on the Celsius scale is a degree Celsius (°C). The degree Celsius is the metric unit of temperature. Water freezes at 0°C. It boils at 100°C.

Scientists working with very low temperatures use the Kelvin scale. The Kelvin scale is part of the SI measurement system. It begins at absolute zero, or 0K. This number indicates, in theory at least, a total lack of heat.

COMPARING TEMPERATURE SCALES			
	Kelvin	Fahrenheit	Celsius
Boiling point of water	373K	212°F	100°C
Human body temperature	310K	98.6°F	37°C
Freezing point of water	273K	32°F	0°C
Absolute zero	0K	−459.67°F	−273.15°C

▲ **Figure 13**

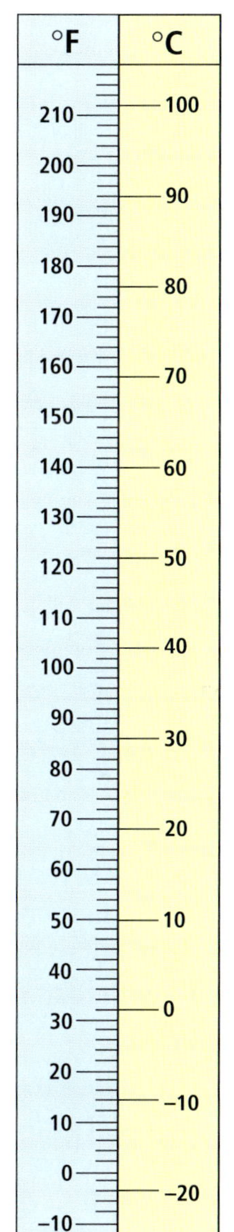

◀ **Figure 14** The Fahrenheit and Celsius scales

13 **NAME:** What are the three scales used to measure temperature?

Hands-On Activity

READING A THERMOMETER

You will need safety goggles, a lab apron, 2 beakers, a heat source, ice water, a wax pencil, a ruler, and a standard Celsius thermometer.

1. Boil some water in a beaker. ⚠**CAUTION:** Be very careful when working with heat. Place your thermometer in the beaker. Do not let the thermometer touch the sides or bottom of the beaker. Wait until the mercury rises as far as it will go. Record the temperature.
2. Fill a beaker with ice water. Place the unmarked thermometer into this beaker. Wait until the mercury goes as low as it will go. Record the temperature.

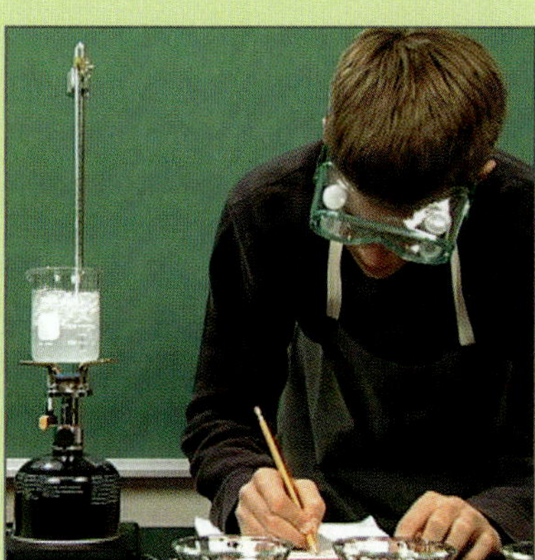

▲ **STEP 1** Record the temperature of the boiling water.

Practicing Your Skills

3. **IDENTIFY:** What is the temperature at which the mercury rose as high as it would go?
4. **IDENTIFY:** What is the temperature at which the mercury went as low as it would go?

5 Analyzing Data and Communicating Results

Key Term

communication: sharing information

Analyzing Data When you organize information, you put it in a logical order. In scientific experiments, it is important to organize your data. Data collected during an experiment are not very useful unless they are organized and easy to read. It is also important to organize your data if you plan to share the results of your experiment.

Scientists often organize information visually by using data tables, charts, graphs, and diagrams. By using tables, charts, graphs, and diagrams, scientists can display a lot of information in a small space. They also make it easier to compare and interpret data.

Tables are made up of rows and columns. Columns run up and down. Rows run from left to right. Tables usually show numerical data. Information in the table can be arranged in time order. It can also be set up to show patterns or trends. A table showing the number of endangered species born over a period of time, for example, can reveal a pattern of extinction rates. Figure 15 shows a table of elements in living things.

ELEMENTS FOUND IN LIVING THINGS	
Element	**Percentage**
Oxygen	64.5
Carbon	18
Hydrogen	10
Sulfur, phosphorus, and others	4.5
Nitrogen	3

▲ **Figure 15**

Graphs, such as bar graphs, line graphs, and circle graphs, often use special coloring, shading, or patterns to represent information. Keys indicate what the special markings represent. Line graphs have horizontal (x) and vertical (y) axes to indicate such things as time and quantities.

14 EXPLAIN: How do tables and graphs help you analyze data?

Sharing Results When you talk to a friend, you are communicating, or sharing information. If you write a letter or a report, you are also communicating but in a different way. Scientists communicate all the time. They communicate to share results, information, and opinions. They write books and magazine or newspaper articles. They may also create Web sites about their work. This is called written **communication.**

Graphs are a visual way to communicate. The circle graph in Figure 16 is showing the same information as Figure 15. The circle graph presents the information in a different way.

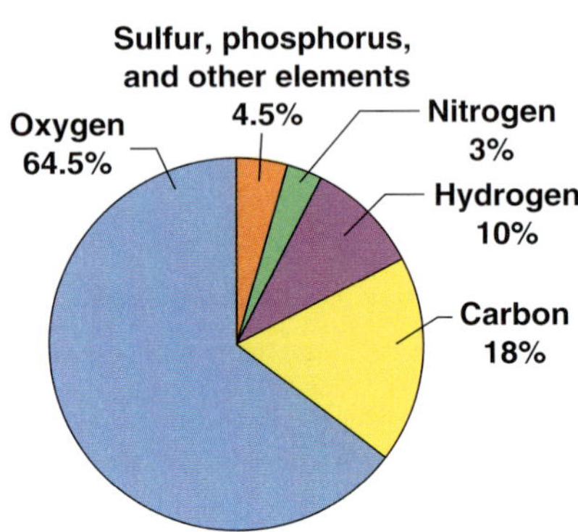

▲ **Figure 16** Circle graphs are a good way to show parts of a whole.

15 LIST: What are some ways to communicate the results of an experiment?

6 Making Predictions

Key Terms

infer: to form a conclusion

predict: to state ahead of time what you think is going to happen

Thinking of Possibilities When you **infer** something, you form a conclusion. This is called making an inference. Your conclusion will usually be based on observations or past experience. You may use logic to form your statement. Your statement might be supported by evidence and perhaps can be tested by an experiment. An inference is not a fact. It is only one possible explanation.

When you **predict,** you state ahead of time what you think will happen. Predictions about future events are based on inferences, evidence, or past experience. The two science process skills of inferring and predicting are very closely related.

16 CONTRAST: What is the difference between inferring and predicting?

How do you conduct a scientific investigation?

By now, you should have a good understanding of the science process skills. These skills are used to solve many science problems. There is also a basic procedure, or plan, that scientists usually follow when conducting investigations. Some people call this procedure the scientific method.

The scientific method is a series of steps that can serve as a guide to solving problems or answering questions. It uses many of the science process skills you know, such as observing and predicting.

Not all experiments use all of the steps in the scientific method. Some experiments follow all of them, but in a different order. In fact, there is no one right scientific method. Each problem is different. Some problems may require steps that another problem would not. However, most investigations will follow the same basic procedure.

1 **DESCRIBE:** What is the scientific method?

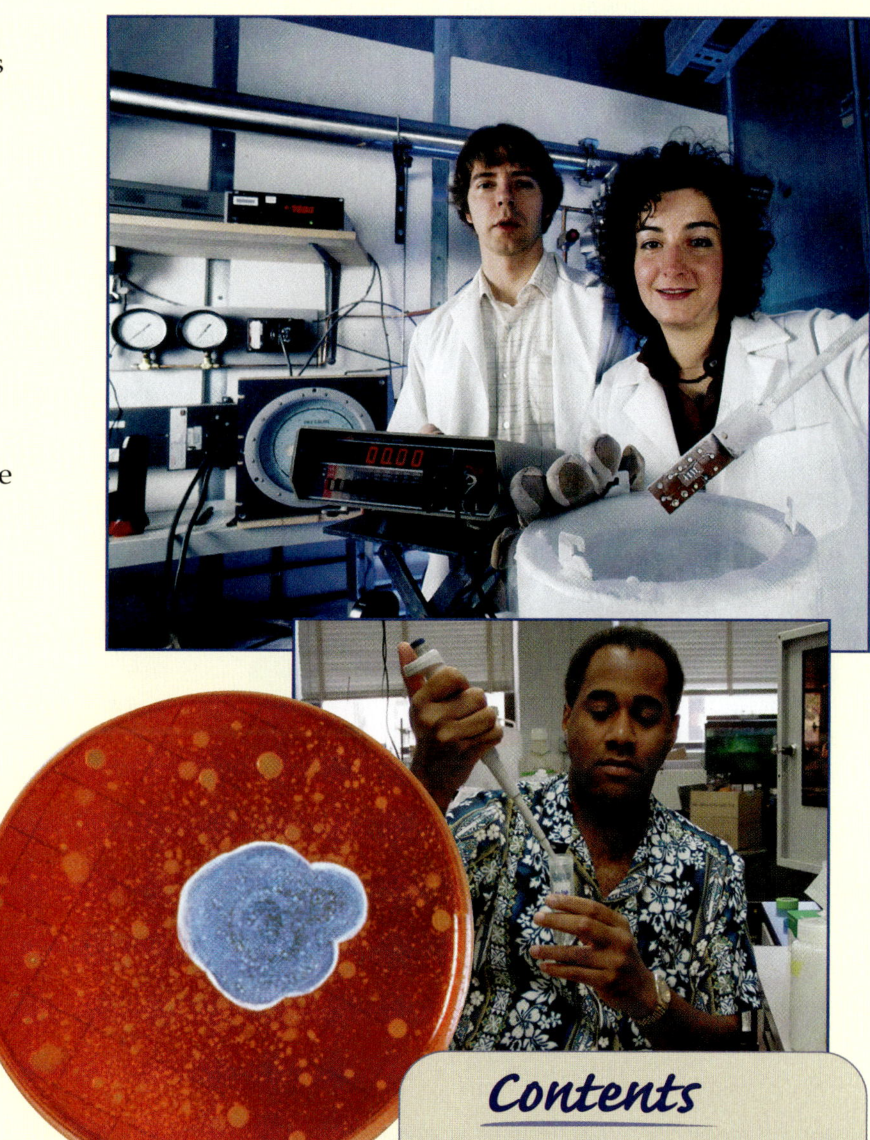

▲ **Figure 1** Scientists use the scientific method to guide experiments.

Contents

1 Identifying a Problem and Doing Research
2 Forming a Hypothesis
3 Designing and Carrying Out an Experiment
4 Recording and Analyzing Data
5 Stating a Conclusion
6 Writing a Report

1 Identifying a Problem and Doing Research

Starting an Investigation Scientists often state a problem as a question. This is the first step in a scientific investigation. Most experiments begin by asking a scientific question. That is, they ask a question that can be answered by gathering evidence. This question is the reason for the scientific investigation. It also helps determine how the investigation will proceed.

Have you ever done background research for a science project? When you do this kind of research, you are looking for data that others have already obtained on the same subject. You can gather research by reading books, magazines, and newspapers, and by using the Internet to find out what other scientists have done. Doing research is the first step of gathering evidence for a scientific investigation.

2 **IDENTIFY:** What is the first step of a scientific investigation?

BUILDING SCIENCE SKILLS

Researching Background Information Suppose you notice that there is moss growing in your backyard. You also notice that the moss in the shady area of your backyard seems to grow faster and look healthier than the moss that grows in sunlight. You wonder if sunlight affects moss growth.

To determine if sunlight affects moss growth, look for information on moss in encyclopedias, in botany books, or on the Internet. Put your findings in a report.

▲ **Figure 2** Moss grows best in shady areas.

2 Forming a Hypothesis

Key Terms

hypothesis: suggested answer to a question or problem

theory: set of hypotheses that have been supported by testing over and over again

Focusing the Investigation Scientists usually state clearly what they expect to find out in an investigation. This is called stating a hypothesis. A **hypothesis** is a suggested answer to a question or a solution to a problem. Stating a hypothesis helps to keep you focused on the problem and helps you decide what to test.

To form their hypotheses, scientists must think of possible explanations for a set of observations or they must suggest possible answers to a scientific question. One of those explanations becomes the hypothesis. In science, a hypothesis must include something that can be tested.

A hypothesis is more than just a guess. It must consider observations, past experiences, and previous knowledge. It is an inference turned into a statement that can be tested. A set of hypotheses that have been supported by testing over and over again by many scientists is called a **theory.** An example is the theory that explains how living things have evolved, or changed, over time.

A hypothesis can take the form of an "if…then" statement. A well-worded hypothesis is a guide for how to set up and perform an experiment.

3 **DESCRIBE:** How does a scientist form a hypothesis?

BUILDING SCIENCE SKILLS

Developing a Hypothesis If you are testing how sunlight affects moss growth, you might write down this hypothesis:

Moss that grows in the shade is healthier than moss that grows in sunlight.

However, what do you mean by healthier? Is the moss greener? Does it grow faster? You need to make your hypothesis specific. Revise the hypothesis above to make it more specific.

3 Designing and Carrying Out an Experiment

Key Terms

variable: anything that can affect the outcome of an experiment

constant: something that does not change

controlled experiment: experiment in which all the conditions except one are kept constant

Testing the Hypothesis Scientists need to plan how to test their hypotheses. This means they must design an experiment. The plan must be a step-by-step procedure. It should include a record of any observations made or measurements taken.

All experiments must take variables into account. A **variable** is anything that can affect the outcome of an experiment. Room temperature, amount of sunlight, and water vapor in the air are just some of the many variables that could affect the outcome of an experiment.

4 **DEFINE:** What is a variable?

Controlling the Experiment One of the variables in an experiment should be what you are testing. This is what you will change during the experiment. All other variables need to remain the same. In this experiment, you will vary the amount of sunlight.

A **constant** is something that does not change. If there are no constants in your experiment, you will not be sure why you got the results you did. An experiment in which all the conditions except one are kept constant is called a **controlled experiment.**

Some experiments have two setups. In one setup, called the control, nothing is changed. In the other setup, the variable being tested is changed. Later, the control group can be compared with the other group to provide useful data.

5 **EXPLAIN:** Explain how a controlled experiment is set up.

Designing the Procedure Suppose you now want to design an experiment to determine if sunlight affects moss growth. You have your hypothesis. You decide your procedure is to grow moss. Your procedure will be to grow one moss plant in sunlight and the other in shade. You will then check your plants after a few days to see if your hypothesis is correct.

Suppose you water the moss that is growing in the sunlight but forget to water the moss in the shade? The moss in the sunlight might grow faster than the moss in the shade. Is the difference caused by the sunlight or by the water? You would have no way of knowing if your experiment had more than one variable.

In designing your experiment, you need to identify the variables. The amount of water you give the mosses, temperature, and the type of soil are all variables that could affect the outcome of your experiment. Everything about growing the mosses needs to be the same except the amount of sunlight each receives.

Finally, you should decide on the data you will collect. How will you measure the "health" of the moss? In this case, you might want to record the thickness of the moss, its color, and whether it reproduces.

The hands-on activity on page 12 is an example of an experiment you might have designed.

6 **LIST:** How do constants and variables affect an experiment?

Hands-On Activity

CARRYING OUT AN EXPERIMENT

You will need 4 clumps of fresh moss, 4 medium-sized paper cups, soil, a hand lens, a metric ruler, water, and safety goggles.

1. Fill the four paper cups with the soil and plant a clump of moss in each cup. Label cups 1 and 2 *Sunlight.* Label cups 3 and 4 *Shade*.
2. Examine each moss plant with a hand lens. Measure the heights of each sample. Record your observations in your notes.
3. Place cups 1 and 2 in an area where the moss plants will receive sunlight for most of the day. Place cups 3 and 4 where the moss plants will be in shade for most of the day.
4. Water the moss plants each day. Be sure to give the same amount of water to each plant.
5. After a week, examine the moss plants with a hand lens. Describe the moss plants in each cup.

▲ **STEP 1** Plant a clump of moss in each cup.

Practicing Your Skills

6. **COMPARE:** Compare the color of the moss plants grown in direct sunlight with the color of the moss plants grown in indirect sunlight.
7. **MEASURE:** Measure the heights of each sample. Is there a relationship between height and sunlight?

4 Recording and Analyzing Data

Dealing With Data During an experiment, you must keep careful notes about what you observe. For example, you might need to note down the time of day that you made your observations. Was there any change of temperature or color? This is important information that might affect your conclusion.

At the end of an experiment, you will need to study the data to find any patterns. Much of the data you will deal with is written text, such as a report or a summary of an experiment. However, scientific information is often a set of numbers or facts presented in other, more visual ways. These visual presentations can make the information easier to understand. Tables, charts, and graphs can help you understand a collection of facts on a topic.

After your data have been organized, you need to ask what the data show. Do they support your hypothesis? Do they show something wrong in your experiment? Do you need to gather more data by performing another experiment?

7 **LIST:** What are some ways to display data?

BUILDING SCIENCE SKILLS

Analyzing Data You made the following notes during your experiment. How would you display this information?

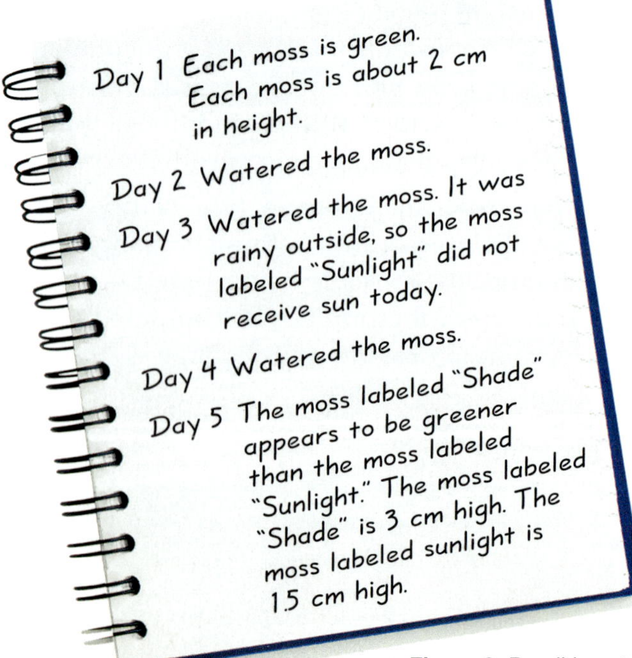

▲ **Figure 3** Possible notes

5 Stating a Conclusion

Drawing Conclusions A conclusion is a statement that sums up what you have learned from an experiment. When you draw a conclusion, you need to decide whether the data you collected supported your hypothesis. You may need to repeat an experiment several times before you can draw any conclusions from it. Conclusions often lead you to ask new questions and plan new experiments to answer them. Sometimes a scientist's conclusion is to find that his or her hypothesis was incorrect. This will then lead to a new hypothesis.

8 **EXPLAIN:** Why might it be necessary to repeat an experiment?

BUILDING SCIENCE SKILLS

Stating a Conclusion Review your hypothesis statement regarding the effect of sunlight on moss plants. Then, review the data you obtained during your experiment.

- Was your hypothesis correct? Use your observations to support your answer.
- Which moss plants grew best? What type of light is best for the growth of moss plants?

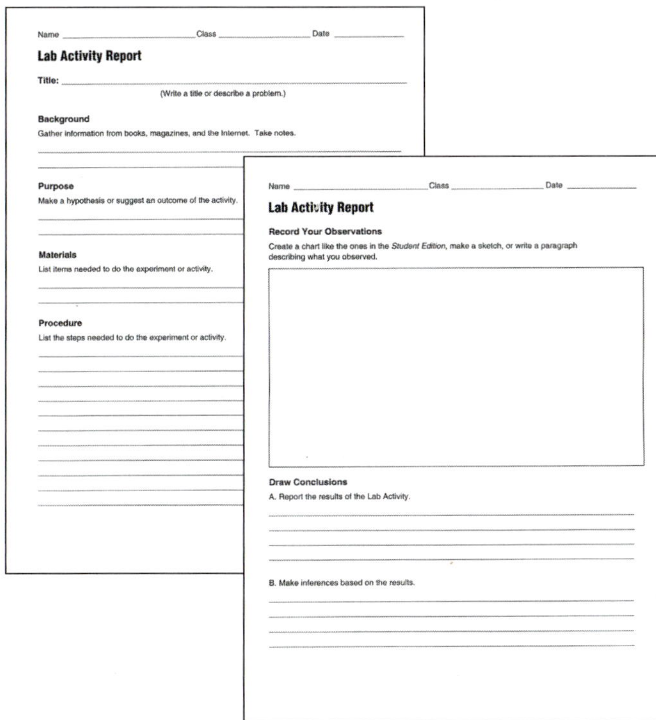
Name ____ Class ____ Date ____

Lab Activity Report

Title: ____
(Write a title or describe a problem.)

Background
Gather information from books, magazines, and the Internet. Take notes.

Purpose
Make a hypothesis or suggest an outcome of the activity.

Materials
List items needed to do the experiment or activity.

Procedure
List the steps needed to do the experiment or activity.

Name ____ Class ____ Date ____

Lab Activity Report

Record Your Observations
Create a chart like the ones in the *Student Edition*, make a sketch, or write a paragraph describing what you observed.

Draw Conclusions
A. Report the results of the Lab Activity.

B. Make inferences based on the results.

▲ **Figure 4** Throughout this program, you may use forms like these to organize your lab reports.

6 Writing a Report

Communicating Results Scientists keep careful written records of their observations and findings. These records are used to create a lab report. Lab reports are a form of written communication. They explain what happened in the experiment. A good lab report should be written so that anyone reading it can duplicate the experiment. It should contain the following information:

- A title
- A purpose
- Background information
- Your hypothesis
- Materials used
- Your step-by-step procedure
- Your observations
- Your recorded data
- Your analysis of the data
- Your conclusions

Your conclusions should relate back to the questions you asked in the "purpose" section of your report. Also, the report should point out any experimental errors that might have caused unexpected results. For example, did you follow the steps in the correct order? Did an unexpected variable interfere with your results? Was your equipment clean and in good working order? This explanation of possible errors should also be part of your conclusions.

9 **EXPLAIN:** Why is it important to explain possible errors in your lab report?

BUILDING SCIENCE SKILLS

Writing a Lab Report Write a lab report to communicate to other scientists your discoveries about the effect of sunlight on moss plants. Your lab report should include a title, your hypothesis statement, a list of materials that you used, the procedure, and your observations, and your conclusions. Try to include one table of data in your report.

LAB SAFETY

Working in a science laboratory can be both exciting and meaningful. However, you must always be aware of safety precautions when carrying out experiments. There are a few basic rules that should be followed in any science laboratory:

- Read all instructions carefully before the start of an experiment. Follow all instructions exactly and in the correct order.
- Check your equipment to make sure it is clean and working properly.
- Never taste, smell, or touch any substance in the lab that you are not told to do so. Never eat or drink anything in the lab. Do not chew gum.
- Never work alone. Tell a teacher at once if an accident occurs.

Experiments that use chemicals or heat can be dangerous. The following list of rules and symbols will help you avoid accidents. There are also rules about what to do if an accident does occur. Here are some rules to remember when working in a lab:

1. Do not use glass that is chipped or metal objects with broken edges. Do not try to clean up broken glassware yourself. Notify your teacher if a piece of glassware is broken.

2. Do not use electrical cords with loose plugs or frayed ends. Do not let electrical cords cross in front of working areas. Do not use electrical equipment near water.

3. Be very careful when using sharp objects such as scissors, knives, or tweezers. Always cut in a direction away from your body.

4. Be careful when you are using a heat source. Use proper equipment, such as tongs or a ringstand, when handling hot objects.

5. Confine loose clothing and hair when working with an open flame. Be sure you know the location of the nearest fire extinguisher. Never reach across an open flame.

6. Be careful when working with poisonous or toxic substances. Never mix chemicals without directions from your teacher. Remove any long jewelry that might hang down and end up in chemicals. Avoid touching your eyes or mouth when working with chemicals.

7. Use extreme care when working with acids and bases. Never mix acids and bases without direction from your teacher. Never smell anything directly. Use caution when handling chemicals that produce fumes.

8. Wear safety goggles, especially when working with an open flame, chemicals, and any liquids.

9. Wear lab aprons when working with substances of any sort, especially chemicals.

10. Use caution when handling or collecting plants. Some plants can be harmful if they are touched or eaten.

11. Use caution when handling live animals. Some animals can injure you or spread disease. Handle all live animals as humanely as possible.

12. Dispose of all equipment and materials properly. Keep your work area clean at all times.

13. Always wash your hands thoroughly with soap and water after handling chemicals or live organisms.

14. Follow the ⚠ CAUTION and safety symbols you see used throughout this book when doing labs or other activities.

Chapter 1 Support and Movement

▲ **Figure 1-1** Physical activities, such as figure skating, require strength and flexibility.

Humans have an internal skeleton made of bone and cartilage. This skeleton acts as a flexible framework that supports the body and allows for a variety of movements. Joints and the muscles attached to the bones allow different types of movements, such as stretching, twisting, and turning.

▶Why do you think strong bones and muscles are important to the athletes in Figure 1-1?

Contents

- **1-1** What are tissues?
- **1-2** What are organs and organ systems?
- **1-3** What is the skeletal system?
- **1-4** What are bones?
- **1-5** How do joints work?
- **1-6** What is the muscular system?
- ■ **Lab Activity:** Modeling Muscle Movement
- **1-7** What are the kinds of muscles?
- ■ **The Big Idea:** How are sports injuries treated?

1-1 What are tissues?

Objective

Describe the four main kinds of tissues.

Key Terms

tissue: group of cells that look alike and work together

epithelial (ehp-ih-THEE-lee-uhl) **tissue:** tissue that covers and protects parts of the body

connective tissue: tissue that holds parts of the body together

ligament: type of tissue that connects bones

tendon: type of tissue that connects muscle to bone

Tissues On a baseball team, the players work together. They wear uniforms that make them look alike. In multicellular organisms, cells work as teams. A group of cells that look alike and work together make up a **tissue.** Tissues are named for the jobs they do. There are four main kinds of tissue.

1 **DEFINE:** What is a tissue?

Muscle Tissue Muscle tissue makes up muscles. Muscle tissue is made up of cells that can become shorter. There are different kinds of muscle tissue. One kind is attached to bones. When these muscles shorten, they pull on bones and make the bones move.

 **RELATE:** How do some muscles and bones work together?

Covering Tissue The skin that covers your body is made of **epithelial tissue.** Epithelial tissue is made up of cells that join tightly together. Epithelial tissue also covers many parts inside your body. It protects your body by keeping harmful microscopic organisms out of your body.

3 **NAME:** What type of tissue is skin?

Connective Tissue Tissue that holds some parts of the body together is called **connective tissue.** Connective tissue also supports and protects the body. Bone is a connective tissue. Other kinds of connective tissue are ligaments and tendons. **Ligaments** connect bones to one another. **Tendons** connect muscles to bones.

Blood is a liquid connective tissue. It has blood cells that float in a yellow liquid. Blood carries food, gases, and other important substances to and from all the cells in the body.

 **LIST:** What are four kinds of connective tissue?

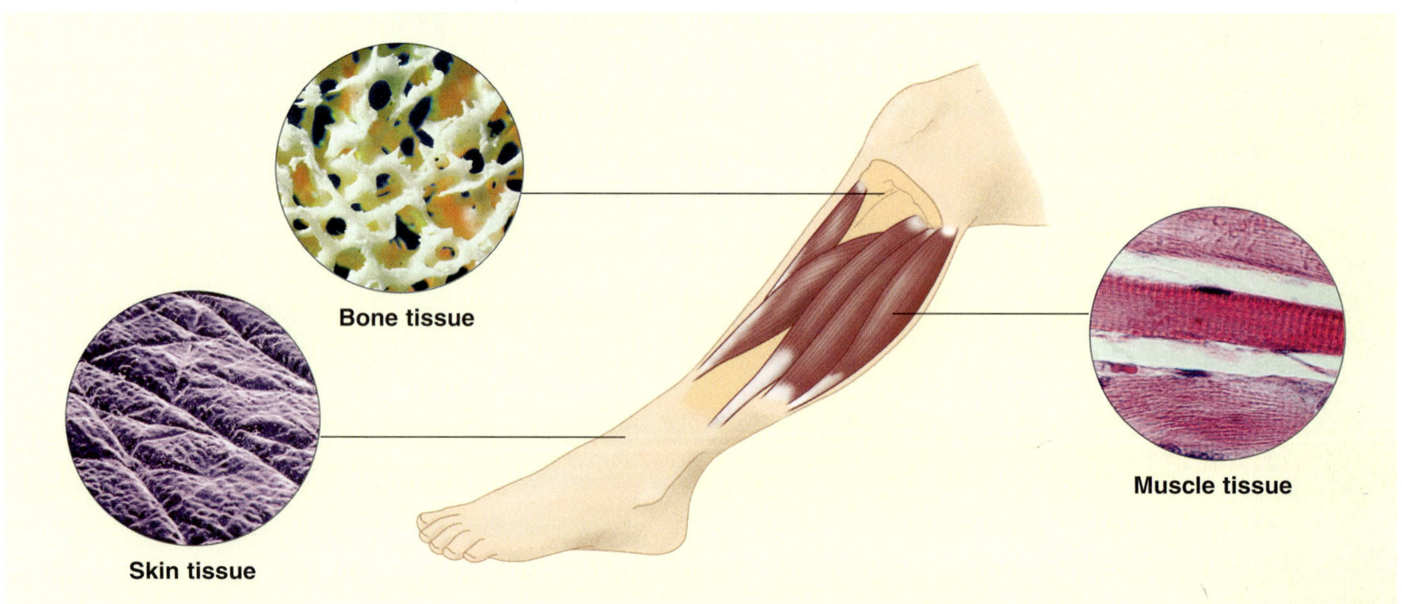

▲ **Figure 1-2** The human body is made of many different kinds of tissue.

Nerve Tissue Nerve tissue is made up of nerve cells, or neurons. Nerve tissue carries messages. It causes muscles to act. It controls breathing, digestion, and heartbeat. Your brain and spinal cord are made mostly of nerve tissue.

 **INFER:** What is the function of the brain?

CHECKING CONCEPTS

1. What are the four main types of tissue?
2. What is one function of muscle tissue?
3. Where could you find epithelial tissue?
4. What type of tissue makes up the brain?
5. What type of tissue connects muscles to bones?

THINKING CRITICALLY

6. **CONTRAST:** What are the functions of muscle, connective, and nerve tissues?
7. **INFER:** Why do you think blood is classified as connective tissue?

HEALTH AND SAFETY TIP

The ligaments in the knee connect the upper and lower leg bones. This area gets injured very easily. The knee carries a large portion of the body's weight. The knee also contains many ligaments that can be strained or even torn. One way to prevent this type of injury is by stretching before and after exercising and by not pushing yourself too far.

Science and Technology

TESTING MUMMY DNA

Three thousand years ago, the ancient Egyptians carefully wrapped, dried, and preserved the bodies of people who died, producing mummies. Although these mummies are very fragile today, some of their tissues have been so well preserved that they still contain fragments of DNA. Recently, scientists have been carefully removing small tissue samples from mummies and studying them.

The teeth are tissues that have most of their DNA still intact. The scientists test the DNA samples from the teeth by comparing them to DNA strands of closely related modern-day people.

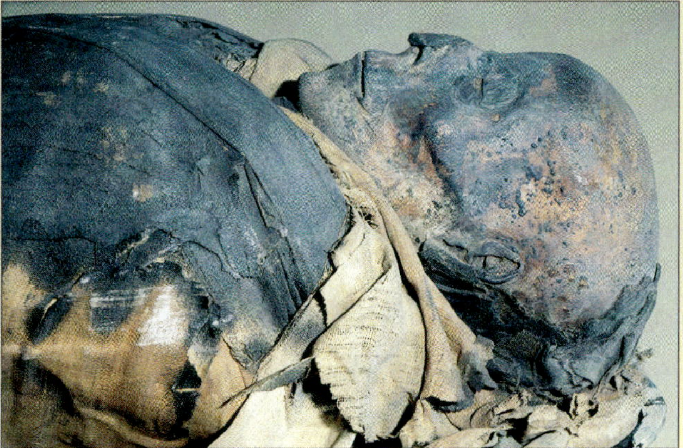

▲ **Figure 1-3** Mummy tissues still contain DNA.

By testing mummy tissue, scientists can learn specific information about the health and family relationships of the person who was preserved. Scientists use the information they discover from mummy tissue to learn about ancient people and cultures. They work together with historians to piece together clues about a mummy's life story.

Thinking Critically Why do you think mummy tissue must be handled carefully?

1-2 What are organs and organ systems?

Objective

Describe organs and organ systems.

Key Terms

organ: group of tissues that work together to do a special job

organ system: group of organs that work together

gland: organ or group of cells that produces and secretes substances used by the body

endocrine (EHN-doh-krihn) **system:** organ system that includes all of the glands of the body

Organs Groups of cells that work together form tissues. Different tissues work together, too. A group of tissues that works together to do a special job is called an **organ.**

Your body has many different organs. Each organ has a special shape and job. Your heart is an organ. It is made of several different tissues. A special type of muscle tissue makes up most of the heart. It pumps blood into the blood vessels. Nerve tissue carries impulses to the heart and controls the heartbeat. Blood vessels surround the heart, supplying its cells with oxygen and nutrients.

1 DEFINE: What is an organ?

Organ Systems Organs do not work alone. Groups of organs work together. These groups of organs form **organ systems.** All the organs in an organ system work together to carry out certain life processes. For example, your heart works together with the blood vessels in your body to make up the circulatory system. This system moves blood throughout the body. All the organ systems of a living thing work together to keep the organism alive. Each organ system carries out a different life process. Some of the major organ systems are listed in Figure 1-4.

2 ANALYZE: What is the job of the circulatory system?

SUMMARY OF ORGAN SYSTEMS		
System	**Major Structures**	**Function**
Skeletal	Bones	Provides structure; supports and protects internal organs
Muscular	Muscles (skeletal, cardiac, and smooth)	Provides structure; supports and moves trunk and limbs
Circulatory	Heart, blood vessels, blood	Transports nutrients and wastes to and from all body tissues
Respiratory	Air passages, lungs	Carries air into and out of lungs, where gases (oxygen and carbon dioxide) are exchanged
Immune	Lymph nodes and vessels, white blood cells	Provides protection against infection and disease
Digestive	Mouth, esophagus, stomach, liver, pancreas, small and large intestines	Stores and digests food; absorbs nutrients; eliminates wastes
Excretory	Kidneys, ureters, bladder, urethra, skin, lungs	Eliminates waste; maintains water and chemical balance
Nervous	Brain, spinal cord, nerves, sense organs, receptors	Controls and coordinates body movements and senses; controls consciousness and creativity; helps monitor and maintain other body systems
Endocrine	Glands (such as adrenal, thyroid, and pancreas), hypothalamus	Maintains homeostasis; regulates metabolism, water and mineral balance, growth and sexual development, and reproduction
Reproductive	Ovaries, uterus, mammary glands (in females), testes (in males)	Produces offspring

▲ **Figure 1-4**

Glands Some organs and groups of cells make and give off substances used by the body. These special organs and groups of cells are called **glands.** Some glands produce chemicals that act as messengers. The blood carries these "messengers" to organs. The glands that produce chemical messengers make up an organ system called the **endocrine system.** Many of the chemical messengers made by glands control the activities of other tissues and organs.

DEFINE: What is a gland?

CHECKING CONCEPTS

1. A group of tissues that works together is called an __________.
2. Groups of organs form __________.
3. Each organ system carries out a life __________.
4. Your heart and blood vessels make up the __________ system.
5. Glands make and give off __________ messengers.

THINKING CRITICALLY

6. **RELATE:** How is your body similar to a machine with many parts?
7. **SEQUENCE:** Place the levels of organization in an organism from smallest to largest. **a.** organism **b.** cells **c.** organ **d.** tissues **e.** organ systems
8. **APPLY:** What organ systems do you think work together to move your leg?

Web InfoSearch

Plant Organs Plant tissues have organs with special jobs. The roots, stems, leaves, and flowers of a plant are all organs.

SEARCH: Use the Internet to find out more about plant organs. Make a chart explaining each organ, its function, and which organ from the human body it is most similar to. Start your search at www.conceptsandchallenges.com. Some key search words are **plant, plant anatomy,** and **botany.**

Real-Life Science

ORGAN TRANSPLANTS

When any of its organs fail to do its job, an organism becomes ill and may die. In an organ transplant, a failing organ is replaced with a healthy organ from a donor. Once a new organ is surgically transplanted, the body may accept the organ as its own and function regularly again.

Medical advances in organ transplant surgery have increased the success rate for patients. However, the demand for organs is so great that many people wait years for an organ. Each day, about 60 people in the United States receive an organ transplant, but another 15 people die waiting for one. As a result, the U.S. government passed an act that set up a waiting system for people in need of organ donations.

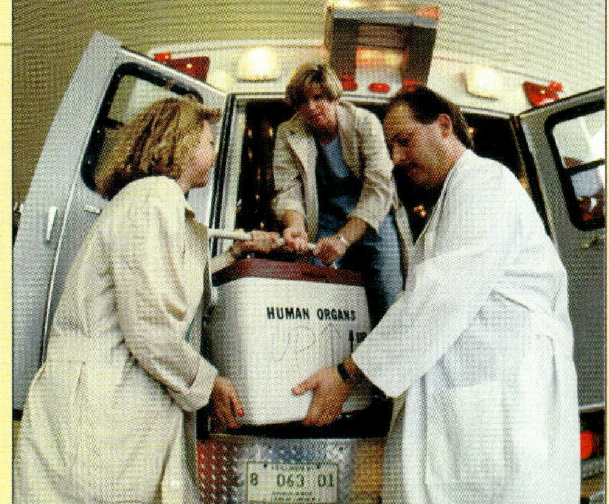

▲ **Figure 1-5** Donated organs must be kept cool until they are transplanted.

Scientists are also looking for ways to help people. Doctors have conducted transplant experiments involving artificial organs. They have also transplanted organs from animals, such as baboons and pigs, into patients waiting for organ transplants.

Thinking Critically Why is it important that individuals fill out donor cards or make their wishes about organ donation known in some other way?

1-3 What is the skeletal system?

Examining Bone Structure and Function

HANDS-ON ACTIVITY

1. Observe a model or poster of the human skeletal system.
2. Create a chart on a separate sheet of paper. In your chart, list at least 10 different bones.
3. Describe the structure or shape of each bone in your chart.
4. Try to guess the function or job of each bone in your chart. Include this in your chart as well.

THINK ABOUT IT: How is the structure of each bone related to its function?

Objective

Describe the functions of the skeletal system and its parts.

Key Terms

skeletal system: system of bones and cartilage that helps to support and protect the body

vertebra, *pl.* **vertebrae:** bone that makes up the backbone

cartilage (KAHRT-uhl-ihj)**:** tough, flexible connective tissue

The Skeletal System Have you ever seen a house being built? If you have, you have probably seen the wooden framework that makes up a house. The framework of a house is important. It gives a house its shape. The framework also supports a house. You also have a frame that supports your body. This frame is your skeleton. Most of your **skeletal system** is made of bone. Bone is a very hard tissue.

 COMPARE: How is a skeleton similar to the frame of a house?

Kinds of Skeletons Some living things do not have a skeleton. Their bodies are entirely soft. Other organisms, such as lobsters and insects, have an exoskeleton, or a skeleton outside their bodies. An exoskeleton is tough and hard. It protects the animal. Humans and many other animals have an endoskeleton, or a skeleton inside their bodies.

 INFER: List three organisms with an exoskeleton and three with an endoskeleton.

Jobs of the Skeleton A major job of the skeletal system is to support the body. The spine, or backbone, supports the body and also allows for a variety of movements. The backbone is made up of separate bones called **vertebrae.** These bones resemble a stack of hollow rings. Because they are separate bones, the backbone can bend and twist.

Besides giving support and shape to your body, your skeletal system has many other important jobs. One of these jobs is to work together with muscles to move the body. Another job of the skeleton is to protect important organs. For example, the skull protects the brain. The backbone protects the spinal cord. Blood cells are made inside some bones. Bones also store minerals, such as calcium, that are required by the body. When the body needs these minerals, the bone releases them into the blood so they can be used.

JOBS OF THE SKELETON		
Bone	**Common Name**	**Job**
Clavicle	collar bone	supports the shoulder and arm bones
Sternum	breast bone	protects the heart; supports the rib cage
Cranium	skull	protects the brain
Vertebrae	backbones	supports the body; protects the spinal cord

▲ Figure 1-6

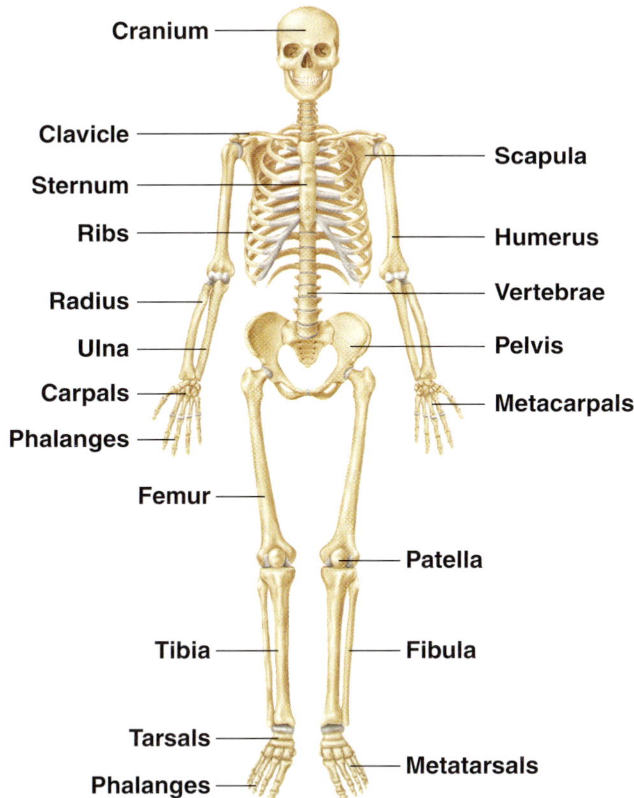

▲ **Figure 1-7** The human skeletal system

3 **INFER:** What do you think the rib cage protects?

Cartilage Feel your knee. The bones of your knee are very hard. Some parts of your skeleton are not as hard. Move the tip of your nose. Bend one of your ears with your hand. These two parts of your body are not made of bone. They are made of cartilage. **Cartilage** is a tough, but flexible, connective tissue. Before you were born, your skeleton was made of cartilage. However, during the second and third months of embryonic development, bone slowly replaced most of the cartilage in your skeleton.

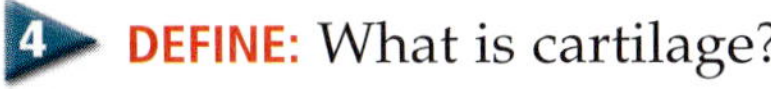

4 **DEFINE:** What is cartilage?

Bone Formation Over time, the cartilage in most bones is replaced by hard, living bone tissue. This process is carried out by several specialized cells. One type of cell produces the calcium-enriched material that makes up most bones. Another cell breaks down bone tissue during the growth and remodeling of bones. It may seem strange to have a cell that destroys bone tissue. However, this process is very important because the size and shape of bones change as a person matures.

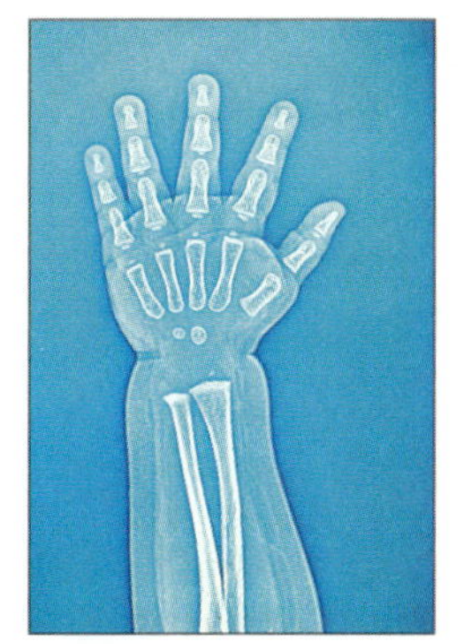
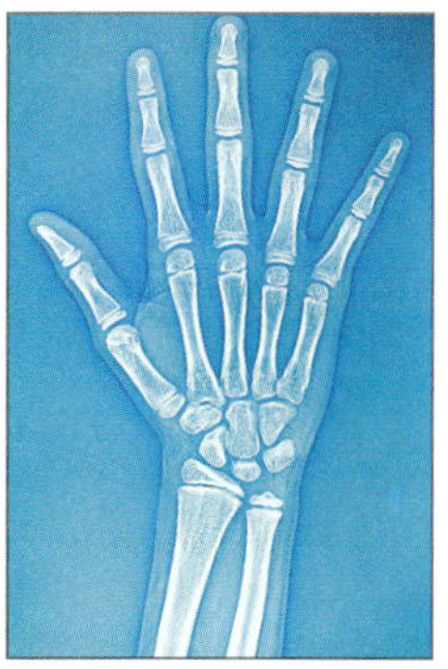

▲ **Figure 1-8** X-rays of infants (left) show that they have fewer bones than older children (right).

5 **EXPLAIN:** How does cartilage become bone?

CHECKING CONCEPTS

1. A very hard tissue that makes up the skeletal system is __________ tissue.
2. An internal skeleton is called an __________.
3. The backbone is made up of __________.
4. The skeletal system works with __________ to move the body.
5. Before a baby is born, most of its skeleton is made up of __________.

THINKING CRITICALLY

6. **RELATE:** How is the structure of the ribs related to their function?
7. **PREDICT:** The backbone is made of 33 separate vertebrae. What might happen if several of those vertebrae were fused together?

INTERPRETING VISUALS

Use Figure 1-7 to answer the following questions.

8. **ANALYZE:** How many bones make up the lower arm?
9. **ANALYZE:** What is another name for the breastbone?

1-4 What are bones?

Objective

Describe the parts of a bone.

Key Terms

periosteum (per-ee-AHS-tee-uhm)**:** thin membrane that covers a bone

compact bone: mostly solid, dense part of a bone

spongy bone: part of a bone with many small pores or spaces

marrow: soft tissue inside bones that produces blood cells

fracture: crack or break in a bone

Bones The adult human skeleton is made up of 206 bones. Bones come in all shapes and sizes. Some bones are very small. There are three small bones in your ear that help you hear. Other bones are quite large. The bone in your thigh is the longest bone in the body. Some bones are tubelike. Others are flat. Although bones are different in size and shape, they all have similar structures.

 INFER: Name some places in your body where there are small bones.

Structure of Bones Bones are made up of both living and nonliving material. Each bone is covered by the **periosteum.** It is a thin membrane. The periosteum has many blood vessels in it that carry food molecules and oxygen to living bone cells.

The hardest part of a bone is called **compact bone.** Compact bone is made up of living bone cells, protein fibers, and nonliving minerals. The mineral calcium makes compact bone hard. Calcium in your diet helps keep your bones hard and strong. Dairy products are rich in calcium.

Bones are not entirely hard, however. The ends of bones are soft and spongy. The soft part of bones is called **spongy bone.** Spongy bone looks like a sponge. It has many holes in it. Spongy bone is lightweight and gives the bone its strength.

 DESCRIBE: What is the function of the periosteum?

Marrow The spaces in spongy bone are filled with bone marrow. Bone **marrow** is a soft connective tissue. It is red or yellow in color. Spongy bone contains red bone marrow. New red blood cells are made in the red bone marrow. When you were younger most of your bones contained red marrow. Adults only have red marrow in certain bones such as the femur and hips. Long bones contain yellow marrow. Yellow marrow contains mostly fat.

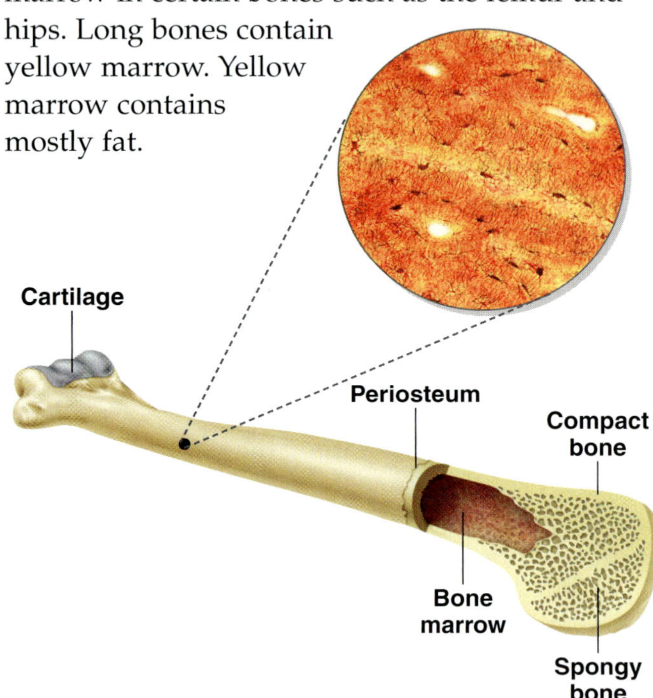

▲ **Figure 1-9** Bone is made up of several layers of living and nonliving material.

 NAME: In which kind of bone marrow are red blood cells made?

Fractures Injuries to bones are quite common. A **fracture** is a crack or break in a bone. Some fractures can be very severe. In open fractures, the bone breaks through the skin. Closed fractures do not break the skin. Another fracture called a hairline fracture is a very thin crack in the bone. Doctors use X-rays to determine the severity and the exact location of the fracture. Many times patients must wear a cast to prevent the injured bone from moving while it heals.

 INFER: Why do you think it is important that a bone with a fracture should not move?

CHECKING CONCEPTS

1. New blood cells are made in __________ bone.
2. The membrane that covers bone is called the __________.
3. The mineral __________ keeps bones strong.
4. Blood vessels in spongy bone supply the bones with food and __________.
5. Red blood cells are made in the __________.
6. A break or crack in a bone is called a __________.

THINKING CRITICALLY

7. **INFER:** Is the periosteum living or nonliving?
8. **PREDICT:** What might happen if the blood vessels in the periosteum were blocked?
9. **RELATE:** Why is living bone tissue important for growth?

DESIGNING AN EXPERIMENT

Design an experiment to solve the following problem. Include a list of materials, variables, a procedure, and a type of data to study.

PROBLEM: Calcium and other minerals give bones their strength and firmness. These minerals can be dissolved by vinegar. Design an experiment that proves that calcium and other minerals are contained in bone.

Science and Technology

BONE MARROW TRANSPLANTS

Bone marrow transplants are used to treat many different blood disorders, such as leukemia and certain kinds of anemia. The marrow in many bones produces new blood cells. A bone marrow transplant is needed when a person's bone marrow produces abnormal blood cells instead of normal blood cells.

A healthy donor is needed for a bone marrow transplant. Radiation treatments are given to the person with the abnormal bone marrow cells. The radiation kills the marrow cells in the body. Healthy bone marrow is then taken from the donor and inserted into the patient's bloodstream.

One factor in the success of a bone marrow transplant is whether the patient's body accepts or rejects the new bone marrow. One of the major drawbacks of transplants is that the body may reject the new bone marrow. Another drawback is the possibility of infection.

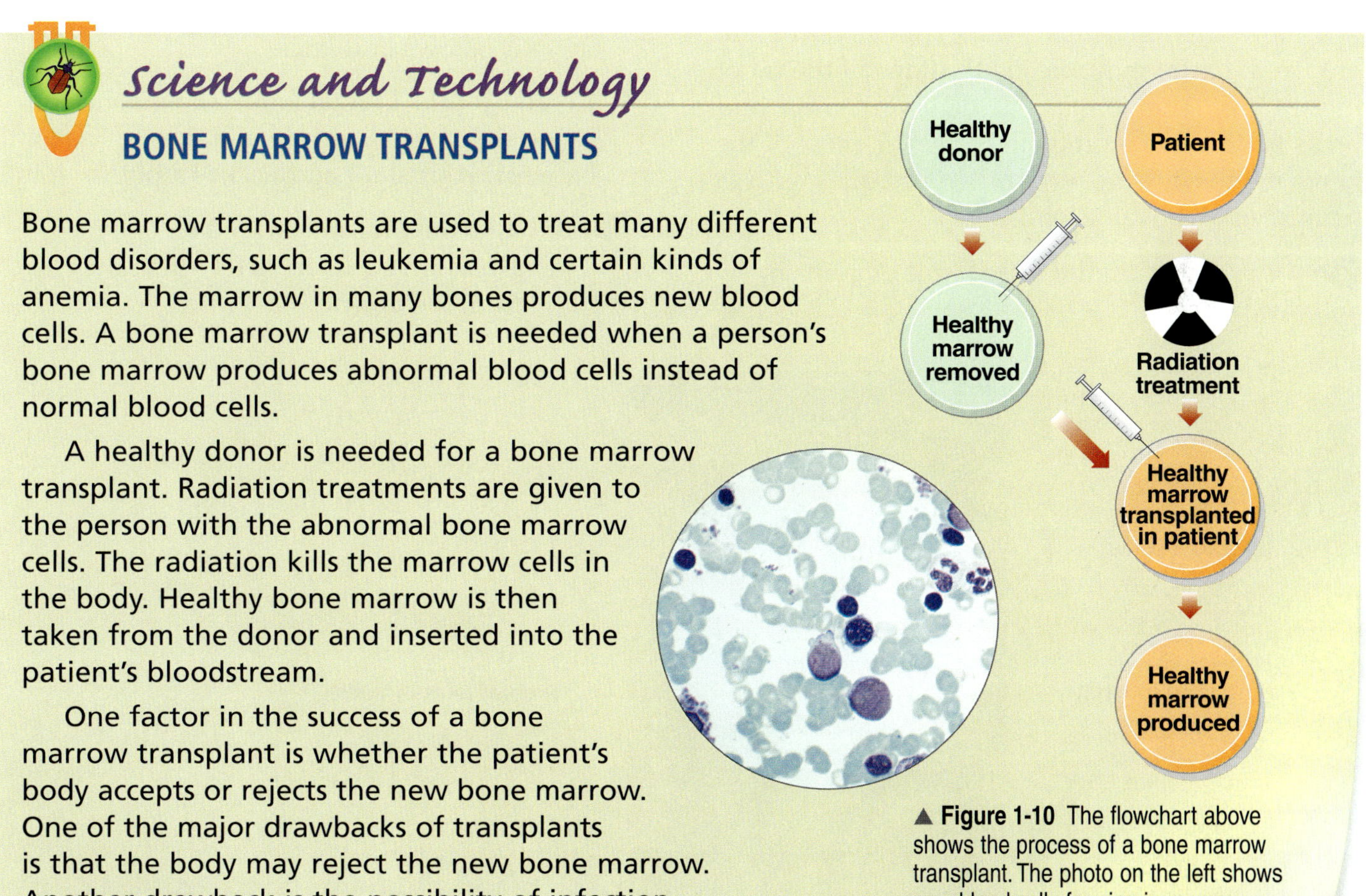

▲ **Figure 1-10** The flowchart above shows the process of a bone marrow transplant. The photo on the left shows new blood cells forming in marrow.

Thinking Critically Why are patients treated with radiation before a bone marrow transplant?

1-5 How do joints work?

Objective

Identify the motions and locations of the four kinds of movable joints.

Key Term

joint: place where two or more bones meet

Joints The place where two bones or more meet is called a **joint.** Some bones are connected directly to other bones at the joint. However, most bones are held together at joints by ligaments.

DEFINE: What is a joint?

Kinds of Joints There are three main kinds of joints in the body. They are fixed joints, partly movable joints, and movable joints. Fixed joints do not allow any movement. The joints in your skull are fixed. Partly movable joints allow a little bit of movement. The joints between your ribs and breastbone move a little bit. However, most of the joints in the body are movable. Your arms and legs have several movable joints.

STATE: What are the three kinds of joints in the body?

Movable Joints There are four major kinds of movable joints. These joints are ball-and-socket joints, gliding joints, hinge joints, and pivotal joints.

- **Ball-and-Socket Joints** Ball-and-socket joints allow bones to move in most directions. The joint between your upper arm and shoulder is a ball-and-socket joint. Your arm can move up and down, side to side, front to back, and around in a circle.
- **Gliding Joints** Gliding joints allow some movement in all directions. In a gliding joint, the bones slide along each other. Your wrist has gliding joints.
- **Hinge Joints** Hinge joints allow bones to move forward and backward in only one direction. This movement is similar to a door opening and closing. Hinge joints are located in your elbows and knees.
- **Pivotal Joints** Pivotal joints allow bones to move side to side and up and down. The joint between your skull and neck is a pivotal joint.

3 **LIST:** List the four major kinds of movable joints and give examples of where they are found in the body.

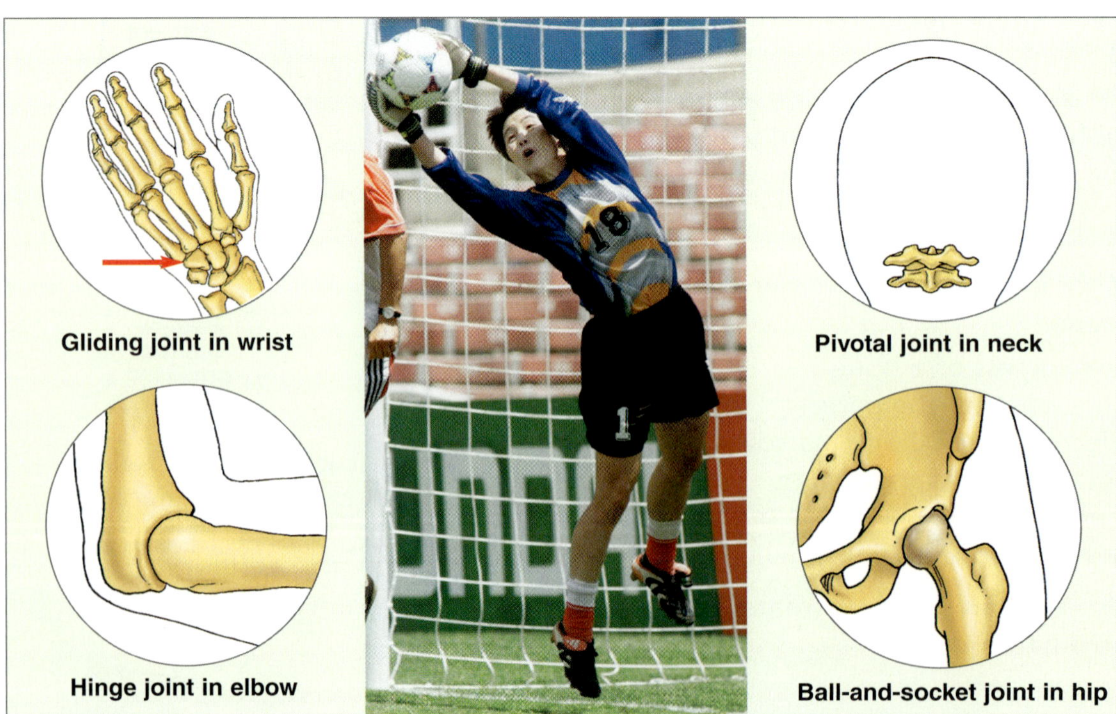

Figure 1-11 The joints inside this soccer goalie allow her to move in many different ways.

Cartilage and Bones Cartilage is found in the joints of many bones. Movable joints such as the knee, shoulder, and hip all have cartilage between the bones. This layer of cartilage cushions the bones and prevents them from rubbing against each other. Cartilage is smoother than bone, so it causes less friction when rubbed together. This allows for easier movement of the bones. Cartilage is also found between the bones of the spinal column. The cartilage there acts as shock-absorbing padding for the vertebrae.

INFER: Would you expect to find more cartilage between your arm and shoulder bones or between the bones of the skull?

CHECKING CONCEPTS

1. Joints can be either fixed, partly movable, or ___________.
2. The joints between your breastbone and ribs are ___________.
3. Most bones are held together at joints by ___________.
4. The joint in your elbow is a ___________ joint.

THINKING CRITICALLY

5. **HYPOTHESIZE:** What would happen if the joint between your arm and shoulder was not a ball-and-socket joint?
6. **INFER:** Why do you think the joints between your rib cage and breastbone are partly movable?

Web InfoSearch

Arthritis Do you know anyone who has arthritis? Arthritis affects people who are both young and old. Arthritis is a term that describes many different joint problems. The most common form of arthritis occurs when the cartilage between the bones is replaced with bone deposits. Movement in these joints is limited and can be very painful.

SEARCH: Use the Internet to find out more about arthritis. Write a report about the different types of arthritis and possible treatments. Start your search at www.conceptsandchallenges.com. Some key search words are **arthritis** and **joint pain.**

Hands-On Activity

OBSERVING JOINT MOVEMENTS

You will need a sheet of paper and a pencil.

1. Move your ankle in as many different ways as possible. Write down all the movements your ankle can make.
2. Move your fingers in as many different ways as possible. ⚠ CAUTION: Do not force movements at the joint. Write down all the movements your fingers can make.
3. Move your head in as many different ways as possible. Write down all the movements your head can make.
4. Move your leg and hip joints in as many different ways as possible. Write down all the movements your leg can make at the hip.

▲ **STEP 1** The human body contains four different kinds of joints.

Practicing Your Skills

5. **INFER:** What kind of joint was used in each step? How can you tell?
6. **OBSERVE:** Based on the movements in your fingers, how many joints do you think are in your fingers?

1-6 What is the muscular system?

Objective

Describe how muscles work.

Key Terms

flexor: muscle that bends a joint

extensor: muscle that straightens a joint

Muscles More than 600 muscles make up the muscular system. Muscles are tissues that can shorten along their length. Without muscles, the bones of the skeletal system could not move the body. Muscles are attached to bones by tendons. A tendon is a strong elastic band of tissue. Tendons make movement possible. When a muscle contracts, or shortens, it pulls on the tendon, which makes the bone move.

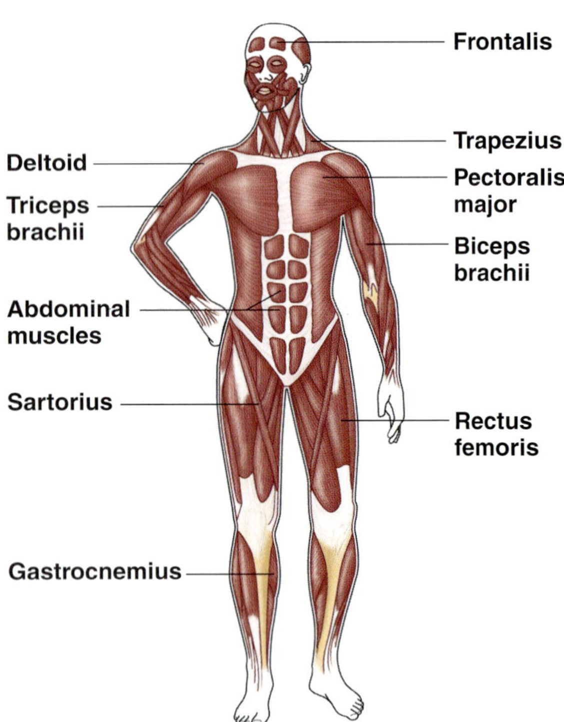

▲ **Figure 1-12** The muscular system

1 **CONTRAST:** What is the difference between a tendon and a ligament?

Muscle Actions Muscles only move bones when the muscles contract. For this reason, muscles can only pull bones. They cannot push bones. For example, there are muscles that bend, or flex, your knee joint. These muscles are called **flexors.** There are other muscles that straighten, or extend, your knee joint. These muscles are **extensors.**

2 **DEFINE:** What does a flexor muscle do?

Teamwork Most muscles must work in teams of two. The muscles that bend and straighten the arm are examples of muscles working together. These muscles are called biceps and triceps. Biceps are flexors. They bend the arm at the elbow. Triceps are extensors. They straighten the arm at the elbow. As you bend your arm, the biceps contract, and the triceps relax. As you straighten out your arm, the biceps relax while the triceps contract and pull the arm straight.

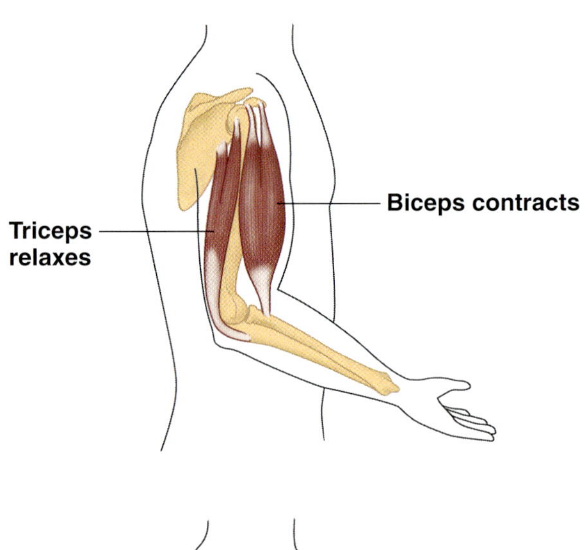

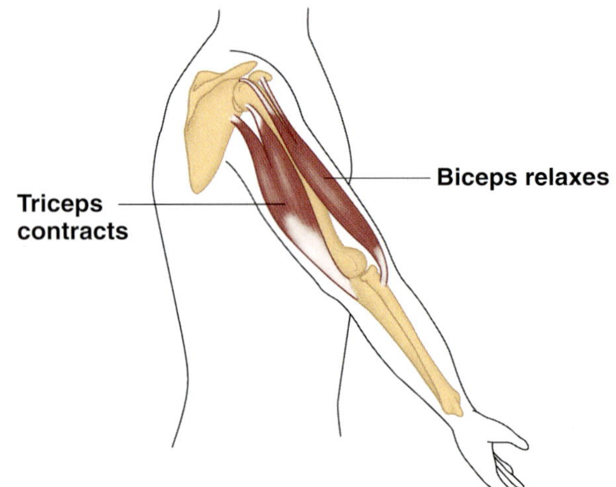

▲ **Figure 1-13** Flexion and extension are opposite movements.

3 **STATE:** Name a muscle in the arm that is a flexor.

✓ CHECKING CONCEPTS

1. What is a tendon?
2. Are muscles relaxed or contracted when they move bones?
3. What is the main function of the muscular system?
4. What do extensor muscles do?
5. Why must muscles work together?

THINKING CRITICALLY

6. **HYPOTHESIZE:** If your biceps muscle was injured, which motion would you be unable to do?
7. **INFER:** When exercising, why do you think it is important to use both muscles in a pair?

Web InfoSearch

Anabolic Steroids Anabolic steroids are drugs that duplicate the male hormone testosterone. Some people take this drug illegally to increase muscle mass. However, these drugs affect many parts of the body, not just the muscles. The steroids have harmful side effects and can even be life threatening.

SEARCH: Use the Internet to research the effects of anabolic steroids. Present your findings to the class in a report or health brochure. Start your search at www.conceptsandchallenges.com. Some key search words are **steroid** and **anabolic steroid.**

Real-Life Science

EXERCISE AND MUSCLES

Keeping the muscles in your body healthy is very important to your overall well-being. The muscles in your body will be stronger and more flexible if you exercise regularly. Exercise will build endurance, or allow your muscles to withstand more activity. Having well-conditioned muscles can also prevent injuries. Examples of exercises that strengthen and condition your muscles are weight training and hiking.

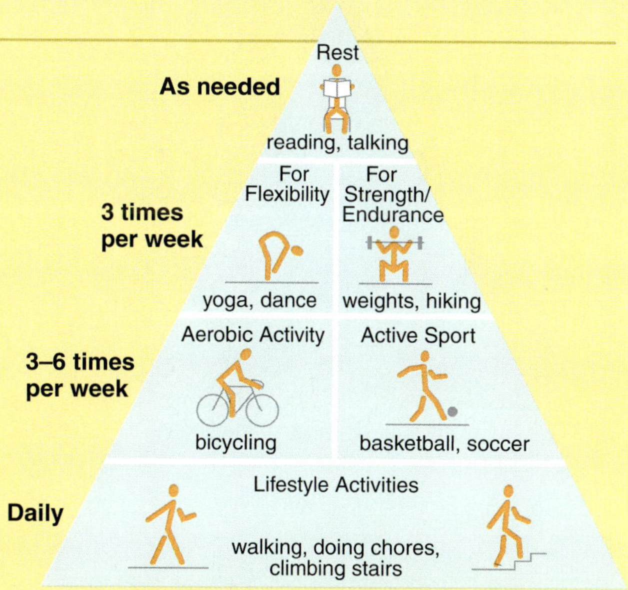

Exercise is also important to your heart. Your heart is made of muscle and requires conditioning. Aerobic activities are those that force the heart to pump blood to the muscles continuously. Examples of aerobic activities include running, bicycling, and swimming. Playing sports such as basketball and soccer also improve the condition of your heart.

Many people do not exercise regularly. It may help if you make an exercise program or schedule and include it in your daily routine. You may also be more likely to exercise if you choose activities that you enjoy or exercise with a friend. Talk with your doctor before starting any exercise program.

Thinking Critically What are some ways that you exercise already? What are some other ways you could include exercise in your life?

As needed — Rest: reading, talking

3 times per week — For Flexibility: yoga, dance; For Strength/Endurance: weights, hiking

3–6 times per week — Aerobic Activity: bicycling; Active Sport: basketball, soccer

Daily — Lifestyle Activities: walking, doing chores, climbing stairs

▲ **Figure 1-14** The exercise pyramid

LAB ACTIVITY
Modeling Muscle Movement

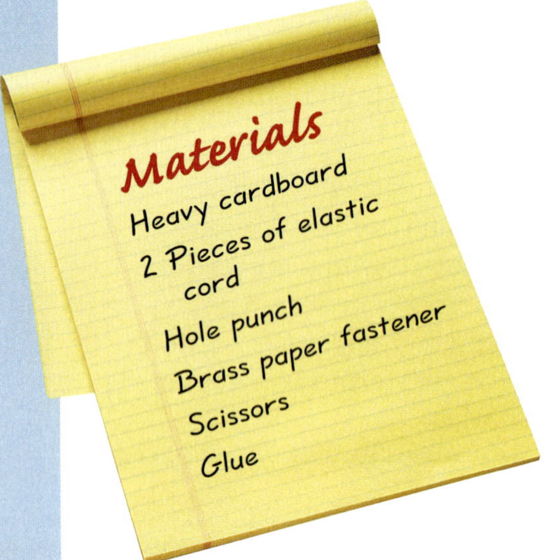

BACKGROUND

Bones are connected to each other at the joints. They cannot move by themselves. Muscles make bones move. Muscles are attached to bones. When muscles contract, they cause bones to move.

PURPOSE

In this activity you will construct a model of an arm to show how muscles and bones work together to cause movement.

PROCEDURE 

1. Trace and cut out the drawings of bones in Figure 1-15. Glue the paper cutouts to a sheet of cardboard. Let the glue dry. Then, cut the shapes out of the cardboard. ⚠ **CAUTION:** Be careful when using scissors.

2. Use the hole punch to make holes in the cardboard bones where the small circles are.

3. Push a paper fastener through the hole marked *elbow joint* in the humerus bone, then through the hole marked *elbow joint* in the forearm bone.

4. Fasten the cardboard bones together. Test the bones to make sure they can move freely.

5. Thread a piece of elastic cord through the *biceps muscle* hole in the forearm bone. Tie a knot behind the bone so that the cord cannot slip through.

6. Pull the cord through the *biceps muscle* hole in the humerus. Pull the cord so that it pulls the two bones nearly together. Then, knot the cord behind the humerus bone.

▲ **STEP 1** Cut out your drawings of the bones.

▲ **STEP 4** Fasten the cardboard bones together.

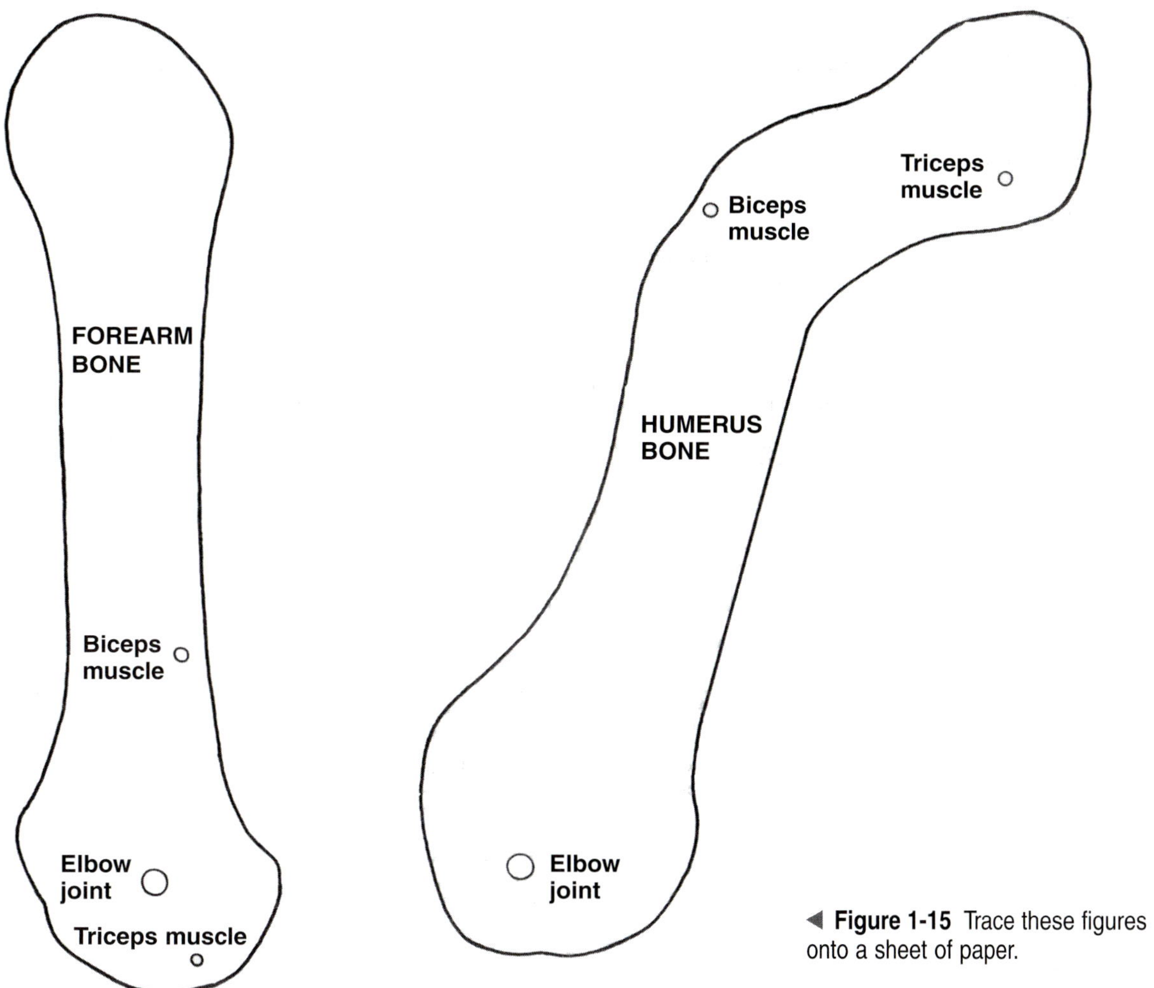

◀ **Figure 1-15** Trace these figures onto a sheet of paper.

7. Use another piece of elastic cord to attach the *triceps muscle* holes of the humerus and forearm bones. Follow Steps 5 and 6. This cord should be tight enough so that it is stretched somewhat between the two holes.

8. Bend your model arm back and forth at the elbow. Watch the elastic cords as you do this.

CONCLUSIONS

1. **OBSERVE:** Which muscle pulls on the model arm to bend it? Which muscle pulls on the model arm to straighten it?
2. **ANALYZE:** What does the fastener represent?
3. **ANALYZE:** Which bones of the arm do the cardboard pieces represent? What muscles do the elastic cords represent?
4. **INFER:** Why do muscles have to work in pairs?

1-7 What are the kinds of muscles?

Objectives

Name three kinds of muscle and identify where they are located in the body.

Key Terms

striated (STRY-ayt-uhd) **muscle:** muscle tissue with stripes, or dark bands

skeletal muscle: muscle attached to the skeleton that makes movement possible

smooth muscle: muscle that causes movements that you cannot control

cardiac (KAHR-dee-ak) **muscle:** type of muscle found only in the heart and major blood vessels

Skeletal Muscle There are three different kinds of muscle tissue in the human body. Each kind of muscle tissue has a different job. Some kinds of muscle tissue are striated. **Striated muscles** have stripes, or dark bands. If you look at Figure 1-16, you can see how striated muscle gets its name.

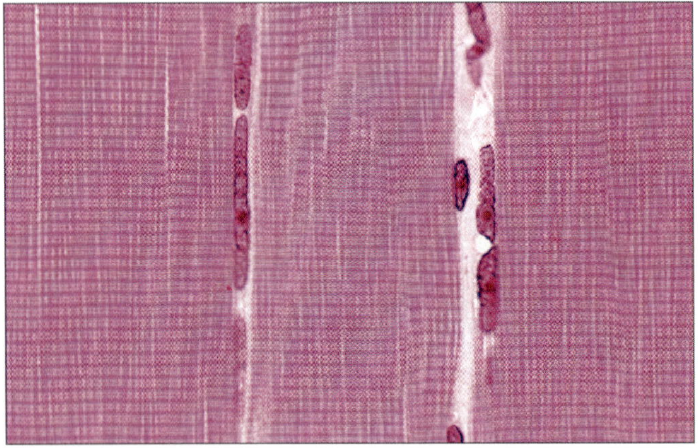

▲ **Figure 1-16** Striated muscle shown at 250 magnification

Skeletal muscle is a type of striated muscle. It is attached directly to the skeleton. Skeletal muscles make the body move. Move your foot. Open and close your fingers. These are movements you can control. Skeletal muscles are usually voluntary muscles. They are voluntary muscles because you can control their movements.

NAME: Name three places in your body where skeletal muscle is found.

Smooth Muscle Muscle tissue that is found in the walls of blood vessels, the stomach, and other internal organs is called smooth muscle. **Smooth muscle** causes movements that you cannot control. For this reason, smooth muscle is sometimes called involuntary muscle. For example, after you eat, you cannot stop the muscles lining your stomach from moving to help digest the food.

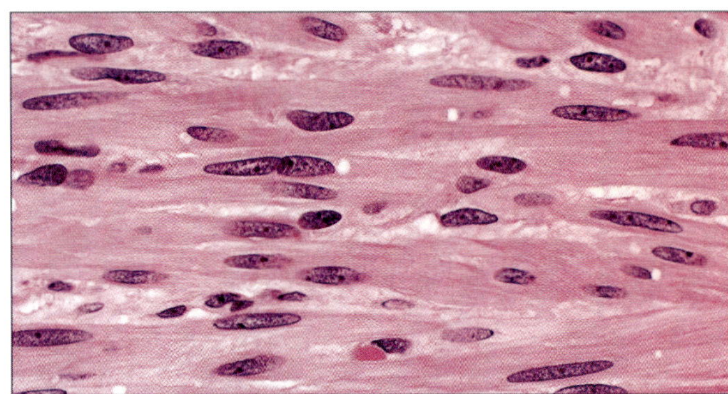

▲ **Figure 1-17** Smooth muscle shown at 160 magnification

INFER: Why do you think smooth muscle is often called involuntary muscle?

Cardiac Muscle The third kind of muscle is called cardiac muscle. The word *cardiac* means "heart." **Cardiac muscle** is found only in the heart and major blood vessels. Cardiac muscle is very strong. The heart must be strong to pump blood throughout the body. Cardiac muscle is striated. Unlike most striated muscle, cardiac muscle is involuntary. You have no control over your heart beating.

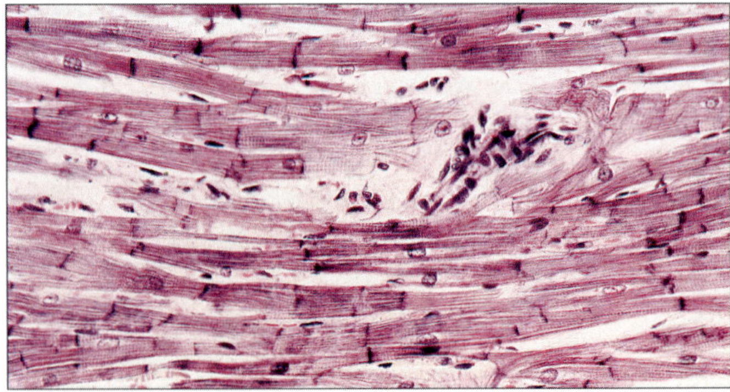

▲ **Figure 1-18** Cardiac muscle shown at 250 magnification

IDENTIFY: Where are the only places cardiac muscle is found?

CHECKING CONCEPTS

1. The word *cardiac* means ___________.
2. Smooth muscles are ___________ muscles.
3. Blinking your eyes is usually caused by ___________ muscles.
4. Striated muscle is usually ___________ muscle.
5. The heart is made of ___________ muscle.

THINKING CRITICALLY

6. **COMPARE:** How are cardiac muscle and smooth muscle similar?
7. **INFER:** Why is the muscular system necessary for the circulatory and digestive systems to function?

BUILDING SCIENCE SKILLS

Classifying When you classify, you group things together based on similarities. Using reference materials, classify the following muscles as being voluntary or involuntary.

a. muscles in the eye that move your eye back and forth

b. cardiac muscle

c. muscles in your abdomen that you use to do sit-ups

d. muscles in the stomach that help digest your food

e. muscles in your blood vessels

f. muscles in your jaw

g. muscles in your legs

People in Science

PHYSICAL THERAPIST

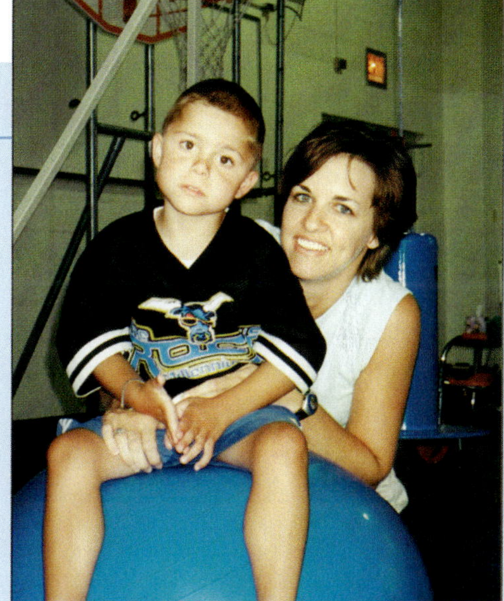

▲ **Figure 1-19** Physical therapists, like Joelle Kelly, help children improve their physical abilities.

Physical therapy is a medical specialty. Physical therapists help restore normal body functioning to patients who have some type of physical impairment. They often use exercise as a form of treatment. Many physical therapists work only with patients in a specific age group or with a specific disability. Physical therapists are employed by hospitals, clinics, and schools. Some work independently and are hired by the family of a disabled person.

Joelle Kelly is a physical therapist. She works only with children. Her day includes traveling to various schools and homes. Joelle treats children with a variety of conditions, such as Down syndrome and autism. She works with the children to improve their flexibility and muscle strength. These exercises help her patients carry out everyday activities such as walking to class and climbing stairs.

In order to become a physical therapist, you need a four-year college degree and a degree in physical therapy. Most physical therapists study biology, chemistry, and human anatomy. Students of physical therapy are often required to observe other physical therapists at work for many hours before they are allowed to treat their own patients.

Thinking Critically How could a physical therapist help a person who was injured in an accident?

Integrating Technology

THE Big IDEA

How are sports injuries treated?

Sports and exercise can strengthen bones and muscles. They also can help make your joints more flexible. Flexibility allows your body to move easily. It also reduces strain on your back and other parts of your body. Sports and exercise are also good for your heart and your lungs.

Even though sports and exercise are good for you, they have risks. Sports injuries send 2.6 million children and young adults to hospitals each year. Some injuries are caused by overuse of a muscle. Other injuries are caused by trauma, such as a fall. Broken bones and sprained ankles are common injuries. Rest, ice, and special exercises heal many injuries.

Medical technology helps doctors examine and treat sports injuries. X-ray machines help doctors see bone injuries. Ultrasound imaging and magnetic resonance imaging are able to show soft tissue, such as ligaments.

An arthroscope helps doctors view joints inside the body. An arthroscope is a tiny video camera that is inserted through tiny cuts in the skin. By looking at a screen, doctors can examine a joint carefully. Doctors also perform surgery in this way with tiny instruments. Patients recover much faster from arthroscopic surgery than from open surgery.

Look at the pictures and text on these two pages. They point out technologies used to examine and treat bone and muscle injuries. Follow the directions in the Science Log to learn more about "the big idea." ✦

Low-level Lasers

Low-level lasers are pen-like devices that give off a concentrated amount of ultraviolet light. This device is not yet approved in the United States but has been used in many European countries for years. Low-level lasers are used to relieve pain related to sprains, muscle inflammation, and other sports injuries.

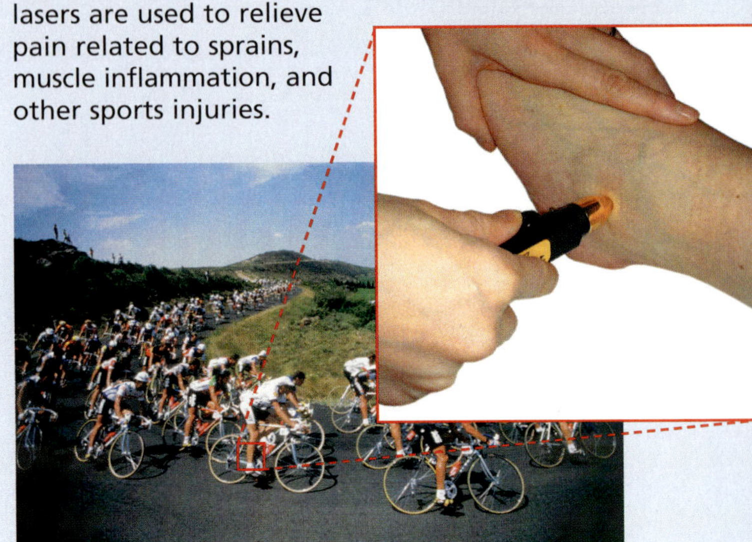

Extracorporeal Shock Wave Therapy

Tennis elbow gets its name because the backhand swing is a common cause of it. Tennis elbow is actually an irritated tendon in the forearm. It causes pain at the outside bump of the elbow. A technology used in Europe and Canada is being tested in the United States. It is called extracorporeal shock wave therapy. The machine uses low-energy shock waves to reduce pain.

Arthroscopes

Surgeons often use arthroscopes to repair torn knee ligaments like the one shown below. An arthroscope is a very thin tube with optical fibers and lenses. The tube is inserted into the joint through tiny cuts in the skin. The arthroscope is connected to a video camera. The surgeon inserts very small surgical tools through other cuts. The arthroscope makes the joint and the tools look large.

Magnetic Resonance Imaging

A torn rotator cuff is a common shoulder injury. The rotator cuff is made up of four muscles that attach to the shoulder blade. The ends of the muscles are tendons that attach to the arm bone. MRI, or magnetic resonance imaging, is a medical tool that can be used to look at shoulder injuries. An MRI machine is a very strong magnet. It works with radio wave pulses of energy. Together they build a map of tissues. MRI can show the same tissue from different angles.

WRITING ACTIVITY

Science Log

Look at the pictures on these two pages. Have you or anyone you know ever suffered a sports injury? In your science log, research and write about the technology that might be used to examine and treat this injury. Start your search at www.conceptsandchallenges.com.

Chapter 1 Challenges

Chapter Summary

Lesson 1-1

- A group of cells that look alike and work together make up a **tissue.** Four types of tissues are muscle tissue, **epithelial tissue, connective tissue,** and nerve tissue.

Lesson 1-2

- A group of tissues that work together to do a job is called an **organ.** A group of organs that works together is called an **organ system.**
- The **endocrine system** is made up of **glands** that make and give off substances used by the body.

Lesson 1-3

- The skeleton supports and gives the body its shape. The bones of the **skeletal system** also protect organs and make red blood cells.
- **Cartilage** is a tough, flexible connective tissue that makes up parts of the skeletal system.

Lesson 1-4

- The mostly solid part of a bone is called **compact bone.** The part of a bone with many spaces is called **spongy bone.** The spaces in spongy bone are filled with red bone **marrow.**

Lesson 1-5

- A **joint** is where two bones meet. The three kinds of joints are fixed joints, partly movable joints, and movable joints.
- The four major kinds of movable joints are ball-and-socket joints, gliding joints, hinge joints, and pivotal joints.

Lesson 1-6

- Muscles are tissues that can shorten along their length. Muscles usually work in pairs to move the body.
- **Flexors** are muscles that bend a joint. **Extensors** are muscles that straighten a joint.

Lesson 1-7

- **Skeletal muscle** is muscle that you control for movement.
- **Smooth muscle** causes movements that you cannot control.
- **Cardiac muscle** is involuntary muscle found only in the heart and major blood vessels.

Key Term Challenges

cardiac muscle (p. 30)
cartilage (p. 20)
compact bone (p. 22)
connective tissue (p. 16)
endocrine system (p. 18)
epithelial tissue (p. 16)
extensor (p. 26)
flexor (p. 26)
fracture (p. 22)
gland (p. 18)
joint (p. 24)
ligament (p. 16)
marrow (p. 22)
organ (p. 18)
organ system (p. 18)
periosteum (p. 22)
skeletal muscle (p. 30)
skeletal system (p. 20)
smooth muscle (p. 30)
spongy bone (p. 22)
striated muscle (p. 30)
tendon (p. 16)
tissue (p. 16)
vertebra (p. 20)

MATCHING **Write the Key Term from above that best matches each description.**

1. outer covering of a bone
2. striated, involuntary muscle found in the heart
3. place where two or more bones meet
4. connective tissue that connects bone to bone
5. bone made up of bone cells, protein fibers, and nonliving minerals
6. connective tissue that connects muscle to bone
7. strong, lightweight bone with many holes in it
8. organ that produces and secretes substances used by the body
9. involuntary muscle
10. group of organs that work together

IDENTIFYING WORD RELATIONSHIPS **Explain how the terms in each pair are related. Write your answers in complete sentences.**

11. extensor, flexor
12. bone, cartilage
13. skeletal muscle, cardiac muscle
14. tissues, organs
15. marrow, spongy bones

Content Challenges TEST PREP

MULTIPLE CHOICE Write the letter of the term or phrase that best completes each statement.

1. The human skeletal system is made up of 206
  a. bones.
  b. muscles.
  c. tendons.
  d. ligaments.

2. Blood cells are made in the
  a. periosteum.
  b. compact bone.
  c. striated muscle.
  d. red bone marrow.

3. The kind of muscle found in the walls of blood vessels is
  a. cardiac muscle.
  b. skeletal muscle.
  c. smooth muscle.
  d. striated muscle.

4. Joints that allow movement in only one direction are
  a. hinge joints.
  b. ball-and-socket joints.
  c. fixed joints.
  d. gliding joints.

5. The joints that are found in the shoulder are
  a. gliding joints.
  b. pivotal joints.
  c. hinge joints.
  d. ball-and-socket joints.

6. As an embryo develops, the cartilage in the skeleton is replaced by
  a. bone.
  b. tendon.
  c. ligaments.
  d. muscle.

7. The connective tissue that connects a muscle to a bone is a
  a. ligament.
  b. tendon.
  c. skeletal muscle.
  d. bone marrow.

8. Skeletal muscle is
  a. found in the heart.
  b. found in the stomach.
  c. involuntary.
  d. voluntary.

9. Spongy bone is strong and
  a. flexible.
  b. lightweight.
  c. fat.
  d. heavy.

10. The backbone is made up of separate bones called
  a. vertebrae.
  b. cranium.
  c. femurs.
  d. tarsals.

TRUE/FALSE Write *true* if the statement is true. If the statement is false, change the underlined term to make the statement true.

11. The solid part of a bone is <u>compact</u> bone.

12. Fixed joints are found in the <u>neck</u>.

13. Muscles can only <u>push</u> bones.

14. Human beings have an <u>exoskeleton</u>.

15. Smooth muscle is <u>voluntary</u> muscle.

Concept Challenges TEST PREP

WRITTEN RESPONSE Answer each of the following questions in complete sentences.

1. **EXPLAIN:** How do muscles work to move bones?
2. **INFER:** Discs of cartilage are found between the vertebrae. What function do you think these discs serve?
3. **INFER:** What happens to the cartilage between your ribs and breastbone when you breathe?
4. **PREDICT:** Calcium adds strength to bones. What might be the effect of a diet without enough calcium?
5. **LOCATE:** What are three parts of the human skeleton that contain cartilage?

INTERPRETING A TABLE Use Figure 1-20 to answer the following questions.

6. **OBSERVE:** How many organ systems does the human body have?
7. **NAME:** Which system includes the kidneys?
8. **IDENTIFY:** What is the function of the endocrine system?
9. **ANALYZE:** Which system is responsible for fighting disease?
10. **INFER:** Which body systems would be involved in an activity such as skateboarding? Explain your answer.

SUMMARY OF ORGAN SYSTEMS		
System	**Major Structures**	**Function**
Skeletal	Bones	Provides structure; supports and protects internal organs
Muscular	Muscles (skeletal, cardiac, and smooth)	Provides structure; supports and moves trunk and limbs
Circulatory	Heart, blood vessels, blood	Transports nutrients and wastes to and from all body tissues
Respiratory	Air passages, lungs	Carries air into and out of lungs, where gases (oxygen and carbon dioxide) are exchanged
Immune	Lymph nodes and vessels, white blood cells	Provides protection against infection and disease
Digestive	Mouth, esophagus, stomach, liver, pancreas, small and large intestines	Stores and digests food; absorbs nutrients; eliminates wastes
Excretory	Kidneys, ureters, bladder, urethra, skin, lungs	Eliminates waste; maintains water and chemical balance
Nervous	Brain, spinal cord, nerves, sense organs, receptors	Controls and coordinates body movements and senses; controls consciousness and creativity; helps monitor and maintain other body systems
Endocrine	Glands (such as adrenal, thyroid, and pancreas), hypothalamus	Maintains homeostasis; regulates metabolism, water and mineral balance, growth and sexual development, and reproduction
Reproductive	Ovaries, uterus, mammary glands (in females), testes (in males)	Produces offspring

▲ **Figure 1-20**

Chapter 2 Digestion and Nutrition

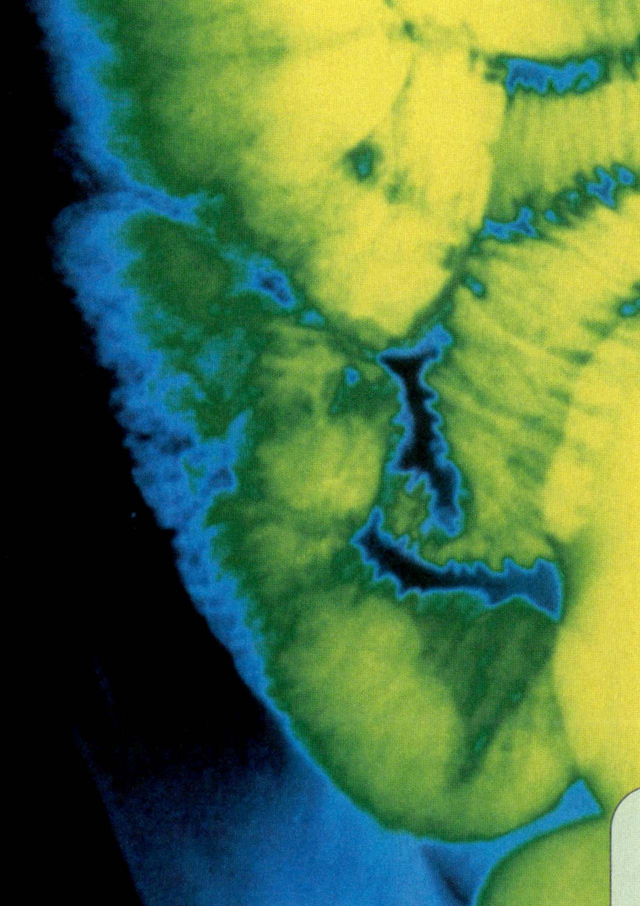

▲ **Figure 2-1** An X-ray of the digestive system

All of the nutrients your body needs come from food. However, the food you eat must be broken down into a form your body can use. This is done through digestion. Digested nutrients are absorbed into the bloodstream and carried to all of the cells in your body. Figure 2-1 shows an X-ray of a healthy digestive system.

▶Why do you think digestive health is so important?

Contents

2-1 What are nutrients?

2-2 Why are proteins important?

2-3 Why are vitamins important?

2-4 Why are minerals important?

■ **Lab Activity:** Testing Foods for Nutrients

2-5 What is a balanced diet?

2-6 What is the digestive system?

2-7 What is digestion?

2-8 What happens to food in the stomach?

2-9 What happens to food in the small intestine?

■ **The Big Idea:** What chemical reactions take place during digestion?

2-10 How do living things get energy?

2-1 What are nutrients?

Objective

Identify the nutrients used by the body.

Key Terms

nutrient (NOO-tree-uhnt): chemical substance that is needed to carry out life processes

carbohydrate (kahr-boh-HY-drayt): nutrient that supplies energy

protein (PROH-teen): nutrient needed to build and repair cells

Nutrients All foods contain nutrients. **Nutrients** are chemical substances in food that your body uses for growth and energy. Nutrients are also needed to carry out life processes. All of the cells of your body need nutrients in order to function. There are five main types of nutrients. They are carbohydrates, fats, proteins, vitamins, and minerals. There are not many foods that contain all five types of nutrients. This is why it is important to eat a variety of different foods.

1 DEFINE: What are nutrients?

Carbohydrates **Carbohydrates** are nutrients that supply your body with energy. Other nutrients such as fats and proteins provide energy as well, but carbohydrates are more easily used by the body. They are your main source of energy.

▲ **Figure 2-2** Common foods rich in carbohydrates

There are two kinds of carbohydrates, simple and complex. Sugars, such as sucrose and fructose, are simple carbohydrates. They give your body short, quick bursts of energy. Starches are complex carbohydrates. They give your body energy over a longer period of time. Breads, cereals, and pasta contain starch.

2 NAME: What are the two kinds of carbohydrates?

Fats Fats are the energy-storage nutrients. The stored energy in fats can be used if energy from carbohydrates is not available. Fat that is stored in the body is used for insulation (ihn-suh-LAY-shuhn). It keeps your body warm. Fat is also used to protect your body organs.

Fats can be either solids or liquids. Solid fats come mostly from animals. Butter and lard are solid fats. Liquid fats are called oils. They usually come from vegetables, such as corn or olives. Many oils are used in cooking.

▲ **Figure 2-3** Common foods rich in fats

3 LIST: Identify three ways the body uses fat.

Proteins Your body needs **proteins** for growth and repair. Proteins are also used to build tissues such as muscles. You get the building blocks for proteins from the foods you eat. Then, proteins are made in your body. When carbohydrates and fats have been used up, proteins can be used for energy. Milk, fish, meat, and cheese are good sources of protein. Peas, peanuts, and beans also contain protein.

▲ **Figure 2-4** Common foods rich in protein

 **EXPLAIN:** Why are proteins needed by the body?

Essential Fluids Although water is not a nutrient, your body needs a constant supply of water. More than two-thirds of your body is made up of water. Water is needed to carry out your life processes. Most of the chemical changes that take place in your body require water. Water also helps control your body temperature. You should try to drink at least six glasses of water each day.

5 **INFER:** What might happen if you do not drink enough water?

CHECKING CONCEPTS

1. Your body needs ___________ for growth, for energy, and to perform life processes.
2. Simple carbohydrates give your body energy over a ___________ period of time.
3. The energy-storage nutrients are ___________.
4. Your body uses ___________ to build and repair cells.
5. Breads and pastas are good sources of ___________ carbohydrates.

THINKING CRITICALLY

6. **HYPOTHESIZE:** Why is some fat a necessary part of your diet?
7. **INFER:** Why should you eat more complex carbohydrates than simple carbohydrates?
8. **EXPLAIN:** Why is water an important part of a diet?

Hands-On Activity

TESTING FOR STARCH

You will need iodine, a medicine dropper, five different types of seeds, a small dish, water, and a knife.

1. Soak the seeds in a dish of water overnight.
2. The next day, remove the seed coats from the seeds. Observe the seed coats.
3. Break apart the seeds. You may need to cut some of the seeds in half with the knife.
   ⚠ **CAUTION:** Be careful when cutting with a knife.
4. Place a drop of iodine on one side of each seed. Iodine changes color when starch is present.

▲ **STEP 4** Place a drop of iodine on each seed.

Practicing Your Skills

5. **OBSERVE:** To what color did the iodine change when starch was present?
6. **APPLY:** Which of the seeds contained starch?
7. **INFER:** What do you think the starch in seeds is used for by plants?

2-2 Why are proteins important?

Objective

List five ways the body uses proteins.

Key Terms

molecule: smallest part of a substance that has all the properties of that substance

amino acid: building block of proteins

Protein Molecules A **molecule** is the smallest part of a substance that has all the properties of that substance. Proteins are giant molecules. In fact, proteins are one of the largest molecules in living things. All proteins contain atoms of carbon, hydrogen, oxygen, and nitrogen.

 NAME: What atoms do protein molecules contain?

Importance of Proteins Proteins are the building blocks of living material. Your body uses proteins in several different ways. One important use of proteins is to build new cells. Another use of proteins is to repair cells that are damaged. Proteins are also used to make enzymes. They can also be used as a source of energy for body cells.

 EXPLAIN: How are proteins used by the body?

Amino Acids Proteins are formed when many smaller molecules join together. The smaller molecules that make up proteins are **amino acids.** There are about 20 different amino acids. Twelve of these amino acids are made in the body. The other eight amino acids must be taken into the body. The foods you eat contain different amino acids. The amino acids are put together in many different ways to form thousands of different proteins. This is like making thousands of words from the 26 letters of the alphabet.

 IDENTIFY: What are the building blocks of proteins?

Protein Synthesis The body uses proteins in foods to make the special proteins it needs. When proteins in food are digested, the amino acids are separated from one another. Cells in your body make their own proteins by putting these amino acids together again in their own special way. This is called protein synthesis. Protein synthesis occurs in the endoplasmic reticulum and ribosomes of your cells. Your genes carry the genetic codes for protein synthesis.

 INFER: Why do you think the body can make so many proteins?

ESSENTIAL AMINO ACIDS		
Amino Acids	**Use in Body**	**Food Sources**
Isoleucine	Works with leucine to promote alertness	Fish, meat, wheat germ, and most seeds and nuts
Lysine	Helps absorb calcium; helps hormones and enzymes	Wheat germ, dairy products, fish, meat, many fruits and vegetables
Valine	Helps in muscle coordination	Found in most foods
Threonine	Assists in digestive processes	Meat, dairy products, and eggs
Phenylalanine	Produces chemicals that transmit signals between nerve cells and the brain	Meat and dairy products
Leucine	Works with isoleucine to promote alertness	Meat, dairy products, wheat germ, and oats
Methionine	Helps reduce cholesterol; reduces liver fat; protects the kidneys; promotes healthy hair growth	Dairy products, eggs, and fish
Tryptophan	Relaxes; helps boost the immune system; helps to reduce cholesterol levels	Meat, eggs, dairy products, and most seeds and nuts
Histidine	Required by infants; helps promote healthy nerve tissue and hearing	Meat, eggs, cheese, lima beans, and peas

▲ Figure 2-5

CHECKING CONCEPTS

1. The smallest part of a substance that has all the properties of that substance is a __________.
2. All proteins contain atoms of carbon, oxygen, hydrogen, and __________.
3. Proteins are the __________ of living material.
4. Proteins are made of __________.
5. There are about __________ different amino acids.
6. Cells make proteins during a process called __________.

THINKING CRITICALLY

7. **ANALYZE:** Why is a diet low in protein unhealthy?
8. **RELATE:** How are amino acids like letters of the alphabet?
9. **INTERPRET:** In which food sources can you find leucine?
10. **INTERPRET:** In which food sources can you find valine?

INTERPRETING VISUALS

Use Figure 2-5 and the list below to answer the following questions.

a. spinach	**d.** meat	**g.** oatmeal
b. milk	**e.** eggs	**h.** wheat germ
c. beans	**f.** fish	**i.** peanut butter

11. Many plant foods do not contain all of the essential amino acids. Which of the essential amino acids can be found in each of the foods listed above?
12. If you were a vegetarian, which foods could you eat in order to get all of the essential amino acids?

Integrating Physical Science

TOPIC: chemical bonds

PEPTIDE BONDS

Proteins are made up of building blocks called amino acids. Amino acids are made up of a molecule containing nitrogen and hydrogen and a molecule containing carbon, oxygen, and hydrogen. When a nitrogen molecule in one amino acid is joined with a carbon molecule from another amino acid, a peptide bond is formed and a molecule of water is given off as a byproduct. Small proteins are called peptides. More amino acids can be added until the peptide chain stretches out to dozens or even hundreds of amino-acid units. These very large peptides are proteins.

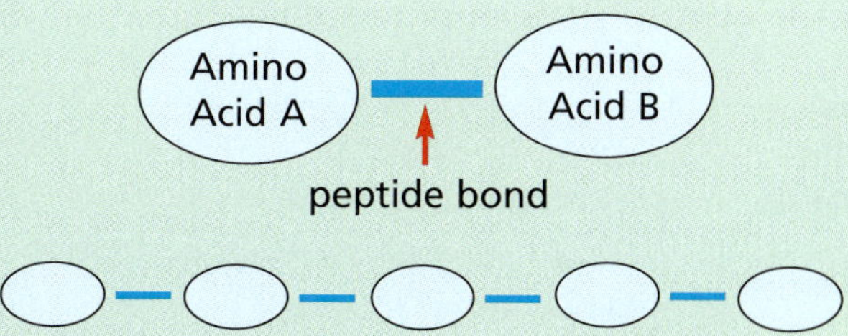

▲ **Figure 2-6** Peptide bonds form between two amino acids. Many amino acids form a chain.

The formation of a peptide bond does not happen by itself. Enzymes, or chemicals, bring the amino acids together and help them to react. Other enzymes help your body change the proteins you eat back into amino acids. To break a peptide bond and release the amino acids, a molecule of water must be added.

Thinking Critically Why is protein an important part of our diets?

2-3 Why are vitamins important?

Objective

Explain why vitamins are important.

Key Terms

vitamin: nutrient found in foods that is required by the body and is made by other organisms

deficiency (dee-FIHSH-uhn-see) **disease:** disease caused by the lack of a certain nutrient

Vitamins Your body needs small amounts of vitamins so it can function properly. **Vitamins** are nutrients that are made by living organisms. You get most of the vitamins you need from food. However, small amounts of vitamins D and K are made in your body. Figure 2-7 lists some vitamins humans need.

DEFINE: What are vitamins?

Importance of Vitamins Vitamins are important for proper growth. They are important for keeping bones, teeth, muscles, and nerves healthy. Vitamins also help control many of the chemical activities that take place in your body. Vitamins can be reused by the body. For this reason, only a small amount are needed in the diet.

Most vitamins work with other vitamins or nutrients. Some vitamins help to change carbohydrates and fats into energy. Unlike carbohydrates and fats, vitamins do not give off energy. Figure 2-7 lists some uses of vitamins in the body.

 EXPLAIN: How are vitamins used in your body?

Deficiency Disease The tissues of your body need small amounts of vitamins every day. If your diet does not include enough of a certain vitamin, you may become sick. This kind of sickness is called a **deficiency disease.** Rickets is a deficiency disease that causes soft bones and teeth. Rickets is caused by a lack of vitamin D. Figure 2-7 lists some other deficiency diseases.

 DEFINE: What is a deficiency disease?

Classifying Vitamins Vitamins are either fat soluble or water soluble. Fat soluble vitamins dissolve in fat. They are stored in fatty tissues. Some fat-soluble vitamins are vitamins A, D, E, and K. Water-soluble vitamins dissolve in water. They are not stored in the body. Vitamin C and all of the B vitamins are water-soluble vitamins.

 INFER: Why is it very important to include water-soluble vitamins in your daily diet?

IMPORTANCE OF VITAMINS			
Vitamin	Use in Body	Sources	Deficiency Disease
A	Growth; healthy skin, eyes, bones, and teeth; ability to see well at night	Orange and dark green vegetables, eggs, fruits, liver, milk	Night blindness
B_1 (thiamine)	Growth; healthy nerves, muscles and heart; helps body get energy from carbohydrates	Pork, whole grain foods, soybeans	Beriberi
B_2 (riboflavin)	Growth; healthy skin and eyes; helps body get energy from carbohydrates, fats, and proteins	Green vegetables, milk, beef, chicken	Skin disorders
B_2 (folic acid)	Also called folate; healthy fetal development	Beans, leafy vegetables, peas, corn, beets, blackberries, strawberries	Birth defects
B_3 (niacin)	Growth; works with other B vitamins to get energy from nutrients in cells	Beans, chicken, eggs, tuna, potatoes	Pellagra
C	Healthy teeth, gums, and blood vessels	Citrus fruits, tomatoes, leafy vegetables	Scurvy
D	Healthy bones and teeth; helps body use calcium	Eggs, milk, made by skin in sunlight	Rickets
E	Healthy blood and muscles; normal reproduction	Leafy vegetables, vegetable oil, milk	Mild anemia
K	Healthy liver, normal blood clotting	Green vegetables, tomatoes	Poor blood clotting

▲ Figure 2-7

✓ CHECKING CONCEPTS

1. Required nutrients in foods that are made by other living organisms are __________.
2. You get most of your vitamins from __________.
3. A __________ is caused by a diet that is missing a certain nutrient.
4. An example of a deficiency disease that causes soft bones is __________.

THINKING CRITICALLY

5. **INFER:** How would eating a balanced diet help prevent a deficiency disease?
6. **HYPOTHESIZE:** Why do you think many foods you eat, such as bread and milk, are "fortified" with vitamins?
7. **INFER:** Why do you think many people take a vitamin supplement?

INTERPRETING VISUALS

Use Figure 2-7 to answer the following questions.

8. **ANALYZE:** You have cut yourself and note that your blood is slow to clot. What vitamin might you be lacking in your diet? Explain
9. **INTERPRET:** What vitamins help the body get energy from carbohydrates?
10. **ANALYZE:** If you have scurvy, what vitamin are you missing in your diet?
11. **INTERPRET:** What is another name for vitamin B_1?
12. **INTERPRET:** What is the deficiency disease for vitamin A?

How Do They Know That?

VITAMIN K AND BLOOD

Many biochemists study how vitamins behave in the body. They use that information to prevent or treat deficiency diseases. Biochemists conduct experiments to study the chemical nature of vitamins. One such study involved vitamin K. Vitamin K dissolves in fat. It is made in the body and is present in certain foods, such as leafy green vegetables.

▲ **Figure 2-8** Vitamin K is found in these foods.

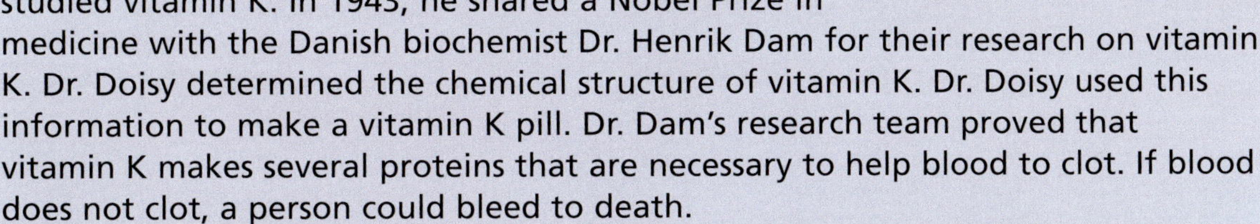

Dr. Edward Doisy was an American biochemist. He studied vitamin K. In 1943, he shared a Nobel Prize in medicine with the Danish biochemist Dr. Henrik Dam for their research on vitamin K. Dr. Doisy determined the chemical structure of vitamin K. Dr. Doisy used this information to make a vitamin K pill. Dr. Dam's research team proved that vitamin K makes several proteins that are necessary to help blood to clot. If blood does not clot, a person could bleed to death.

Dr. Dam and Dr. Doisy's research led others to conclude that vitamin K could be used to cure diseases in which a person cannot stop bleeding.

Thinking Critically Why is the ability to reproduce vitamin K in a pill an important discovery?

2-4 Why are minerals important?

Objective

Explain why minerals are important.

Key Term

mineral: nutrient needed by the body to develop and function properly

Minerals Your body needs minerals as well as vitamins. **Minerals** are nutrients needed for the body to develop and function properly. You need small amounts of some minerals and large amounts of other minerals. For example, you need small amounts of iron, iodine, and zinc. You need larger amounts of calcium, phosphorus (FAHS-fuh-ruhs), and sodium.

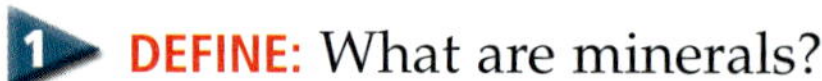

1 DEFINE: What are minerals?

Important Uses of Minerals Each mineral has a different job. For example, iron is needed to form red blood cells. Calcium and phosphorus are needed to build strong teeth and bones. Bones contain calcium. It gives them strength. If calcium is removed from bones, they become soft and weak. Sodium is needed for healthy muscles and nerves. Chlorine is needed to make hydrochloric acid, a chemical used in digestion. Iodine controls body growth and the oxidation of food. Figure 2-9 lists some important minerals and their uses.

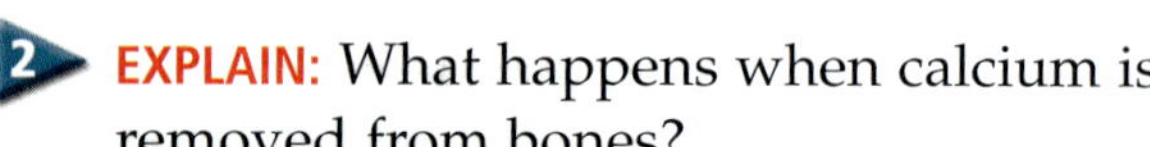

2 EXPLAIN: What happens when calcium is removed from bones?

Deficiency Disease A deficiency disease can be caused if certain minerals are missing from the diet. For example, if you take in too little iron, a deficiency disease called anemia can result. Anemia is sometimes called iron-poor blood. If you are deficient in iodine, a deficiency disease called goiter can result. Figure 2-9 lists some signs of mineral deficiency.

3 IDENTIFY: What deficiency disease is caused by too little iodine?

IMPORTANCE OF MINERALS			
Mineral	**Use**	**Sources**	**Signs of Deficiency**
Calcium	Builds strong bones and teeth; healthy functioning of heart and muscles	Milk and milk products, fish, green leafy vegetables	Soft bones, poor teeth
Phosphorus	Builds strong bones and teeth; forms nucleic acids and energy molecules	Red meat, fish, milk products, poultry, whole grain cereal	None known
Iron	Builds red blood cells	Red meat, whole grains, liver, egg yolks, nuts, green leafy vegetables	Paleness, weakness, tiredness, brittle fingernails
Sodium	Helps keep muscles and blood healthy; helps nerves function properly	Table salt, found naturally in many foods	None known
Iodine	Is used to make a chemical that controls oxidation	Seafood, iodized salt	Goiter
Potassium	Helps keep muscles and nerves healthy	Bananas, oranges, apricots, vegetables	Loss of water from cells, heart problems, high blood pressure
Magnesium	Builds strong bones and muscles, nerve action	Nuts, whole grains, green leafy vegetables	None known
Zinc	Helps in the formation of enzymes	Milk, eggs, seafood, whole grains	None known

▲ Figure 2-9

CHECKING CONCEPTS

1. Your body needs __________ as well as vitamins.
2. The body needs large amounts of calcium, phosphorus, and __________.
3. Sodium is needed for healthy muscles and __________.
4. Bones are hard because they contain __________.

THINKING CRITICALLY

5. **INTERPRET:** What foods contain iodine?
6. **INTERPRET:** Which minerals help build strong teeth and bones?
7. **INTERPRET:** What foods are good sources of potassium?
8. **INFER:** You are feeling tired and weak. What mineral might you be deficient in?

Web InfoSearch

Calcium Ninety-nine percent of the calcium you need is in your teeth and bones. The other 1% is in body tissues such as blood and muscle. The only way that you get calcium is through your diet or from the calcium in your bones. If your body takes more calcium from your bones than it can replace, your bones become weak. This can lead to a disease called osteoporosis.

SEARCH: Use the Internet to find out more about calcium. Then, create a brochure encouraging people to make sure they have enough calcium in their diets. Start your search at www.conceptsandchallenges.com. Some key search words are **calcium** and **osteoporosis.**

Integrating Earth Science

TOPICS: Earth's crust, rocks, minerals

MINERALS FROM EARTH

▲ **Figure 2-10** Minerals are found in rocks. Pyrite, shown above, contains the mineral iron.

The minerals that our bodies need are natural substances, but they are not produced by living things. Scientists call them inorganic compounds. Substances that are produced by living organisms are organic compounds. Minerals come from rocks in Earth's crust.

Can you imagine eating rocks? Rocks are mixtures of minerals. Different processes on Earth change rock minerals into forms that we can use. Water flowing over a rock may dissolve small amounts of minerals and carry them into the soil and into rivers, streams, and oceans. Plants play an important role in supplying us with minerals we can use. They take up minerals through the film of moisture that surrounds their roots. They change these minerals into a form that can be digested. We take in minerals when we eat plants. We also get some minerals by eating animals that have eaten plants and by drinking water.

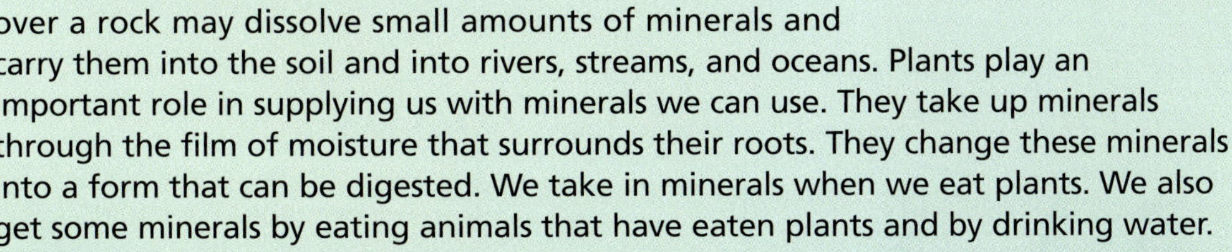

When nutritionists list minerals in foods, they use the names of the elements, such as sodium or calcium. Actually, minerals are often in the form of compounds, in which the elements are chemically bonded to other elements. Table salt, for example, is sodium chloride. Calcium can be obtained from the compound calcium carbonate.

Thinking Critically How do plants supply us with the minerals we need?

LAB ACTIVITY
Testing Foods for Nutrients

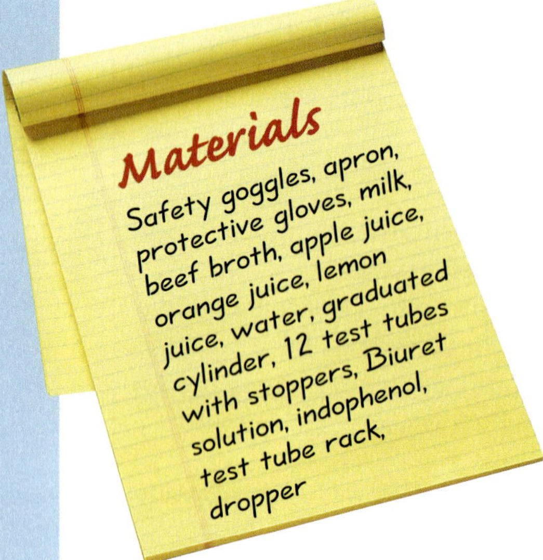

BACKGROUND

The useful parts of the food you eat are called nutrients. Carbohydrates, such as starches and sugars, are nutrients. Another important group of nutrients is proteins. Your body needs proteins to help build and repair its cells. Minerals and vitamins are also nutrients.

PURPOSE

In this activity, you will learn how to test foods to see whether they contain proteins and vitamin C. Biuret solution will be used to test for proteins and indophenol will be used to test for vitamin C.

PROCEDURE 

1. Copy the data chart in Figure 2-11 onto a sheet of paper.

2. Make a hypothesis to predict which of the foods in the materials list will contain proteins and which will contain vitamin C. Put on your safety goggles, apron, and protective gloves.

3. Use a graduated cylinder to measure out 10 mL of milk into one of the test tubes.

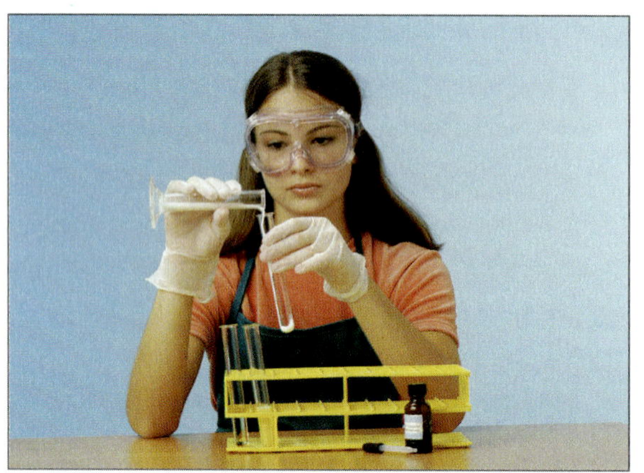

▲ **STEP 3** Measure 10 mL of milk into a test tube.

Testing for Food Nutrients

Food	Test	Chemical	Observation	Nutrient

▲ **Figure 2-11** Copy this data chart onto a sheet of paper.

4. Add five drops of Biuret solution to the milk. Put a stopper in the test tube and shake it.
5. Compare the color of the tested milk to the color of the original milk. Record your observations.
6. Rinse out the dropper and the graduated cylinder. Measure out 10 mL of indophenol into a clean test tube.
7. Add milk drop by drop into the test tube of indophenol. Observe what happens to the color of the indophenol. Note how many drops were needed to cause a color change. Record your observations in your data chart.
8. Repeat Steps 3-7 for beef broth, apple juice, orange juice, lemon juice, and water. Make sure you rinse out the graduated cylinder and dropper after each food test.
9. In your data chart, underline the foods that turned color with the Biuret solution. Circle the foods that produced a color change with the indophenol most quickly.

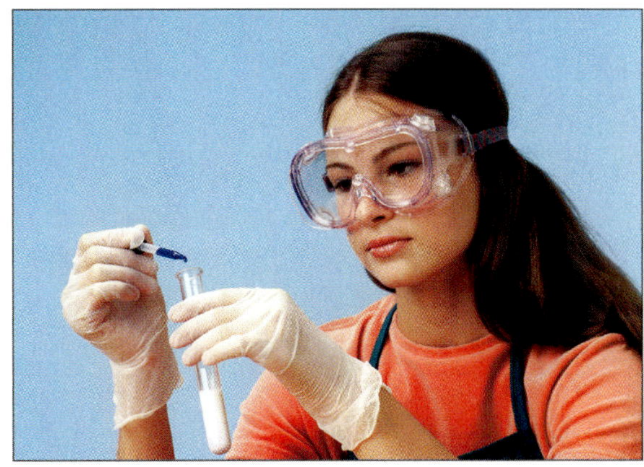

▲ **STEP 4** Add five drops of Biuret solution.

▲ **STEP 5** Record any changes in the milk in your data chart.

CONCLUSIONS

1. **IDENTIFY:** Biuret solution turns purple in the presence of protein. Which of the foods tested contain protein? Was your hypothesis correct?
2. **APPLY:** The darker the purple color of the Biuret solution, the more protein is present. Which of the foods tested contain the greatest amount of protein?
3. **IDENTIFY:** Indophenol turns colorless when vitamin C is present. Which of the foods tested contain vitamin C? Was your hypothesis correct?
4. **APPLY:** The more vitamin C there is in a liquid, the less liquid it takes to turn indophenol colorless. Which of the liquids tested has the most vitamin C?

2-5 What is a balanced diet?

Objective

Describe how to use the Food Guide Pyramid to plan a balanced diet.

Key Term

malnutrition (mal-noo-TRISH-uhn): poor nutrition caused by an unbalanced diet

A Balanced Diet Diets that contain the right amount of nutrients are called balanced diets. Eating a balanced diet will help you stay healthy. Many people think that eating a balanced diet is difficult. Eating a balanced diet is really quite simple.

1 EXPLAIN: Why is a balanced diet important?

The Food Guide Pyramid The U.S. Department of Agriculture has developed a simple way for people to know what to eat each day to maintain good health. The Food Guide Pyramid shows the kinds of foods and the number of servings of those foods a person should have each day. The pyramid does not tell you exactly what foods to eat. Rather it shows you how to choose the right kinds of food to eat. The pyramid calls for eating a variety of foods to get the nutrients you need.

2 STATE: What is the Food Guide Pyramid?

Reading Food Labels The U.S. Food and Drug Administration requires that all processed foods have a food label. A food label lists the nutritional information of the food. It also lists all the ingredients in the food. Figure 2-13 is a food label.

The first item listed on a food label is the serving size. This is the recommended amount you should eat. The rest of the information found on the label is based on the serving size. If you eat twice the recommended serving size, you consume twice the number of nutrients and calories listed on the label. Next to each nutrient is the percent daily value. This tells you how the nutritional content of the food fits into your diet. The daily values are based on the diet of someone who consumes 2,000 calories a day.

3 OBSERVE: What is the percent daily value of sodium listed on the food label in Figure 2-13?

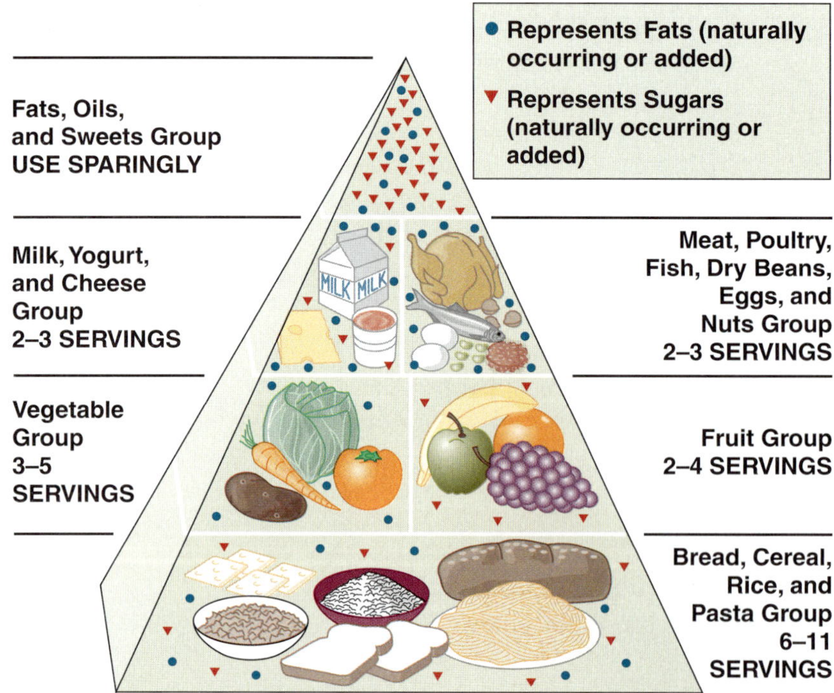

▲ **Figure 2-12** The Food Guide Pyramid

Nutrition Facts

Serving Size: 1 cup
Servings Per Container: About 9

Calories 100	
Calories from fat 0	
	% Daily Value
Total fat 0g	0%
Saturated Fat 0g	0%
Cholesterol 0mg	0%
Sodium 10mg	0%
Total Carbohydrate 31g	10%
Dietary Fiber 2g	9%
Sugars 29g	

▲ **Figure 2-13** A food label

Planning a Balanced Diet You can see in Figure 2-12 that foods are classified into six groups. The food group that should make up the largest part of your diet—breads, cereals, rice, and pasta—is at the bottom of the pyramid. The top of the pyramid shows foods that should make up the smallest part of your diet—fats, oils, and sweets.

The pyramid also tells you how many servings you should eat from each food group. Be sure to eat at least the lowest number of servings from each of the major food groups.

EXPLAIN: How can you use the Food Guide Pyramid to plan a balanced diet?

Malnutrition When your body is not properly nourished, it becomes weak. This disorder is called **malnutrition.** Many people think malnutrition occurs only from a lack of food. However, anyone can be malnourished. If you eat too many foods from one group and not enough foods from another group, you can become malnourished.

STATE: What might happen if you eat too much from one food group and not enough from another food group?

CHECKING CONCEPTS

1. What is a balanced diet?
2. What is a food label?
3. Name two foods from each of the groups in the Food Guide Pyramid.

THINKING CRITICALLY

4. **HYPOTHESIZE:** How can an overweight person be malnourished?
5. **EXPLAIN:** Is an all-protein diet healthy? Explain.

HEALTH AND SAFETY TIP

Eating Disorders Bulimia (byoo-LEE-mee-uh) and anorexia (an-uh-REHKS-ee-uh) are harmful eating disorders. Bulimia and anorexia threaten good health and even life. People with bulimia eat large amounts of food at one time. Then, they either throw up the food or use laxatives. People with anorexia are usually underweight. They refuse to eat food. There are many self-help groups that can help people with bulimia and people with anorexia. Create a prevention poster warning someone against eating disorders.

Real-Life Science

CHOLESTEROL

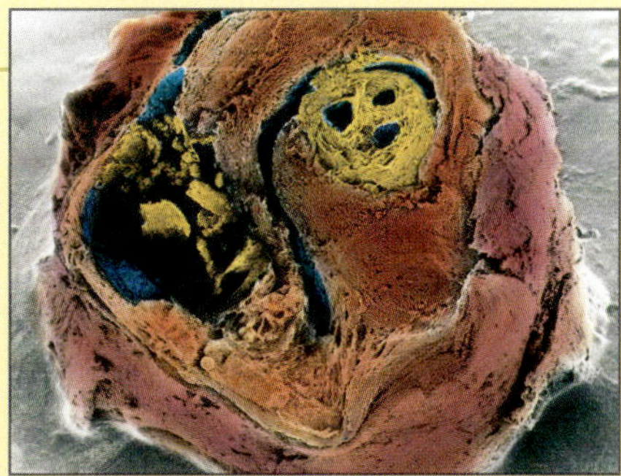

▲ **Figure 2-14** Thick plaque, shown in yellow, clogs arteries.

You have probably heard of people with high cholesterol watching what they eat. Cholesterol can form a yellow plaque on the inside of your arteries. The plaque can become thick enough to reduce the flow of blood to your heart. This may lead to a heart attack. This type of cholesterol is called low density lipoprotein, or LDL. This cholesterol is harmful to your body.

Not all cholesterol is bad. High density lipoprotein, or HDL, is good. Without HDL, the cell membranes of animals would have no support. HDL is also part of the chemical messengers that regulate many body functions.

The ratio of LDL to HDL in your blood can tell a physician if you are at risk for some types of heart disease. If you exercise regularly, the amount of HDL will increase and the amount of LDL may decrease. Once you are over the age of 20 years, you should have your cholesterol levels and ratios checked regularly.

Thinking Critically Fatty foods are usually high in LDL. Do you think someone with a high level of LDL should eat fatty foods?

2-6 What is the digestive system?

Objective

Identify the organs in the human digestive system.

Key Terms

digestion (dih-JEHS-chuhn)**:** process of breaking down food so that it can be used by living things

saliva: liquid in the mouth that helps in digestion

pharynx (FAR-inks)**:** tube connecting the mouth to the esophagus; throat

epiglottis (ehp-uh-GLAHT-ihs)**:** flap of tissue that prevents food from entering the windpipe

esophagus (ih-SAHF-uh-guhs)**:** tube that connects the mouth to the stomach

peristalsis (per-uh-STAL-sihs)**:** wavelike movement that moves food through the digestive tract

Digestion Most of the foods that you eat are not in a form that your body can use. The foods you eat must be changed so that they can be used by the body. The process by which foods are changed into usable forms is called **digestion.** During digestion, larger pieces of food are broken down into smaller pieces. Complex molecules in food are changed into simpler ones.

 DEFINE: What is digestion?

The Digestive Tract The foods that you eat move through a coiled tube inside the body. This tube is called the digestive tract. It is about 10 m long. Some parts are narrow. Other parts are wide. The digestive tract and all of the organs that help with digestion make up your digestive system. The digestive organs that help with digestion are the liver, the pancreas (PAN-kree-uhs), and the gall bladder. These organs are not part of the digestive tract. However, they play an important role in digestion.

 IDENTIFY: What organs help with digestion but are not part of the digestive tract?

Parts of the Digestive System Figure 2-15 shows the digestive system. Food enters the digestive system through the mouth. In the mouth, food is chewed and mixes with a liquid called **saliva,** which is produced by the salivary glands.

Once food is swallowed, it enters the **pharynx,** or throat. The pharynx is a passageway for both food and air. Air moves from the pharynx to the windpipe. As you swallow, a thin flap of tissue keeps food from entering the windpipe. This flap of tissue is called the **epiglottis.** Food moves into a long tube called the **esophagus.** The esophagus connects the mouth to the stomach. From the stomach, food moves into another narrow tube called the small intestine. The small intestine leads into the large intestine. The end of the large intestine is called the rectum.

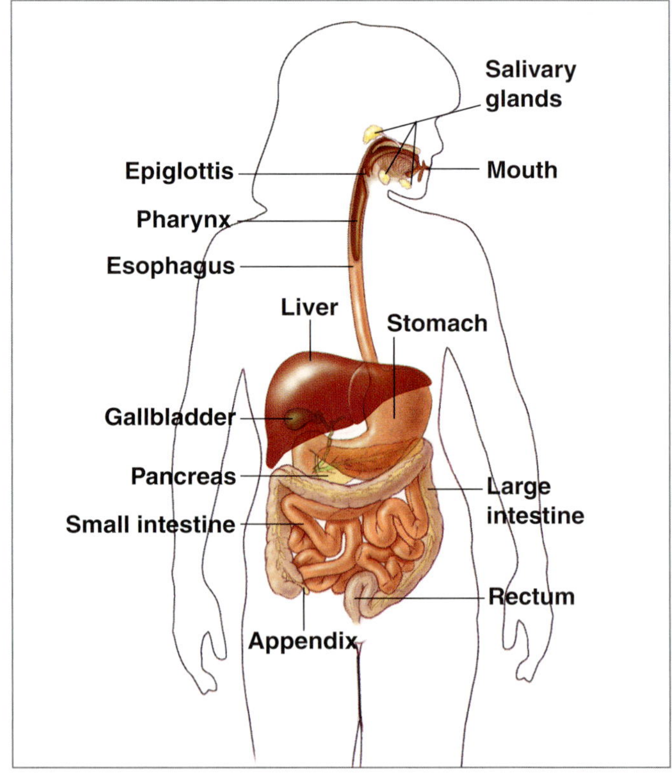

▲ **Figure 2-15** The digestive system

 NAME: What are the organs of the digestive system?

Peristalsis Once food leaves the mouth, it enters the esophagus. The walls of the esophagus secrete mucus. The mucus helps the food move easily through the esophagus. Once food leaves the esophagus, it continues along the digestive tract. Food is moved through the digestive tract by wavelike movements of muscles. The wavelike movement that moves food through the digestive tract is called **peristalsis.**

 DEFINE: What is peristalsis?

CHECKING CONCEPTS

1. What is the process by which food is turned into usable forms?
2. What is the end of the large intestine called?
3. How does food move through the digestive tract?
4. What connects the mouth to the stomach?
5. What prevents food from entering the windpipe?

THINKING CRITICALLY

6. SEQUENCE: Develop a flowchart to show the parts of the digestive tract through which food passes, in order, beginning with the mouth.
7. INFER: Why do you think food must be broken down into smaller pieces?

HEALTH AND SAFETY TIP

Sometimes a piece of food accidentally enters the windpipe. When this happens, choking occurs. To help prevent choking, you should chew your food carefully, eat slowly, and avoid talking or running with food in your mouth. If you should choke on anything, give the universal sign of choking shown in Figure 2-16. Use library references to find out what to do if someone you are eating with begins to choke.

▲ **Figure 2-16** The universal sign of choking

Hands-On Activity

MODELING PERISTALSIS

You will need a clear, flexible plastic straw and a small bead. The bead should fit snugly inside the straw.

1. Insert the bead into the straw.
2. Pinch the straw directly above the bead so that the bead moves down the straw. Release the straw when the bead moves.
3. Continue to pinch and release the straw to move the bead until the bead exits the straw.

▲ **STEP 2** Pinch the straw above the bead.

Practicing Your Skills

4. APPLY: What does the bead represent?
5. APPLY: What does the plastic straw represent?
6. EXPLAIN: How does this activity model peristalsis?
7. INFER: What might happen if you try to swallow a large piece of food?

2-7 What is digestion?

Objectives

Compare mechanical and chemical digestion.
Explain the function of enzymes.

Key Terms

mechanical digestion: process by which large pieces of food are cut and crushed into smaller pieces

enamel: hard, outer coating of the tooth

dentin: spongy substance below the enamel of the tooth

chemical digestion: process by which large food molecules are broken down into smaller food molecules

enzyme: protein that controls chemical reactions in the body

Digestion Digestion is the process of changing foods into usable forms. Food is changed two ways, physically and chemically. Changes in shape and size are examples of physical changes. If you tear a sheet of paper, that is a physical change. A chemical change results in new substances. For example, a log burning is a chemical change. The wood is changed into ash and soot.

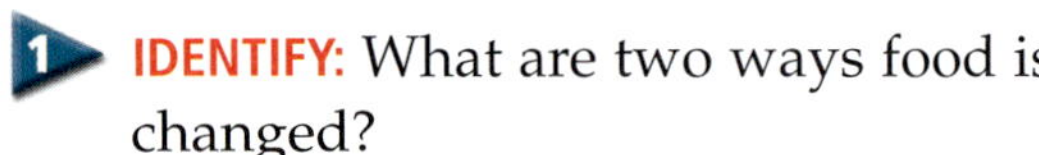

1 IDENTIFY: What are two ways food is changed?

Mechanical Digestion The physical change of food is called **mechanical digestion.** Mechanical digestion breaks large pieces of food into smaller pieces. In the mouth, teeth begin the mechanical digestion of food. You use your teeth to cut, tear, grind, and crush foods.

The part of the tooth that is visible is called the crown. The crown is covered with **enamel.** Enamel is the hardest substance in the human body. Underneath the enamel is a spongy substance called **dentin.** Dentin absorbs the shock of chewing. The roots secure the teeth in the jaw. The root canal is a space for nerves and blood vessels to get to the tooth. Look at Figure 2-17.

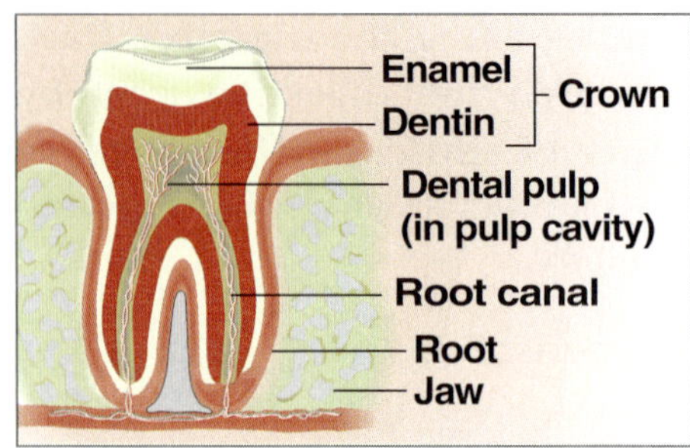

◀ **Figure 2-17** Parts of a tooth

Adults have 32 teeth. There are four different kinds of teeth. Incisors and canines cut and tear food. Bicuspids and molars grind and crush food. When food is crushed by the teeth, it is broken into small pieces. Your tongue moves the food around. This crushing of food is a physical change.

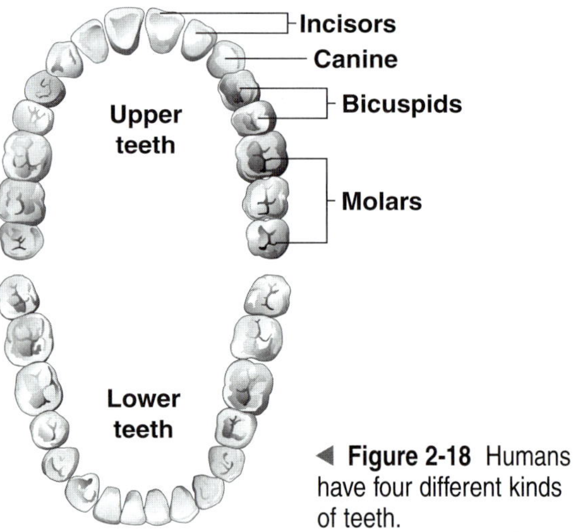

◀ **Figure 2-18** Humans have four different kinds of teeth.

2 INTERPRET: Look at Figure 2-18. How are the shapes of teeth adapted to their functions?

Chemical Digestion The process by which large food molecules are broken down into smaller food molecules is called **chemical digestion.** Chemical digestion begins in the mouth with saliva. Saliva mixes with foods and makes them soft and moist.

Saliva contains enzymes. **Enzymes** are proteins that control chemical reactions in the body. Enzymes help digest food. They break down the complex molecules in food into simpler molecules. Each enzyme can break down only one specific kind of food molecule. For example, one enzyme in saliva helps digest starch. It changes starch into sugar.

3 DEFINE: What is an enzyme?

Process of Digestion Enzymes act only on the outside surface of food particles. The mechanical breakdown of food provides a larger surface area for the enzymes to work on. The chemical digestion of food takes a number of steps. With each step, the food is broken down into smaller particles and then molecules. The body can use only the smallest, simplest molecules.

4 **INFER:** Why is the mechanical breakdown of food important?

CHECKING CONCEPTS

1. Shape and size are __________ properties.
2. The crushing of food by the teeth is a __________ change.
3. The liquid found in the mouth is called __________.
4. Enzymes in saliva change __________ into sugars.
5. The breakdown of large food molecules into small food molecules is __________ digestion.

THINKING CRITICALLY

6. **INFER:** Why do you think it is important to chew your food into small pieces?
7. **EXPLAIN:** What nutrient begins to be digested in the mouth?

HEALTH AND SAFETY TIP

Tooth Decay Tooth decay causes cavities. A cavity is a hole in the tooth. Saliva, food, and bacteria in the mouth mix to form a film called plaque (PLAK). Plaque breaks down the enamel of the tooth. If plaque is allowed to build up, it spreads to the soft parts of the tooth. Brushing and flossing your teeth daily can help prevent the buildup of plaque. Make a poster promoting good dental health. Include proper techniques for brushing and flossing. Present your poster to the class.

People in Science

DENTAL HYGIENIST

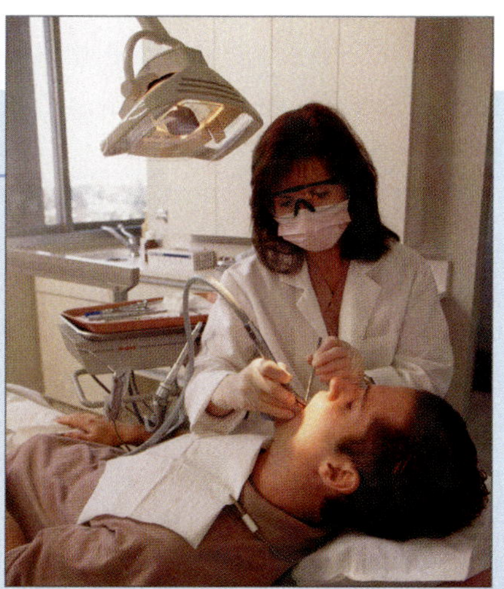

▲ **Figure 2-19** Dental hygienists examine teeth.

A trip to the dentist often includes a session with a dental hygienist. Dental hygienists help find, prevent, and treat mouth diseases. They examine teeth and gums, take X-rays, and clean and polish patients' teeth. They also remove plaque from under the gums. After oral surgery, dental hygienists may remove stitches or change dressings. Many dental hygienists work with dentists in private offices. Many work in other health-care facilities or in public health jobs. Often, dental hygienists specialize in education, teaching people how to take better care of their teeth and gums.

To be a dental hygienist, a person needs to complete a two-year course at a college or professional school. Some students take additional courses and training to earn a four-year college degree and sometimes even a graduate degree. Dental hygienists need to be skillful in working with their hands. They also need to be good at making worried patients feel comfortable.

Thinking Critically Why do you think it is important for people in all situations to take care of their teeth?

2-8 What happens to food in the stomach?

Modeling Digestion
HANDS-ON ACTIVITY

1. Fill two glasses with water.
2. Place a mint in one of the glasses of water.
3. Break another mint into several small pieces. Put the pieces of mint in the second glass of water.
4. Observe which mint dissolves more quickly.

THINK ABOUT IT: Based on your observations, do you think food is digested more quickly when it is broken down into smaller pieces?

Objective
Describe what happens to food once it enters the stomach.

Key Terms
gastric juice: juice produced in the stomach that contains mucus, pepsin, and hydrochloric acid

pepsin (PEHP-sihn)**:** enzyme that digests proteins

chyme (KYM)**:** thick liquid form in which food leaves the stomach

The Stomach Once food leaves the esophagus, it enters the stomach. The stomach is a J-shaped, baglike organ that stores food. The stomach also breaks down food. In fact, mechanical digestion takes place in the stomach as well as in the mouth. The walls of the stomach are made up of layers of strong muscles. These muscles tighten and squeeze the food, changing it into smaller pieces.

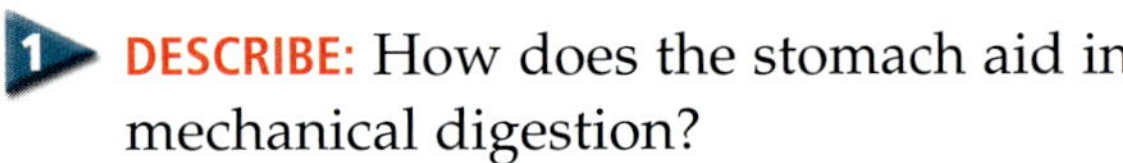

1 DESCRIBE: How does the stomach aid in mechanical digestion?

Gastric Juice The small pieces of food in the stomach are mixed with stomach juice. This juice makes the food soft. The juice the stomach produces is called **gastric juice.** Gastric juice contains hydrochloric (hy-droh-KLAWR-ihk) acid, mucus, and pepsin.

2 IDENTIFY: What does gastric juice contain?

Chemical Digestion in the Stomach One of the enzymes in gastric juice is **pepsin.** Pepsin begins the digestion of proteins. Hydrochloric acid is a very strong acid. It is needed to make the stomach acidic. Pepsin can work only in an acidic environment. Hydrochloric acid kills bacteria in the stomach and helps to break down food. The mucus in gastric juice protects the stomach lining from the hydrochloric acid and pepsin.

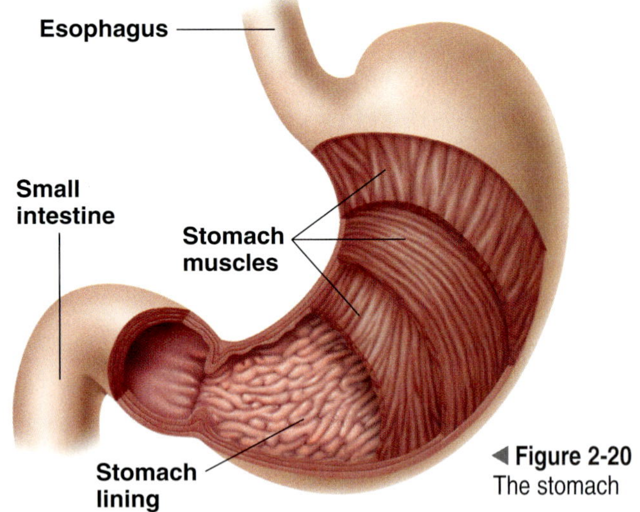

◀ **Figure 2-20** The stomach

3 DEFINE: What is pepsin?

Chyme Once food has been crushed by the stomach and mixed with gastric juice, it is ready to leave the stomach. Food that leaves the stomach is in the form of a thick liquid. This liquid is called **chyme.** Chyme is released slowly from the stomach into the small intestine.

 **DEFINE:** What is chyme?

CHECKING CONCEPTS

1. What does mucus in the gastric juice do?
2. How is food mechanically digested in the stomach?
3. How is food chemically digested in the stomach?
4. What enzyme digests proteins?
5. In what form is food that leaves the stomach?
6. What does the stomach look like?

THINKING CRITICALLY

7. **EXPLAIN:** Why is the stomach an important part of the digestive system?
8. **INFER:** What would happen if the stomach did not produce mucus?
9. **EXPLAIN:** Why is hydrochloric acid important to digestion?
10. **SEQUENCE:** Describe the change that food undergoes from the time it enters the mouth to the time it enters the small intestine. Put your answer in a flowchart.

BUILDING SCIENCE SKILLS

Researching A hole that occurs in the stomach lining is called an ulcer. A stomach ulcer is caused by bacteria. Ulcers can also occur in the small intestine. Use library references to find out the causes of ulcers, the signs and symptoms of ulcers, and the treatment of ulcers. Present your findings in a table.

How Do They Know That?

DR. WILLIAM BEAUMONT (1785–1853)

William Beaumont was an American army doctor in the early 1800s. On June 6, 1822, an 18-year-old named Alexis St. Martin was accidentally shot in the stomach. Dr. Beaumont saved the young man's life. However, the wound never completely closed. For the rest of his life, St. Martin had a two-and-a-half-inch opening in his left side.

William Beaumont discovered that he could view the workings of the stomach through the opening. For the next eight years, with St. Martin's cooperation, Dr. Beaumont studied the stomach. At that time, most information about human digestion was obtained by examining the remains of the deceased. The use of X-rays had not been discovered yet. Therefore, the ability to view a functioning body system was extraordinary. Dr. Beaumont published his findings in 1833, providing other doctors with valuable information about human digestion. Much of what people know today about the functions of the stomach is based on the observations of Dr. Beaumont.

▲ **Figure 2-21** Dr. Beaumont studied St. Martin's stomach.

Thinking Critically Why do you think the work of Beaumont was important?

2-9 What happens to food in the small intestine?

Modeling Fat Digestion

HANDS-ON ACTIVITY

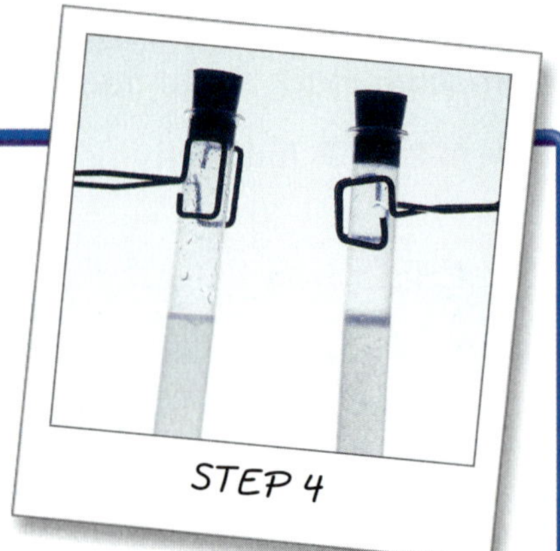

1. Half-fill two test tubes with water.
2. Using a medicine dropper, put four drops of cooking oil into each test tube.
3. Add 1/4 teaspoon of baking soda to one of the test tubes.
4. Put a stopper in each test tube and shake them well. Observe what happens.

THINK ABOUT IT: How did the baking soda affect the cooking oil? How might this effect speed the digestion of fats?

Objectives

Describe what happens to food in the small intestine. Describe what happens to food after it leaves the small intestine.

Key Terms

lipase (LY-pays)**:** enzyme that digests fats and oils

bile: green liquid that breaks down large droplets of fat into smaller droplets of fat

emulsification (ee-mul-suh-fih-KAY-shuhn)**:** process of breaking down large droplets of fat into smaller droplets of fat

absorption (ab-SAWRP-shuhn)**:** movement of food molecules from the digestive system to the blood

villus, *pl.* **villi:** fingerlike projection on the lining of the small intestine

The Small Intestine The small intestine is a long, coiled tube. It is about 6.5 m long and 2.5 cm wide. Like the stomach, the walls of the small intestine are muscular. Food moves through the small intestine by peristalsis. Most of the chemical digestion of food takes place in the small intestine. Look at the location of the small intestine in Figure 2-22 on the next page.

1 **EXPLAIN:** What happens in the small intestine?

Digestion in the Small Intestine Digestive juices in the small intestine contain many enzymes that complete digestion. One of these enzymes is **lipase.** Lipase digests fats and oils. Fats are digested only in the small intestine.

DEFINE: What is lipase?

The Pancreas The pancreas is a large gland that lies below the stomach (see Figure 2-22). When food first enters the small intestine, the pancreas releases digestive juices. These digestive juices travel to the small intestine through a small tube called the pancreatic duct. Pancreatic digestive juices contain enzymes. These enzymes change starches, proteins, and fats into simpler forms.

IDENTIFY: How does the pancreas aid in chemical digestion?

The Liver The liver is the largest organ in the human body. One job of the liver is to produce bile. **Bile** is a green liquid that breaks down large droplets of fat into smaller droplets of fat. The breaking down of large fat droplets into smaller fat droplets is called **emulsification.** The smaller droplets can then be used by the body.

Bile does not move directly from the liver to the small intestine. Bile is stored in a small sac under the liver. The sac is called the gallbladder. Bile moves from the gallbladder into the small intestine through a small tube.

DEFINE: What is emulsification?

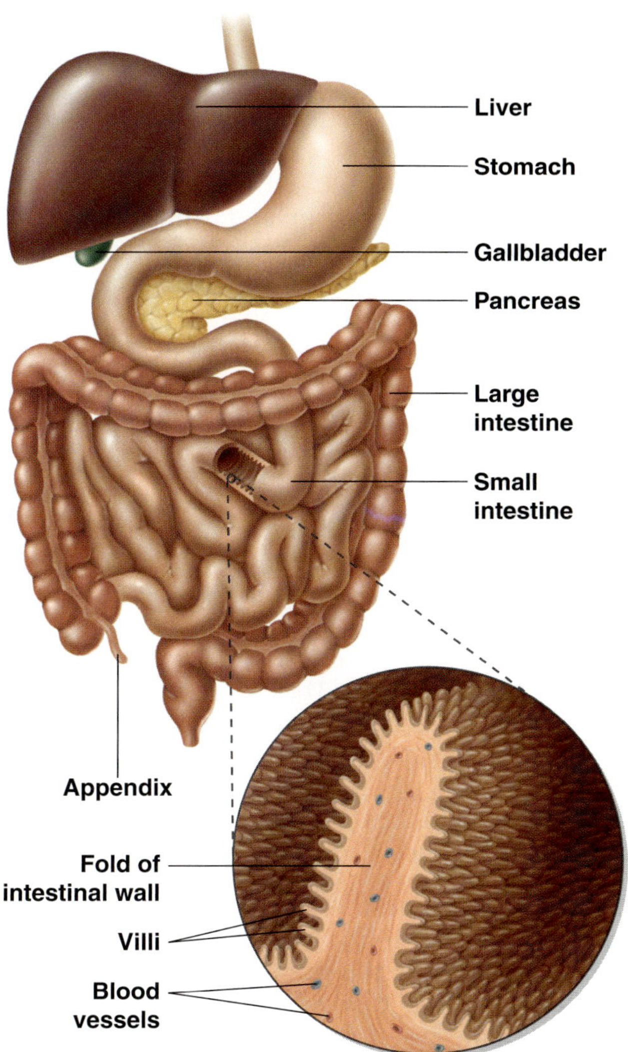

▲ **Figure 2-22** The small and large intestines

Absorption in the Small Intestine After food has been changed to usable molecules, it is ready to be absorbed. **Absorption** is the movement of food from the digestive system to the blood. Absorption of food molecules and water takes place through the walls of the small intestine. Once inside the blood, digested food is carried to all of the cells of your body .

The inner lining of the small intestine is folded. The folds have millions of tiny fingerlike projections called **villi.** The folds and villi make the surface area of the small intestine larger. Digested food passes through the layers of the villi and into the blood vessels.

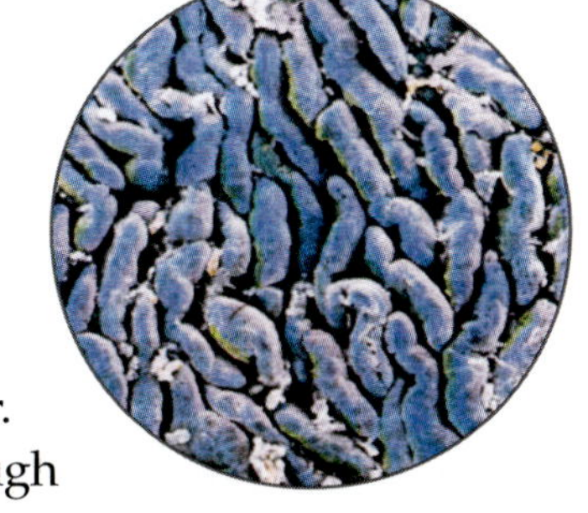

▲ **Figure 2-23** Villi

5 **EXPLAIN:** What is absorption?

The Large Intestine The large intestine is the last part of the digestive system. Some undigested food, minerals, and water are not absorbed in the small intestine. They form a watery mixture. This mixture enters the large intestine. Water and minerals are absorbed into the blood in the large intestine. The remaining solid wastes are stored temporarily in the rectum. Then, they are eliminated from the body.

6 **DESCRIBE:** What happens to food in the large intestine?

CHECKING CONCEPTS

1. Most __________ digestion takes place in the small intestine.
2. Lipase is an enzyme that digests __________.
3. The gallbladder stores __________.
4. Bile is responsible for the __________ of fat.

THINKING CRITICALLY

5. **INFER:** Why must food be absorbed?
6. **HYPOTHESIZE:** How do folds and villi increase the surface area of the small intestine?

Web InfoSearch

The Appendix The appendix is located where the small intestine and large intestine meet. It does not have a known use in humans. An infection of the appendix is called appendicitis. An infected appendix must be removed.

SEARCH: Use the Internet to find out more about the appendix. Write your findings in a report. Start your search at www.conceptsandchallenges.com. Some key search words are **appendix** and **appendicitis.**

THE Big IDEA

What chemical reactions take place during digestion?

Chemistry is a branch of physical science. It is the study of all forms of matter and changes in matter. Digestion changes food into usable forms. This involves chemistry.

Chemical digestion breaks large food molecules into smaller food molecules. For this to happen, a chemical change must take place in the food. The process by which a chemical change takes place is called a chemical reaction. In some chemical reactions, substances combine to form a more complex substance. This is called a synthesis reaction. In digestion, the opposite occurs. Complex substances are broken down into simpler substances. This is called a decomposition reaction. Enzymes are chemicals that speed up these reactions. Each enzyme works on only one type of food molecule.

The stomach secretes enzymes called pepsin. Pepsin enzymes start to digest protein. Proteins are giant molecules. Pepsin enzymes split proteins into small fragments. These fragments are still too big to be absorbed. In the small intestine, proteins break down further into substances that are called amino acids. Amino acids are the building blocks of protein. Amino acids pass easily through the lining of the small intestine.

In addition to protein, the digestive system breaks down carbohydrates and fats. Look at the boxes of text that appear on this page and the next. They point out parts of the digestive tract where chemical reactions take place to digest food. Follow the directions in the Science Log to learn more about "the big idea." ✦

1 Gastric Juices

Gastric juices are released into the stomach. They contain mucus, pepsin, and hydrochloric acid. Hydrochloric acid breaks up particles of food. Pepsin splits proteins into fragments. These fragments are still not small enough to be absorbed. Food leaves the stomach as a thick liquid called chyme.

2 Bile

The liver secretes bile. Bile is stored in the gallbladder, which squirts it into the small intestine. Bile salts help in the digestion and absorption of fats. They coat the fat droplets. The chemical makeup of bile salts keeps the droplets from rejoining. They also combine with other substances to form particles that can dissolve in water.

3 Bicarbonate

The chyme moves to the small intestine. The chyme that enters is very acidic from the hydrochloric acid in the stomach. The pancreas secretes a chemical called bicarbonate that neutralizes the chyme.

4 Pancreatic Enzymes

Pancreatic juices enter the small intestine. These juices contain enzymes that change starches, proteins, and fats into simpler forms. Lipase splits fat molecules into more easily absorbed droplets. Enzymes in the wall of the small intestine break protein fragments into amino acids. Pancreatic amylase breaks down starch into simpler substances. Enzymes in the wall of the small intestine split these molecules further.

5 Small Intestine

Digestion is completed in the small intestine. Most nutrients move into the bloodstream through the intestinal lining by active transport. Energy pumps them from a less-crowded area to a more-crowded area. The other process, diffusion, does not require energy. Material moves from an area where molecules are crowded to an area where they are less crowded.

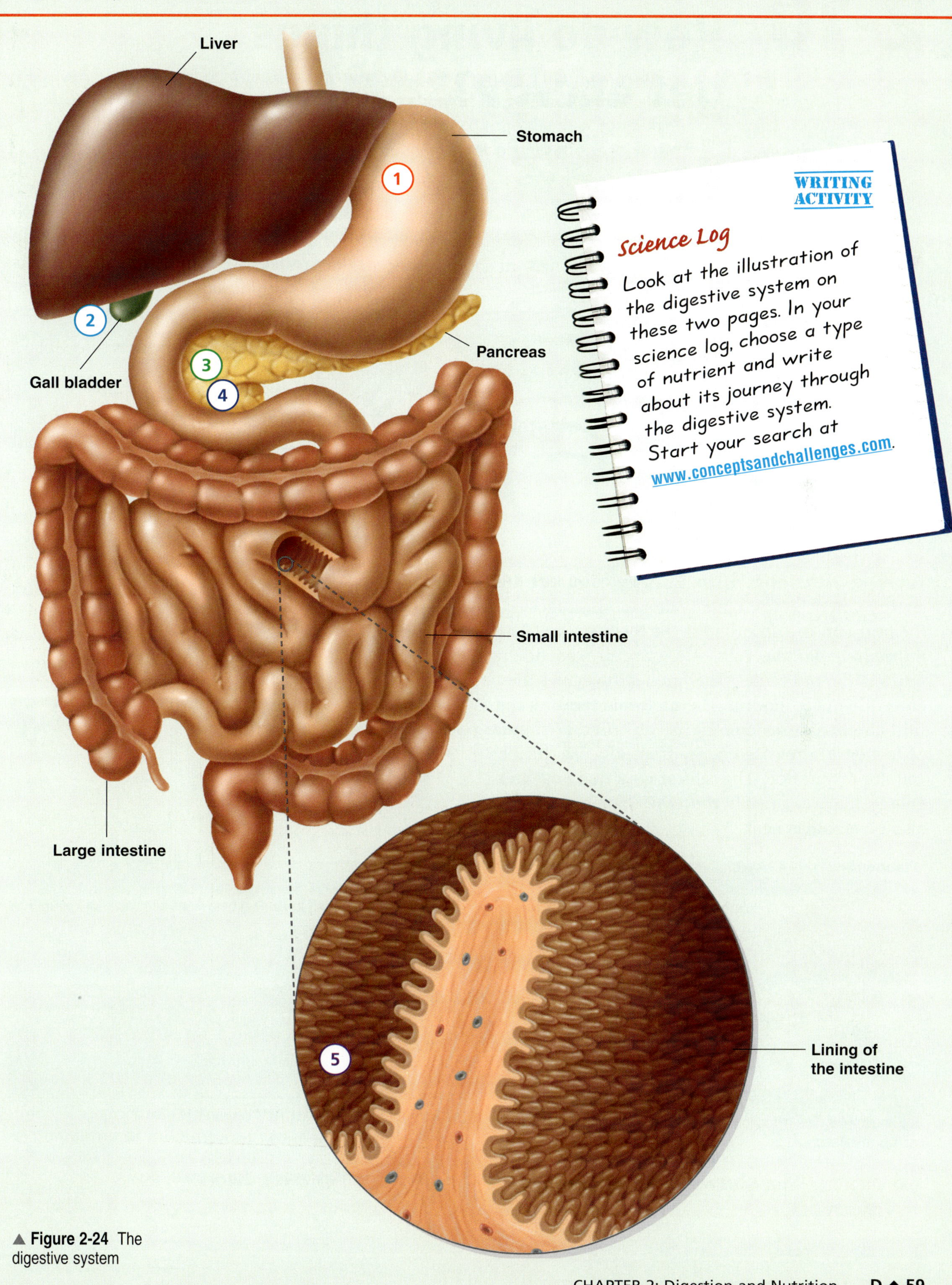

▲ **Figure 2-24** The digestive system

2-10 How do living things get energy?

Objective

Explain how organisms turn food into energy.

Key Term

Calorie (KAL-uh-ree)**:** unit used to measure energy from foods

Energy Your body needs energy to stay alive. Everything you do requires energy. You need energy to walk, to run, and even to sleep. Your heart needs energy to pump blood through the body. Right now, your body is growing. You need energy to grow.

 STATE: Why does your body need energy?

Turning Nutrients into Energy You get the energy you need from food. After food is digested, the nutrients are absorbed in the bloodstream. The nutrients enter the cells. They are broken down into smaller molecules. The smaller molecules then enter the mitochondria. The molecule used by the mitochondria for energy is glucose, a sugar. Mitochondria release energy from glucose during cellular respiration. The cells of your body use this energy to carry out life processes. Some energy is also given off as heat.

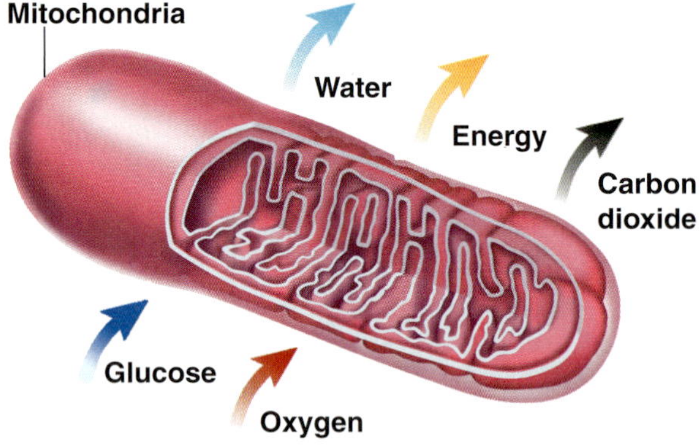

▲ **Figure 2-25** The mitochondria release energy during cellular respiration.

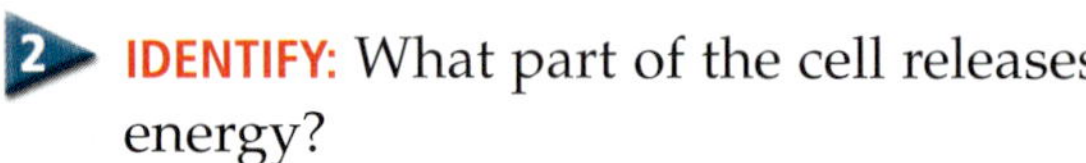 IDENTIFY: What part of the cell releases energy?

Byproducts of Cellular Respiration During cellular respiration, carbon dioxide and water are given off as byproducts. To show that your body gives off water, breathe on a mirror. What do you see? Water collects on the mirror. The water is a byproduct of cellular respiration going on in your body.

 IDENTIFY: What are the byproducts of cellular respiration?

Measuring Food Energy Different foods contain different amounts of energy. The amount of energy contained in foods is measured in **Calories.** A Calorie is a unit used to measure food energy. Fat contains the most energy. Each gram of fat contains approximately 9.5 Calories of energy. No more than 30% of the Calories that you consume should be from fat. Proteins and carbohydrates each give off about the same amount of energy. Each gram of protein or carbohydrate gives off about 4 Calories of energy.

▲ **Figure 2-26** These marathon runners burn approximately 800 Calories per hour.

 DEFINE: What is a Calorie?

CHECKING CONCEPTS

1. What process produces the energy your body needs?
2. What are the byproducts of cellular respiration?
3. Do all foods give off the same amount of energy?
4. What unit is used to measure food energy?
5. Where do you get the energy you need?
6. What nutrient supplies the most energy?

THINKING CRITICALLY

7. **CALCULATE:** If food contains 5 g of fat, how many Calories of fat are in the food?
8. **INFER:** Why do foods with high amounts of fat have more Calories than do foods that are high in carbohydrates?
9. **HYPOTHESIZE:** Boys ages 12 to 15 years need about 2,800 Calories each day. Girls the same age need about 2,400 Calories each day. What do you think would happen if you ate more Calories than what you needed?

INTERPRETING VISUALS

Use Figure 2-25 to answer the following questions.

10. **SYNTHESIZE:** What is the chemical equation for cellular respiration?
11. **ANALYZE:** What are the byproducts?

Hands-On Activity

CALCULATING CALORIES

You will need a sheet of paper and a pencil.

1. To find the total number of Calories in food, multiply the total number of grams of fat the food contains by 9.5. Record the product.
2. Then, multiply the total number of grams of carbohydrates the food contains by 4. Record the product.
3. Multiply the total number of grams of protein the food contains by 4. Record the product.
4. Add the three products together to find out the total number of Calories in a serving of food.

Calories from fat =
$9.5 \times$ number of fat grams

Calories from carbohydrate =
$4 \times$ number of carbohydrate grams

Calories from protein =
$4 \times$ number of protein grams

▲ **Figure 2-27** Use these formulas to calculate the number of calories in food.

Practicing Your Skills

Find out the total number of Calories in each of the following examples.

5. 8 g Protein, 11 g carbohydrates, 1 g fat
6. 4 g Protein, 10 g carbohydrates, 8 g fat
7. 0 g Protein, 1 g carbohydrates, 5 g fat
8. 14 g Protein, 4 g carbohydrates, 3 g fat
9. 5 g Protein, 7 g carbohydrates, 6 g fat
10. 7 g Protein, 4 g carbohydrates, 0 g fat

Chapter 2 Challenges

Chapter Summary

Lesson 2-1

- **Nutrients** are chemical substances in food that are needed by the body for growth, energy, and life processes.

Lessons 2-2, 2-3, and 2-4

- **Proteins** are used to build new cells, repair damaged cells, make enzymes, control chemical activities, and are a source of energy.
- **Vitamins** are important for growth and for proper body function. **Minerals** are nutrients needed by the body for it to develop and function properly.

Lesson 2-5

- Balanced diets contain the right amounts of nutrients to keep the body healthy.

Lesson 2-6

- **Digestion** is the process by which foods are changed so that they can be used by the body. The digestive tract and digestive organs make up your digestive system.

Lesson 2-7

- Large pieces of food are cut and crushed into smaller pieces of food during **mechanical digestion.**
- Large food molecules are broken down into smaller food molecules during **chemical digestion.**

Lesson 2-8

- The stomach is a baglike organ that stores food.
- **Gastric juice** contains mucus, **pepsin,** and hydrochloric acid, and is produced by the stomach. **Chyme** is a thick liquid form of food that leaves the stomach.

Lesson 2-9

- The pancreas releases digestive juices into the small intestine to break up starch, protein, and fat. The liver produces **bile,** which emulsifies fats and oils. Bile is stored in the gallbladder.

Lesson 2-10

- Your body needs energy to stay alive. Cells produce energy during cellular respiration.
- The amount of energy food gives off is measured in **Calories.**

Key Term Challenges

absorption (p. 56)
amino acid (p. 40)
bile (p. 56)
Calorie (p. 60)
carbohydrate (p. 38)
chemical digestion (p. 52)
chyme (p. 54)
deficiency disease (p. 42)
dentin (p. 52)
digestion (p. 50)
emulsification (p. 56)
enamel (p. 52)
enzyme (p. 52)
epiglottis (p. 50)
esophagus (p. 50)
gastric juice (p. 54)
lipase (p. 56)
malnutrition (p. 48)
mechanical digestion (p. 52)
mineral (p. 44)
molecule (p. 40)
nutrient (p. 38)
pepsin (p. 54)
peristalsis (p. 50)
pharynx (p. 50)
protein (p. 38)
saliva (p. 50)
villus (p. 56)
vitamin (p. 42)

MATCHING Write the Key Term from above that best matches each description.

1. finger like projections on the lining of the small intestine
2. enzyme that begins the digestion of protein
3. breaking down of large food molecules into small food molecules
4. process by which foods are changed into forms the body can use
5. chemical substance in food needed by the body for growth, energy, and life processes
6. protein that controls chemical activity
7. nutrient needed by the body to develop properly
8. thick, liquid like form of food

IDENTIFYING WORD RELATIONSHIPS Explain how the words in each pair are related. Write your answers in complete sentences.

9. lipase, emulsification
10. amino acid, protein
11. saliva, carbohydrate
12. bile, fat

Content Challenges 

MULTIPLE CHOICE **Write the letter of the term or phrase that best completes each statement.**

1. The wavelike movement that moves through the digestive system is called
- **a.** chyme.
- **b.** mechanical digestion.
- **c.** peristalsis.
- **d.** chemical digestion.

2. The largest organ inside the body is the
- **a.** stomach.
- **b.** gallbladder.
- **c.** liver.
- **d.** pancreas.

3. Soft bones and teeth may be caused by a diet that lacks
- **a.** zinc.
- **b.** protein.
- **c.** calcium.
- **d.** vitamin A.

4. Starches are
- **a.** proteins.
- **b.** simple carbohydrates.
- **c.** fats.
- **d.** complex carbohydrates.

5. The largest amount of food energy comes from
- **a.** fats.
- **b.** carbohydrates.
- **c.** vitamins.
- **d.** proteins.

6. Mechanical digestion begins in the
- **a.** esophagus.
- **b.** pharynx.
- **c.** mouth.
- **d.** stomach.

7. Undigested food from the small intestine moves into the
- **a.** pancreas.
- **b.** appendix.
- **c.** stomach.
- **d.** large intestine.

8. Saliva begins the chemical digestion of
- **a.** proteins.
- **b.** starches.
- **c.** fats.
- **d.** nutrients.

9. Amino acids make up
- **a.** proteins.
- **b.** fats.
- **c.** water.
- **d.** carbohydrates.

10. Your body needs proteins for
- **a.** malnourishment.
- **b.** insulation.
- **c.** energy.
- **d.** growth and repair.

FILL IN **Write the term that best completes each sentence.**

11. Many chemical reactions that take place in the body are controlled by ___________.

12. Gastric juice contains pepsin, ___________, and mucus.

13. Bile is produced in the ___________.

14. The ___________ releases digestive juices into the small intestine.

15. When food is swallowed, it enters the ___________.

16. A weakened condition that results from a lack of a certain nutrient is called a ___________.

Concept Challenges TEST PREP

WRITTEN RESPONSE **Answer each of the following questions in complete sentences.**

1. **EXPLAIN:** Is the action of bile on fat part of mechanical digestion or chemical digestion? Explain.
2. **INFER:** What role does the large surface area of the small intestine play in absorption?
3. **EXPLAIN:** Why is absorption important?
4. **HYPOTHESIZE:** Why do you think low-carbohydrate "liquid diets" are unhealthy?
5. **APPLY:** What would you eat before an athletic competition, a bowl of spaghetti or a steak? Explain.

INTERPRETING A DIAGRAM **Use Figure 2-28 to answer the following questions.**

6. What is the function of the part labeled *A*?
7. What letter indicates a organ that has no known function?
8. What letter indicates where gastric juice is produced?
9. What is the function of the part labeled *E*?
10. What does letter *F* represent?

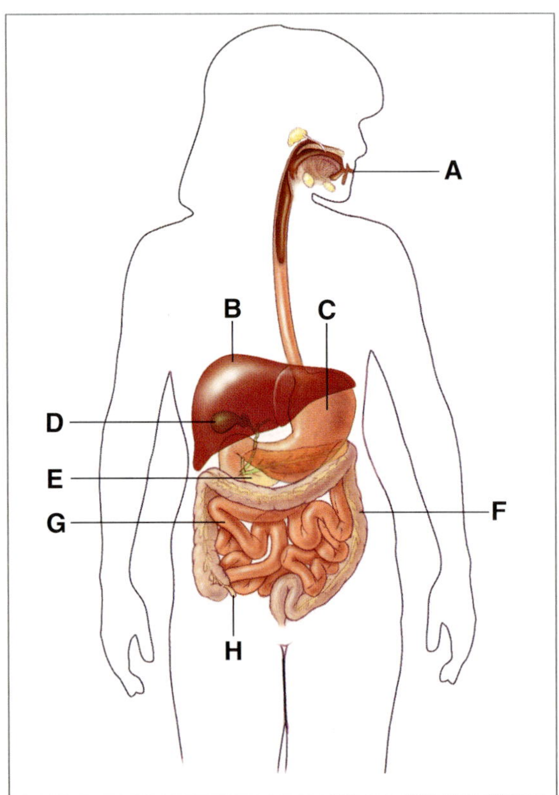

▲ **Figure 2-28** The digestive system

Chapter 3 Transport in the Body

▲ **Figure 3-1** The oxygen these swimmers need is transported through the body by the circulatory system.

All of the cells in the human body require oxygen and nutrients to function. These materials need to be transported to the cells. Waste products from the cells have to be taken away. During activity such as swimming, muscle cells require more oxygen than usual. Oxygen is transported by blood, which is pumped throughout the body by the heart.

▶Why do you think it is important for the heart to be able to adapt to the changing needs of the body?

Contents

3-1 What is the circulatory system?

3-2 What are the parts of the heart?

3-3 What are blood vessels?

3-4 What is blood?

■ **Lab Activity:** Observing Blood Cells

3-5 What happens to blood as it circulates?

3-6 What is heart disease?

■ **The Big Idea:** How is technology used to treat cardiovascular disease?

3-1 What is the circulatory system?

Objective

Describe the circulatory system and its functions.

Key Terms

circulation: movement of blood through the body

closed circulatory system: organ system in which blood moves through vessels

hormone (HAWR-mohn)**:** chemical substance that regulates body functions

Circulation Most large cities have a complex network of railroads, highways, and subways. This transport system is necessary for people to get around and for materials to go into and out of the city. Your body also has a transport system. It is your circulatory system. The circulatory system transports, or moves, blood throughout the body. The movement of blood through the body is called **circulation.**

1 DEFINE: What is circulation?

The Circulatory System Your circulatory system is made up of your heart, blood vessels, and blood. The blood vessels form a closed circulatory system. All vertebrates, including fish, birds, and humans, have a closed circulatory system. In a **closed circulatory system,** the blood moves through blood vessels. The arteries are connected to the veins by capillaries. The arteries, veins, and capillaries form a large network of tubes that form a continuous closed system.

2 LIST: What makes up your circulatory system?

Jobs of the Circulatory System The main job of the circulatory system is to transport various materials. However, the circulatory system has many other jobs as well.

- **Transport of Food and Oxygen** The circulatory system transports nutrients from the small intestines to the cells of the body. It also delivers oxygen from the lungs to the cells of your body. A compound called hemoglobin in red blood cells carries the oxygen.
- **Transport of Wastes** The circulatory system carries away wastes and byproducts of cellular processes. One important byproduct is carbon dioxide.
- **Protection** Another job of the circulatory system is protection. Certain cells in your blood called white blood cells defend your body against invading microorganisms. This helps the body fight disease.
- **Transport of Hormones** The circulatory system carries chemicals called **hormones.** Hormones carry chemical "messages" from one part of your body to another part of your body.
- **Regulation** The circulatory system helps regulate your body temperature. Blood distributes heat evenly around your body. This is important for all warm-blooded animals, including humans.

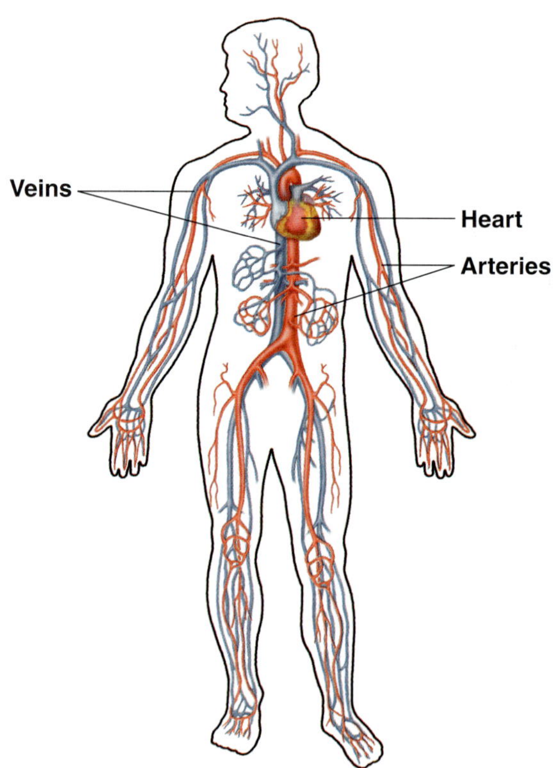

▲ **Figure 3-2** The circulatory system transports materials throughout the body.

3 LIST: What are some jobs of the circulatory system?

CHECKING CONCEPTS

1. The circulatory system __________ blood and oxygen to all parts of the body.
2. Arteries, veins, and capillaries form a __________ circulatory system.
3. Carbon dioxide is a __________ that is removed from the body by blood.
4. Chemical "messengers" that are carried in the blood are called __________.
5. The job of __________ blood cells is to fight disease.

THINKING CRITICALLY

6. **INFER:** Why is the human circulatory system called a closed system?
7. **RELATE:** How is the circulatory system like a network of highways?

Web InfoSearch

Artificial Hearts In July 2001, advancement in medical scienc made. The world's first wire-fre heart was implanted into a patien type of procedure could help thous patients who have been waiting yea natural heart to be donated.

SEARCH: Use the Internet to find out more about artificial hearts. Write a repo that describes different kinds of artificial hearts, how they work, and how they can help patients. Start your search at www.conceptsandchallenges.com. Some key search words are **artificial heart** and **mechanical heart.**

How Do They Know That?

BLOOD TRANSFUSIONS

▲ **Figure 3-3** Charles Drew

One of the most important parts of the circulatory system is blood. Blood transports all of the nutrients needed by the body to survive. The circulatory system cannot function properly without the correct amount of blood moving throughout the body. Sometimes, due to an injury or disease, people need blood that has been donated by other people. This blood is delivered to the patient in a process called a transfusion.

One scientist, Charles Drew, led the way for more effective blood transfusions. Charles Drew was an American doctor who concluded that plasma could be used in blood transfusions instead of whole blood. Plasma is the liquid part of blood. Using plasma in blood transfusions has two advantages. Whole blood stays fresh for only about one week. Plasma can last for a longer period of time. Plasma can also be used in a transfusion for any blood type.

Charles Drew did most of his research at Columbia University in New York City between 1938 and 1940. Drew's research was very important for his time. During World War II, Drew set up blood banks in the United States to collect plasma. The blood plasma was then sent to the American armed forces who were fighting in other countries. The blood plasma that was collected saved many lives.

Thinking Critically What are the advantages of using plasma in blood transfusions?

are the parts of the heart?

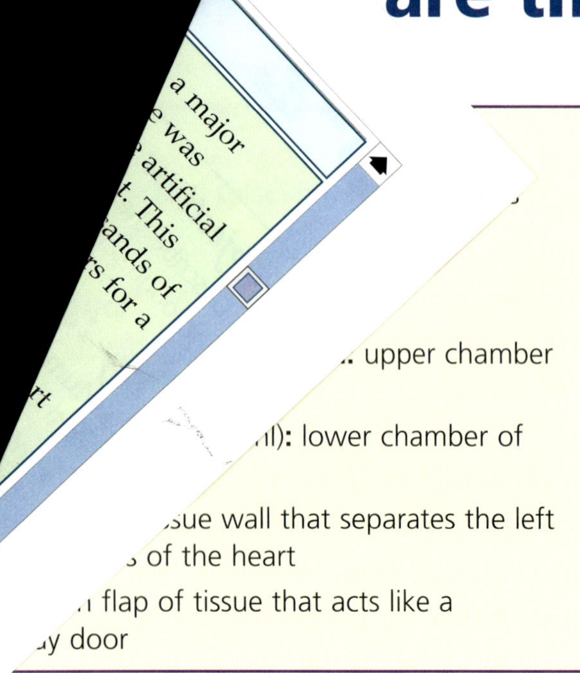

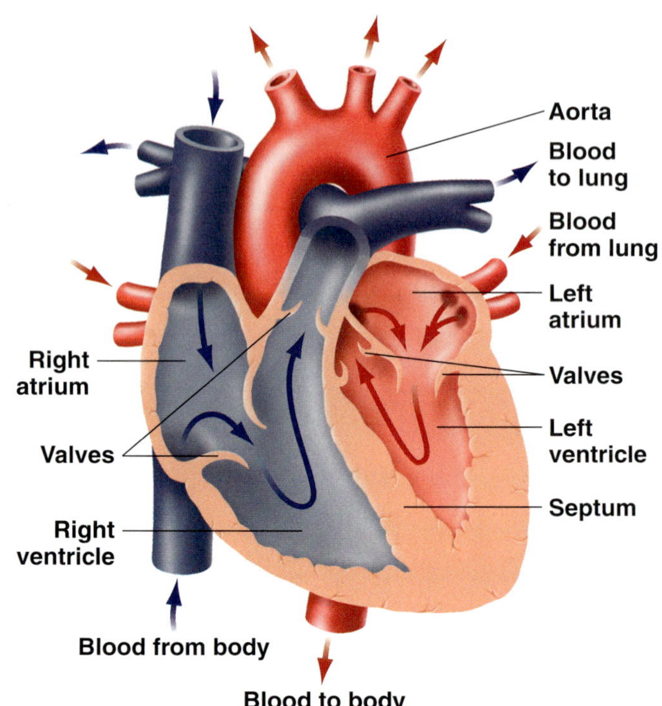

▲ **Figure 3-4** Trace the flow of blood through the heart.

Muscular Organ The central organ of the circulatory system is the heart. The heart is a muscular organ about the size of your fist. It is located in the chest cavity behind the sternum, or breastbone.

The function of the heart is to pump blood. The heart is divided into four parts, or chambers. There are two upper and two lower chambers. Each upper chamber of the heart is called an **atrium.** The atria receive blood. The lower chambers are called **ventricles.** The ventricles pump blood out of the heart. The walls of the ventricles are thicker than the walls of the atria. This is because the ventricles need to work hard to pump blood to all parts of the body.

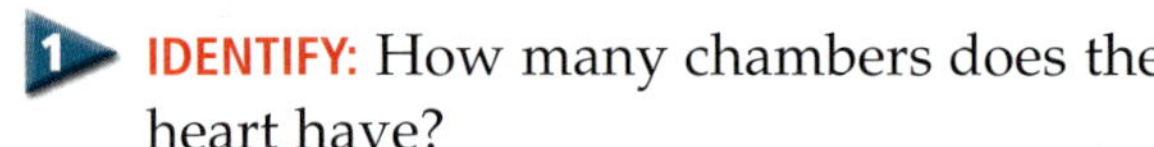

1 IDENTIFY: How many chambers does the heart have?

Blood Flow in the Heart Look at Figure 3-4. You can see that the heart is divided into two sides—a left side and a right side. A thick tissue wall separates the two sides of the heart. This tissue wall is called the **septum.**

Blood flows into the atria of the heart. When the atria are filled with blood, they contract. This motion pumps the blood into the ventricles. Once the ventricles are filled with blood, they contract. This motion pushes the blood out of the heart. The strong muscles of the ventricle walls give the heart enough force to send blood to all parts of the body.

2 SEQUENCE: Trace the flow of blood from the time it enters the heart until it leaves the heart.

Heart Valves Inside the heart, there are four valves. A **valve** is a thin flap of tissue. It acts like a one-way door. The valves keep the blood moving in only one direction. Blood is supposed to flow only from the atria to the ventricles. The valves are located between the atria and the ventricles. If the blood tries to flow backward, the valve shuts. There also are valves between the ventricles and the blood vessels. As blood leaves the ventricles, it passes through the valves.

3 IDENTIFY: What keeps blood from flowing backward in the heart?

Heartbeat Your heart will beat over 2 billion times in your lifetime. Your heartbeat is the rhythm of your heart as it pumps blood. A stethoscope (STEHTH-uh-skohp) is an instrument doctors use to listen to your heartbeat. If you were to listen to it, you would hear a lub-dub sound. The lub-dub sound is made by your valves opening and closing. When the valves between the atria and ventricles snap shut, they make a lub sound. When the valves between the ventricles and blood vessels snap shut, they make a dub sound.

 **DEFINE:** What is a stethoscope?

CHECKING CONCEPTS

1. The heart is a __________ organ.
2. The __________ divides the heart into left and right sides.
3. The upper chambers of the heart are called __________.
4. The __________ pumps blood out of the heart.
5. The heart has __________ valves.
6. The sound of your heartbeat is caused by the opening and closing of __________.

THINKING CRITICALLY

7. **INFER:** What do you think would happen if a valve were damaged?
8. **HYPOTHESIZE:** What might cause your heartbeat rate to increase?

BUILDING MATH SKILLS

Calculating If a person's heart beats 80 times a minute, how many times would it beat in 10 minutes? Calculate the number of heartbeats in an hour, a day, a week, a month, and a year.

Science and Technology

HEART VALVE REPLACEMENT

When heart valves do not work properly, the heart cannot pump blood effectively, and the body cells may not receive enough blood to supply their need for oxygen and nutrients. Surgeons may be able to repair damaged heart valves, or they may replace them. The faulty valve is carefully removed, and a new valve is attached in its place.

▲ **Figure 3-5** Synthetic valves are used to replace damaged heart valves.

Doctors use several kinds of replacements for damaged heart valves. They may transplant a human heart valve obtained from an organ donor. Valves taken from pig hearts or constructed from cow tissues can also be used. Mechanical heart valves, made from materials such as stainless steel or other materials, may also be used. Valves made of human or other animal tissues are less likely to be rejected by the body, but they are not as durable. Over a period of years, they may break down and have to be replaced. Mechanical heart valves are very durable, but blood clots tend to form on them and can cause a heart attack or stroke. Patients with these valves must take drugs to prevent clotting throughout their lives.

Thinking Critically How could a blood clot that formed on a mechanical he- valve cause a heart attack or stroke?

3-3 What are blood vessels?

Objective

Describe the three kinds of blood vessels.

Key Terms

artery (AHRT-uhr-ee)**:** blood vessel that carries blood away from the heart

vein (VAYN)**:** blood vessel that carries blood back to the heart

capillary (KAP-uh-ler-ee)**:** tiny blood vessel that connects arteries to veins

aorta (ay-AWR-tuh)**:** largest artery in the body

Blood Vessels Blood moves through a closed system of tubes called blood vessels. The human body has three kinds of blood vessels. The **arteries** are blood vessels that carry blood away from the heart. Blood vessels that carry blood back to the heart are **veins.** Veins and arteries are connected by tiny blood vessels called **capillaries.**

1 NAME: Name the three kinds of blood vessels.

Arteries As the heart beats, it pumps blood through the arteries at high pressure. The arteries must be strong to be able to handle this pressure. Arteries have thick muscular walls that prevent the arteries from bursting. The largest artery in the body is the **aorta.**

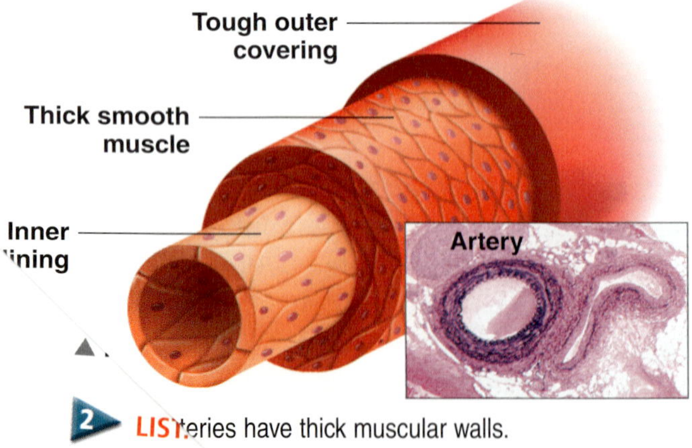

▲ .

2 LIS teries have thick muscular walls.

arterie

some characteristics of

Pulse As your heart beats, it pushes blood through the arteries in spurts. With each spurt of blood, a beat can be felt. The beat you feel is your pulse. You can feel a pulse wherever an artery is close to the skin's surface. Your pulse rate and heartbeat are the same.

3 IDENTIFY: Can you feel your pulse in a vein, artery, or capillary?

Veins Veins have thinner walls than arteries do. Blood pumps through the veins at less pressure than it does through arteries. The blood flow through veins is not as forceful as it is through arteries. The contraction of muscles in veins keeps the blood flowing. Some veins also have valves that keep the blood from flowing backward.

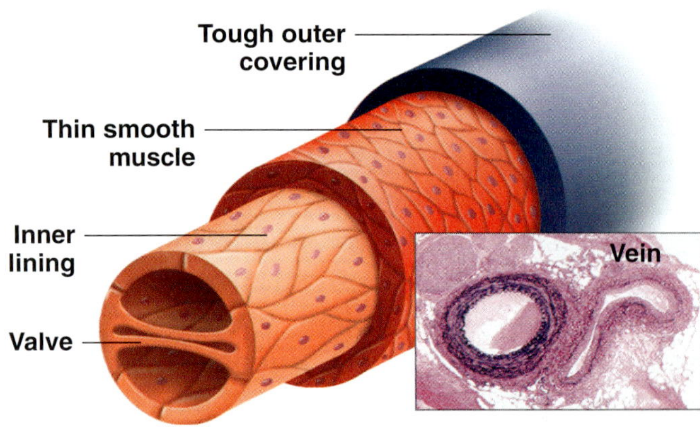

▲ **Figure 3-7** The walls of veins are thinner than those of arteries.

4 EXPLAIN: Why are the walls of veins thinner than the walls of arteries?

Capillaries Capillaries have walls that are only one cell thick. Blood cells travel through capillaries in a single file. Look at the diagram in Figure 3-8. In the capillaries, blood and body cells exchange nutrients and waste. For example, carbon dioxide and waste products move from body cells into the blood through capillaries. Food and oxygen in the blood move through the capillaries into the body cells.

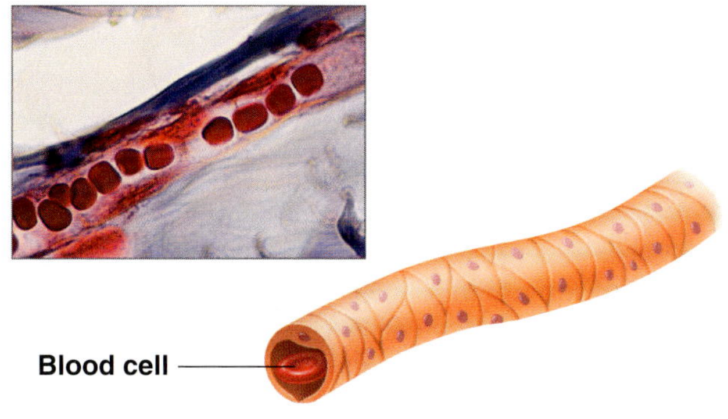

▲ **Figure 3-8** Capillaries are only wide enough for blood cells to pass through one at a time.

 **DESCRIBE:** What happens in capillaries?

✓ CHECKING CONCEPTS

1. How many types of blood vessels are found in the human body?
2. Through which vessel is blood pumped at a greater pressure?
3. In what areas of the body can you feel your pulse?
4. How is blood prevented from flowing backward in a vein?

✓ THINKING CRITICALLY

5. **CONTRAST:** What are the differences between arteries and veins?
6. **INFER:** Why do you think a pulse cannot be detected in a vein?

Web InfoSearch

High Blood Pressure Blood pressure is a measure of the force of blood on the arteries. High blood pressure causes the heart to overwork. Over time, high blood pressure causes the arteries and the heart to weaken.

SEARCH: Use the Internet to find out more about high blood pressure. Write a report about the possible prevention and treatment of high blood pressure. Start your search for information at www.conceptsandchallenges.com. A key search word is **high blood pressure.**

Hands-On Activity

MEASURING PULSE RATE

You will need a clock or watch with a second hand.

1. Sit quietly for 2 minutes.
2. Have a partner take your pulse for 30 seconds by placing his or her middle and index fingers over the inside of your wrist. Multiply this number by 2 to find your heart rate per minute. Record your answer.
3. Stand up for 2 minutes. Repeat Step 2.
4. Jog in place for 2 minutes. Repeat Step 2.
5. Rest for 2 minutes. Repeat Step 2.

▲ **STEP 2** Have a partner take your pulse.

Practicing Your Skills

6. **ANALYZE:** How did your pulse change when you stood up?
7. **ANALYZE:** How did your pulse change when you jogged?
8. **ANALYZE:** What effect did exercise have on your heart rate?

3-4 What is blood?

Objective

Describe the different parts of blood.

Key Terms

plasma (PLAZ-muh)**:** liquid part of blood

hemoglobin (HEE-muh-gloh-bihn)**:** protein found in red blood cells that carries oxygen

platelet (PLAYT-liht)**:** piece of cell that is involved in blood clotting

transfusion: transfer of blood from one person into the body of another person

Blood Blood is a fluid tissue. You have about 5 liters of blood in your body. Blood makes up about 9% of your body weight.

Blood is a mixture. It has a liquid part and a solid part. Scientists use a centrifuge (SEHN-truh-fyooj) to separate blood into its two parts. A test tube filled with blood is spun around in the centrifuge. The solid part of the blood is forced to the bottom of the test tube. The liquid part of the blood remains on top.

1 DEFINE: What is a centrifuge?

Plasma The straw-colored liquid part of blood is called **plasma.** It is made up mostly of water. Digested nutrients, dissolved vitamins, and minerals are found in plasma. Hormones and waste products from the cells of the lungs and kidneys are also dissolved in the plasma.

2 LIST: What are some things found in plasma?

▲ **Figure 3-9** Blood will separate into layers after it has been centrifuged.

Red Blood Cells Red blood cells are different from any other cell in the body because they have no nucleus. This means that they cannot divide. Because red blood cells do not reproduce themselves through cell division, they have to be continuously replaced. A typical red blood cell will function for about 120 to 130 days. Then, it has to be replaced. Red blood cells are made in the bone marrow of long bones.

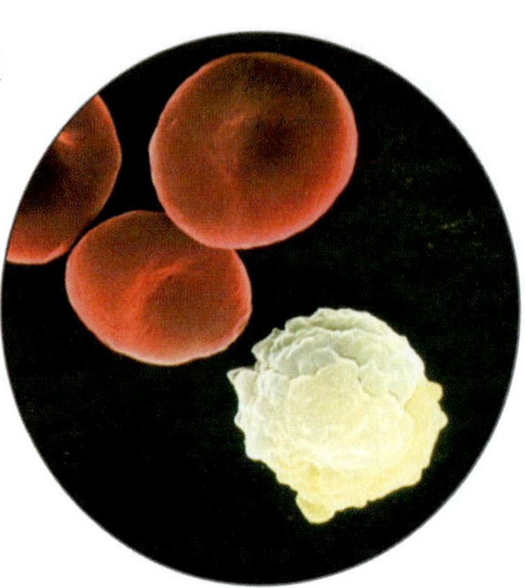

▲ **Figure 3-10** Red and white blood cells

The job of red blood cells is to carry oxygen. Red blood cells contain a compound called hemoglobin. **Hemoglobin** is an iron-containing protein that carries oxygen. Up to four molecules of oxygen can attach to a single molecule of hemoglobin. The color of the blood can vary, depending on the amount of oxygen its hemoglobin molecules are carrying. Blood with the maximum amount of oxygen is usually a brighter red than blood carrying less oxygen.

3 DEFINE: What is the function of hemoglobin?

White Blood Cells White blood cells are larger than red blood cells. They also have a different shape than red blood cells. White blood cells have an irregular shape and a rough surface. They have a nucleus and can function for many years. There are several different kinds of white blood cells.

White blood cells defend the body against foreign substances. By destroying bacteria and other microorganisms, white blood cells help fight disease. There are many more red blood cells than white blood cells. For every white blood cell, there are about 1,000 red blood cells.

4 DESCRIBE: What does a white blood cell do?

Platelets Have you ever cut yourself? What happens to the wound? Soon after you cut yourself, a clot forms. Clotting is controlled by platelets. **Platelets** are tiny, colorless pieces of cells. When tissues are injured, many platelets clump together near the wound and form a temporary plug. Then, the blood produces a chemical that forms long sticky threads. These threads form a net that traps red blood cells. This lump of red blood cells and sticky threads hardens and becomes a clot. The clot prevents the body from losing any more blood. White blood cells in the clot will attack bacteria to help prevent infection.

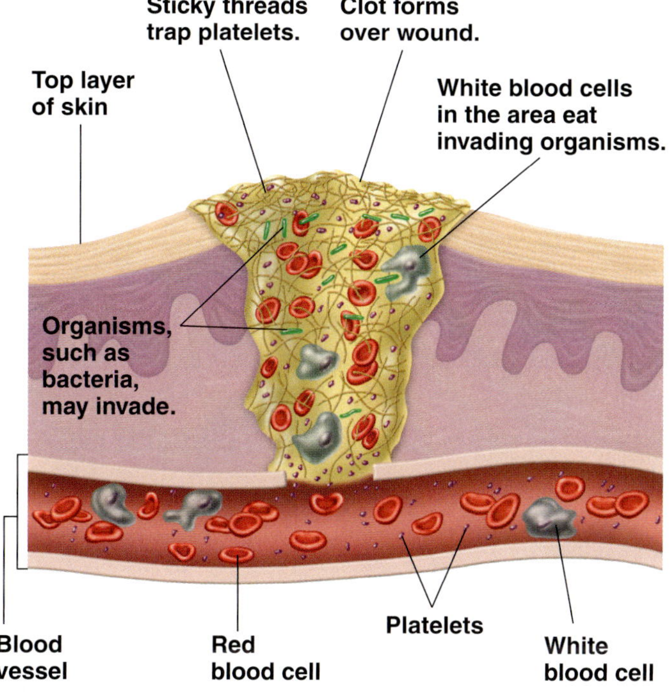

▲ **Figure 3-11** Platelets help the blood form clots.

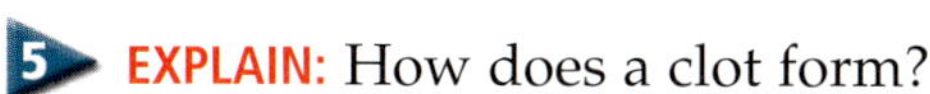

5 **EXPLAIN:** How does a clot form?

Blood Types The four major blood types are A, B, AB, and O. Your blood type depends on a specific chemical signal on the red blood cells in your blood. Scientists have labeled two different chemical signals, A and B. People with the A signal have blood type A. People with the B signal have blood type B. Some people have both signals—they have blood type AB. Others have neither the A nor B signal—they have blood type O.

You should know what your blood type is in case of an emergency. Your blood type determines what type of blood you can receive in a transfusion. A **transfusion** is a transfer of blood from one person to another. If you do not know your blood type, ask your doctor.

BLOOD TYPES		
Blood Types	Can Get Blood from	Can Give Blood to
A	O, A	A, AB
B	O, B	B, AB
AB	A, B, AB, O	AB
O	O	A, B, AB, O

▲ **Figure 3-12** Your blood type determines what types of blood you can give and get for transfusions.

6 **IDENTIFY:** If a person has type AB blood, what type of blood can that person receive in a transfusion?

CHECKING CONCEPTS

1. Red blood cells do not have a ___________.
2. The liquid part of blood is called ___________.
3. Blood gets its red color from ___________.
4. Platelets help the body to form ___________.
5. Type ___________ blood indicates that there are no signals on the red blood cells.

THINKING CRITICALLY

6. **PREDICT:** What would happen if there were no platelets in the blood?
7. **EXPLAIN:** Why is it important to know your own blood type?

Web InfoSearch

Artificial Blood The Food and Drug Administration has approved use of four blood substitutes. Using artificial blood can help doctors during blood shortages. Each type of artificial blood has its advantages and disadvantages.

SEARCH: Use the Internet to find out more about artificial blood. Write your findings in a report. Start your search at www.conceptsandchallenges.com. A key search word is **artificial blood.**

LAB ACTIVITY
Observing Blood Cells

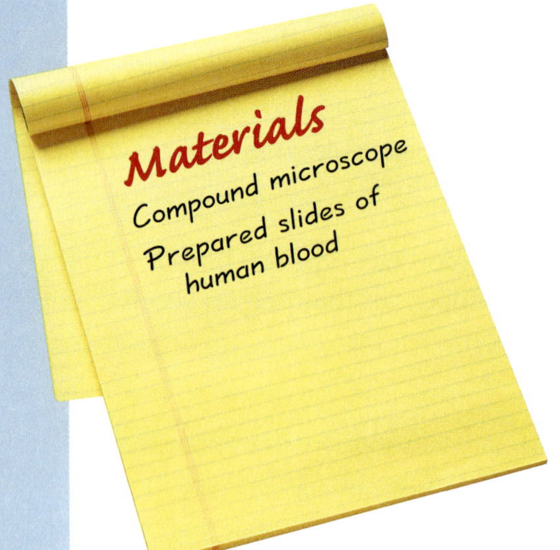

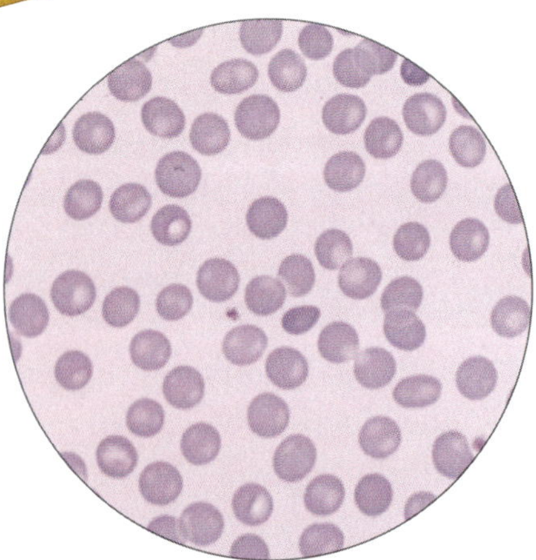

▲ **Figure 3-13** Red blood cells at low magnification

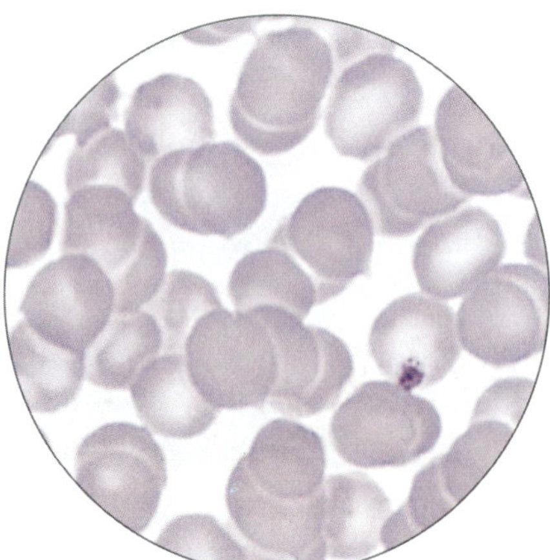

▲ **Figure 3-14** Red blood cells at high magnification

BACKGROUND

Blood is a liquid connective tissue. It carries oxygen and nutrients to your body's cells and it carries away byproducts. Blood contains a liquid part and a solid part. The liquid part is plasma, which makes up about 55% of the blood. The remaining 45% is composed of three types of cells: red blood cells, white blood cells, and platelets. Red blood cells are the most numerous. White blood cells defend the body against disease. Platelets are tiny, colorless fragments of cells made in the bone marrow. They are involved in clotting.

PURPOSE

In this activity, you will examine the solid part of blood. You will use a microscope to observe different types of blood cells.

PROCEDURE

1. Obtain a prepared slide of red blood cells from your teacher. Make sure the low power objective is in place. Place the slide on the stage of the microscope. Secure the slide in place with the stage clips.

2. Copy the chart in Figure 3-16 onto a sheet of paper. Use the low power objective lens to observe the slide. Use the coarse and fine adjustments to focus the image. Examine the blood under low power. Record your observations in your table. Then, draw what you see on a sheet of paper. Be sure to include the power of magnification.

3. Switch to the high power objective lens. Observe the same slide of red blood cells under high power. Record your observations in your table. Draw what you see on a separate sheet of paper.

4. Using the same slide, try to find platelets. If you need to move the slide, switch to low power first. After you find a few platelets, switch back to high power. Record your observations in your table. Make a drawing of the platelets on a sheet of paper.

5. Now, try to find a white blood cell. You may use the same slide or get a different slide from your teacher. Observe the white blood cell under low power first; then switch to high power. Record your observations in your chart. Make a drawing of the white blood cell also.

6. Try to find other types of white blood cells. Observe as many as you can under low and high power. Record your observations in the table. Make drawings of each white blood cell you observe.

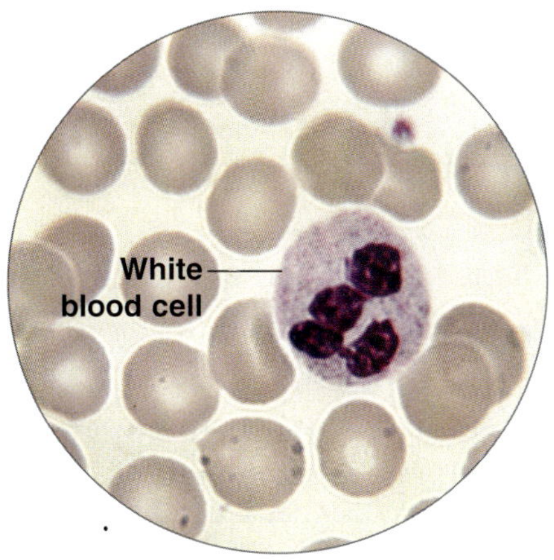

▲ **Figure 3-15** A white blood cell at high magnification

Type of Cell	Low Magnification	High Magnification
Red blood cell		
Platelet		
White blood cell		

▲ **Figure 3-16** Copy this chart onto a separate sheet of paper.

CONCLUSIONS

1. **OBSERVE:** Does the red blood cell have a nucleus? Does the white blood cell have a nucleus?

2. **CONTRAST:** In what other ways are red and white blood cells different from each other?

3. **CONTRAST:** How does the shape and size of platelets differ from the other blood cells?

4. **RELATE:** How are the shapes of each of the blood cells related to their functions?

3-5 What happens to blood as it circulates?

Objective

Describe what happens to blood as it circulates.

Key Term

pulmonary (PUL-muh-ner-ee) **artery:** artery that carries blood from the heart to the lungs

Exchange of Substances The flow of blood throughout the body is quite simple. Blood is pumped from the left ventricle into the aorta. The aorta is the largest artery in the body. Blood that enters the aorta carries food and oxygen to the body cells.

Once the aorta leaves the heart, it branches into many smaller arteries. These arteries divide again and again until they form capillaries in all the body tissues. Substances are exchanged through the walls of the capillaries. Food and oxygen pass out of the blood in the capillaries and into the body cells. At the same time, carbon dioxide and other wastes or byproducts pass from the body cells into the blood in the capillaries. Look at Figure 3-17 to trace the flow of blood throughout the body.

IDENTIFY: Where are materials exchanged between the blood and the body cells?

Return to the Heart Once the exchange of substances has taken place, the blood must be returned to the heart. The capillaries in the body tissues join to form small veins. Blood containing carbon dioxide and other wastes are carried in the veins to the right atrium of the heart. Before it can be sent out to the body tissues again, the blood must get a fresh supply of oxygen. It also must get rid of its carbon dioxide. To do this, the blood must be sent to the lungs.

NAME: To what part of the heart does blood containing wastes and byproducts return?

Heart and Lung Circulation Once the blood is received in the right atrium, it passes into the right ventricle. The right ventricle pumps blood into the pulmonary artery. The **pulmonary artery** carries blood from the heart to the lungs. The pulmonary artery has two branches. One branch goes to each lung. In the lungs, the pulmonary arteries divide many times until they form capillaries. As blood passes through these lung capillaries, it picks up oxygen and gets rid of carbon dioxide. The carbon dioxide is then exhaled from the body.

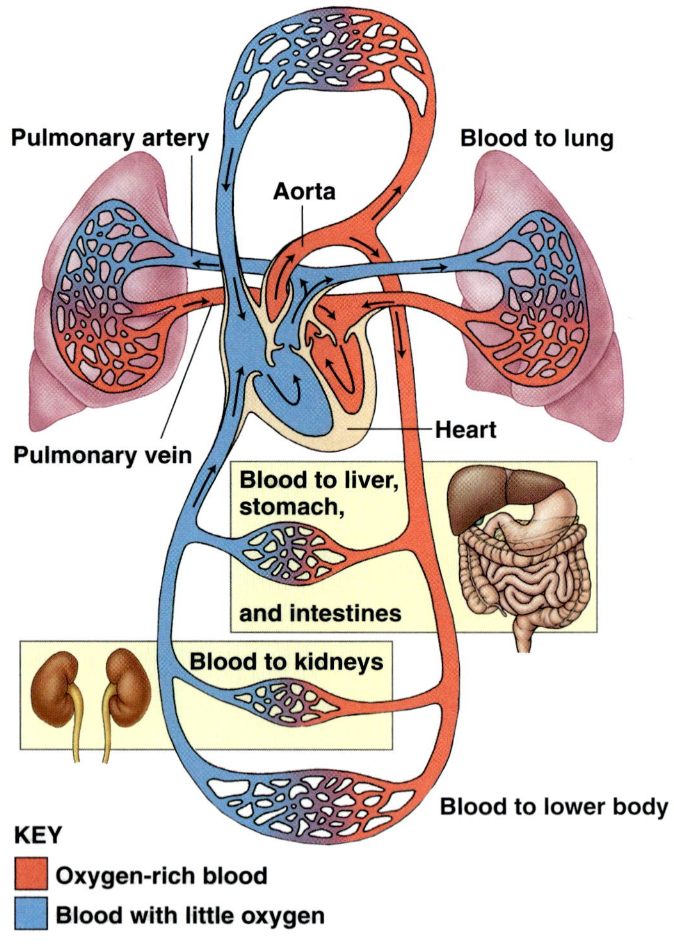

▲ **Figure 3-17** Circulation in the body takes place in two parts or loops.

Once the blood has picked up a fresh supply of oxygen, it is ready to be circulated through the body again. The capillaries in the lungs join together to form veins. The pulmonary veins carry the blood from the lungs to the left atrium of the heart. The left atrium pumps blood into the left ventricle. The left ventricle pumps blood throughout the body.

IDENTIFY: Where does the blood pick up oxygen and get rid of carbon dioxide?

CHECKING CONCEPTS

1. Blood is pumped through the __________ to the lungs.
2. Arteries divide many times until they form __________.
3. Blood picks up oxygen in the __________.
4. Blood is returned to the heart through __________.
5. Materials are exchanged between the blood and the body cells through the walls of __________.
6. Blood is carried to the lungs by the __________.
7. Blood leaving the right atrium passes into the __________.

THINKING CRITICALLY

8. **SEQUENCE:** Develop a flowchart that illustrates the flow of blood through the body and lungs.
9. **INFER:** What changes take place in the blood as it circulates?

BUILDING LANGUAGE ARTS SKILLS

Building Vocabulary You can sometimes infer where an artery carries blood to just by knowing its name. Some of the major arteries of the body include the carotid artery, the femoral artery, the bronchial artery, the brachial artery, the renal artery, and the coronary artery. Use library references to look up the meaning of each of these words. Find out where each of these arteries carries blood to in the body.

Integrating Physical Science

TOPIC: elements in blood

IRON IN HEMOGLOBIN

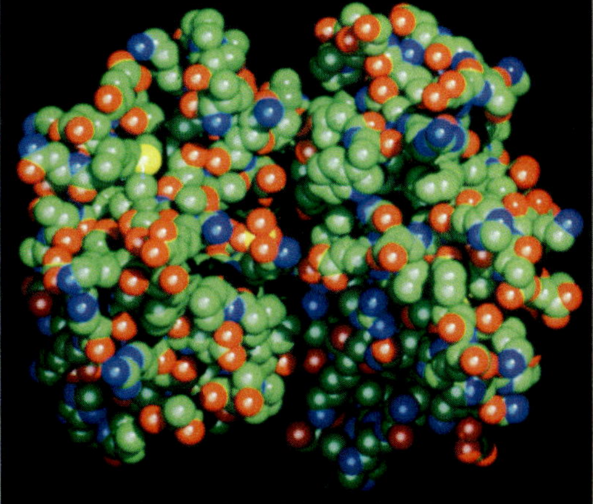
▲ **Figure 3-18** Hemoglobin is a complex molecule made up of proteins and iron.

Hemoglobin is the red protein in red blood cells that moves oxygen from your lungs to all the cells of your body. Almost one-third of red blood cells is hemoglobin. When hemoglobin is carrying oxygen, it is called oxyhemoglobin. When hemoglobin has given up its oxygen, it is known as deoxyhemoglobin. Oxyhemoglobin is bright red. Deoxyhemoglobin is much darker.

The element in hemoglobin that is attracted to oxygen is iron. Atoms in iron bond, or combine, with atoms in oxygen. Iron oxidizes well, which means it reacts easily with oxygen. Evidence for the oxidation of iron can be seen when metal is left out and rusts. By oxidating iron, hemoglobin in red blood cells carries oxygen. The rest of the hemoglobin is a twisted pretzel-like protein chain that surrounds the iron. Scientists know the exact structure and shape of hemoglobin by studying X-ray patterns of the molecule after it has been turned into a crystal.

Thinking Critically Which type of hemoglobin do you think is found in arteries, oxyhemoglobin or deoxyhemoglobin?

3-6 What is heart disease?

Objective

Identify types of heart disease and their causes.

Key Terms

atherosclerosis (ath-uhr-oh-skluh-ROH-sis)**:** buildup of fat deposits on artery walls

coronary (KAWR-uh-ner-ee) **artery:** artery that carries blood and oxygen to the tissues of the heart

heart attack: failure of a part of the heart due to a lack of blood and oxygen

Heart Disease More than half of all deaths in the United States are caused by heart disease. Heart disease affects both the heart and the blood vessels. Some kinds of heart disease are genetic, or passed from parent to offspring. If someone in your family has heart disease, there is a chance that you also may develop heart disease. Other kinds of heart disease are the result of a person's lifestyle and environment. Figure 3-19 lists some of the factors that contribute to heart disease.

FACTORS CONTRIBUTING TO HEART DISEASE	
Age	Gender
High blood pressure	Physical inactivity
Family history	Smoking
Obesity	Drinking alcohol
High cholesterol levels	

▲ **Figure 3-19** Heart disease may be caused by several different factors.

 **INFER:** What are some ways you can prevent heart disease?

Atherosclerosis In one kind of heart disease, fatty substances coat the inside walls of the arteries. One of these fatty substances is cholesterol. Cholesterol is found in animal products. As fat builds up in an artery, the opening becomes narrower. The artery walls may also harden and thicken. This condition is known as **atherosclerosis.** This may result in higher blood pressure and other problems related to the circulatory system.

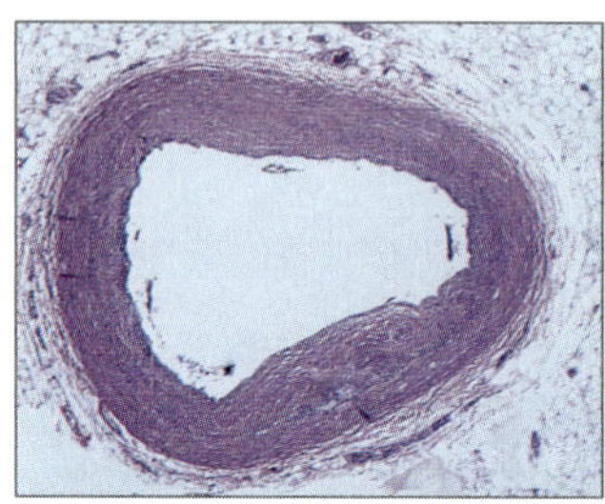

◀ **Figure 3-20** This photo shows a healthy artery.

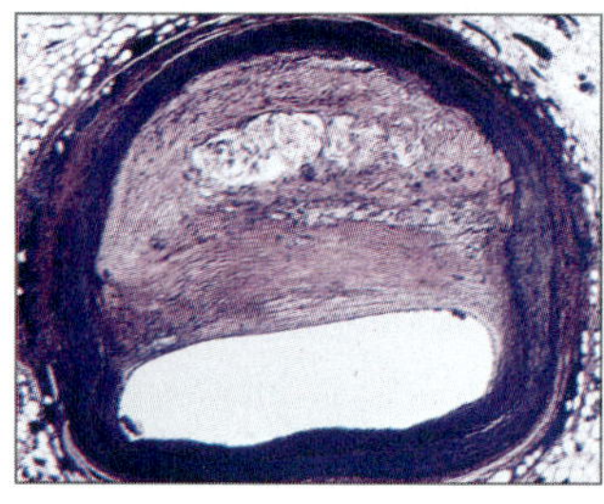

◀ **Figure 3-21** This photo shows an artery clogged by fatty deposits.

 **EXPLAIN:** What is atherosclerosis?

Heart Attack Like other body cells, the cells of the heart need food and oxygen. Heart cells also need to get rid of waste materials and byproducts. The heart has its own system of blood vessels to take care of these needs. This system is called the coronary system. **Coronary arteries** carry oxygen and blood to the heart muscle.

Atherosclerosis may make the openings in coronary arteries narrower. Coronary arteries can also be blocked by a blood clot. Either form of blockage stops blood and oxygen from reaching the muscles of the heart. The affected part of the heart cannot do its work. This condition is called a **heart attack.** A person having a heart attack usually feels a sharp pain in the chest. Heart attacks often are fatal.

 **DESCRIBE:** What is a heart attack?

CHECKING CONCEPTS

1. More than half of all deaths in the United States are caused by __________.
2. The __________ arteries carry blood and oxygen to all parts of the heart.
3. A blockage in a coronary artery can cause a person to suffer a __________.
4. A fatty substance that can coat the inside walls of arteries is __________.

THINKING CRITICALLY

5. **HYPOTHESIZE:** Does the width of an artery increase or decrease as a person ages?
6. **HYPOTHESIZE:** What do you think you can do to reduce the chance that you will be affected by atherosclerosis later in life?
7. **ANALYZE:** Which of the factors listed in Figure 3-19 can be controlled?
8. **EXPLAIN:** Pick three factors in Figure 3-19. How can you lower your risk of getting heart disease for each of the three factors chosen?

Web InfoSearch

Pacemakers The heart sends out electrical signals that keep all four chambers beating in a familiar rhythm. If this electrical signal is not working properly, the heart loses its rhythm. Doctors must then implant a mechanical pacemaker to keep the heart beating normally.

SEARCH: Use the Internet to find out more about pacemakers. Write a report comparing the body's natural pacemaker to mechanical pacemakers. Start your search at www.conceptsandchallenges.com. Some key search words are **pacemaker, heart,** and **heart disease.**

People in Science

CARDIOLOGIST

Cardiologists are doctors who treat patients with heart problems. The field of cardiology is considered a medical specialty, not a surgical one. However, cardiologists often work closely with heart surgeons. Cardiologists may also perform tests, prescribe drugs, and monitor patient progress.

Dr. Mark Blum is a cardiologist. He has been treating patients with heart conditions for 18 years. He specializes in disorders of the coronary arteries. Dr. Blum works with a team of other health care professionals. This team may include family doctors, surgeons, technicians, and nurses. Together the team diagnoses problems of the heart. They may also help patients recover from heart attacks or other related conditions.

▲ **Figure 3-22** Dr. Mark Blum

According to Dr. Blum, a student interested in becoming a cardiologist should work in a hospital or clinic to get an idea about what the job requires. He also feels students need to be hardworking and committed to learning in order to succeed.

Thinking Critically Why do you think it is important that cardiologists, surgeons, nurses, and technicians work together?

Integrating Technology

THE Big IDEA

How is technology used to treat cardiovascular disease?

About 12.4 million people have coronary heart disease. Heart disease is a factor in seven out of 10 deaths each year in the United States.

Technology is the application of science to produce things that make life better. Technology can be simple or advanced. A stethoscope is not complex, but it is a very important technological tool. Doctors use it to listen to the heartbeat. An abnormal heartbeat can signal a problem.

Today, doctors have many advanced tools to help them find and correct heart problems. An ultrasound uses sound waves to create an image of the heart. An electrocardiogram shows the electrical activity of the heart. First done in 1977, angioplasty is now a common way for doctors to open clogged arteries.

Technology in heart medicine has reached a new frontier. Robots, under the control of surgeons, fix heart valves. New blood vessels grow from genetic material injected into the heart. An artificial heart provides hope for patients waiting for transplants.

Medical technology has helped saved the lives of many people with heart disease. Look at the boxes of text that appear on this page and the next. They point out some devices used by heart doctors today and others that may become common in the future. Follow the directions in the Science Log to learn more about "the big idea."✦

Defibrillator

Sometimes the heart quivers instead of beating and pumping blood. This irregular heartbeat can be fatal. An electrical shock can reset the heart's rhythm. The device that delivers this shock is called a defibrillator. In an emergency, an external defibrillator is used on the outside of the chest. Some patients have one placed inside their chest. This is called an implantable cardioverter defibrillator. It resets the heart if it beats too fast or quivers.

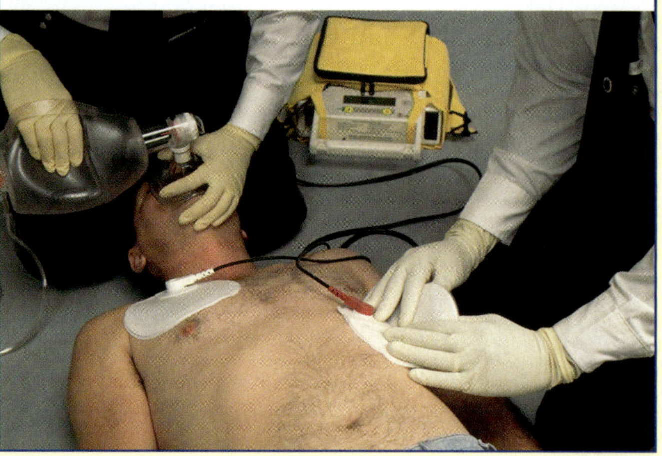

Angioplasty

Angioplasty is used to open blocked arteries. Fat deposits called plaque block arteries. A special catheter is inserted into the coronary artery. The catheter has a balloon attached to it. The balloon inflates inside the artery. The plaque is pressed against the artery wall. In laser angioplasty, bursts of laser light sent through the catheter break down the plaque. The opened artery improves blood flow to the heart.

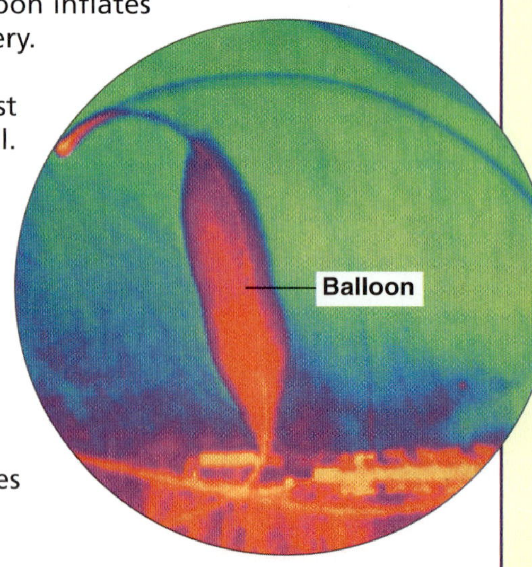

Arteriogram

An arteriogram is a picture of the arteries. A long, hollow tube called a catheter is inserted into an artery. It is threaded through the aorta into one of the coronary arteries. A dye is injected into the tube. A special X-ray shows the dye moving through the arteries. It reveals places where the artery is clogged.

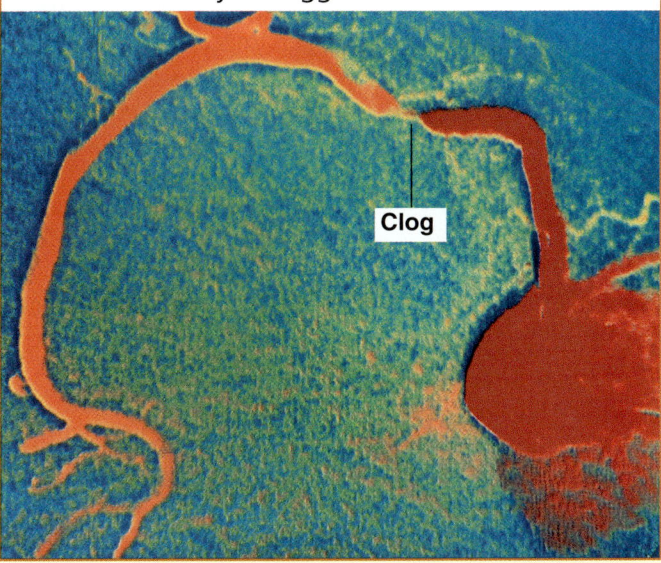

Artificial Heart

An artificial heart is designed to replace a diseased heart. Most early models were large and clumsy. They had to be connected to an outside power source. They failed terribly. The first self-contained artificial heart was recently developed. It fits inside the chest. No tubes or wires stick out. It must be tested on many patients to see how well it works and to see if it is safe.

Robotics

A few surgeons are using robots to repair mitral valves and for other open-heart surgery. The robotic arms can grip, cut, and sew arteries and valves. Surgeons view the heart on a video monitor. They control the robot's movements with joysticks and foot pedals. Robotic surgery requires a relatively small incision. This allows for a faster recovery.

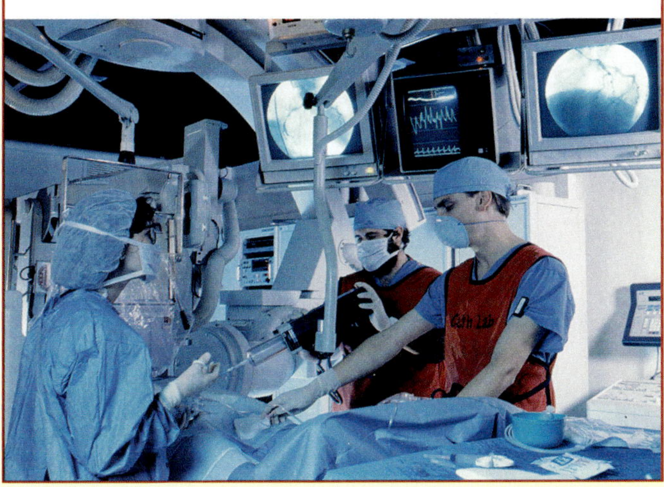

WRITING ACTIVITY

Science Log

Look at the photos on these two pages. Do you know anybody who has had heart problems? In your science log, research and write about a technology that is used to help heart patients. Describe the benefits of this medical technology. Start your search at www.conceptsandchallenges.com.

Chapter 3 Challenges

Chapter Summary

Lesson 3-1

- **Circulation** is the movement of blood through the body. In a **closed circulatory system,** blood travels within a system of blood vessels.
- The circulatory system transports food and oxygen, and it carries away wastes and byproducts such as carbon dioxide.
- The circulatory system protects your body from disease, carries **hormones,** and regulates body temperature.

Lesson 3-2

- The heart is divided into **atria** and **ventricles.** The **septum** is a thick tissue wall that separates the left and right sides of the heart.
- Heart **valves** prevent blood from flowing backward.

Lesson 3-3

- **Arteries** have thick muscular walls and are strong and elastic. **Veins** have thin walls and valves to keep blood flowing toward the heart.
- **Capillaries** are where the exchange of oxygen, carbon dioxide, food, and wastes takes place between the blood and body cells.

Lesson 3-4

- Blood is a fluid connective tissue. **Plasma** is the liquid part of blood.
- Red blood cells transport oxygen and give blood its color.
- White blood cells destroy germs and help fight disease.
- **Platelets** form clots, which prevent the body from losing blood.

Lesson 3-5

- As the blood is circulated around the body, it picks up nutrients and oxygen and gets rid of wastes and byproducts, such as carbon dioxide.

Lesson 3-6

- **Atherosclerosis** is a condition in which fat deposits build up on the walls of arteries.
- **Coronary arteries** carry blood to the heart.
- A **heart attack** occurs when part of the heart does not receive blood and oxygen.

Key Term Challenges

aorta (p. 70)
artery (p. 70)
atherosclerosis (p. 78)
atrium (p. 68)
capillary (p. 70)
circulation (p. 66)
closed circulatory system (p. 66)
coronary artery (p. 78)
heart attack (p. 78)
hemoglobin (p. 72)
hormone (p. 66)
plasma (p. 72)
platelet (p. 72)
pulmonary artery (p. 76)
septum (p. 68)
transfusion (p. 72)
valve (p. 68)
vein (p. 70)
ventricle (p. 68)

MATCHING Write the Key Term from above that best matches each description.

1. cell parts that control clotting
2. protein in red blood cells that carries oxygen
3. liquid part of blood
4. movement of blood through the body
5. transfer of blood from one person to another
6. thick wall of tissue that separates the left and right sides of the heart
7. flap of tissue that prevents blood from flowing backward

FILL IN Write the Key Term that best completes each statement.

8. When it reaches the lungs, the ___________ divides into two branches.
9. Blood is pumped out of the heart by the ___________.
10. Blood vessels with thick muscular walls are ___________.
11. The upper chambers of the heart are the ___________.
12. The blood vessels that carry blood back to the heart are the ___________.
13. The largest artery is the ___________.
14. The exchange of food, oxygen, and wastes takes place through the ___________.

Content Challenges TEST PREP

MULTIPLE CHOICE Write the letter of the term or phrase that best completes each statement.

1. The heart is divided into four
- **a.** valves.
- **b.** chambers.
- **c.** atria.
- **d.** ventricles.

2. The instrument doctors use to listen to your heartbeat is a
- **a.** stethoscope.
- **b.** telescope.
- **c.** thermometer.
- **d.** centrifuge.

3. When blood is pushed through the arteries, the resulting beat felt at the skin's surface is your
- **a.** blood pressure.
- **b.** artery.
- **c.** pulse.
- **d.** contraction.

4. The blood vessels through which blood flows at high pressure are
- **a.** arteries.
- **b.** veins.
- **c.** capillaries.
- **d.** valves.

5. The tiniest blood vessels are
- **a.** arteries.
- **b.** veins.
- **c.** capillaries.
- **d.** valves.

6. Disease-causing germs within the body are destroyed by
- **a.** red blood cells.
- **b.** hemoglobin.
- **c.** platelets.
- **d.** white blood cells.

7. The substance that gives red blood cells their color is
- **a.** plasma.
- **b.** carbon dioxide.
- **c.** iron.
- **d.** platelets.

8. The circulatory system is made up of the heart, the blood vessels, and
- **a.** oxygen.
- **b.** hormones.
- **c.** blood.
- **d.** enzymes.

9. The main job of the circulatory system is
- **a.** regulation of temperature.
- **b.** transport of blood.
- **c.** protection against disease.
- **d.** exchange of substances.

10. In the lungs, blood picks up oxygen and gives off
- **a.** hormones.
- **b.** food.
- **c.** oxygen.
- **d.** carbon dioxide.

TRUE/FALSE Write *true* if the statement is true. If the statement is false, change the underlined term to make the statement true.

11. The structures that prevent blood from flowing backward in the heart are called valves.

12. Blood flows from the atria to the ventricles, then back into the body.

13. The walls of arteries are thinner than the walls of veins.

14. With each heartbeat, a pulse can be felt in a capillary.

15. Scientists use a stethoscope to separate blood into liquid and solid parts.

Concept Challenges TEST PREP

WRITTEN RESPONSE **Complete the exercises and answer each question in complete sentences.**

1. **SEQUENCE:** Describe the complete flow of blood starting from where it leaves the heart to where it enters the heart once again.
2. **DESCRIBE:** Describe the process of blood clotting.
3. **PREDICT:** What happens to the number of white blood cells in your body when you become sick? Why?
4. **INFER:** Explain how the circulatory system provides protection for the body. Give several examples for your answer.

INTERPRETING A DIAGRAM **Use Figure 3-23 to answer the following questions.**

5. What is represented by letter *A*?
6. What is represented by letter *B*?
7. Where is the septum located?
8. Where is the aorta located?
9. What is the job of the aorta?
10. Which letter represents the part of the heart that receives blood from the lungs?
11. In which direction does blood flow in the heart?
12. What blood vessels carry blood to the left atrium?
13. Is blood leaving the right ventricle carrying more oxygen or more carbon dioxide?
14. Is blood carried from the heart to the lungs by a vein or an artery?

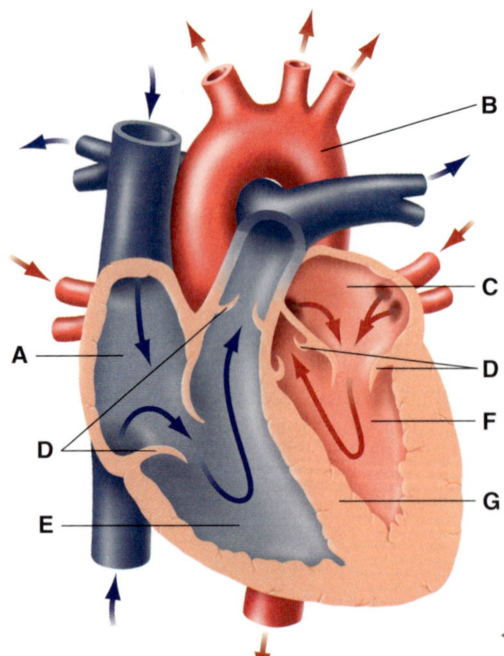

◀ **Figure 3-23** The human heart

Chapter 4 Respiration and Excretion

▲ **Figure 4-1** Hiking is a demanding physical activity.

Have you ever been outside when the air was so cold you could see your breath? All humans breathe. Breathing is important for cellular respiration, which releases energy from food. When you breathe in, you take in oxygen. This oxygen is used in cellular respiration. When you breathe out, you get rid of water and carbon dioxide. Breathing out is part of excretion, or the removal of waste products from the body. When you see your breath on cold days, you are seeing some of the waste products of respiration.

▶Why do you think you breathe harder when you are engaged in a physical activity?

Contents

4-1 What is the respiratory system?

4-2 What are breathing and respiration?

■ **Lab Activity:** Modeling Breathing

4-3 What happens to air before it reaches the lungs?

4-4 How does oxygen get into the blood?

4-5 How does tobacco affect the body?

4-6 What is the excretory system?

4-7 How do the kidneys work?

4-8 How does the skin remove wastes?

■ **The Big Idea:** What happens when the body overheats?

4-1 What is the respiratory system?

Objective

Describe the parts of the respiratory system.

Key Terms

trachea (TRAY-kee-uh)**:** windpipe

bronchus (BRAHN-kuhs), *pl.* **bronchi:** tube leading to the lungs

alveolus (al-VEE-uh-luhs), *pl.* **alveoli:** microscopic air sacs in the lungs

larynx (LAR-inks)**:** organ located on top of the trachea that contains the vocal cords

The Respiratory System Each time you breathe in, your lungs fill with air. The lungs, tubes, and passageways through which air moves in your body make up the respiratory system. The job of this system is to take oxygen into the lungs and to get rid of carbon dioxide and water.

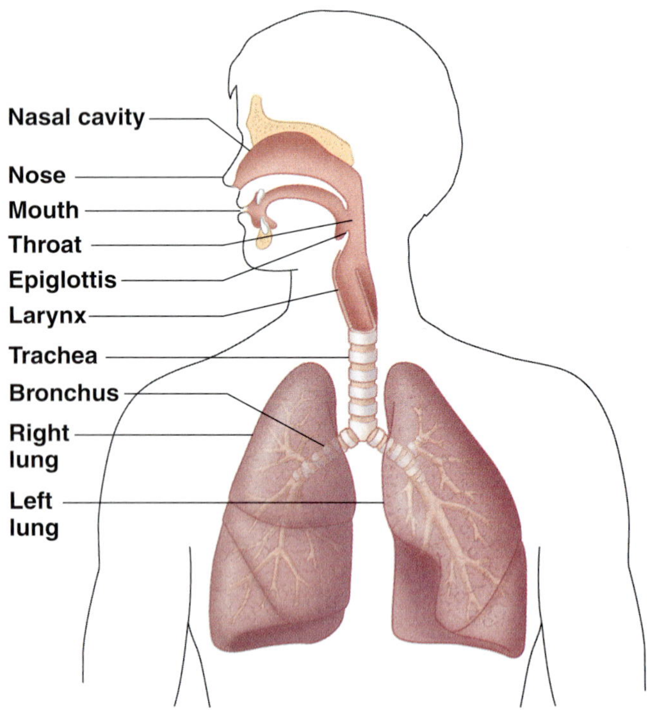

▲ **Figure 4-2** The respiratory system

1 ANALYZE: What are the waste products of respiration?

Passages to the Lungs Air enters your body through your nose and mouth. Then, air moves into your throat and enters the **trachea,** or windpipe. The trachea is a tube about 10 cm long. The end of the trachea divides into two smaller tubes. These tubes are the **bronchi.** Each bronchus extends into a lung.

 OBSERVE: How many bronchi are there?

Lungs The lungs are the main organs of the respiratory system. In the lungs, the bronchi divide many times. The tubes become smaller and smaller. At the ends of the smallest tubes are microscopic air sacs. These air sacs are called **alveoli.** Each lung contains about 300 million alveoli.

 NAME: What are the main organs of the respiratory system?

Larynx At the top of the trachea is an organ called the **larynx.** It is made up of cartilage. The human larynx contains two thin folds of skin called vocal cords. During normal, quiet breathing, the vocal cords are relaxed. However, when you speak, your vocal cords tighten. As you breathe out, air passing over the vocal cords causes them to vibrate and produce sounds.

When you swallow, a flap of tissue called the epiglottis, automatically closes the larynx. This prevents food and liquid from entering the windpipe. If food or water does enter the windpipe, the cough reflex usually forces the material out.

▲ **Figure 4-3** The vocal cords are in the larynx.

 INFER: Why do you think that you should not talk while you are eating?

CHECKING CONCEPTS

1. The organ system that helps you breathe is the __________.
2. Microscopic air sacs in the lungs are called __________.
3. The windpipe branches into two tubes called __________.
4. The main organs of the respiratory system are the __________.
5. Air enters the body through your mouth and __________.

THINKING CRITICALLY

6. **COMPARE:** The windpipe, bronchi, and branches of the bronchi are sometimes called the bronchial tree. How is the arrangement of these structures similar to the arrangement of a tree?

7. **SEQUENCE:** Place the following words in order to show how air moves through the respiratory system.

   a. trachea
   b. nose
   c. bronchi
   d. throat
   e. lungs
   f. alveoli

HEALTH AND SAFETY TIP

Asthma Many people suffer from asthma (AZ-muh). Asthma usually is caused by an allergy to airborne particles. The muscles react by getting narrower. Air cannot pass easily into and out of the alveoli. Particles in the air can also cause the lungs to produce mucus. Breathing becomes very difficult. Drugs prescribed by a doctor often are used to help relax muscles in the air tubes, allowing them to open up.

People in Science

RESPIRATORY THERAPIST

People sometimes have trouble breathing because of lung or heart disease. Helping people breathe more easily is the job of respiratory therapists. They work with other medical specialists to figure out why patients have trouble breathing. They use special equipment, such as breathing machines and oxygen monitors. They give medications to help people with asthma and other breathing problems.

Steven Sittig is a medical specialist who works with children. He does respiratory therapy while riding in a rescue helicopter. When he gets a call on the job at Mayo Medical Transport in Minnesota, Sittig has 15 minutes to get into a helicopter and take off. The helicopter has the medical equipment and medication needed for moving a patient quickly and safely to a hospital. It is Sittig's job to make sure that his patient is breathing well during the flight. Some patients are very young infants, while others are as old as sixteen.

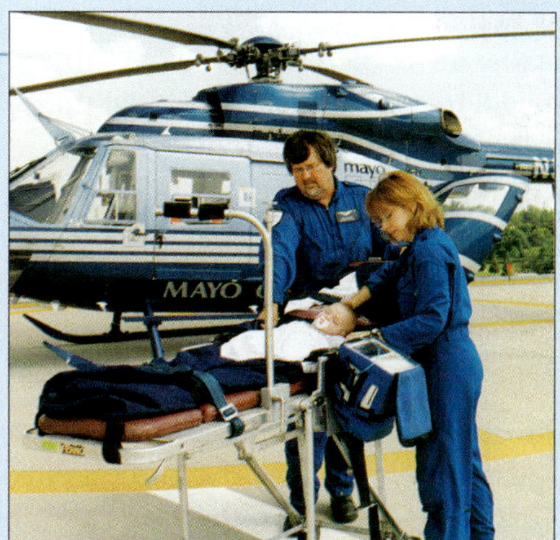

▲ **Figure 4-4** Steven Sittig is a respiratory therapist who works with children.

To become a respiratory therapist, Sittig earned a two-year college degree, specializing in science. Then, he passed a nationwide exam to become a registered respiratory therapist. He also passed another national exam to become a pediatric specialist, which allows him to treat children.

Thinking Critically Why do you think respiratory therapists need specialized training to work with children?

4-2 What are breathing and respiration?

Objectives

Compare breathing and respiration. Explain the process of breathing.

Key Terms

respiration (rehs-puh-RAY-shuhn)**:** process of carrying oxygen to cells, getting rid of carbon dioxide, and releasing energy

diaphragm (DY-uh-fram)**:** sheet of muscle below the lungs

inhale: to breathe in

exhale: to breathe out

Comparing Breathing and Respiration Breathing is the process by which air is taken into the body. It is a mechanical process. When you breathe in, oxygen is carried to your lungs. It is not carried to your cells. Breathing does not release energy for your body to use.

Carrying oxygen to your cells, getting rid of carbon dioxide, and releasing energy is called **respiration.**

Respiration is a chemical process. It has three parts.

- **External Respiration** During external respiration, oxygen and carbon dioxide are exchanged between the lungs and the blood.
- **Internal Respiration** During internal respiration, oxygen and carbon dioxide are exchanged between the blood and the cells of the body.
- **Cellular Respiration** Cellular respiration is the chemical process by which energy from food molecules is released by cells. Carbon dioxide and water are given off as byproducts.

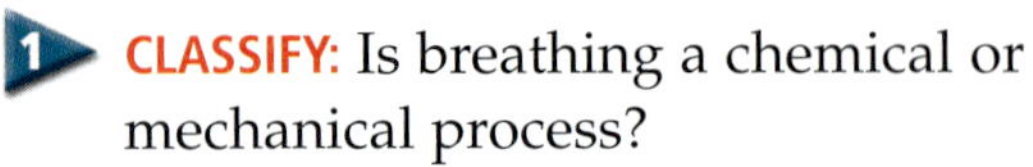

1 CLASSIFY: Is breathing a chemical or mechanical process?

The Diaphragm Below the lungs, there is a sheet of muscle called the **diaphragm.** Look at the position of the diaphragm in Figure 4-5. The diaphragm helps you breathe. It works with the ribs and rib muscles. Many body parts work together to help you breathe.

2 LIST: What parts of the body work together to help you breathe?

Inhaling When you **inhale,** or breathe in, your rib muscles contract, causing the ribs to move up and out. The diaphragm moves downward, away from the lungs. The space inside the chest becomes larger. Because of this, there is less air pressure in the lungs than outside the body. The outside air pressure causes air to rush into the lungs. The lungs fill with air and expand.

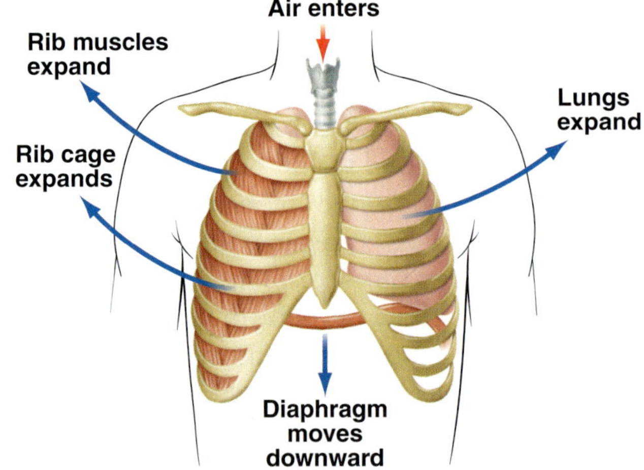

▲ **Figure 4-5** Inhaling

3 DEFINE: What does the word *inhale* mean?

Exhaling When you **exhale,** or breathe out, the rib muscles relax, causing the ribs to move down and in. The diaphragm relaxes and moves upward, toward the lungs. The space inside the chest becomes smaller. Because of this, the air pressure in the lungs is greater than the air pressure outside the body. Air moves out of the lungs. The lungs deflate and take up less space in the chest.

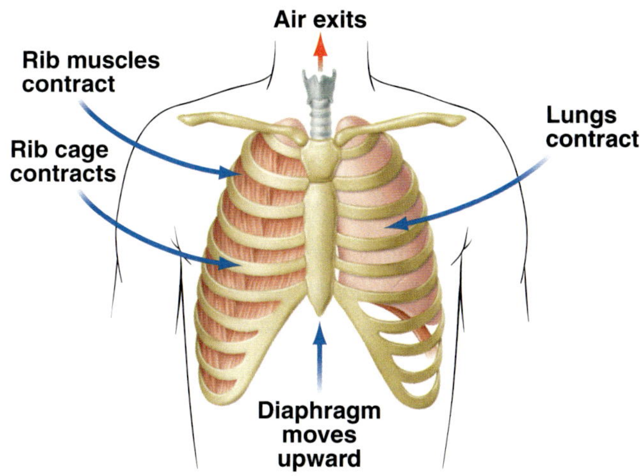

▲ **Figure 4-6** Exhaling

 **DESCRIBE:** What happens to the size of the space in the chest when you exhale?

CHECKING CONCEPTS

1. How does the diaphragm move when you exhale?
2. What is breathing?
3. Does breathing release energy?
4. What are the waste products of cellular respiration?
5. What happens to the space inside your chest when you inhale?

THINKING CRITICALLY

6. **SEQUENCE:** List the steps your body goes through to get oxygen into your bloodstream.
7. **ANALYZE:** What body systems allow you to breathe?
8. **APPLY:** How are breathing and respiration related?

INTERPRETING VISUALS

Use Figures 4-5 and 4-6 to answer the following questions.

9. **ANALYZE:** Look at the red and blue arrows in each diagram. What is the relationship between the directions in which they point? Tell how they explain the actions of inhaling and exhaling.

Hands-On Activity

EXERCISE AND BREATHING RATE

You will need a watch or clock with a second hand.

1. Breathe in and out normally. Have your partner count the number of breaths you take in 1 minute. Record the number of breaths.
2. Jog in place for 20 seconds. Then stop. Have your partner count the number of breaths you take in 1 minute. Record this number.
3. Jog in place for 40 seconds. Then stop. Have your partner count the number of breaths you take in 1 minute. Record.
4. Change places with your partner and repeat the activity.

▲ **Figure 4-7** Have your partner count the number of breaths you take in 1 minute.

Practicing Your Skills

5. **MEASURE:** How many breaths did you take in a minute at rest? After 20 seconds of jogging? After 40 seconds of jogging?
6. **COMPARE:** How did your breathing rates compare to your partner's breathing rates?
7. **INFER:** What effect does exercise have on breathing rate?

LAB ACTIVITY
Modeling Breathing

BACKGROUND

You are always breathing. When you inhale, you breathe in fresh air. When you exhale, you breathe out used air. The diaphragm is a sheet of muscle that helps you breathe. It is located just under your lungs. The diaphragm moves up and down to change the amount of space in your chest. This changes the amount of air pressure in your chest. It is the changing air pressure that forces air in and out of your lungs.

PURPOSE

In this activity, you will make a simple model that shows how you breathe.

PROCEDURE

1. Place a small balloon on the end of the straw. Wrap some wire around the neck of the balloon so that it will not slip off the straw.

2. Push the drinking straw through the hole in the bottom of the plastic cup. Then pull the straw back so that the balloon goes up into the cup, just above the hole.

3. Seal the space around the straw with rubber cement. Allow it to dry.

4. Cover the mouth of the cup with a rubber sheet. Use a rubber band to hold the sheet tightly in place.

▲ **STEP 1** Wrap wire around the neck of the balloon.

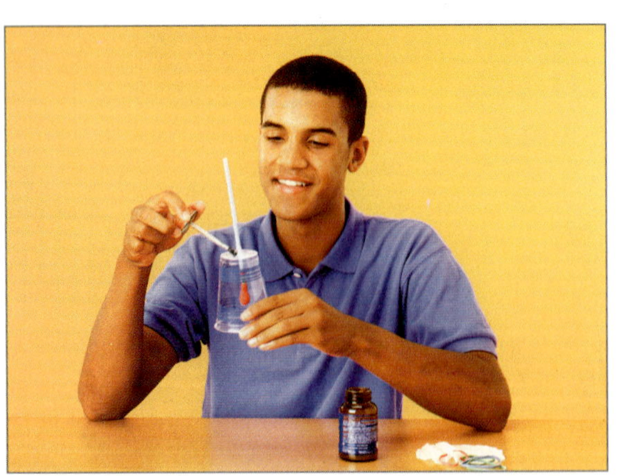

▲ **STEP 3** Seal the space around the straw with rubber cement.

5. Copy the data chart in Figure 4-8 onto your own paper. Then, use your thumb and forefinger to grasp the rubber sheet at its center. Pull the sheet out a little bit. Watch the balloon. How did you change the space inside the cup. What happened to the balloon? Write your observations in your data chart.

6. Use your forefinger to push the rubber sheet a little bit in toward the balloon. Watch the balloon. Write your observations in your data chart.

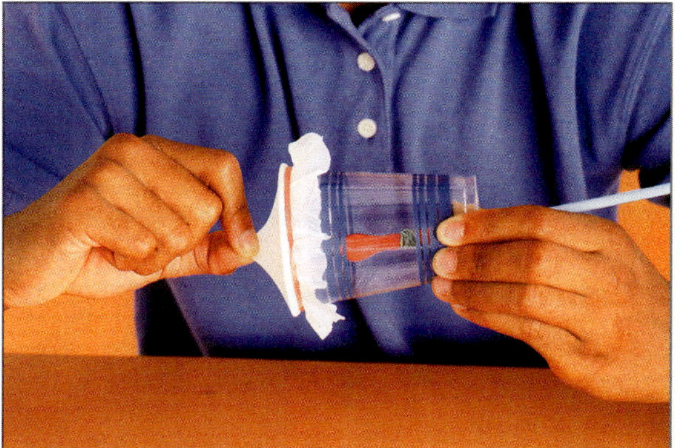

▲ **STEP 5** Pull the sheet out.

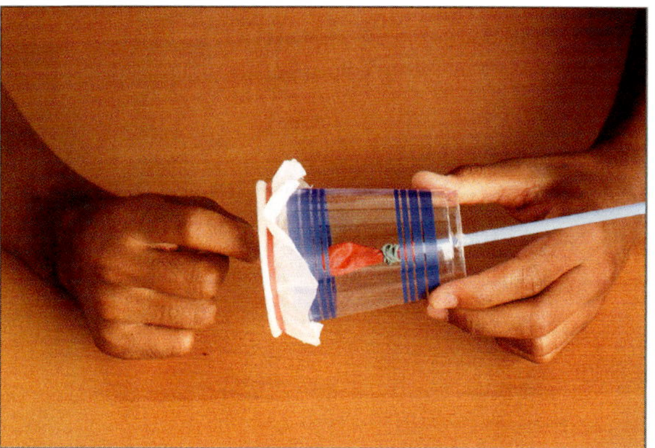

▲ **STEP 6** Push the sheet in.

Action	Change in Amount of Space Inside Cup	Change in Air Pressure	Change in Balloon

▲ **Figure 4-8** Copy this chart onto a sheet of paper.

CONCLUSIONS

1. **APPLY:** What did the balloon in this experiment represent?
2. **APPLY:** What did the rubber sheet in this experiment represent?
3. **ANALYZE:** When you pushed the rubber sheet in, did you model exhaling or inhaling?
4. **EXPLAIN:** How does your diaphragm help you breathe?

4-3 What happens to air before it reaches the lungs?

Modeling Filtering Hairs
HANDS-ON ACTIVITY

1. Your teacher will give you a small dish filled with water.
2. Sprinkle about one teaspoonful of pepper over the surface of the water.
3. Gently run a popsicle stick over the water. How much pepper did you pick up?
4. Repeat Step 3 with a toothbrush. How much pepper did you pick up?

THINK ABOUT IT: What do you think caused the difference in the results?

Objective
Explain how air is cleaned, warmed, and moistened as it moves through the respiratory system.

Key Terms
mucus (MYOO-kuhs)**:** sticky liquid
cilia (SIHL-ee-uh)**:** tiny hairlike structures

Filtering Air You normally breathe through your nose. The air that you inhale contains dirt and dust particles. These particles may be harmful to the lungs. Inside your nose, there are many hairs. These hairs filter out and trap many dust and dirt particles.

 **INFER:** Why do you think that it is better to breathe through your nose than through your mouth?

Mucus The cells inside the nose and windpipe produce a sticky liquid called **mucus.** Mucus lines the inside of the nose and windpipe. Dust, dirt, bacteria, and other harmful particles stick to the mucus. Mucus stops many particles from reaching the lungs. Mucus also keeps the tissues of the respiratory system from drying out.

 **EXPLAIN:** What are the two jobs of mucus?

Cilia **Cilia** are tiny hairlike structures. Your trachea and nose are lined with millions of cilia. The cilia move back and forth, pushing mucus toward the back of the throat. Trapped particles are pushed along the throat with the mucus. Some mucus with its trapped particles is swallowed.

▲ **Figure 4-9** Cilia

Sometimes mucus and the particles stuck in it can irritate the lining of your nose. When this happens, you respond by sneezing. A sneeze is a burst of air. Sneezing blows harmful particles out of the nose.

 **NAME:** Where are cilia located in the respiratory system?

Warm, Moist Air Sometimes the air you inhale is cold and dry. When the air enters your body, it is warmed by heat from the body. Remember humans are warmblooded. Your body temperature is about 37°C, except when you have a fever. Air that enters the lungs has been warmed in your nose and throat. The body also adds water vapor to the air you inhale. The air is made moist as it moves through the nose and trachea. Air reaching the lungs is warm and moist. Warm, moist air prevents damage to the lungs.

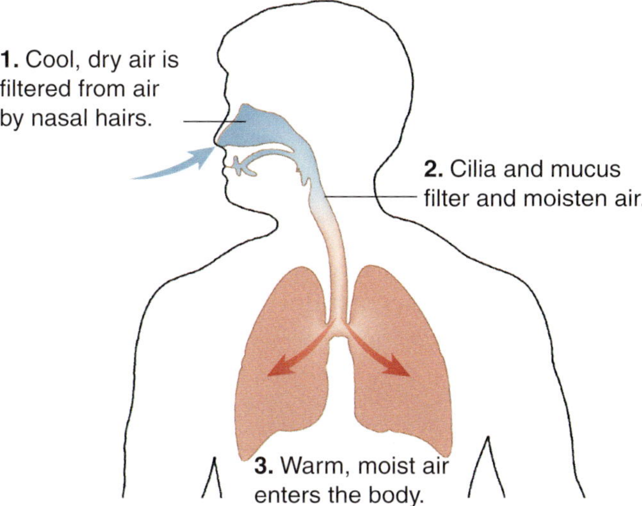

▲ **Figure 4-10** Air is filtered and warmed before entering the lungs.

4 INFER: Why do you think it is better for air to be filtered and warmed before it reaches the lungs?

CHECKING CONCEPTS

1. A burst of air that blows harmful particles out of the nose is a ___________.
2. The trachea is lined with tiny hairlike structures called ___________.
3. Air that enters the lungs is warm and ___________.
4. The sticky liquid that traps harmful particles in the respiratory tubes is ___________.
5. You normally breathe through your ___________.

THINKING CRITICALLY

6. **EXPLAIN:** How is the air you breathe in changed before it reaches the lungs?
7. **DIAGRAM:** Develop a flowchart that traces the pathway of air from the nose to the lungs. List each organ the air passes through. Beneath each organ, identify how air passing through the organ is changed.

Real-Life Science

PROTECTING THE RESPIRATORY SYSTEM

Some chemicals found in the environment can weaken a person's respiratory system. Automobile fumes, smoke, chalk dust, and other common air pollutants are known dangers. Serious damage can occur after prolonged exposure to air pollutants. Workers in occupations that produce air pollutants are at the highest risk for respiratory illness. Coal miners and construction workers fall into this category.

Asbestos (eh-SPEH-stahs) is a material that was used in the past to insulate buildings. Inhaling asbestos fibers can cause lung diseases. Today, asbestos is being removed from buildings to eliminate the danger.

▲ **Figure 4-11** Workers removing asbestos must wear special protective gear.

Another disease that affects the lungs is miner's asthma. Miner's asthma is caused by the inhalation of quartz dust. Quartz dust is usually created during dynamiting in mining. Prolonged exposure to asbestos or quartz dust can cause scar tissue to form in the lungs. There are federal regulations to protect workers from respiratory diseases. Coal miners, for example, are required to wear air masks with filters.

Thinking Critically Why do you think there is usually a large number of cases of asthma in cities?

4-4 How does oxygen get into the blood?

Objectives

Explain gas exchange in the lungs and between the blood and body cells. Compare the gas makeup of inhaled air and exhaled air.

Oxygen in the Air Air is a mixture of gases. It is made up mostly of nitrogen and oxygen. Your body cells need oxygen to carry out respiration. Oxygen enters the lungs in the air you inhale. One of the jobs of the lungs is to take in oxygen from the air.

PERCENTAGE OF GASES IN THE AIR	
Gas	**Percentage**
Nitrogen	78.00%
Oxygen	21.00%
Argon	00.90%
Carbon dioxide	00.03%
Other	00.07%

▲ Figure 4-12

 ANALYZE: What percentage of air is made up of oxygen?

Alveoli The alveoli are where gases are exchanged in the lungs. Alveoli are shaped like a bunch of grapes. They have very thin walls and are surrounded by many capillaries. Capillaries are very tiny blood vessels. Red blood cells move through the capillaries in single file.

The most important part of respiration is the exchange of the gases oxygen and carbon dioxide. In the lungs, oxygen and carbon dioxide are exchanged between the alveoli and the blood. Oxygen molecules pass through the walls of the alveoli into the capillaries. The oxygen molecules attach to the red blood cells. At the same time, carbon dioxide molecules pass from the blood plasma through the capillary walls into the alveoli.

How does this exchange of gas take place? Fresh air in the alveoli has a high level of oxygen and a low level of carbon dioxide. Blood in the capillaries surrounding the alveoli is low in oxygen and high in carbon dioxide. These differences in concentration of gases allow for diffusion, or movement across cell membranes, to take place. The oxygen diffuses, or moves out, of the alveoli into the capillaries. At the same time, carbon dioxide diffuses from the capillaries into the alveoli.

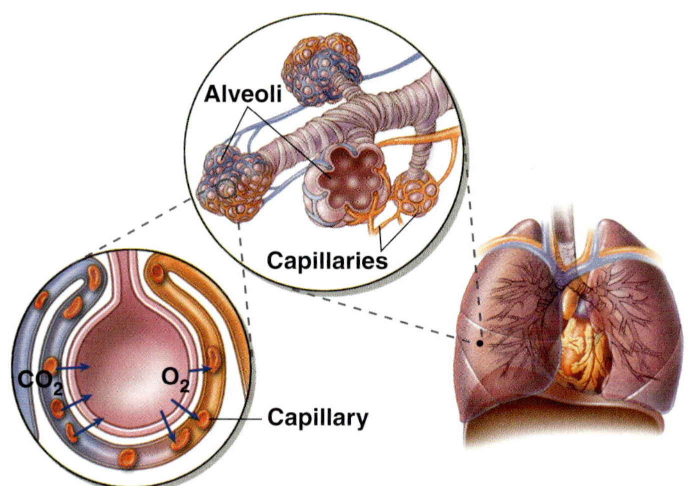

▲ Figure 4-13 The alveoli

 DESCRIBE: What happens to oxygen molecules in the lungs?

Gas Exchange in Cells Once oxygen is picked up by the blood in the lungs, it is brought to body cells. Then, oxygen and carbon dioxide are exchanged between the body cells and red blood cells. Oxygen moves from the red blood cells into the body cells. Carbon dioxide moves from the body cells into the capillaries. The carbon dioxide is carried back to the lungs by the red blood cells, where it can be exhaled.

 DESCRIBE: What happens to carbon dioxide molecules in the body cells?

Air In and Air Out The gas makeup of the air you breathe in is different from the gas makeup of the air you breathe out. Inhaled air contains more oxygen than does exhaled air. Exhaled air contains more carbon dioxide than does inhaled air. Exhaled air is different because oxygen in the air is absorbed by the lungs. In addition, your cellular respiration adds carbon dioxide to air exhaled. Water vapor is also added to the air you exhale.

ANALYZE: Why is there more carbon dioxide in exhaled air than inhaled air?

CHECKING CONCEPTS

1. What is air?
2. Where are gases exchanged in the lungs?
3. What are capillaries?
4. How is carbon dioxide removed from the body?
5. Does inhaled air contain more oxygen or more carbon dioxide than exhaled air?
6. Does exhaled air contain more oxygen or more carbon dioxide than inhaled air?

THINKING CRITICALLY

7. INTERPRET: How much of the air is made up of nitrogen?
8. INFER: Which percentages would most likely be contained in inhaled air?
   - **a.** 78% nitrogen, 21% oxygen
   - **b.** 78% nitrogen, 17% oxygen
9. INFER: Which percentages would most likely be contained in exhaled air? How do you know?
   - **a.** 21% oxygen; 0.03% carbon dioxide
   - **b.** 17% oxygen; 4% carbon dioxide

BUILDING MATH SKILLS

Graphing A graph is a good way to organize and present information. Use the percentages of the gases contained in air shown in Figure 4-12 to make a circle graph of this data. Make sure you include a title, labels, and units. Add together the gases that make up less than 1% of air. Label these "Other" in your graph.

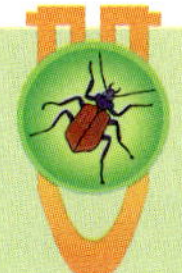

Hands-On Activity

ANALYZING EXHALED AIR

You will need safety goggles, a shallow piece of glass, such as a watchglass or petri dish, 50 mL of limewater, a beaker or glass, and a straw.

1. Breathe out onto the watchglass. Record your observation.
2. Add the 50 mL of limewater to the beaker or glass. Limewater is used to test for carbon dioxide. If carbon dioxide is present, the limewater becomes cloudy.
3. Put the straw into the limewater. Gently blow bubbles through the straw into the glass of limewater. ⚠ CAUTION: Do not inhale while the straw is in the limewater. Do not drink the limewater.

▲ **STEP 3** Blow bubbles into the limewater. Do not inhale.

Practicing Your Skills

4. OBSERVE: What forms on the watchglass? Where did it come from?
5. INFER: What happens to the limewater when you bubble exhaled air into it? Explain your answer.
6. INFER: What does this tell you about the air you exhale?

4-5 How does tobacco affect the body?

Objective

Explain the effects of tobacco on the body.

Key Term

nicotine (NIHK-uh-teen): stimulant found in tobacco

Tobacco Tobacco contains more than 100 chemical substances. When tobacco burns, many new substances are formed. All of these substances are taken into the body with the tobacco smoke. One of the harmful substances in tobacco smoke is nicotine. **Nicotine** is a stimulant drug that causes both physical and mental addiction. Tars and carbon monoxide are other harmful substances found in tobacco smoke. When inhaled, tar coats the lining of the lungs. Experiments have shown that tar causes cancer in some laboratory animals. Carbon monoxide is a poisonous gas that may cause dizziness, headaches, and drowsiness. In large doses, carbon monoxide is fatal.

SOME CHEMICALS IN TOBACCO	
Chemical Name	**Other Uses**
Acetone	Nail polish remover
Arsenic	Rat poison
Carbon monoxide	Car exhaust fumes
Formaldehyde	Preserving dead bodies
Methanol	Rocket fuel
Nicotine	Insecticides

◀ **Figure 4-14**

 **IDENTIFY:** What are three harmful substances found in tobacco smoke?

Effect on Breathing The air tubes in the lungs are lined with cells. These cells have tiny hairlike structures called cilia. The cilia beat back and forth to push mucus from the lungs toward the throat. Foreign substances trapped in the mucus get pushed out of the lungs. Smoking causes the cilia to stop working. Without the action of the cilia, mucus collects in and blocks the air tubes. This trapped air causes the air sacs, or alveoli, to break. With fewer air sacs at work, less oxygen flows into the lungs with each breath. Less carbon dioxide is released from the body with each exhalation. The smoker must breathe harder and more often to get enough oxygen.

 **EXPLAIN:** What effect does smoking have on the cilia in the air tubes of the lungs?

Illnesses When the cilia stop beating, foreign substances remain trapped in the lungs. There, these substances may cause infection and disease. Smokers are more likely to get heart disease, cancer, and lung disease than nonsmokers are. Emphysema (ehm-fuh-SEE-muh) is a lung disease in which the air sacs are destroyed. This leads to a poor exchange of oxygen and carbon dioxide between the lungs and the bloodstream. Smokers have a higher death rate from these diseases than do nonsmokers. Compare the healthy lung on the left in Figure 4-15 with the smoker's lung on the right.

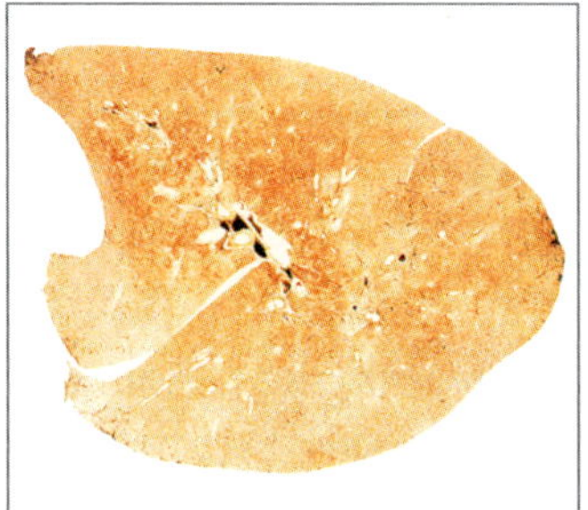

▲ **Figure 4-15** The photo on the left is the healthy lung of a nonsmoker. The photo on the right is the diseased lung of a smoker.

Smoking also places a great strain on the heart. With fewer air sacs in the lungs, the blood gets less oxygen. The heart must work harder to supply enough blood to the body cells. This raises blood pressure. Nicotine also makes the blood vessels narrow. The heart must work harder to pump the blood through the smaller openings. This puts an even greater strain on the heart.

 **DESCRIBE:** What effect does nicotine have on blood vessels?

Secondhand Smoke Researchers have discovered that tobacco smoke can also affect nonsmokers. For example, children living with smokers are twice as likely to have respiratory problems as children living with nonsmokers. Due to the dangers of secondhand smoke, or the smoke from a burning tobacco product, smoking is banned in many public places. Other public places are required to provide a nonsmoking section.

DEFINE: What is secondhand smoke?

CHECKING CONCEPTS

1. Nicotine, carbon monoxide, and ___________ are examples of harmful substances found in tobacco smoke.
2. When cilia in the air tubes stop beating, ___________ collects and blocks the tubes.
3. Nicotine makes blood vessels ___________.
4. Smoking puts a great strain on the ___________.

THINKING CRITICALLY

5. **INFER:** What effect would cigarette smoking have on a person's ability to exercise?
6. **HYPOTHESIZE:** Nicotine is an addictive drug. Why do you think it may be difficult for a person to quit smoking?

BUILDING WRITING SKILLS

Writing to Persuade When you write to persuade, you try to get someone to agree with your point of view. Create an antismoking pamphlet to persuade people about the dangers of smoking.

Real-Life Science

EFFECTS OF SMOKING ON THE HUMAN BODY

You already know that smoking can cause heart and lung disease. You know that nicotine is addictive. Studies show that along with these diseases, there are outward signs of smoking on the human body as well.

Did you know that people who smoke are five times more likely to develop wrinkles earlier than nonsmokers are? The chemicals in smoking can weaken a person's bones. As a result, smokers are more likely to break their bones than nonsmokers are.

Smoking damages the inside of the human body as well. Smoking has been linked to several different forms of cancer, including some forms of leukemia, cancer of the larynx, esophageal, lung, kidney, pancreatic, stomach, and urinary cancers.

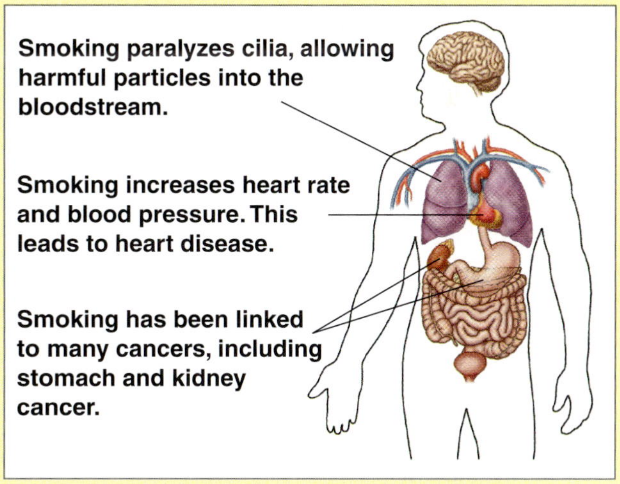

Smoking paralyzes cilia, allowing harmful particles into the bloodstream.

Smoking increases heart rate and blood pressure. This leads to heart disease.

Smoking has been linked to many cancers, including stomach and kidney cancer.

▲ **Figure 4-16** Smoking can damage the entire body.

Despite the information about tobacco's effect on the body, an estimated 48 million people in the United States continue to smoke each year. More than 400,000 of those people will die from cigarette-related illnesses.

Thinking Critically Why do some people who smoke look older than nonsmokers who are the same age?

4-6 What is the excretory system?

Objective

Explain how waste products are formed and removed by the body.

Key Terms

excretion (ehks-KREE-shuhn)**:** process of removing waste products from the body

kidney: excretory organ that removes waste products from the blood

ureter (yoo-REET-uhr)**:** tube that carries liquid waste from the kidneys to the bladder

bladder: excretory organ that stores liquid wastes

Forming Waste Products Foods are combined with oxygen in your cells. As the food is used by the body, heat and other kinds of energy are produced. The energy released is used by the body to carry out its life processes. When the foods are used to produce energy, waste products are formed.

Many waste products are formed by the cells of your body. Carbon dioxide and water are byproducts of cellular respiration. Other byproducts made by the cells are salts and nitrogen compounds. Heat also is a waste product.

 LIST: What are some waste products formed by your body?

Excretion The many waste products formed by your body must be removed from your body. If these waste products build up in your body, they will be harmful to you. The process of removing waste products from the body is called **excretion.**

2 DEFINE: What is excretion?

The Excretory System Removing waste products from the body is the job of the excretory system. It is made up of many different organs. The lungs are part of the excretory system. You know that the lungs get rid of carbon dioxide and of water. The **kidneys** also are organs of the excretory system. They get rid of liquid waste and dissolved solids. The largest organ of the excretory system is your skin. It gets rid of liquid waste and salts and helps you get rid of extra heat.

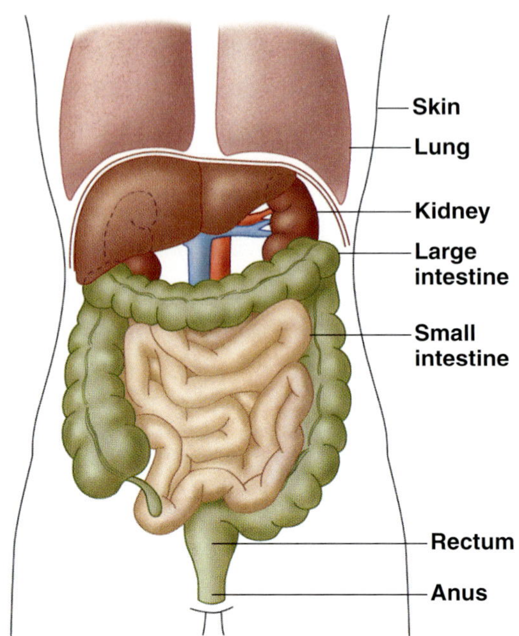

▲ **Figure 4-17** The excretory system

 LIST: What are three organs of excretion?

Liquid Waste Much of the liquid waste in blood is removed by the kidneys. This liquid is collected. It then flows through the **ureters** into the **bladder.** From there, the liquid waste is excreted through the urethra.

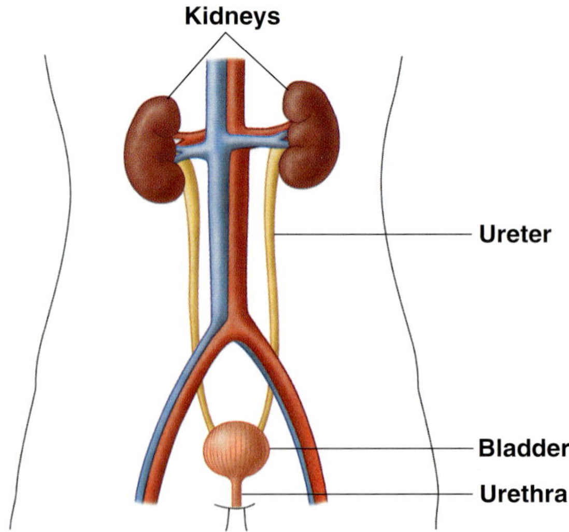

▲ **Figure 4-18** Liquid waste is removed by the kidneys.

 DEFINE: What is the job of the bladder?

Solid Wastes Some parts of the foods that you eat cannot be digested. They cannot pass through the villi. Undigested foods form waste. This waste moves along in the small intestine. It enters the large intestine. Water is removed from the waste in the large intestine, shown in Figure 4-17. As water is removed, the waste becomes solid. The solid waste moves along in the large intestine and into the rectum. From there, the solid waste is excreted through the anus (AY-nuhs).

5 **DESCRIBE:** What is the job of the large intestine?

CHECKING CONCEPTS

1. What are the waste products of cellular respiration?
2. What is excretion?
3. What does the excretory system do?
4. What does skin do?
5. What is the job of the large intestine?
6. How does solid waste leave the body?
7. How do liquid wastes leave the body?

THINKING CRITICALLY

8. **CONTRAST:** How is the excretory system different from the respiratory system?

INTERPRETING VISUALS

Use Figures 4-17 and 4-18 to answer the following questions.

9. Which organs in the diagrams excrete liquid waste?
10. Which organ in the diagrams is used to rid the body of excess heat?
11. Through which organ is solid waste excreted?

Science and Technology

USING SOUND TO BREAK APART KIDNEY STONES

Mineral compounds that are not excreted by the body can build up and form kidney stones. Kidney stones form inside the kidneys. Large kidney stones can completely block the passage of liquid waste from the kidneys. The liquid waste then backs up into the kidneys. Waste products can quickly destroy kidney cells.

Doctors use X-rays or ultrasound images to diagnose kidney stones and find out exactly where they are. The hard minerals in the stones show up just as clearly as bones in X-ray pictures. Ultrasound imaging bounces sound waves off structures inside the body to form pictures.

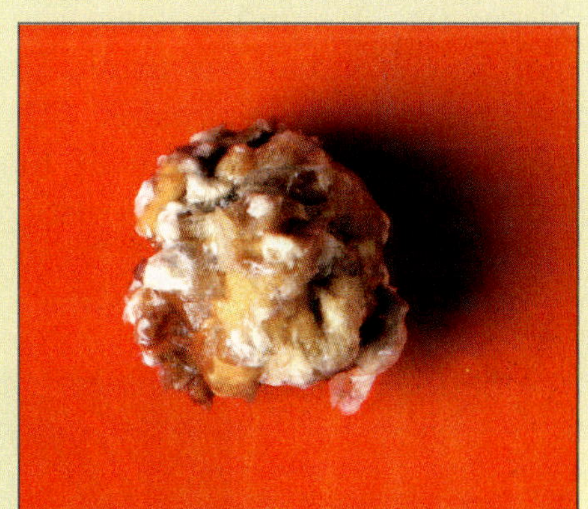

▲ **Figure 4-19** A kidney stone

Some kidney stones will pass out of the body if the patient drinks a lot of water to help push them along. Surgery used to be the only way to get rid of larger stones, but now doctors can use a new method. Lithotripsy sends high-pressure shock waves into the kidneys. The energy from the shock waves produces cracks in the edges of the kidney stone. When new waves hit the stone, the kidney stone breaks into smaller pieces. Eventually the kidney stone may break down into sand-size particles, which can pass out easily with the liquid waste.

Thinking Critically If you had a kidney stone, would you rather have it removed by surgery or by lithotripsy? Explain.

4-7 How do the kidneys work?

Objective

Describe how the kidneys act as a filtering system for the blood.

Key Terms

urine (YOOR-ihn)**:** liquid waste formed in the kidneys

urea (yoo-REE-uh)**:** nitrogen compound formed as a waste product

nephron (NEHF-rhon)**:** filtering structure of the kidneys

The Kidneys Most people have two kidneys. Each kidney is about 10 cm long. The kidneys are located just above your waist. One kidney is behind your liver. The other is behind the stomach. The main job of the kidneys is to remove waste products from the blood.

 **IDENTIFY:** What is the main job of the kidneys?

Liquid Waste Like the skin, the kidneys help the body get rid of liquid wastes. The liquid waste formed in the kidneys is **urine.** Urine is mostly water, but it also contains other materials, including many salts. Some of these salts give urine its yellow color. Urine also contains urea. **Urea** is a waste product formed when proteins are used by the body. It is a nitrogen compound.

 **NAME:** What is the liquid waste formed in the kidneys called?

Nephrons The inside of each kidney is made up of millions of tiny tubes called **nephrons.** Nephrons are filtering structures in the kidneys. They remove wastes from blood. Each nephron has a small cup at one end. This cup is called Bowman's capsule. Many coiled capillaries are found inside each capsule. Blood flows through the capillaries. Water and other materials are filtered out of the blood here. These materials move through the walls of the capsule and into the nephron.

How do the nephrons filter waste products from the blood? As you read each step below, look at the nephron in Figure 4-20.

- Blood enters the nephron.
- In the nephron, the blood passes into a cluster of capillaries in Bowman's capsule.
- Water, salts, urea, and nutrients are forced out of the capillaries and into Bowman's capsule.
- In the coiled part of the tube, any nutrients pass back into the blood. Excess water, salts, and urea remain in the last part of the tube, called the collecting duct.

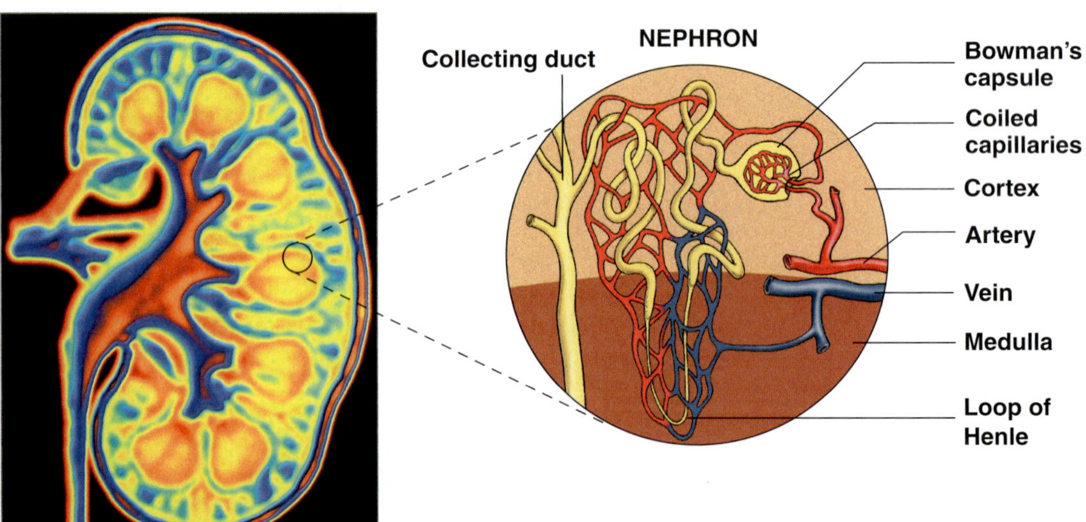

Figure 4-20 ▶ The kidneys filter liquid waste out of blood. The photo on the left shows a CT scan image of a kidney.

- The filtered blood returns to the heart. The water, salts, and urea are carried out of the kidney as urine.

 **SEQUENCE:** How do materials get into the kidney tubes?

Excretion of Urine Urine forms in the collecting duct. Then it moves into the hollow, middle part of the kidney. Urine passes out of the kidneys through the ureters. Urine collects in the bladder. Urine passes out of the body through the urethra.

4 **INFER:** What happens to urine when it leaves the kidney?

CHECKING CONCEPTS

1. Urea is a __________ compound.
2. Most people have __________ kidneys.
3. The kidneys help to get rid of __________ wastes.
4. The liquid waste formed in the kidneys is __________.
5. Urine leaves the kidneys through the __________.
6. Urine leaves the body through the __________.

THINKING CRITICALLY

7. **MODEL:** Develop a flowchart that traces the path of urine from the kidneys out of the body.
8. **INFER:** What element do you think is present in all proteins?
9. **APPLY:** What happens to nutrients that are removed from the blood in the kidneys?

BUILDING MATH SKILLS

Calculating Blood filters through the kidneys at a rate of 125 mL per minute. How many milliliters filter through the kidneys in an hour? A day?

Science and Technology

DIALYSIS

A field of study that uses engineering concepts to design machines that help or replace diseased organs is called biomedical engineering. Biomedical engineers have developed a machine that acts like a kidney. The machine is called a dialysis (dy-AL-uh-sis) machine. People who have lost their kidneys or have kidney damage are kept alive by using a dialysis machine.

A patient is connected to the machine by a tube. The tube is connected to an artery in the patient's arm. Blood from the artery flows from the tube into the dialysis machine. The machine filters the patient's blood, removing waste materials. The blood then flows out of the machine through a tube connected to a vein in the patient's arm.

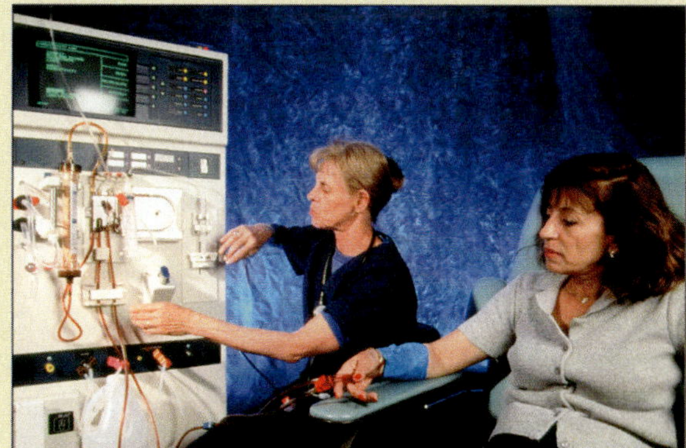

▲ **Figure 4-21** A patient with kidney damage can use a dialysis machine while waiting for a transplant.

Many people use a dialysis machine three times a week. However, depending on how serious kidney damage is, some patients may need to use the machine every two days.

Thinking Critically How can biomedical engineering help people with diseases?

4-8 How does the skin remove wastes?

Observing Evaporation and Cooling
HANDS-ON ACTIVITY

1. Hold two fingers in front of your mouth. Blow on them. Record if one finger feels cooler.
2. Dip one finger in water. Blow on the wet finger and a dry finger. Record which feels cooler.
3. Wet a cotton ball with isopropyl alcohol. Wet one finger. Blow on the wet finger and a dry finger. Record which feels cooler.
4. Wet one finger with water and one finger with isopropyl alcohol. Blow on them. Record which feels cooler.

THINK ABOUT IT: Which finger felt cooler? Explain why you think it felt cooler.

Objectives

Identify the layers and some of the structures of the skin. Explain why the skin is an organ of excretion.

Key Terms

epidermis (ehp-uh-DUR-mihs)**:** outer layer of skin

dermis: inner layer of skin

perspiration (pur-spuh-RAY-shuhn)**:** waste water and salts that leave the body through the skin

pore: tiny opening in the skin

evaporation (ee-vap-uh-RAY-shuhn)**:** changing of a liquid to a gas

The Largest Organ The skin is the largest organ of the human body. It covers the entire outside of your body. The main function of skin is to cover and protect the body. The skin is made up of two layers. There is an outer layer and an inner layer. Skin also contains blood vessels, nerves, and other tissues.

1 **OBSERVE:** Look at Figure 4-22. Which is thicker, the outer layer or the inner layer of skin?

Epidermis The outer layer of skin is called the **epidermis.** The epidermis covers and protects the body. It is made up of living and dead skin cells. The dead skin cells are replaced constantly by the living skin cells beneath them. Each time you scrape the surface of your skin or wash, thousands of dead skin cells are carried away.

2 **INFER:** Why do you think skin cells are constantly being replaced?

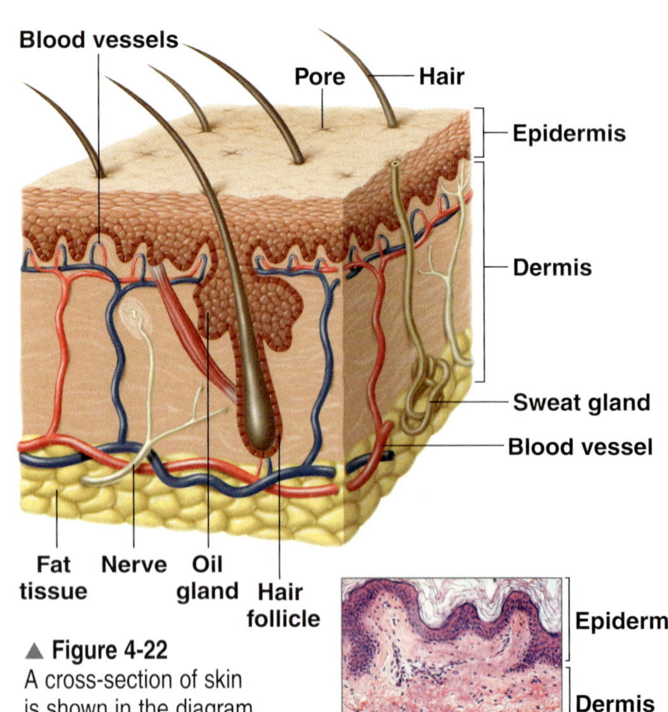

▲ **Figure 4-22** A cross-section of skin is shown in the diagram and photo.

Dermis The inner layer of the skin is called the **dermis.** The dermis is a living layer of skin. It is much thicker than the epidermis. The dermis has many different structures in it.

Hair follicles are one structure in the dermis. Each hair on your body grows from a hair follicle. Oil glands are located near the hair follicles. Oil glands produce oil, which softens and moistens the skin. Nerve endings and many tiny blood vessels are also located in the dermis.

3 **NAME:** What are three structures found in the dermis?

Perspiration Some waste water leaves your body through your skin. This waste water is called **perspiration,** or sweat. Perspiration is made up of waters and salts.

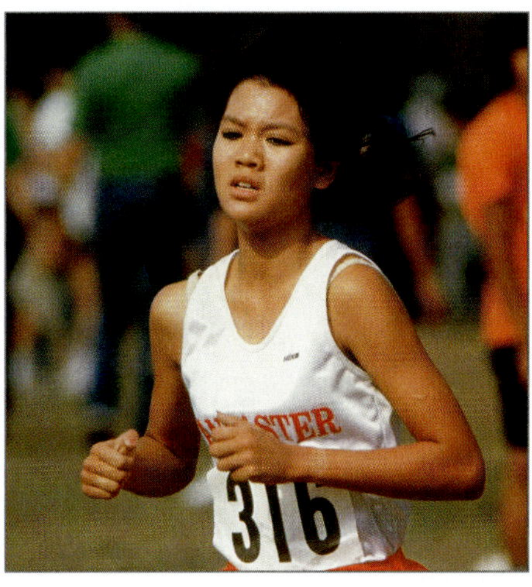

◀ **Figure 4-23** Perspiration cools the body.

4 **DEFINE:** What is perspiration?

Sweat Glands The dermis also contains many sweat glands. A sweat gland is a coiled tube surrounded by capillaries. Water molecules in the blood pass through the walls of the capillaries into the sweat gland. Each sweat gland extends to a tiny opening in the skin called a **pore.** Waste water leaves the sweat gland through the pore.

▲ **Figure 4-24** The surface of your skin has openings like this called pores.

5 **DESCRIBE:** What is a sweat gland?

An Air-Conditioning System Your body has a built-in cooling system. When it is very hot, do you sweat? Do you sweat after you exercise or do heavy work? Perspiration, or sweating, helps your body "cool off." The evaporation of perspiration from your skin cools the body. **Evaporation** is the changing of a liquid to a gas. As perspiration evaporates, it removes heat from your body.

6 **PREDICT:** Are you likely to perspire if your body temperature drops below 37°C? Explain.

CHECKING CONCEPTS

1. The outer layer of skin is the __________.
2. Hair follicles, oil glands, and nerve endings are located in the __________.
3. A sweat gland is a coiled tube surrounded by __________.
4. Perspiration leaves the body through __________ in the skin.
5. The changing of a liquid to a gas is called __________.
6. Evaporation of perspiration helps to __________ the body.

THINKING CRITICALLY

7. **INFER:** When you are cold, you shiver. What do you think shivering does for the body?
8. **HYPOTHESIZE:** Why do you think it is important to take in more salts when the weather is hot?

DESIGNING AN EXPERIMENT

Design an experiment to solve the following problem. Include a hypothesis, variables, a procedure, and a type of data to study.

PROBLEM: During which types of activities from the list below does your body perspire more heavily?

a. jogging
b. playing basketball
c. climbing stairs
d. walking
e. dancing
f. jumping rope

THE Big IDEA

What happens when the body overheats?

Humans are warmblooded organisms. This means that our bodies try to keep a constant body temperature, no matter the temperature outside of it. Your body systems work together to maintain a temperature of 37°C. The systems involved in temperature control include your skin, excretory system, respiratory system, and endocrine system.

Sometimes your body temperature rises in response to fighting a virus or bacteria. This is called a fever. When you have a fever, you will sweat to get cool. If you sweat a lot, the kidneys may filter less water out of the blood. However, you should drink liquids to replace the lost water and salts. With a high fever, you may breath faster, which cools you and gets rid of extra carbon dioxide. Usually, a fever can be controlled with medicine.

Your body temperature also rises slightly during exercise. The same kinds of system changes that occur during a fever will help cool you when exercising. If you exercise in very hot weather, however, it can be dangerous. Heat illness happens when the body is heated beyond the control of normal systems. If your body loses too much water because of sweating, you may get dehydrated. This means the amount of liquid in your blood is less than it should be. When this happens, all of your body systems react!

With heat exhaustion, your body systems cause you to feel faint or collapse. This makes you STOP what you are doing. Fast shallow breathing and fever are symptoms. You need to drink liquids, replace lost salts, and get cool. It is important to prevent a more life-threatening illness called heat stroke.

Look at the illustrations and text on these pages. They show the dangerous steps that lead to heat stroke. Follow the directions in the Science Log to learn more about "the big idea." ✦

1 Sweating Leads to Dehydration

Working or exercising in hot weather makes you sweat a lot. When you sweat a lot, you have to drink to replace the fluids and salts leaving your body. If you do not, you can become dehydrated. You may also become overheated.

2 Blood Volume Decreases

When you are dehydrated the amount of liquid, or plasma, in you blood is decreased. The total volume of blood in your body is less. This means that the circulatory system cannot function properly. To help, the heart works harder, but less blood gets to organs.

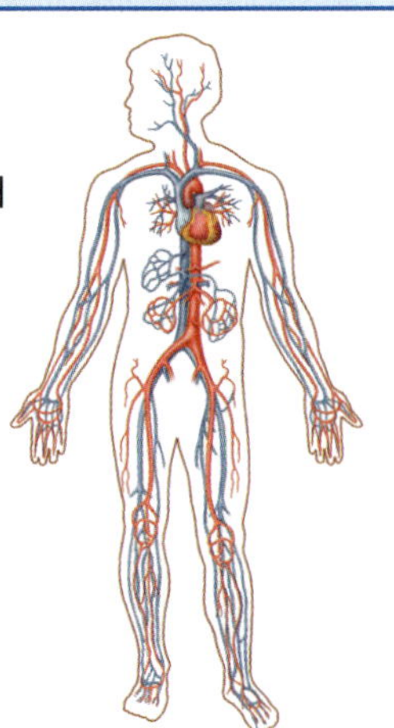

Circulatory system

3 Skin Gets More Blood

When you are overheating, your body sends more blood to the skin. This is a way to help cool it. As you sweat, the blood gets cool. However, less blood is going to the other organs.

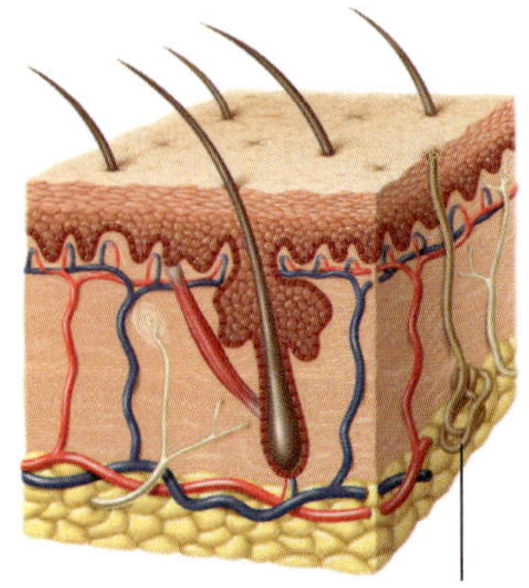

Sweat gland

4 Carbon Dioxide Builds Up

Cells normally release carbon dioxide into the blood. This happens during gas exchange with blood. When the body is overheating, carbon dioxide builds up in the cells because of the problems with circulation.

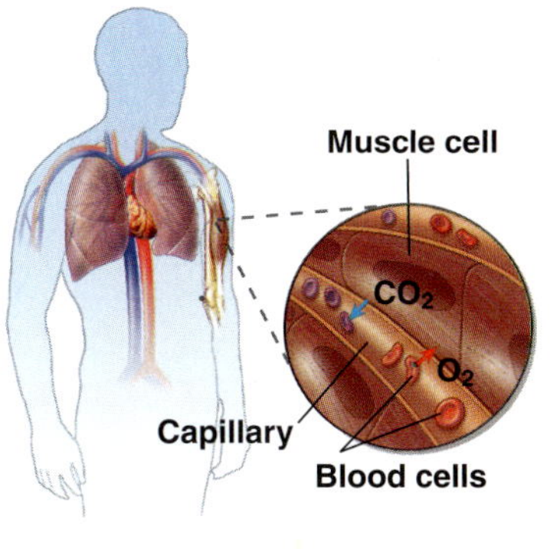

5 Breathing Becomes Rapid

Rapid breathing is one way the body responds to overheating. Breathing becomes fast and deep. This decreases the level of carbon dioxide in the blood and increases oxygen. It also cools the body a bit.

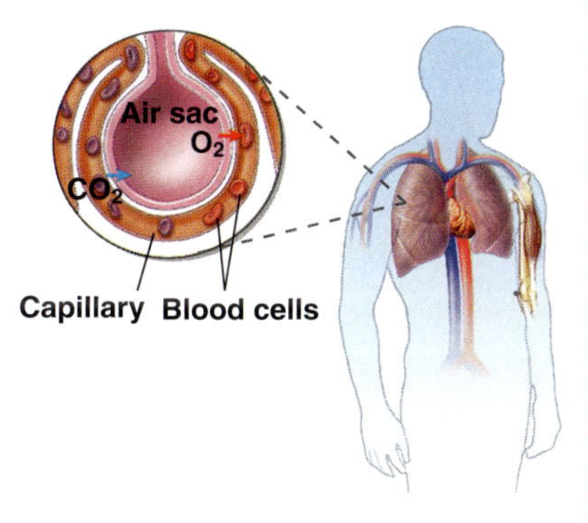

6 Kidneys Respond

When the body is dehydrated, the kidneys try to keep more fluids inside the body. When they detect less blood flowing to them, a chemical signal is sent that causes the nephrons to excrete more salts and absorb more water. The urine will be concentrated.

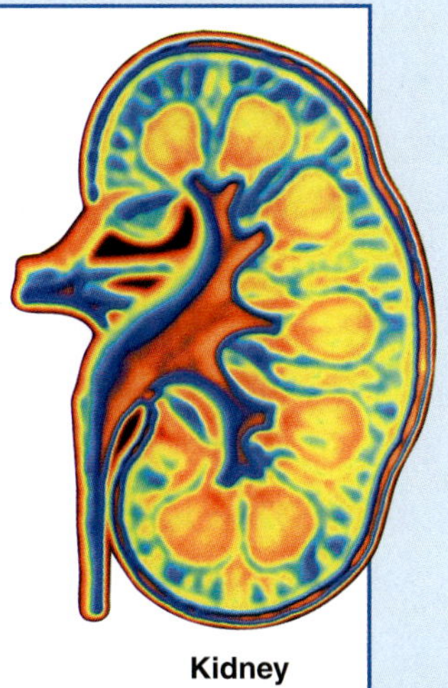

Kidney

7 Heat Stroke Occurs

If the body systems cannot reverse overheating, heat stroke may occur. At this point, the sweating system stops working. The body has no way to cool itself and body temperature rises. One by one, the body systems shut down. Immediate medical treatment is needed to prevent death.

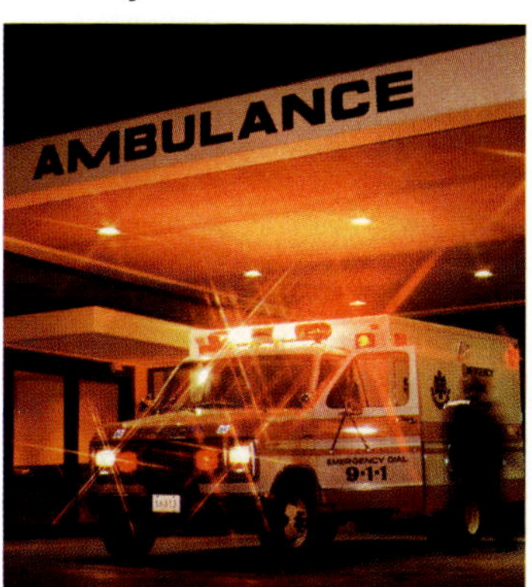

WRITING ACTIVITY

Science Log

Look at the pictures on these two pages. Have you ever felt sick from spending too much time in the heat? In your science log, research heat illnesses and ways to prevent them. Then create a poster that shows how to stay safe in the heat. Start your search at www.conceptsandchallenges.com.

Chapter 4 Challenges

Chapter Summary

Lesson 4-1

- The respiratory system is made up of the lungs, tubes, and passageways through which air moves in the body.

Lesson 4-2

- **Breathing** is the process by which air enters and leaves the body. **Respiration** is the process of carrying oxygen to cells, getting rid of carbon dioxide, and releasing energy.

Lesson 4-3

- Hairs in the nose filter dust particles from the air. **Mucus** in the nose and windpipe helps trap harmful particles contained in air. **Cilia** in the windpipe and nose push mucus and trapped particles toward the back of the throat.

Lesson 4-4

- In the lungs, oxygen and carbon dioxide are exchanged between the **alveoli** and the blood.
- Oxygen and carbon dioxide are exchanged between body cells and red blood cells in the capillaries.

Lesson 4-5

- Tobacco smoke contains many different kinds of harmful chemicals. Smoking can lead to cancer and heart disease.

Lesson 4-6

- Carbon dioxide, water, salts, nitrogen compounds, and heat are waste products formed by the body.
- Waste products are removed from the body in a process called **excretion**. The lungs, kidneys, and skin are the three main organs of the excretory system.

Lesson 4-7

- The main job of the kidneys is to filter wastes from the blood. **Urine** formed in the kidneys leaves the body through the urethra.

Lesson 4-8

- **Perspiration** is a waste excreted by the skin. It is formed by sweat glands and is excreted through **pores** in the skin.

Key Term Challenges

alveolus (p. 86)
bladder (p. 98)
bronchus (p. 86)
cilia (p. 92)
dermis (p. 102)
diaphragm (p. 88)
epidermis (p. 102)
evaporation (p. 102)
excretion (p. 98)
exhale (p. 88)
inhale (p. 88)
kidney (p. 98)
larynx (p. 86)
mucus (p. 92)
nephron (p. 100)
nicotine (p. 96)
perspiration (p. 102)
pore (p. 102)
respiration (p. 88)
trachea (p. 86)
urea (p. 100)
ureter (p. 98)
urine (p. 100)

MATCHING Write the Key Term from above that best matches each description.

1. microscopic air sacs in the lungs
2. breathe out
3. tube leading into the lung
4. liquid waste excreted by the skin
5. sticky liquid
6. liquid waste excreted by the kidneys
7. process of carrying oxygen to cells, getting rid of carbon dioxide, and releasing energy
8. sheet of muscle below the lungs
9. process by which air is taken into the body
10. filtering structure of the kidney

FILL IN Write the Key Term from above that best completes each statement.

11. When you breathe in, you ___________.
12. Tiny hair-like structures called ___________ line the windpipe.
13. The removal of wastes from the body is called ___________.
14. The changing of a liquid to a gas is called ___________.
15. Perspiration leaves the body through openings in the skin called ___________.

Content Challenges TEST PREP

MULTIPLE CHOICE Write the letter of the term or phrase that best completes each statement.

1. The waste products of cellular respiration are
   - **a.** water and carbon dioxide.
   - **b.** water and oxygen.
   - **c.** salts.
   - **d.** nitrogen compounds.
2. A sweat gland is a coiled tube surrounded by
   - **a.** alveoli.
   - **b.** mucus.
   - **c.** capillaries.
   - **d.** cilia.
3. Urine passes out of the body through the
   - **a.** ureters.
   - **b.** urethra.
   - **c.** kidneys.
   - **d.** urea.
4. When you inhale, the
   - **a.** ribs move up and out.
   - **b.** ribs move down and in.
   - **c.** diaphragm moves upward.
   - **d.** chest cavity becomes smaller.
5. The largest organ of the excretory system is the
   - **a.** large intestine.
   - **b.** kidney.
   - **c.** small intestine.
   - **d.** skin.
6. Air enters the body through the
   - **a.** lungs.
   - **b.** skin.
   - **c.** nose and mouth.
   - **d.** windpipe.
7. The windpipe divides into two tubes called
   - **a.** alveoli.
   - **b.** capillaries.
   - **c.** bronchi.
   - **d.** ureters.
8. Air reaching the lungs is
   - **a.** cold and dry.
   - **b.** warm and moist.
   - **c.** cold and moist.
   - **d.** warm and dry.
9. Oxygen and carbon dioxide are exchanged between the lungs and the blood during
   - **a.** external respiration.
   - **b.** internal respiration.
   - **c.** cellular respiration.
   - **d.** breathing.
10. When tobacco burns, it releases harmful substances such as tar, nicotine, and
    - **a.** carbon dioxide.
    - **b.** carbon monoxide.
    - **c.** nitrogen.
    - **d.** oxygen.
11. The process of removing waste products from the body is called
    - **a.** respiration.
    - **b.** digestion.
    - **c.** evaporation.
    - **d.** excretion.

TRUE/FALSE Write *true* if the statement is true. If the statement is false, change the underlined term to make the statement true.

12. Breathing is a <u>chemical</u> process.
13. Inhaled air contains more <u>oxygen</u> than exhaled air.
14. Water is removed from wastes in the <u>bladder</u>.
15. Perspiration is made up mostly of <u>salts</u>.
16. Smoking causes the <u>cilia</u> to stop working.
17. Waste water leaves sweat glands through <u>capillaries</u>.
18. When particles irritate your nose, you respond by <u>sneezing</u>.

Concept Challenges TEST PREP

WRITTEN RESPONSE **Answer each of the following questions in complete sentences.**

1. **SEQUENCE:** Through what tubes and passageways does air pass from the outside of the body to the lungs?
2. **EXPLAIN:** How do mucus and cilia help you fight infection?
3. **CONTRAST:** What is the difference between breathing and respiration?
4. **RELATE:** How do the respiratory system and circulatory system work together?
5. **COMPARE:** How is the skin like an air-conditioning system?

INTERPRETING A DIAGRAM **Use Figure 4-25 to answer the following questions.**

6. Which two labels represent places where air enters the body?
7. What does letter *F* represent? What is the function of this structure?
8. Which letter represents the structure sometimes called the windpipe? What is the name of this structure?
9. How does the nose help in purifying air?
10. Where are cilia found in the respiratory system?

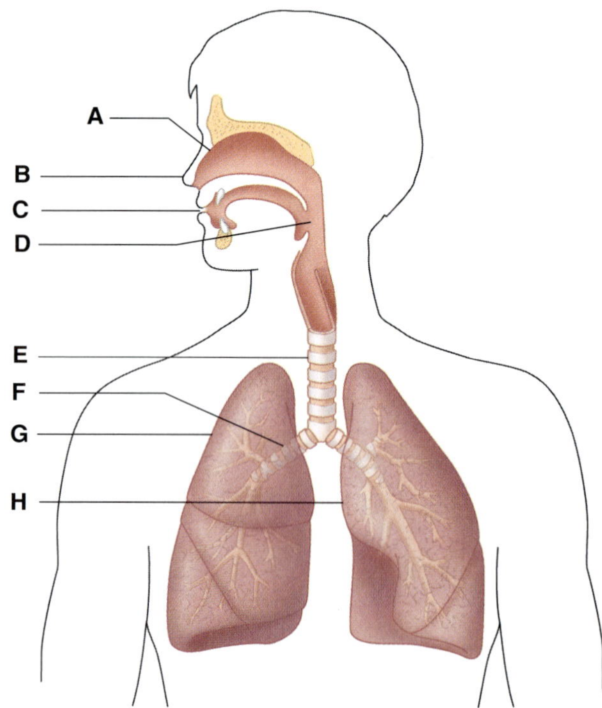

▲ **Figure 4-25** The respiratory system

Chapter 5 Fighting Disease

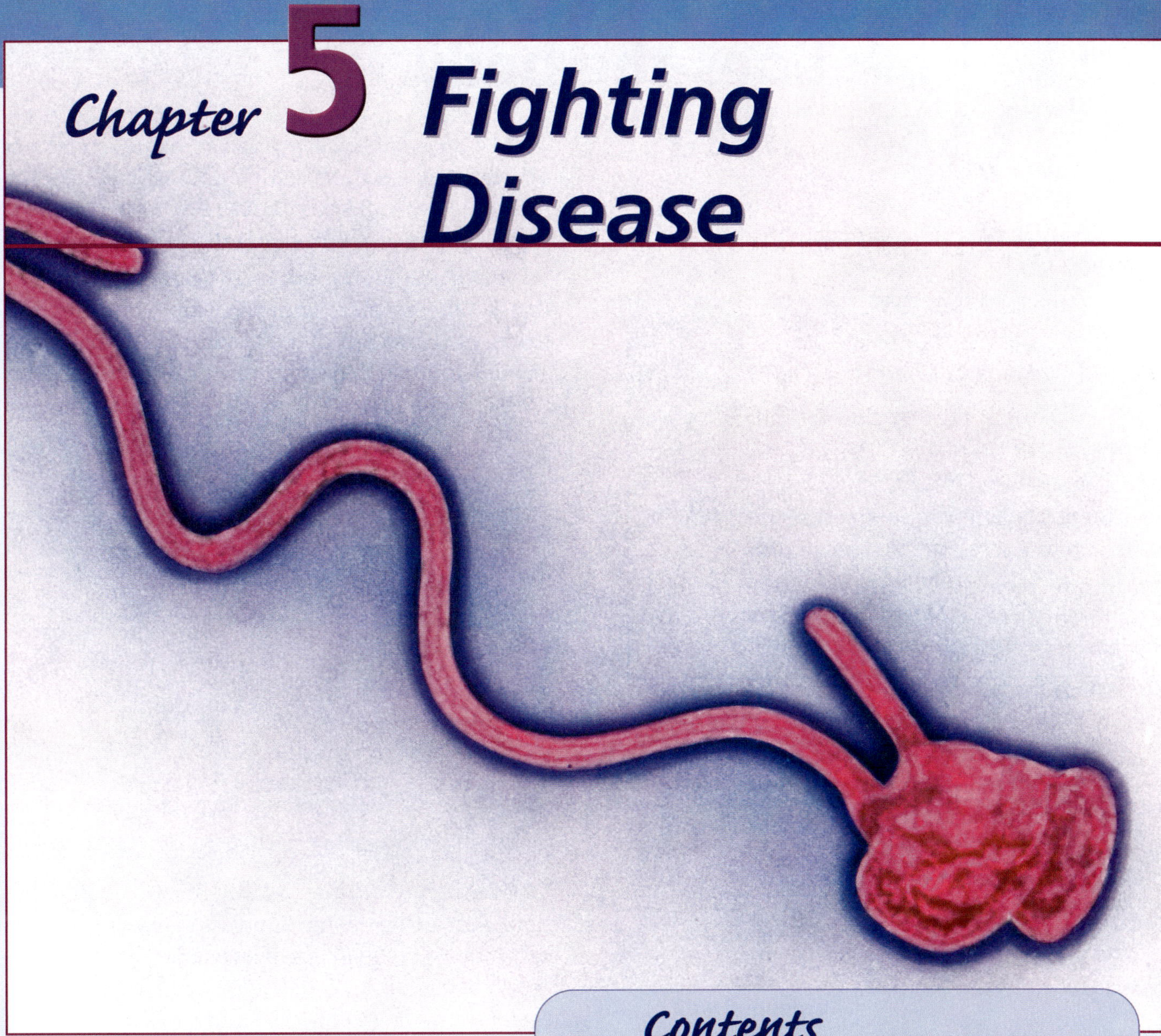

▲ **Figure 5-1** The Ebola virus causes Ebola fever, a disease that can be deadly.

Humans have always been victims of disease. Many diseases, such as the flu, can be passed from one person to another. Other diseases, like cancer, are not contagious. Cures for many human diseases have been found. Many more, including Ebola fever, do not have a cure. More research into these diseases is needed.

► Why do you think research into diseases is necessary?

Contents

5-1 How does the body fight disease?

5-2 What is immunity?

5-3 What are some bacterial diseases?

■ **Lab Activity:** Determining the Effectiveness of Antiseptics

5-4 What are some viral diseases?

5-5 What are noninfectious diseases?

■ **The Big Idea:** How has disease affected us over time?

5-1 How does the body fight disease?

Objective

Identify the ways your body fights disease.

Key Terms

pathogen: any agent that causes disease

white blood cell: blood cell that protects the body against disease

antigen: signal molecule that produces an immune response

antibody: molecule the body makes to protect itself from disease

Defense Systems Your body is under constant attack by agents such as bacteria or viruses. Agents that cause diseases are called **pathogens.** Your body usually can protect itself from illness because it has defenses against disease. These defenses may be physical barriers that actually block the pathogen from entering the body. They may also be chemical defenses that fight the pathogen once it has entered the body.

 IDENTIFY: What is a pathogen?

Skin The skin is a barrier that covers your body. It is made up of several layers of cells. Working together, the layers of the skin act like a wall to prevent pathogens from entering the body. Your skin is your first line of defense against disease.

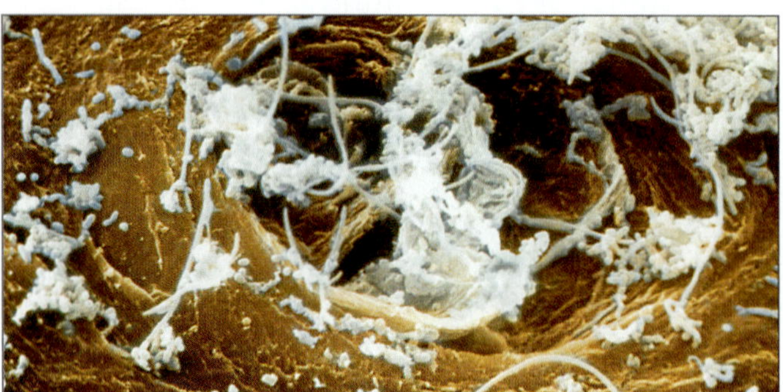

▲ **Figure 5-2** The skin prevents the bacteria, shown in white in this photo, from entering the body.

 DESCRIBE: How does the skin protect the body?

Digestive System Although the skin protects the body from most germs, bacteria and viruses can enter the body through the mouth. The digestive system helps to destroy these agents. Hydrochloric acid in the stomach helps to destroy bacteria and viruses that enter the stomach.

 EXPLAIN: How does the digestive system help to protect the body from pathogens?

Respiratory System Bacteria and viruses also can enter the body through the nose. Hairs in the nose filter the air and trap many small particles. Cilia and mucus in the respiratory system also trap germs before they can enter the lungs. The body gets rid of the trapped particles by sneezing and coughing. Sneezing and coughing force mucus and trapped particles out of the body.

 EXPLAIN: How does mucus in the nose and windpipe protect the body?

Circulatory System When germs get past the defenses of the skin and the digestive and respiratory systems, the **white blood cells** go to work. White blood cells are part of the circulatory system. There are several different kinds of white blood cells, and each works in a different way.

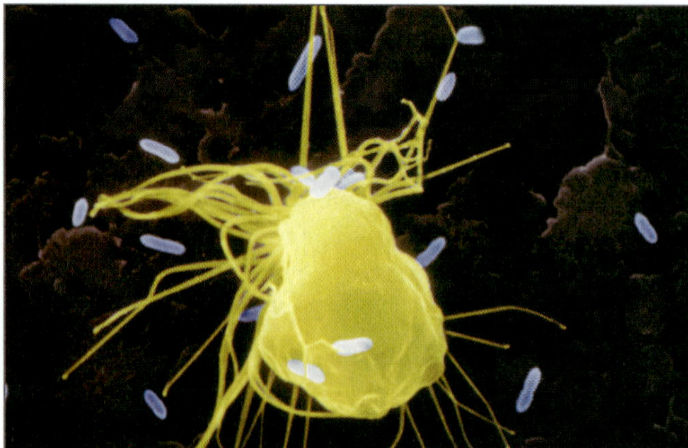

▲ **Figure 5-3** The white blood cell, shown in yellow, is attacking *E. coli* bacteria.

One kind of white blood cell, called a phagocyte, can move and change shape like an amoeba. Phagocytes travel around the body in the bloodstream in search of bacteria or other pathogens. When phagocytes find the pathogens, they surround them. The phagocytes then destroy the bacteria by digesting them.

5 **DESCRIBE:** How do white blood cells help protect the body?

The Lymphatic System Other types of white blood cells, called lymphocytes, play a role in fighting disease as well. Special white blood cells can be found in lymph vessels, which are part of the lymphatic system of the body. The lymphatic system is a transport system, like the circulatory system.

The lymphatic system does not transport blood, but a clear fluid called lymph. This system drains excess fluid from tissues and returns it to the circulatory system. The lymphatic system contains many bean-shaped structures called lymph nodes. The nodes filter the fluid before it is returned to the bloodstream. These lymph nodes sometimes get bigger during an infection.

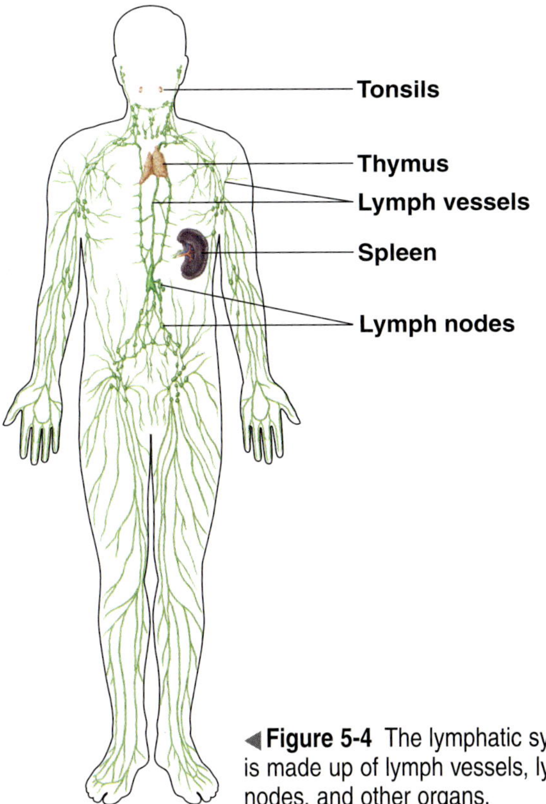

◀ **Figure 5-4** The lymphatic system is made up of lymph vessels, lymph nodes, and other organs.

6 **INFER:** Why do you think lymph nodes swell during an infection?

The Immune System The body's specific defenses are part of the immune system. This system includes several organs that also belong to other systems. The immune system also includes lymph and certain white blood cells. B and T cells are part of this system. These white blood cells are more specific in their attack than the other defenses. They recognize and attack only certain pathogens. These pathogens contain a chemical signal that tells the immune system that it is a foreign substance. These signals are called **antigens.**

Antigens can be whole pathogens or parts of pathogens. They can also be insect venom or pollen. Some white blood cells in the body find foreign substances that contain antigens and produce antibodies. **Antibodies** are molecules that help destroy substances that carry antigens.

7 **EXPLAIN:** What is the function of the immune system?

CHECKING CONCEPTS

1. What are two agents that can cause disease?
2. What is your first line of defense against disease?
3. How does the respiratory system defend against disease?
4. How do white blood cells travel?
5. What are antigens?

THINKING CRITICALLY

6. **INFER:** Tonsils are part of the lymphatic system. Why do you think some people have to have their tonsils taken out?
7. **ORGANIZE:** Make a chart showing how each body system is involved in fighting disease.

HEALTH AND SAFETY TIP

You can help your body fight disease. Always wash your hands before eating and after using the restroom. You can fight infection by washing a cut and putting a bandage over it. Finally, you can help your body fight disease by eating a proper diet. This keeps your body better prepared to deal with disease-causing substances.

5-2 What is immunity?

Objective

Explain the difference between natural immunity and acquired immunity.

Key Term

immunity (ihm-MYOON-uh-tee): resistance to a specific disease

Resisting Disease Antibodies protect the body against foreign substances. After these foreign substances are destroyed, many of the antibodies remain. If the same kind of foreign substances enter the body once again, the remaining antibodies destroy the substances before they can do any harm. The body has become resistant to these diseases. This resistance to a specific disease is called **immunity.**

1 IDENTIFY: What is immunity?

Types of Immunity There are two kinds of immunity. One kind is called natural immunity. The other is called acquired immunity. Natural immunity is one that people are born with. Some people have certain kinds of antibodies in their bodies at birth. Natural immunity is your body's natural defense against certain diseases. Acquired immunity is an immunity that people develop, or acquire, at some time during their lives.

2 COMPARE: What is the difference between natural and acquired immunity?

Active Acquired Immunity There are two kinds of acquired immunity. One kind is called active acquired immunity. With this kind of immunity, the body resists a certain disease because it has already developed antibodies against the disease. In most cases, once you have been exposed to certain diseases, your body continues to make the antibodies for that disease. For example, most people who have had chickenpox will not get it again. Their bodies have developed immunity against chickenpox.

3 EXPLAIN: How do you develop active acquired immunity?

T Cells and B Cells T cells and B cells are special white blood cells that are part of the lymphatic system. They are also part of the body's immune system because they help fight disease. T cells identify pathogens by detecting the signal molecules, or antigens. Some T cells then attack and kill the pathogen. They may also kill the damaged body cells that the pathogen has already harmed. Other T cells work by calling the B cells to action. The B cells produce substances that react with the antigens. These substances are called antibodies. Some antibodies cause the antigens to break up or clump together. Then, they can be easily attacked by the phagocyte white blood cells.

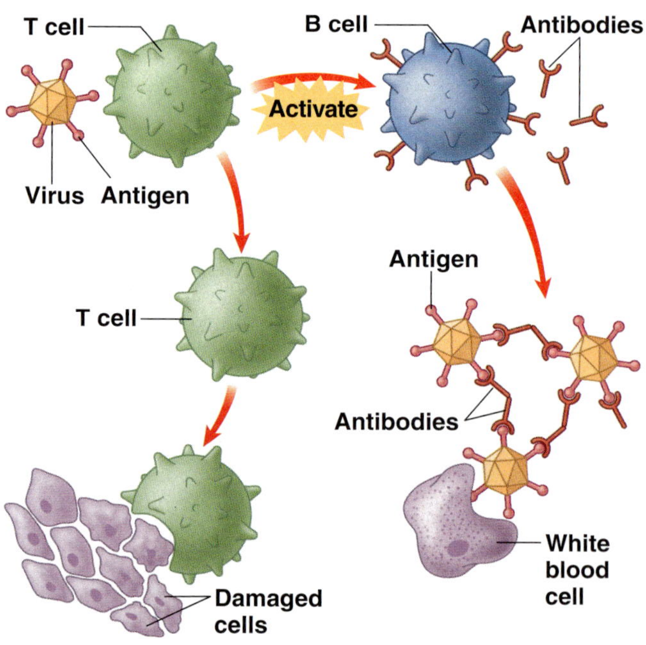

▲ **Figure 5-5** T cells attack some antigens. For others, they signal the B cells to make antibodies.

4 EXPLAIN: In what ways do antibodies work?

Passive Acquired Immunity The second kind of acquired immunity is passive acquired immunity. In this kind of immunity, antibodies are not produced by your body. The antibodies are obtained from somewhere else. You may be injected with antibodies against a certain disease. Then you have passive acquired immunity against that disease. However, this kind of immunity does not last long. Antibodies that are not made by the body usually are destroyed by white blood cells after a short time.

5 **COMPARE:** Which type of acquired immunity lasts the longest?

Vaccines One way of getting immunity is through a vaccine. A vaccine is a serum made from a dead or a weakened form of bacteria or viruses. The serum is injected into the body. Vaccines do not cause you to get the disease. The body responds to the vaccine by making antibodies against the pathogens. The antibodies remain in the body and protect it from the disease. Polio, measles, and mumps have all been controlled by vaccines. The disease smallpox has been completely eliminated because of vaccinations. Scientists continue to try to find vaccines for more diseases.

EXPLAIN: How does a vaccine give you immunity?

CHECKING CONCEPTS

1. A resistance to disease is called __________.
2. Immunity a person is born with is called __________ immunity.
3. Immunity a person develops is called __________ immunity.
4. When a body makes antibodies against a disease, __________ acquired immunity may result.
5. Passive acquired immunity is __________.

THINKING CRITICALLY

6. **COMPARE:** How are natural immunity, active acquired immunity, and passive acquired immunity similar?
7. **RELATE:** Sometimes a developing baby receives antibodies from its mother. Is this immunity a natural or an acquired immunity? Explain.

How Do They Know That?

EDWARD JENNER'S DISCOVERY OF VACCINATIONS

The first vaccine was developed and used in 1796 by Edward Jenner, an English doctor. Jenner noticed that many people who worked near cattle got a mild disease called cowpox. He also noticed that these same people did not get the fatal disease smallpox. To find out why, Jenner tried injecting material from cowpox sores into people. Antibodies against cowpox were produced in these people. Jenner found that these same antibodies were able to destroy the smallpox virus. The people did not get smallpox because the cowpox antibodies protected them against smallpox too.

The vaccine Edward Jenner developed was made directly from a pathogen. Today many vaccines are made from inactive parts of bacteria and viruses. The human body responds to these vaccines by making antibodies. Diseases that were once widespread, such as polio, have been almost eliminated due to the creation of vaccines.

Thinking Critically Why do you think the cowpox antibodies prevented people from getting smallpox as well?

▲ **Figure 5-6** Dr. Jenner gives a child a vaccine against smallpox.

5-3 What are some bacterial diseases?

Objectives

Describe the causes of different types of disease.
Explain how antibiotics are used to fight disease.

Key Terms

contagious: can be spread from one person to another

antibiotic (an-tih-by-AHT-ihk)**:** chemical made by a living organism that kills bacteria

Germ Theory About 150 years ago, Louis Pasteur showed that some diseases are caused by bacteria and other microscopic organisms. The idea that diseases are caused by microscopic organisms, or germs, is called the germ theory of disease.

1 EXPLAIN: What is the germ theory?

Identifying Germs To fight a disease, it is important to identify the kind of bacteria that causes the disease. Robert Koch studied many bacterial diseases. He discovered how to grow bacteria outside a living body. This made it possible to study and find ways of destroying the bacteria. Figure 5-7 lists some common bacterial diseases.

COMMON BACTERIAL DISEASES		
Disease	**Bacteria**	**Body Part Affected**
Cholera	*Vibrio cholerae*	Small intestine
Lyme disease	*Borrelia burgdorferi*	Skin, joints, heart
Salmonella food poisoning	*Salmonella*	Intestine
Strep throat	*Streptococcus pyogenes*	Upper respiratory tract, blood, skin
Tetanus	*Clostridium tetani*	Nerves at synapse
Tuberculosis	*Myocobacterium tuberculosis*	Lungs, bones, other organs

▲ Figure 5-7

DESCRIBE: Why is it important to find the germ that causes a disease?

Spread of Bacterial Diseases Cholera, strep throat, and Lyme disease are all examples of diseases caused by bacteria. Most diseases that are caused by bacteria are **contagious.** This means they can be spread from one person to another. Some diseases are spread by coughing or sneezing. If you inhale air that contains the bacteria, you can get sick. Other bacterial diseases, such as Lyme disease, are spread by another living organism. The bacteria that cause Lyme disease are carried by ticks. Diseases can also be spread when people share drinking glasses, utensils, or makeup.

There are other ways that diseases can be spread. Bacteria can be found in foods and in drinking water. To prevent developing a disease from these bacteria, you should wash all foods thoroughly. You should also cook foods, especially meats, properly.

LIST: What are three ways diseases can be spread?

Treating Disease Sometimes your body needs help in fighting off disease. Your doctor may prescribe medicine or you may get an injection. If you are suffering from a disease caused by bacteria, you may be treated with an antibiotic. An **antibiotic** is a chemical substance that kills bacteria.

IDENTIFY: What is an antibiotic?

Discovery of Antibiotics The use of antibiotics to treat disease is a fairly recent discovery. In 1928, Alexander Fleming, an English bacteriologist, was the first person to observe the action of an antibiotic. Fleming was growing bacteria in a dish. He noticed that the bacteria did not grow in a part of the dish where some mold had grown. Fleming guessed that the mold produced a substance that was harmful to bacteria.

Thirteen years later, scientists were able to separate this substance from the same kind of mold. The scientists called this substance penicillin (pen-uh-SIL-in). Penicillin was the first antibiotic.

Since the discovery of penicillin, many other antibiotics have been discovered. Most antibiotics

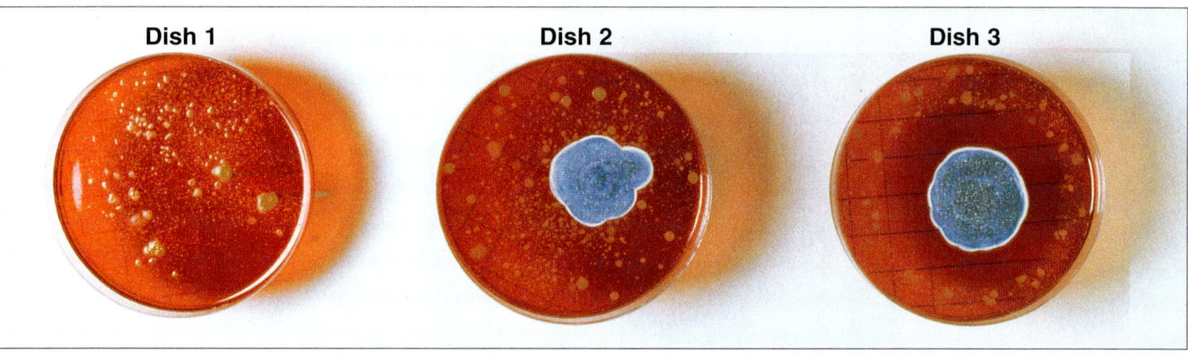

▲ **Figure 5-8** Dish 1 shows the growth of bacteria. Penicillin mold (blue) is growing in Dish 2. In Dish 3, the bacteria around the mold has died.

are produced from molds. Others are made from fungi and bacteria. Certain kinds of plants and animals also produce some types of antibiotics.

5 **EXPLAIN:** How did Fleming discover penicillin?

How Antibiotics Work Antibiotics are not all the same. Different antibiotics have different effects on a particular disease. This means that each antibiotic can be used to fight only certain kinds of organisms. For example, penicillin works only against certain bacteria. The penicillin destroys the bacteria and stops them from reproducing. Penicillin does not work against viruses. No single antibiotic can destroy all types of bacteria.

Allergic reactions can be a drawback to the use of antibiotics. For example, some people are allergic to penicillin. If they take this antibiotic, a fever or rash may develop. In severe reactions, they may not be able to breathe. For this reason, it is important to tell the doctor about any drug allergies.

6 **APPLY:** Why is it important to tell your doctor about any drug allergies you might have?

Overuse of Antibiotics The overuse of antibiotics has become a concern in the field of medicine. One reason is because antibiotics kill useful bacteria in your body along with the bacteria causing the illness. This is why some antibiotics cause side effects such as intestinal problems.

Another problem with overusing antibiotics is that bacteria can become resistant to the antibiotic. This means that the antibiotic may no longer work against certain bacteria. Resistance can become a problem if an antibiotic is needed for a more serious illness.

For these reasons, many doctors do not prescribe antibiotics as often as they used to. They also ask patients to take all of their antibiotics so that the bacteria in the body are completely destroyed and do not have a chance to form a resistance.

7 **EXPLAIN:** Why should you finish all of the medication given to you by a doctor?

CHECKING CONCEPTS

1. The work of __________ showed that diseases are caused by microscopic organisms.
2. Diseases can be spread by __________.
3. The first antibiotic was discovered by __________.
4. Most antibiotics are made from __________.
5. Diseases that can be spread from one person to another are called __________.

THINKING CRITICALLY

6. **ANALYZE:** What are two diseases that affect the intestines?
7. **INFER:** Why is it important to cover your nose when you sneeze?

DESIGNING AN EXPERIMENT

Design an experiment to solve the following problem. Include a hypothesis, variables, a procedure, and a type of data to study.

PROBLEM: Bacteria can be found in almost every place on Earth. There are bacteria on your desk, on the floor, even on your skin! Bacteria can be collected and grown in petri dishes that contain nutrient bases. Lori wants to know which parts of her school or home have the most bacteria. How can she find an answer?

LAB ACTIVITY

Determining the Effectiveness of Antiseptics

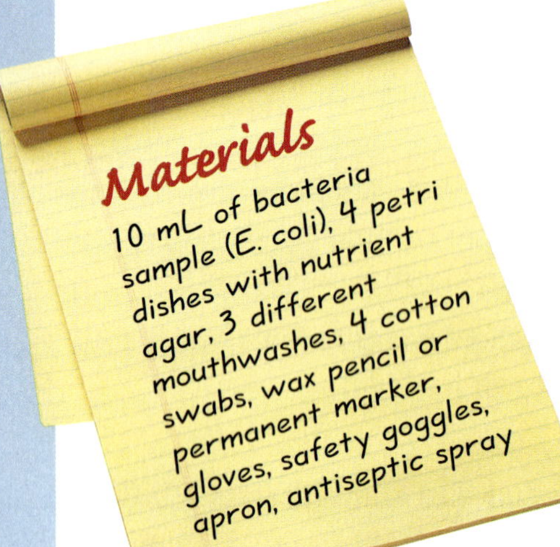

BACKGROUND

Many diseases are caused by some type of bacteria. Diseases can be spread from one person to another or they can be spread by ingesting contaminated foods or drinking water. Antiseptics are substances that are used to fight harmful bacteria. Mouthwash is a type of antiseptic used to fight bacteria that cause tooth decay. Antiseptics such as mouthwash work by stopping or slowing the growth of bacteria and other microorganisms.

PURPOSE

In this activity you will investigate the effectiveness of several different brands of mouthwash.

PROCEDURE

1. Put on your goggles, gloves, and apron. Label four petri dishes *1* to *4*.

2. Add approximately 10 mL of the first type of mouthwash to petri dish 1. Replace the lid and write the name of the mouthwash on the label.

3. Add approximately 10 mL of the second type of mouthwash to petri dish 2. Replace the lid and write the name of the mouthwash on the label.

4. Add approximately 10 mL of the third type of mouthwash to petri dish 3. Replace the lid and write the name of the mouthwash on the label.

5. Add no mouthwash to petri dish 4. This will be the control sample. Label it *control*.

6. Dip the cotton swab into the bacteria sample. Slowly rub the cotton swab back and forth across the agar in the first petri dish. Be careful not to tear the agar. ⚠ **CAUTION:** Do not touch any of the bacteria. Using a clean swab each time, repeat for petri dishes 2, 3, and 4.

▲ **STEP 2** Pour the mouthwash into 3 of the petri dishes.

▲ **STEP 6** Rub the cotton swab back and forth across the petri dish.

7. Set the petri dishes aside in a cool, dark place. Keep the lids on the petri dishes at all times.

8. Remove your gloves. ⚠ **CAUTION:** Dispose of your gloves and used swabs in a disposal bag provided by your teacher. Wash your hands with soap and warm water. Clean your workspace with antiseptic spray.

9. After four to six days, return to the petri dishes. Put on gloves before touching the dishes but do not open them. Copy Figure 5-9 into your notebook. Record your observations in this table.

10. Give the dishes and gloves to your teacher for proper disposal. ⚠ **CAUTION:** Do not throw them in the garbage. Wash your hands with soap and warm water.

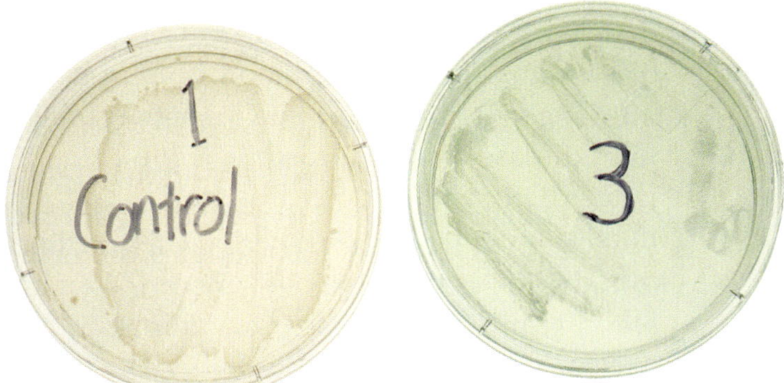

▲ **STEP 9** Observe the petri dishes.

Petri Dish	Observations
1	
2	
3	
4	

▲ **Figure 5-9** Copy this table onto a separate sheet of paper.

CONCLUSIONS

1. **OBSERVE:** Which petri dish had the most bacterial growth in it? Which had the least bacterial growth?

2. **INFER:** Which antiseptic do you think is the most effective?

3. **ANALYZE:** What factors or variables, besides brand of antiseptic, could have caused the results?

5-4 What are some viral diseases?

Objectives

Describe several examples of diseases caused by viruses. Describe the causes and symptoms of AIDS.

Key Term

AIDS: viral disease that attacks a person's immune system

Viral Diseases Some kinds of disease are caused by viruses. The invention of the electron microscope has helped scientists learn about viruses and disease. Scientists have discovered that different kinds of viruses attack different parts of the body. Each virus usually attacks only a certain kind of cell or tissue. For example, the viruses that cause warts seem to attack only cells in the skin. Viruses that cause yellow fever attack cells in the liver. Information about how viruses attack the body helps in the fight against the disease the virus causes.

DESCRIBE: In what way are viruses particular?

Common Viral Diseases

Viruses cause many different kinds of diseases. You have probably had several types of viral diseases in your lifetime. The common cold and the flu are both caused by viruses. Other diseases caused by viruses are listed in Figure 5-11.

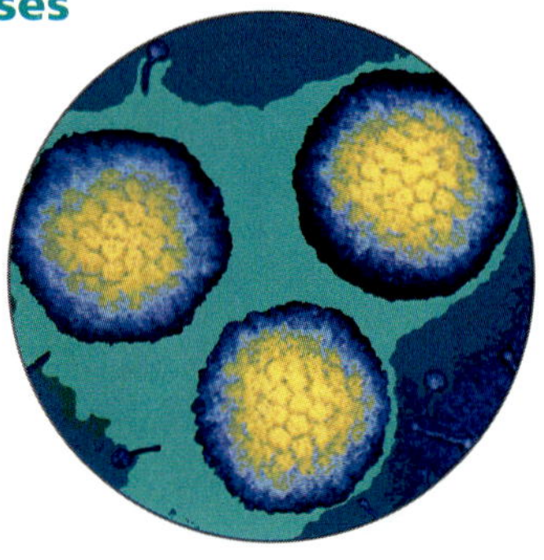

▲ **Figure 5-10** Cold viruses

VIRAL DISEASES	
Disease	**Symptoms**
Influenza (flu)	Muscle aches, fever, and chills
Chickenpox	Skin rash in spots and fever
Measles	Pink rash all over the body
Mumps	Swollen glands and fever
Hepatitis	Jaundiced skin, swollen liver, and loss of appetite

▲ **Figure 5-11**

There are many different kinds of cold and flu viruses. However, most of them cause the same set of symptoms. These symptoms may include sneezing, coughing, sore throat, headache, and fever.

INFER: Which body systems does the common cold affect?

HIV Viruses cause disease. They are selective in the cells or tissues that they attack. A particular virus, called human immunodeficiency virus (HIV), attacks a person's immune system. The illness caused by HIV is called acquired immune deficiency syndrome, or AIDS. **AIDS** is a viral disease that kills white blood cells in a person's immune system. The person loses the ability to fight disease. For this reason, people with AIDS easily get diseases that most healthy people can fight off. These diseases often are fatal for a person with AIDS.

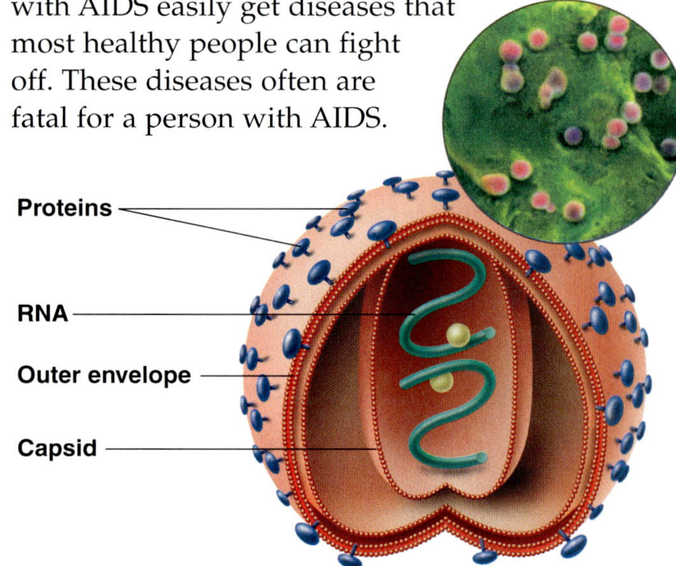

▲ **Figure 5-12** This diagram shows the basic structure of HIV. The photo above shows HIV in pink.

DESCRIBE: What effect does HIV have on the body?

Transmission of AIDS AIDS cannot be transmitted by casual contact. It cannot travel through air, food, or water. People with AIDS have HIV in their blood and body fluids. In order to contract AIDS, you must exchange bodily fluids with an infected person. The virus can enter the bloodstream by sexual contact with someone who has HIV. Another way HIV enters the bloodstream is through a blood transfusion of infected blood.

For this reason, blood banks test donated blood for the HIV virus. Today, it is extremely rare to get HIV from a transfusion given in the United States. You cannot get HIV by donating blood.

4 **EXPLAIN:** How is HIV transmitted?

CHECKING CONCEPTS

1. The invention of the ___________ helped scientists study viruses.
2. Particular kinds of ___________ usually attack only certain types of cells and tissues.
3. The common cold and the flu are both caused by ___________.
4. HIV attacks the body's ___________.

THINKING CRITICALLY

5. **INFER:** Why do you think the invention of the electron microscope helped in the study of viruses?
6. **PREDICT:** Could a person with AIDS transmit the virus to another person sitting across the room?
7. **INFER:** How does making the immune system stronger lengthen the life of a person with AIDS?

Web InfoSearch

Virus Mutations Many viruses have the ability to mutate, or change their genetic material. This ability to mutate makes studying viruses difficult. It also makes it harder for scientists to find treatments or cures for viral diseases.

SEARCH: Use the Internet to find out more about the ability of viruses to mutate. Write a report about how this affects health and medicine. Start your search at www.conceptsandchallenges.com. Some key search words are **virus, viral disease,** and **virus mutation.**

Science and Technology

TREATMENTS FOR AIDS

HIV is an RNA virus. It causes the disease known as AIDS. The virus attacks T cells, which are a major part of our immune system. Millions of people throughout the world have AIDS.

Researchers are trying to find a vaccine that can help stop the spread of AIDS. Vaccines are dead or weakened forms of viruses that allow the person to build up an immunity to the virus. If an effective vaccine were to be found, the number of new AIDS victims could decrease dramatically. Scientists have developed drugs that can treat the disease to extend the life expectancy of patients. These drugs show promise in the slowing of the disease's progress in the body. However, the virus mutates and evolves so quickly that new drugs must be designed constantly.

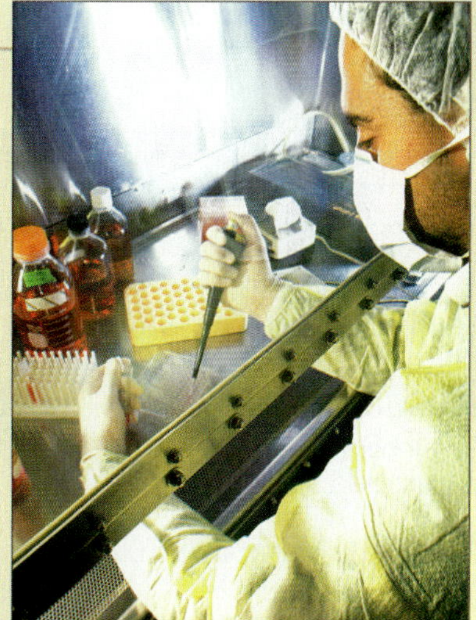

▲ **Figure 5-13** Researchers are trying to find a vaccine for AIDS.

There is no cure as yet for AIDS. The vaccines that exist have not yet been fully tested. People in many nations of the world are now suffering from the HIV virus. More research is needed to find a cure for patients with the disease. For now, education is the best way to stop the disease from spreading to more people.

Thinking Critically Why do you think AIDS is such a difficult disease to treat or cure?

5-5 What are noninfectious diseases?

Objective

Describe several noninfectious diseases and their effect on the body.

Key Terms

tumor (TOO-muhr)**:** mass or lump of cells

benign (bih-NYN) **tumor:** mass of cells that is usually harmless

malignant (muh-LIHG-nuhnt) **tumor:** harmful mass of cells that can spread throughout the body

Noninfectious Diseases Not all diseases are caused by microorganisms. Those that are not are called noninfectious diseases. They cannot be spread from one person to another. Cancer, Alzheimer's disease, and diabetes are all types of noninfectious diseases. The immune system also reacts to noninfectious diseases.

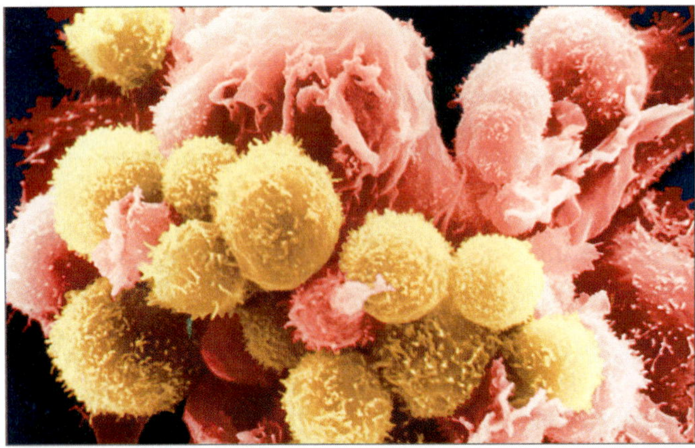

▲ **Figure 5-14** The cancer cells, shown in pink in this photo, are being attacked by T cells, shown in yellow.

 NAME: What are three noninfectious diseases?

Cancer Most cells in the body divide and produce new cells only when necessary. Sometimes new cells grow where they are not needed. Their growth becomes rapid and uncontrolled. The new cells crowd nearby cells and rob them of their nutrients. The new cells form a mass, or lump, called a **tumor.**

There are two kinds of tumors. **Benign tumors** do not spread to other parts of the body and usually are not a serious health problem. **Malignant tumors** are more harmful because they can spread to other parts of the body. As a tumor spreads, it causes harm to the body. The disease caused by the spread of malignant tumors is called cancer.

 CONTRAST: How are benign and malignant tumors different?

Causes of Cancer Scientists are not exactly sure what causes cancer to start growing. They do know that certain chemicals increase the chance of getting cancer. Studies have shown that exposure to too much sunlight and X-rays can cause cancer. Scientists believe that certain viruses and hormones also may cause cancer. Research also has shown that people who smoke cigarettes are more likely to get lung cancer than nonsmokers.

 LIST: What are three things that may lead to cancer?

Alzheimer's Disease Alzheimer's disease affects the brain. Most people with Alzheimer's develop the disease in their later years. However, it is not a normal part of the aging process. Alzheimer's disease causes memory loss. It may also reduce a person's ability to think and speak clearly. The nerve cells and nerve connections of these patients have been tangled or destroyed. Scientists are still unsure of the exact causes of Alzheimer's disease. Most think that the disease may be caused by many different factors, including genetics.

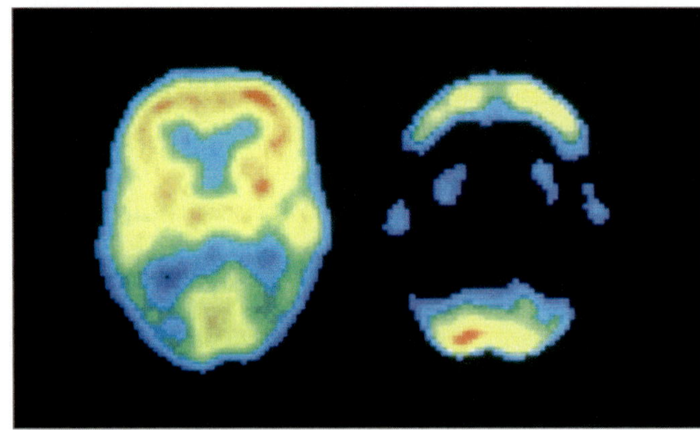

▲ **Figure 5-15** This image shows the brain (left) of a healthy person compared with one of an Alzheimer's patient (right).

 IDENTIFY: Which body system does Alzheimer's disease affect?

Diabetes The pancreas normally produces a hormone called insulin, which regulates the amount of sugar in the bloodstream. If too little insulin is produced, an excess amount of sugar can build up in the blood. This condition is called diabetes mellitus. If untreated, diabetes can lead to kidney failure, blindness, and even death. Most diabetics can control their disease by taking insulin injections and by watching their diet.

5 **EXPLAIN:** How does diabetes affect the body?

CHECKING CONCEPTS

1. A disease that is not caused by a microorganism is called a __________.
2. A tumor that does not spread to other parts of the body is a __________ tumor.
3. Cancer is the spread of __________ tumors.
4. The hormone __________ regulates the amount of sugar in the bloodstream.
5. Patients with __________ disease may have tangled nerve cells.

THINKING CRITICALLY

6. **INFER:** Why do X-ray technicians wear lead aprons when taking X-rays?
7. **RELATE:** How is diabetes related to the endocrine, digestive, and circulatory systems?

HEALTH AND SAFETY TIP

One way to prevent cancer is to avoid the things that contribute to the disease. Not smoking is a way to greatly decrease your chances of getting lung cancer. Wearing sunscreen when outdoors can help prevent developing skin cancer. Eating a healthy diet, with the right amount of vitamins and minerals, can also help reduce your chances of developing cancer. Research cancer using library references or the Internet. Design a health brochure that provides information about cancer prevention.

Science and Technology

PARKINSON'S DISEASE RESEARCH

Parkinson's disease (PD) is a disorder of the central nervous system that tends to progress slowly over time. People with PD often have tremors. Their limbs are stiff, their movements are slow, and they may have balance problems. Researchers have discovered that all these difficulties are caused by damage to nerve cells in a small area in the middle of the brain. This results in a decrease in the production of an important chemical messenger called dopamine.

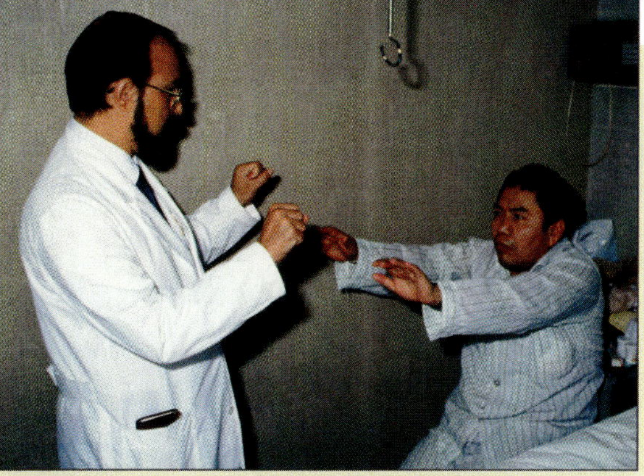

▲ **Figure 5-16** A doctor tests the movement of a patient with Parkinson's disease.

There is no cure for Parkinson's disease although there are a number of treatments. Researchers are working on a new type of drug that helps the brain to rebuild damaged nerve cells. Other scientists believe that injections of neural stem cells, special cells that have the ability to regenerate nerve tissue, may be an effective treatment. Operations in which small areas of nerve fibers are removed from certain parts of the brain can stop tremors. One of the latest advances is deep brain stimulation. A tiny electrode is placed deep inside the brain and stimulates nerve cells. The patient can turn its action on and off with a magnetic control device.

Thinking Critically Dopamine is a chemical messenger used by nerve cells in the brain. How can a decrease of dopamine result in problems in the movement of the body?

Integrating History

THE Big IDEA

How has disease affected us over time?

More than any other time in history, people today live longer, more healthy lives. We owe a lot to heroes in medicine. Edward Jenner invented the smallpox vaccine in 1796. In 1977, naturally occurring smallpox was erased from the planet.

Knowledge, effort, and luck play a role in history. Alexander Fleming didn't set out to discover penicillin. The mold grew in his dish of bacteria by accident. Researchers were working on a polio vaccine for many years before Jonas Salk. But with the financial support of a major foundation, Salk got there first.

What is happening in society influences medicine. During the Industrial Revolution, poor living conditions led to many diseases. In the

Folk Medicine 1400s

Early efforts to fight disease involved magic, faith, and plants. Many modern medicines are based on plants used thousands of years ago. Scientists today are learning more about the power of the mind to help in healing.

Nursing 1854

Florence Nightingale pioneered the field of nursing. In 1854, she led a group of fellow nurses to Turkey to help wounded British soldiers of the Crimean War. Almost all modern nursing methods can be traced back to her.

Radiation 1897

Marie Curie was a Polish-born French chemist who studied the radioactive properties of elements. This knowledge would become useful in the development of many types of radiotherapy.

1400 | 1800 | 1860 | 1870 | 1880 | 1890 | 1900

Smallpox Vaccine 1796

Smallpox killed many people in the 18th century. Cowpox was a form of the disease that affected cattle. Edward Jenner discovered the concept of vaccination. He found that when he gave people small doses of cowpox, they were immune to smallpox.

Germ Theory 1860s–1870s

Germ theory is the idea that specific microscopic organisms cause specific diseases. Louis Pasteur developed this theory and vaccines to prevent diseases. Today, preventing the spread of germs is a very important principle in medicine.

1860s, diseases that killed sheep and silkworms threatened the French economy. Louis Pasteur worked to solve these problems. This work with industry led to important medical discoveries. The desire to treat soldiers in World War II led to mass production of penicillin.

Today, technology is changing at a whirlwind speed. This is fueling amazing advances in the way we detect, prevent, and fight disease.

Look at the timeline on these two pages. They point out important dates in the history of fighting disease. Follow the directions in the Science Log to learn more about "the big idea."✦

WRITING ACTIVITY

Science Log

Look at the timeline on these two pages. In your science log, research and write about a person who played an important role in the history of fighting disease. Tell why you chose that person. Start your search at www.conceptsandchallenges.com.

Leukemia Drug 1953

Leukemia is a form of cancer that affects the blood. Gertrude Belle Elion invented a drug that has been used to fight leukemia.

Heart Transplant 1967

Christiaan Barnard was a South African surgeon. He performed the first human heart transplant. Organ transplants save the lives of many people. But donated organs are in short supply.

Cancer 1971

President Nixon declared war on cancer, and the federal government spends billions of dollars on cancer research. Research led to many advancements in treatment. Still, almost 30 years later, cancer is still the second leading cause of death.

Human Genome Project 2000

Scientists published the first physical map of the human genome. It is a set of instructions for building each human cell. Researchers now are working on ways to turn this knowledge into new treatments for disease.

1930 1940 1950 1960 1970 1980 1990 2000

Penicillin 1928

This lifesaving drug was discovered by Alexander Fleming. This discovery changed forever the way we treat bacterial infections. Penicillin has saved millions of lives.

Polio Vaccine 1954

The polio virus causes paralysis. In epidemics in the 1940s and 1950s, thousands of children were crippled each year. Building on the work of other scientists, Dr. Jonas Salk developed a polio vaccine. The disease has been erased in most parts of the world.

AIDS Treatment 1996

Doctors began prescribing a new drug treatment for AIDS. It was a combination of three drugs. The number of deaths from AIDS quickly dropped. Scientists continue their search for a vaccine and a cure.

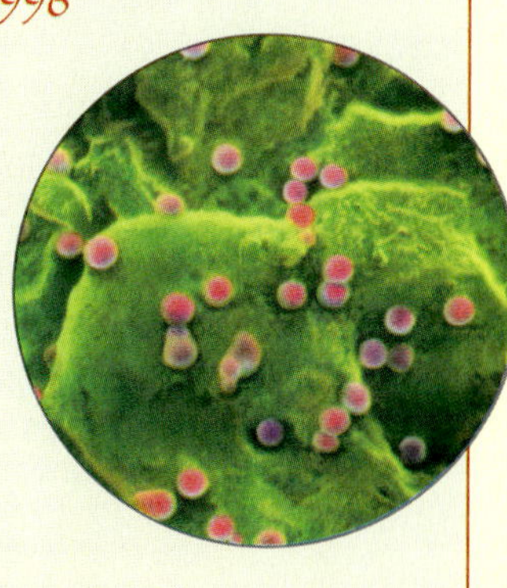

Chapter 5 Challenges

Chapter Summary

Lesson 5-1

- The first line of defense against disease is your skin. The defense systems of the body include the respiratory, digestive, circulatory, lymphatic, and immune systems.
- Certain types of **white blood cells** surround and destroy **pathogens** throughout the body.
- The body produces **antibodies** that can destroy foreign substances called **antigens.**

Lesson 5-2

- **Immunity** is a resistance to a specific disease. There are two kinds of immunity, natural immunity and acquired immunity.
- Active acquired immunity develops after the body has developed antibodies against a certain disease. Passive acquired immunity develops when antibodies are injected into the body.

Lesson 5-3

- The germ theory of disease states that diseases are caused by microscopic organisms.
- **Antibiotics** are chemical substances that kill harmful bacteria.
- Alexander Fleming was the first person to discover the use of antibiotics to treat disease.

Lesson 5-4

- Diseases caused by viruses include colds, the flu, and the measles.
- Viruses usually attack a specific kind of cell.
- **AIDS** is a viral disease that kills white blood cells in a person's immune system.

Lesson 5-5

- Diseases that are not caused by a microorganism are called noninfectious diseases. Alzheimer's disease, cancer, and diabetes are examples of noninfectious diseases.
- A **tumor** is a mass or lump of cells. **Benign tumors** are harmless growths of cells. **Malignant tumors** are tumors that spread to other parts of the body and cause harm.

Key Term Challenges

AIDS (p. 118)
antibiotic (p. 114)
antibody (p. 110)
antigen (p. 110)
benign tumor (p. 110)
contagious (p. 114)
immunity (p. 112)
malignant tumor (p. 120)
pathogen (p. 110)
tumor (p. 120)
white blood cell (p. 110)

MATCHING **Write the Key Term from above that best matches each description.**

1. cells that protect the body against disease
2. substances produced by white blood cells to help fight disease
3. resistance to a certain disease
4. mass or lump of cells
5. viral disease that attacks a person's immune system
6. microscopic organism that causes disease
7. disease that can be spread from one person to another

IDENTIFYING WORD RELATIONSHIPS **Explain how the words in each pair are related. Write your answers in complete sentences.**

8. benign tumor, malignant tumor
9. antibiotic, bacteria
10. antigen, antibodies
11. white blood cells, immune system
12. vaccine, virus

Content Challenges TEST PREP

MULTIPLE CHOICE Write the letter of the term or phrase that best completes each statement.

1. The cells that produce antibodies are called
   a. B cells.
   b. red blood cells.
   c. T cells.
   d. antigens.
2. A treatment made from dead or weakened viruses is
   a. an antibiotic.
   b. a vaccine.
   c. an antibody.
   d. an antivirus.
3. AIDS is a disease of the
   a. endocrine system.
   b. immune system.
   c. digestive system.
   d. respiratory system.
4. Alzheimer's disease affects the
   a. digestive system.
   b. endocrine system.
   c. nervous system.
   d. reproductive system.
5. Hepatitis usually is caused by a
   a. virus.
   b. bacterium.
   c. fungus.
   d. protozoan.
6. The disease that results from rapid, uncontrolled growth of cells is called
   a. diabetes.
   b. Alzheimer's disease.
   c. allergies.
   d. cancer.
7. The system made up of various organs, tissues, and other systems that fight disease is the
   a. lymphatic system.
   b. immune system.
   c. respiratory system.
   d. circulatory system.
8. The body's first line of defense against disease is the
   a. mouth.
   b. white blood cells.
   c. skin.
   d. nose.
9. All of the following are caused by bacteria except
   a. influenza.
   b. meningitis.
   c. tetanus.
   d. strep throat.
10. T cells identify pathogens by detecting the signal molecules called
   a. antigens.
   b. bacteria.
   c. germs.
   d. lymphocytes.

FILL IN Write the term that best completes each statement.

11. Louis Pasteur showed that some diseases are caused by ___________.
12. Some antibiotics cause an ___________ reaction.
13. Alexander Fleming discovered ___________.
14. Vaccines are used to acquire ___________ immunity.
15. Active acquired immunity lasts a ___________ time.

Concept Challenges TEST PREP

WRITTEN RESPONSE Answer each of the following questions in complete sentences.

1. **EXPLAIN:** How has the discovery of vaccines helped in the prevention of disease?
2. **INFER:** A person has smoked cigarettes for more than ten years. Do you think it is too late for this person to quit smoking? Explain your answer.
3. **RELATE:** How is good hygiene related to preventing infectious diseases?
4. **INFER:** Why do you think dentists often wear masks and rubber gloves when examining patients?
5. **PREDICT:** If you have already had chickenpox, what are your chances of getting the disease again?

INTERPRETING VISUALS Use Figure 5-17 to answer the following questions.

6. What are the symptoms of mumps?
7. Is the disease hepatitis caused by a virus or a bacteria?
8. If you had a loss of appetite, which of the diseases might you have?
9. How are the symptoms of measles and chickenpox similar?
10. How many diseases cause fever?

VIRAL DISEASES	
Disease	**Symptoms**
Influenza (flu)	Muscle aches, fever, and chills
Chickenpox	Skin rash in spots and fever
Measles	Pink rash all over the body
Mumps	Swollen glands and fever
Hepatitis	Jaundiced skin, swollen liver, and loss of appetite

▲ Figure 5-17

Chapter 6 Control and Regulation

▲ **Figure 6-1** Being part of an orchestra requires a great deal of concentration.

Have you ever played a musical instrument? If you have, you know it takes a great deal of concentration and control. Different parts of your body have to work together to play an instrument. Getting different parts of the body to work together is the job of the nervous system, which includes the brain and sense organs. For example, your ears send the message of sound to your brain, which interprets the sound as music.

►What other body parts need to work together to play a musical instrument?

Contents

- **6-1** What is the nervous system?
- **6-2** What are the parts of the brain?
- **6-3** What are reflexes?
- **6-4** What are sense organs?
- ■ **Lab Activity:** Identifying Taste Receptors
- **6-5** How do you see?
- **6-6** How do you hear?
- **6-7** What is the endocrine system?
- **6-8** What are hormones?
- ■ **The Big Idea:** How do we respond to artistic expression?
- **6-9** How do some drugs affect the body?
- **6-10** How does alcohol affect the body?

6-1 What is the nervous system?

Objectives

Identify the function of the nervous system. Name the parts that make up the nervous system.

Key Terms

neuron (NOOR-ahn)**:** nerve cell

dendrite (DEHN-dryt)**:** fiber that carries messages to the nerve cell body

axon: fiber that carries messages away from a nerve cell body

synapse (SIHN-aps)**:** gap between the axon of one cell and the dendrite of another

The Nervous System The nervous system controls all of your body's activities. The nervous system is made up of the brain, the spinal cord, and nerves. Nerves carry information to the spinal cord and brain. Other nerves then carry messages from the brain and spinal cord to the muscles and glands. The muscles and glands carry out the orders of the brain and spinal cord.

◀ **Figure 6-2**
The nervous system

1 IDENTIFY: Name the parts of the nervous system.

The Central Nervous System Your brain is the control center of your body. The brain is made up of a mass of nervous tissue. The brain is protected by your skull. The spinal cord is made up of many nerves that extend down your back. The spinal cord is protected by the backbone. The brain and spinal cord make up the central nervous system.

NAME: What structure protects the spinal cord?

Nerve Cells Thirty-one pairs of nerves branch out from your spinal cord. These nerves branch many times and extend to all parts of your body. Each of the nerves in your body is made up of nerve cells called **neurons.** Neurons can be either large or small. Some neurons are among the largest cells in your body. In fact, one neuron in your leg can be as long as 1 m.

The job of a neuron is to carry messages. Messages travel through a neuron in only one direction. You can see the structure of a neuron in Figure 6-3.

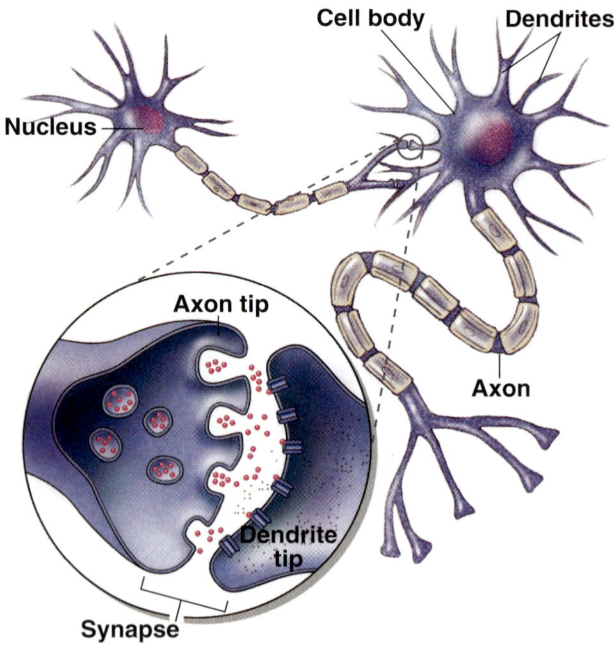

▲ **Figure 6-3** The structure of two neurons

The **dendrites** carry messages toward the nerve cell body, or center of the neuron. The **axon** carries messages away from the cell body. The cell body contains the nucleus of the neuron. It contains most of the cytoplasm.

 **DESCRIBE:** Describe the structure of a neuron.

Synapses The axon of one nerve cell normally does not touch the dendrites of the next nerve cell. Usually, there is a small gap between the two cells. This gap is called a **synapse.** Chemicals released by the axon carry messages across the synapse to the dendrites of the next neuron.

 **DEFINE:** What is the gap between two cells called?

CHECKING CONCEPTS

1. What is the job of the nervous system?
2. What are the parts of the nervous system?
3. What parts make up the central nervous system?
4. What is a neuron?
5. How many pairs of nerves branch out from the spinal cord?
6. What are the parts of a neuron?

THINKING CRITICALLY

7. **INFER:** What is the job of nerve tissue?
8. **MODEL:** Draw and label a neuron. Draw arrows on the diagram to show the direction a message travels through the neuron.
9. **PREDICT:** Unlike other body cells, most nerve cells cannot reproduce themselves. What might happen if many of the nerve cells in your hand were destroyed?

BUILDING LANGUAGE ARTS SKILLS

Writing Analogies When you make an analogy, you are comparing two things that are similar in some way. Write an analogy about how the nervous system is similar to a computer. Your analogy should be at least two paragraphs long.

Hands-On Activity

MODELING TOUCH RECEPTORS

You will need a pencil and a paper clip. You will need to work with a partner.

1. Straighten the paper clip. Then, bend the paper clip until its ends are about 2 cm apart.
2. Ask your partner to close his or her eyes. Gently touch the end of the paper clip to your partner's arm.
3. Ask you partner how many points touched his or her arm.
4. Repeat this three times, each time touching a different part of your partner's arm, hand, and fingers. Also, vary the number of points you use. Record the responses.
5. Repeat Steps 3 to 5 with your partner recording your responses.

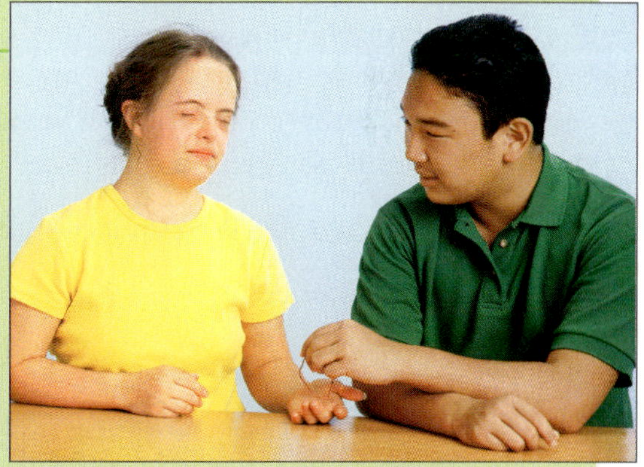

▲ **STEP 2** Gently touch the paper clip to your partner's arm.

Practicing Your Skills

6. **INFER:** Were your responses always correct? Explain.
7. **INFER:** Which part of your arm, hand, or fingers was most sensitive? Why do you think this part of your body is so sensitive?

6-2 What are the parts of the brain?

Objectives

Identify and describe the functions of the three parts of the brain.

Key Terms

cerebrum (suh-REE-bruhm)**:** part of the brain that controls the senses and thinking

cerebellum (ser-uh-BEHL-uhm)**:** part of the brain that controls balance and body motion

brainstem: bundle of nerves at the base of the brain

medulla (mih-DUL-uh)**:** lower part of the brain stem that controls heartbeat and breathing rate

The Brain The main job of the brain is to receive, interpret, and react to messages. These messages may come from inside or outside your body. Your brain responds to the messages and then controls all of your body's activities. For example, movement, thinking, breathing, and sleeping all are controlled by your brain.

The brain often is called the control center of the body. It is made up of three main parts: the cerebrum, the cerebellum, and the brainstem. Each part of the brain performs a different function.

1 EXPLAIN: What is the main job of the brain?

The Cerebrum The largest part of the brain is the **cerebrum.** Figure 6-4 shows that the cerebrum makes up more than two-thirds of the brain. One job of the cerebrum is to interpret information from the sense organs. Your sense organs are your eyes, ears, nose, tongue, and skin. A second job of the cerebrum is to control thinking. Your cerebrum is the part of the brain that controls learning, remembering things, and making decisions. The cerebrum also controls movement and speech.

2 EXPLAIN: What are three jobs of the cerebrum?

The Cerebellum The part of the brain located at the back of the brain is the **cerebellum.** The cerebellum is much smaller than the cerebrum. All motor nerve impulses that begin with the cerebrum pass through the cerebellum. Motor nerve impulses are used in movement. The cerebellum adjusts the impulses so your movements are coordinated.

The cerebellum also helps to maintain balance. As your body changes position, the cerebellum receives messages. Then, the cerebellum sends messages out to your muscles. The muscles work to help you keep your balance.

3 IDENTIFY: Where is the cerebellum located?

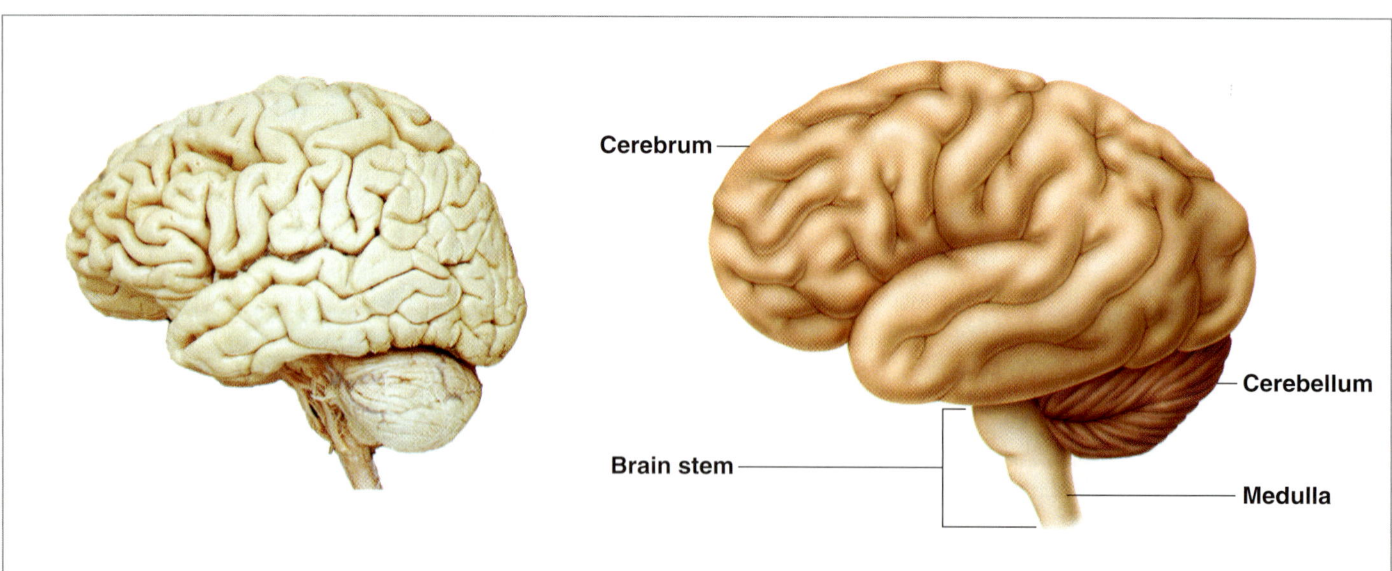

▲ **Figure 6-4** The brain

The Brainstem Bundles of nerves that pass from the cerebrum and the cerebellum form a thick stalk at the base of the skull. This is called the brainstem. The lower part of the brainstem is called the **medulla.**

The medulla connects the brain to the spinal cord. The medulla controls digestion, breathing, and heartbeat rate. It also controls the activities of many glands.

 CLASSIFY: Does the medulla control voluntary or involuntary body activities?

Safety and the Brain Just like other parts of your body, your brain can suffer injuries. A common injury of the brain is a concussion, a bruiselike injury of the brain that occurs when the soft tissue of the cerebrum bumps against the inside of the skull. Concussions can occur during a car accident, a bad fall, or any other accident in which you hit your head. Some symptoms of a concussion are a headache, dizziness, and loss of consciousness. To reduce your risk of brain injury, wear a helmet when riding a bicycle, skating, or performing other physical activities where you risk hitting your head.

 DEFINE: What is a concussion?

CHECKING CONCEPTS

1. What are the three parts of the brain?
2. What is the largest part of the brain?
3. Where is the cerebellum located?
4. Where is the medulla located?
5. What is the main job of the brain?

THINKING CRITICALLY

Determine what part of the brain controls the following activities.

6. You memorize someone's telephone number.
7. You walk to the store.
8. You breathe faster when you run.
9. You smell smoke.
10. You begin to fall, but then regain your balance.

Science and Technology

TAKING PICTURES OF THE BRAIN

X-rays can take clear pictures of the bones, but soft tissues, such as the brain, do not show up as well. To see images of soft tissues, doctors use a technique known as magnetic resonance imaging, or MRI. This technique involves the use of magnets and radio waves to form pictures of organs. Using MRI, doctors can pinpoint the exact location of tumors in soft tissues.

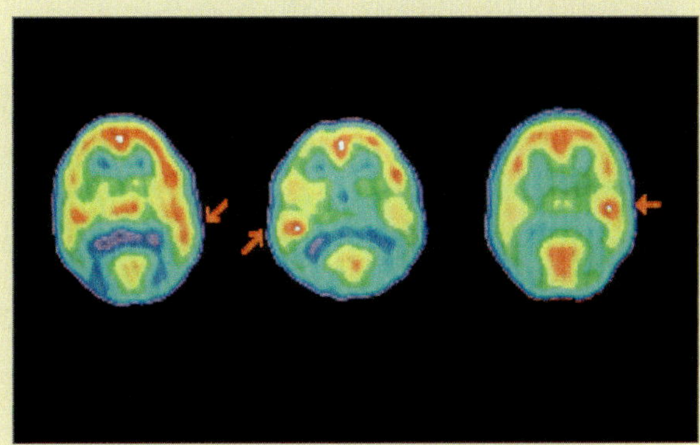

▲ **Figure 6-5** A PET image of a brain

Another technique, called positron emission tomography, or PET, is also used to study body organs, especially the brain. The patient is injected with glucose, a form of sugar. A computer records information about the amount of glucose in the brain. The computer uses this information to make an image showing brain structure and activity. PET is used to diagnose brain tumors and strokes. It is also used to study how the brain reacts to stimuli, such as music.

Thinking Critically Why are MRI and PET technologies important?

6-3 What are reflexes?

Observing Reactions

HANDS-ON ACTIVITY

1. Work with a partner. Have your partner sit so his or her feet do not touch the floor. Your partner should close his or her eyes. Use the side of your hand to gently tap your partner on the knee, just below the kneecap. What happens?
2. Switch places with your partner. Close your eyes. Ask your partner to lightly tap your knee. What happens?

THINK ABOUT IT: Could you control your reaction when your partner tapped your knee?

Objectives

Define reflex. Relate reflexes to the stimuli that cause them.

Key Terms

reflex: automatic response to a stimulus

receptor: part of a nerve cell that receives stimuli from the environment

reflex arc: path of a message in a reflex

Stimuli and Responses Do you jump at a sudden loud noise? Does your mouth water when you smell food? Do you pull your hand away quickly if you touch something hot? Loud sounds, the smell of food, and heat all are examples of stimuli. A stimulus is something that causes you to react in some way. The reaction to a stimulus is called a response.

1 **RELATE:** How are stimuli and responses related?

Reflexes Some responses are simple. You cannot control them. They happen without your thinking about what you are doing. An automatic, or involuntary, response to a stimulus is called a **reflex.**

A reflex usually is a response that protects you in some way. For example, when dust gets into your nose, you sneeze. Dust is a stimulus. Sneezing is the response. Sneezing helps to prevent harmful substances from entering your lungs.

▲ **Figure 6-6** Sneezing is a reflex.

When dirt gets into your eyes, you blink. Your eyes may also water or form tears. Blinking your eyes and forming tears are your body's way of protecting your eyes from harmful substances. Blinking and tearing are examples of reflexes.

 **APPLY:** Is answering a ringing telephone an example of a reflex? Explain.

A Reflex Arc Reflexes usually occur very quickly. One reason reflexes occur so quickly is that they do not involve the brain. Some reflexes are controlled by the spinal cord.

When a reflex takes place, nerves and muscles work together. The stimulus is received by special parts of the nerve cells called **receptors.** Receptors receive stimuli from the environment. Other nerve cells carry a message to the spinal cord. Another nerve carries a message from the spinal cord to a muscle. A muscle causes you to move some part of your body. The message travels along a path formed by nerve cells. This path is called a **reflex arc.** You can trace the path of a reflex in Figure 6-7.

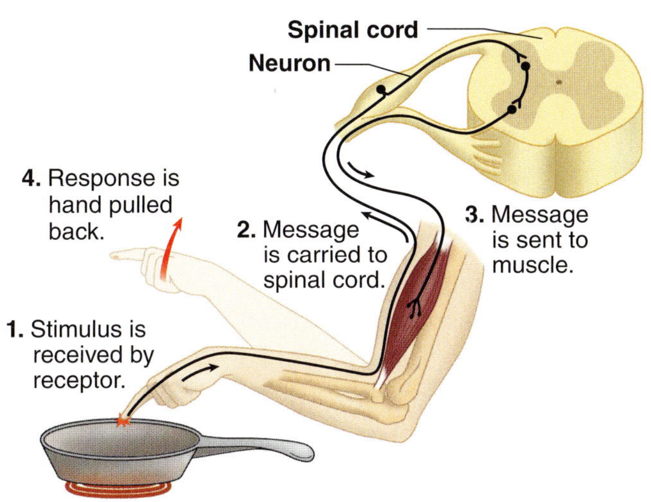

▲ **Figure 6-7** A reflex arc

OBSERVE: What is the stimulus in Figure 6-7? What is the response?

CHECKING CONCEPTS

1. What is a reflex arc?
2. How are stimuli and responses related?
3. What are receptors?

THINKING CRITICALLY

Identify the stimulus and response in the following.

4. You step on a tack and pull your foot away.
5. You blink when a light is shined in your eyes.
6. Food in your windpipe causes you to cough.

DESIGNING AN EXPERIMENT

Design an experiment to solve the following problem. Include a hypothesis, variables, a procedure, and a type of data to study.

PROBLEM: How does the size of the eye's pupil relate to the amount of light in a room?

Integrating Engineering

TOPICS: electronics, bionics, computers

TREATING SPINAL INJURIES WITH BIONICS

People that are paralyzed have lost the ability to move certain body parts. This is often due to a spinal cord injury. The degree of paralysis depends on where the injury occurred. A person might be paralyzed from the waist down or from the neck down.

A new kind of treatment called functional electrical stimulation (FES) has helped patients who have lost control of their muscles due to paralysis. This technique uses electrodes implanted in the patient's skin to control muscle movement. When combined with a prosthetic hand or arm, this system allows patients to carry out everyday activities such as dialing a phone or writing a letter.

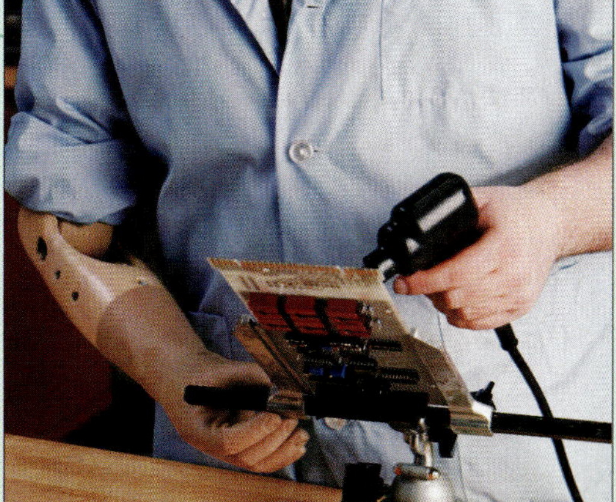

▲ **Figure 6-8** FES and a prosthetic hand allow patients to perform everyday tasks.

Currently, a movement of the individual must control this type of device. For example, the patient could control the movement of a prosthetic hand by shrugging his shoulder. Engineers are now working on a system that would allow the patient to control a prosthetic limb with their own thoughts. This technology, known as brain computer interface, is not yet perfected. However, researchers hope that in the future, computers and bionics will come together to give patients abilities they never thought possible.

Thinking Critically How has engineering helped paralysis patients?

6-4 What are sense organs?

Objective

Name the five sense organs and their jobs.

Key Term

sense organ: special organ that receives and processes stimuli from the environment

Sense Organs Sound, light, and heat are examples of stimuli. Stimuli are messages your brain interprets. You have special organs that receive and process stimuli from your environment. These organs are the **sense organs.** They are the eyes, nose, skin, ears, and tongue.

1 **NAME:** What are the sense organs?

Jobs of the Sense Organs Sense organs work to help you respond to your environment. Sense organs are receptors because they receive messages or stimuli. Each sense organ receives only certain kinds of messages. The eyes are sensitive to light. They help the brain create pictures of things you look at. These pictures are formed by changes in light. The nose responds to different smells. Your skin responds to changes in temperature and pressure. Your skin also responds to pain and touch. Your ears receive sounds from the environment. Your tongue helps you identify different tastes. Each organ senses a different stimulus.

SENSE ORGANS AND THEIR FUNTIONS	
Organ	**Sense**
Skin	Touch, temperature, pressure, pain
Eyes	Sight
Nose	Smell
Tongue	Taste
Ears	Sound

▲ **Figure 6-9**

2 **DESCRIBE:** What do sense organs do?

Senses Work Together Your senses do not work alone. What do you do when you walk into a darkened room? Your hands reach out to touch things that might be in front of you. Your ears listen for the slightest sound. Your eyes search the dark for some sign of light. Your senses work together to help you.

Your senses help you gather many different kinds of information about your surroundings. In this way, your senses help you to learn. Much that you see, hear, taste, smell, and feel is stored in your brain. This information becomes part of your memory. You remember things when you need to use them. Using information gathered by the senses is important for your safety and for all the things you do.

3 **EXPLAIN:** How do the senses help you to learn?

Taste Buds Your tongue is covered with receptors called taste buds. Your taste buds can detect four basic tastes: sweet, sour, bitter, and salty. The taste buds that detect each taste are located on different parts of your tongue. Your taste buds cannot taste dry substances. They can only taste substances that are moist. For this reason, foods must be moistened before your taste buds will recognize the food. When the receptor cells in your taste buds are activated, nerve impulses are sent to the brain where they are interpreted as taste.

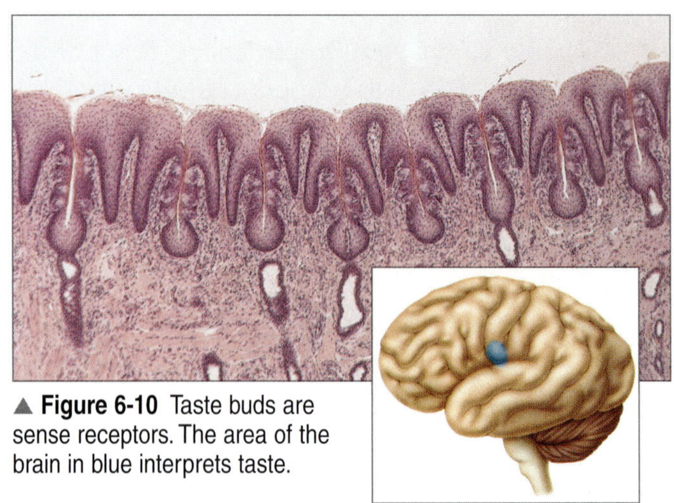

▲ **Figure 6-10** Taste buds are sense receptors. The area of the brain in blue interprets taste.

4 **IDENTIFY:** What organ do you use for taste?

Smell The flavor of food is also detected by receptors in your nose. When your nose is blocked, your odor receptors do not function as well. This is why food often tastes bland when you have a cold. Some odor receptors respond to gas molecules. When gas molecules dissolve in the mucus layer inside the nose, the molecules are detected by the odor receptors. Impulses are sent to the brain where they are interpreted as different odors.

▲ **Figure 6-11** Odor receptors in your nose send messages to your brain. The area in the brain in pink interprets smell.

5 **INFER:** What other sense is related to smell?

Touch Your skin is the largest sense organ in your body. Your skin senses touch, pressure, pain, heat, and cold. Each of these sensations stimulates a different kind of sensory receptor in the skin.

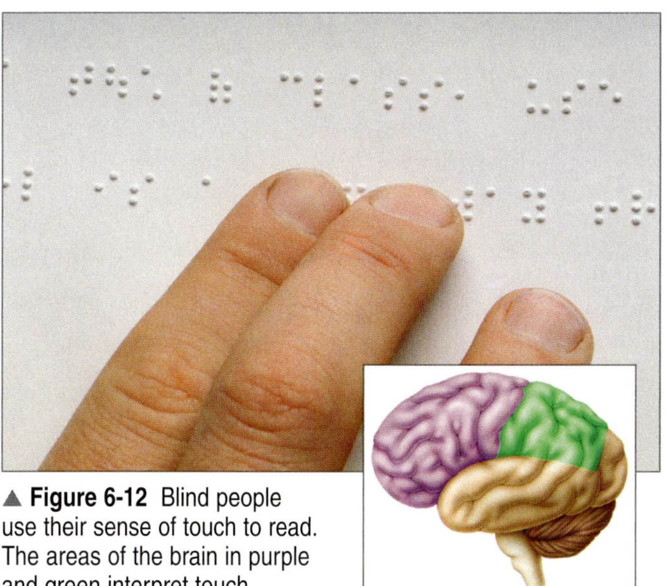

▲ **Figure 6-12** Blind people use their sense of touch to read. The areas of the brain in purple and green interpret touch.

Most touch receptors are found near the surface of the skin. They inform the brain of even the lightest touch. Pressure and pain receptors are found deep within the skin. These receptors alert the brain to dangerous situations in the environment.

Blind people rely heavily on their sense of touch for information. One way that blind people use their sense of touch is by reading Braille. Braille is a series of "letters" made up of a combination of raised dots.

ANALYZE: You have more touch receptors in your fingertips than on your back. Why do you think this is important?

CHECKING CONCEPTS

Which sense organ receives the following messages?

1. pain, temperature, pressure, and touch
2. smells
3. sounds
4. tastes
5. changes in light

THINKING CRITICALLY

6. **ANALYZE:** How do the senses work together?
7. **RELATE:** How do your senses protect you from danger?
8. **INFER:** How does your body respond to cold temperatures?

Web InfoSearch

Braille The Braille system was developed by the French inventor Louis Braille. Braille lost his sight when he was 3 years old. When he was 15 years old, he developed the Braille system.

SEARCH: Use the Internet to find out more about Louis Braille's reading system. Then, make a poster showing the position of dots of your name in Braille. Start your search at www.conceptsandchallenges.com. Some key search words are **Louis Braille** and **Braille system.**

LAB ACTIVITY

Identifying Taste Receptors

BACKGROUND

Your tongue is covered with taste receptors called taste buds. These receptors can detect whether a substance is sweet, sour, bitter, or salty.

PURPOSE

In this activity, you will be tasting four different substances to determine which area of your tongue has receptors for tasting sweetness, sourness, bitterness, and saltiness.

PROCEDURE 

1. Gather the materials needed, shown in Figure 6-13. Copy Figure 6-14 onto a sheet of paper.

2. Put on the goggles. Wet a clean cotton swab in the water. Place the cotton swab in the sugar.

3. Touch your tongue with the cotton swab. Observe what part of your tongue detects the sweetness of the sugar. Shade in this part of the tongue in your drawing.

4. Rinse your mouth with water.

5. Repeat Steps 2, 3, and 4 for the table salt. Use a different color to shade in your drawing.

6. Dip a clean cotton swab in the lemon juice. Touch the swab to your tongue as you did in Step 2. Use a different color to shade in the part of the tongue drawing that detected the lemon juice. Rinse your mouth.

7. Repeat Step 6 using the tonic water. Use a different color to shade in your drawing.

▲ **Figure 6-13** Taste receptors in your tongue can detect sweetness, sourness, bitterness, and saltiness.

▲ **STEP 2** Place the cotton swab in sugar.

▲ **STEP 3** Touch your tongue with the cotton swab.

▲ **STEP 4** Rinse your mouth with water between each test.

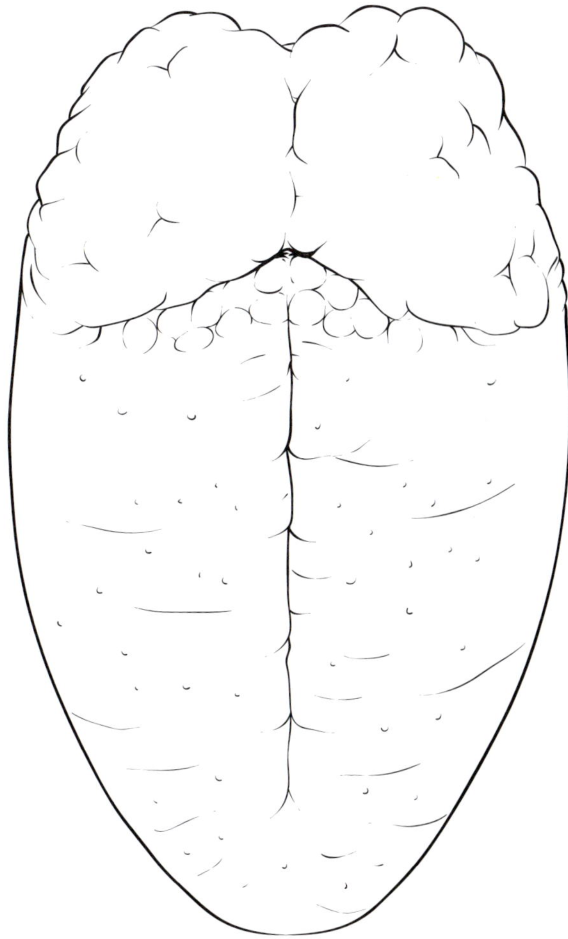

▲ **Figure 6-14** Copy this diagram onto a sheet of paper.

CONCLUSIONS

1. **OBSERVE:** Describe the taste of each substance using the terms salty, bitter, sweet, and sour.

2. **COMPARE:** Look at the drawings made by two of your classmates. How are your drawings the same? How are your drawings different?

6-5 How do you see?

Objectives

Name and describe the functions of the parts of the eye.

Key Terms

cornea (KAWR-nee-uh)**:** clear covering at the front of the eye

iris (EYE-ris)**:** colored part of the eye that controls the amount of light entering the eye

pupil (PYOO-puhl)**:** opening in the center of the iris

lens: part of the eye that focuses an image on the retina

retina (REHT-uhn-uh)**:** part of the eye that receives images from the lens and transmits them to the brain

The Eyes The eyes are the organs of sight. The eyes work by responding to light. In order to see an object, your eyes must respond to light from that object. Different parts of the eye work together to send a signal that is produced from the light to your brain. Your brain then receives messages from your eye and interprets what your eyes are looking at, thereby producing a picture.

1 IDENTIFY: What kinds of stimuli do your eyes respond to?

Parts of the Eye Different parts of the eye work together to help you see. Figure 6-15 shows the parts of the eye. As you read about each part of the eye, locate that part on Figure 6-15.

- **Cornea** The **cornea** is a clear, curved, protective covering at the front of the eye.
- **Iris** Behind the cornea is a round, colored disk called the **iris.** The iris controls the amount of light entering the eye.
- **Pupil** At the center of the iris is a hole called the pupil. Light must pass through the pupil to get to the inside of your eye.

In dim light, the iris widens to let more light in. This makes the pupil larger. In bright light, the iris narrows to let less light in. This makes the pupil smaller. The movement of the iris is controlled by muscles of the eye.

- **Lens** After light passes through the pupil, it passes through the **lens** of the eye. The lens is a curved structure that focuses the light entering the eye.
- **Retina** At the back of the eye is the **retina.** The lens of the eye focuses light onto the retina. There are two types of light sensitive receptor cells in the retina, rods and cones. Rods are sensitive to dim light. They can detect only black and white. Cones are sensitive to bright light and allow you to see different colors. When light strikes the rods and cones, nerve signals are produced.
- **Optic Nerve** Nerve signals formed by the retina are carried to the brain by the optic nerve. The brain then interprets the signals it receives from the optic nerve and produces an image or picture.

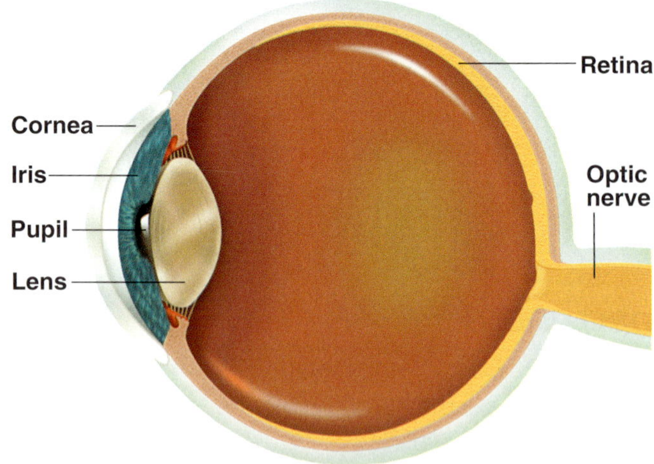

▲ **Figure 6-15** Parts of the eye

2 SEQUENCE: List, in the correct order, the parts of the eye through which light passes.

Protecting the Eyes The eyes are protected in many ways. The bones of the face extend in front of the eyes. These bones keep large objects from hitting and damaging the eyes. Eyelids and eyelashes help keep small pieces of matter from entering the eyes. Any particles that do reach the eyes usually are washed away by tears. Tears also keep the eyes from becoming too dry.

IDENTIFY: How do the bones of the face protect the eyes?

CHECKING CONCEPTS

1. The eyes work by responding to ___________.
2. The clear covering at the front of the eye is the ___________.
3. Pupil size is controlled by the ___________.
4. Light is focused on the part of the eye called the ___________.
5. Nerve signals from the eye are carried to the brain by the ___________.

THINKING CRITICALLY

6. **APPLY:** What color are the pupils of your eyes? What color are your irises?
7. **RELATE:** What structure of the eye forms images on the retina?
8. **INFER:** What are some activities or jobs that would require protective eyewear?

BUILDING SCIENCE SKILLS

Applying Concepts Two problems often corrected with eyeglasses are myopia and astigmatism. Use library references to find out what these problems are and what features eyeglasses must have to correct them. Take a class poll to see how many students wear corrective lenses. Do they have myopia or astigmatism?

Hands-On Activity

ANALYZING OPTICAL ILLUSIONS

You will need a metric ruler, tracing paper, and a pencil.

1. Look at Figure A. Which line appears longer?
2. Look at Figure B. Which arc is longer?
3. Look at Figure C. Which post is tallest?
4. Measure and record the length of each line in Figure A.
5. Trace the top arc in Figure B on a sheet of tracing paper. Place the top arc over the bottom arc. Describe your observation.

Practicing Your Skills

6. a. **OBSERVE:** Which line looked longer than the other? b. **MEASURE:** How long is each line?
7. **ANALYZE:** Are the arcs the same size?
8. a. **OBSERVE:** Which post looked shortest? Which looked tallest? b. **MEASURE:** How tall is each post?
9. **EXPLAIN:** Why was your eye fooled by the optical illusion in each figure?

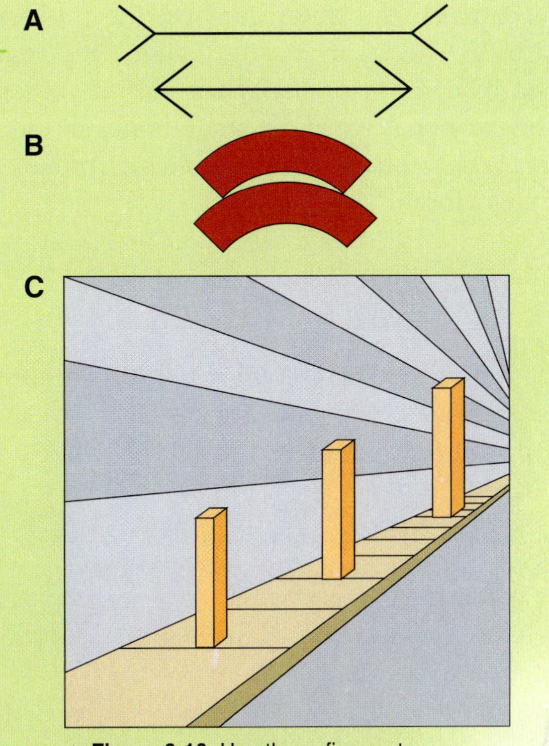

▲ **Figure 6-16** Use these figures to complete the activity.

6-6 How do you hear?

Objective

Describe the jobs of the main parts of the ear.

Key Terms

eardrum: sheet of tissue that vibrates when sounds strike it

cochlea (KAHK-lee-uh)**:** part of the ear that changes vibrations into nerve signals

The Ears The ears are the organs of hearing. The three sections of the ear are the outer ear, the middle ear, and the inner ear. Each part of the ear has a different job. As you read about how the ear works, locate each part in Figure 6-17.

The outer ear acts like a funnel to gather sound. The larger the outer ear, the more sound it can gather. Rabbits have larger outer ears than humans. This is one reason why rabbits have better hearing than humans.

Between the outer ear and the middle ear is a thin sheet of tissue called the **eardrum.** The eardrum vibrates when sound waves hit it. The ear bones are three small bones in the middle ear. When the eardrum vibrates, it makes the ear bones vibrate.

A coiled structure called the **cochlea** is located in the inner ear. The cochlea receives the vibrations of the ear bones.

 STATE: What makes the ear bones vibrate?

Sound Waves When someone speaks to you, sound waves are formed. The sound waves are different for each word. These sound waves travel in the air and are gathered by your outer ear. They make your eardrum vibrate. Your ear bones also vibrate. The vibrations are different for each word. The cochlea changes these vibrations into nerve signals. Then the signals are carried by the auditory nerves to the brain. The brain interprets the signals so that you can understand what they mean.

 EXPLAIN: How do sound signals get from the ear to the brain?

What You Hear Some sounds are too low pitched to hear. The sounds are not detected by the cochlea. No signal is sent to the brain. You hear nothing. Other sounds are too high pitched to hear. The cochlea cannot change these sounds into nerve signals. You do not hear anything.

 EXPLAIN: Why are certain sounds not detected by the ear?

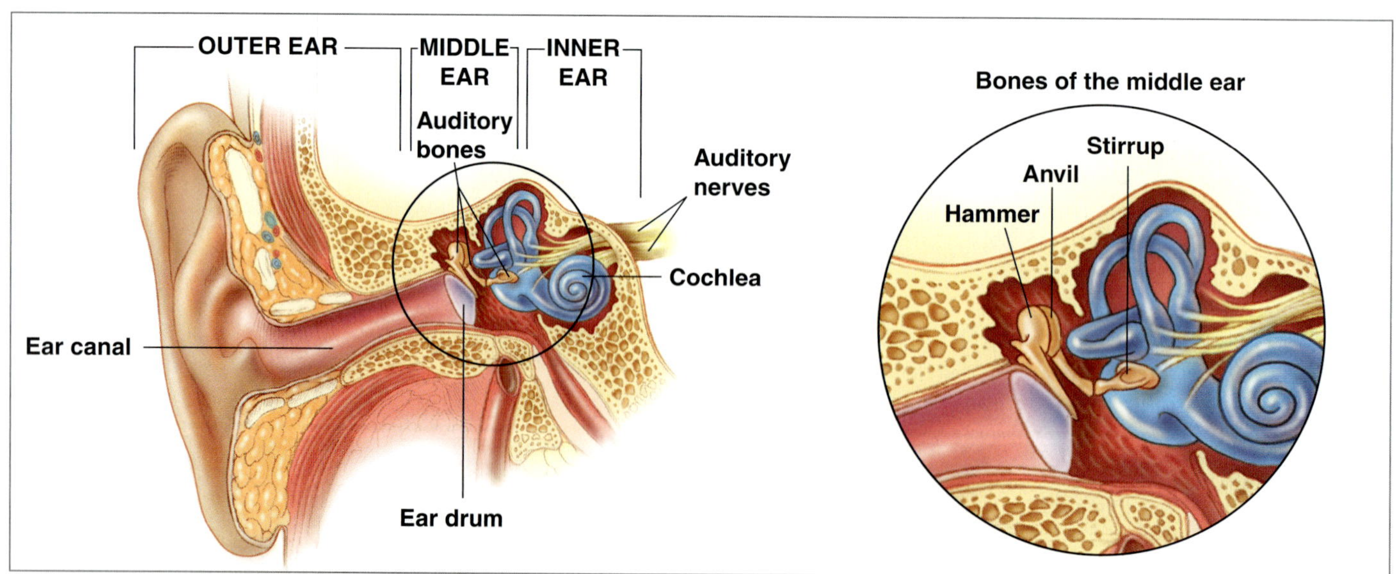

▲ **Figure 6-17** Parts of the ear

Hearing Aids Anything that stops part of the ear from working can cause deafness. Each part of the ear is needed for good hearing. Sometimes the ear can be damaged but still work a little bit. This is partial deafness. Sometimes deafness is caused by an infection of the ear bones. After the infection, the bones may no longer be able to vibrate.

Partial deafness can be often corrected by using hearing aids. Hearing aids are like small amplifiers that fit near or into the ear. They make sounds louder, so even damaged parts of the ear may vibrate.

4 **EXPLAIN:** What are hearing aids?

CHECKING CONCEPTS

1. The sense organs of hearing are ___________.
2. The three main sections of the ear are ___________.
3. The cochlea receives the vibrations of the ear bones and changes them to ___________.
4. Ear vibrations changed to nerve signals are sent to the ___________.

THINKING CRITICALLY

5. **APPLY:** How do a rabbit's large ears help it to hear?
6. **HYPOTHESIZE:** Why can't we hear certain kinds of sounds?
7. **INFER:** What is the brain's role in hearing?

Web InfoSearch

Hearing in Animals Many animals can hear higher-pitched sounds than humans can. Many animals also can hear lower-pitched sounds than humans can.

SEARCH: Use the Internet to find out more about hearing in other animals. Write your findings in a report. Start your search at www.conceptsandchallenges.com. Some key search words are **hearing** and **ears.**

Integrating Physical Science

TOPICS: sound waves, frequency, amplitude

PITCH AND FREQUENCY

Sound is a form of energy that makes molecules vibrate. Sound waves can move through solids, liquids, or gases.

The number of waves produced by a vibrating sound source each second is called the frequency. Frequency is measured in units called Hertz. A sound's frequency determines its pitch, or how high or low it sounds. Animals such as bats, dogs, and dolphins can hear very high-pitched sounds, which humans cannot hear. Elephants communicate over long distances by making low-pitched sounds, which humans also cannot hear.

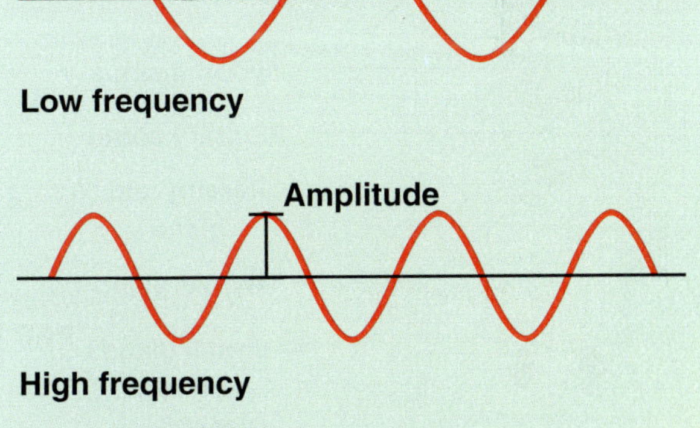

▲ **Figure 6-18** The frequency of a sound wave determines its pitch.

When sound waves vibrate, each molecule moves back and forth from its original position. The farther it moves, the greater the amount of energy flowing through the sound waves and the louder the sound seems. The greatest distance the vibrating molecules move from their original position is called the amplitude of the vibration. A sound wave's amplitude determines how loud the sound is. Loudness is measured in units called decibels.

Thinking Critically Why do you think other animals can hear pitches humans cannot?

6-7 What is the endocrine system?

Objective

Describe the function of the endocrine system.

Key Terms

gland: organ that makes chemical substances used or released by the body

exocrine (EHKS-oh-krihn) **gland:** gland that has ducts

endocrine (EHN-doh-krihn) **gland:** gland that does not have ducts

hypothalamus (hy-poh-THAL-uh-muhs)**:** part of the brain that tells the pituitary gland to release certain chemicals

Glands with Ducts A **gland** is an organ that makes substances used or released by the body. Some glands have ducts, or tubes. These are called **exocrine glands.** Substances made by these glands leave the gland through the ducts. Your skin has many sweat glands. Perspiration, or sweat, is made by these glands. Sweat moves from the sweat gland to the surface of the skin by passing through a duct. Salivary glands also have ducts. Saliva passes from the salivary glands into the mouth through these ducts.

1 NAME: What are two glands that have ducts?

Endocrine Glands Some glands do not have ducts. They are called **endocrine glands.** Substances made by endocrine glands pass from the glands directly into the bloodstream. The blood vessels then carry the substances to the parts of the body where they are needed.

2 IDENTIFY: How do substances made by endocrine glands get to other parts of the body?

The Endocrine System There are ten main endocrine glands in the human body. Together, these glands make up the endocrine system. Eight of the glands that make up the endocrine system are shown in Figure 6-19.

3 OBSERVE: Where are the adrenal glands located?

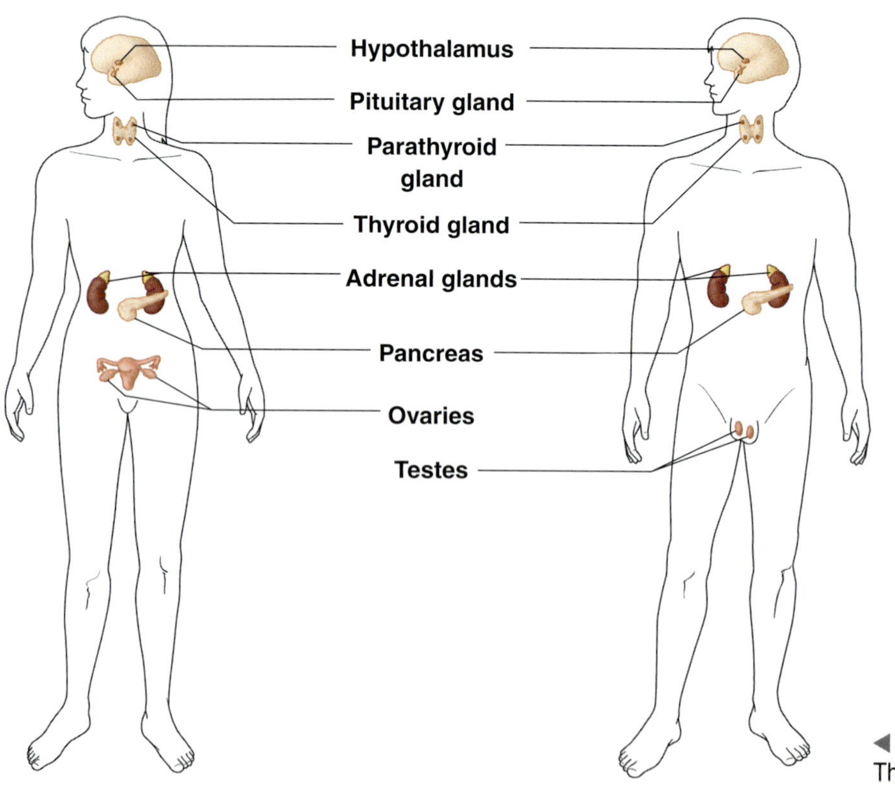

◀ **Figure 6-19** The endocrine systems

Control of Body Functions The job of the endocrine system is to help control bodily functions. Each gland in the endocrine system has a different job. The way each gland works is similar to the way a thermostat and a furnace work. If the temperature of a room goes down, the thermostat then signals the furnace to turn up the heat. The "thermostat" of the body is the **hypothalamus.** If the hypothalamus senses a need for a certain chemical substance in the body, it stimulates the pituitary gland to produce a chemical. This chemical sends a message to one of the other endocrine glands.

STATE: What is the function of the endocrine system?

CHECKING CONCEPTS

1. An organ that makes substances used or released by the body is called a __________.
2. Glands that do not have ducts are called __________ glands.
3. The substances made by endocrine glands are carried by __________ to other parts of the body.
4. Sweat glands are __________ glands.
5. There are about __________ endocrine glands in the body.

THINKING CRITICALLY

6. CONTRAST: What is the difference between an endocrine and an exocrine gland?

INTERPRETING VISUALS

Use Figure 6-19 to answer the following questions.

7. OBSERVE: What endocrine glands are found only in males?
8. OBSERVE: Where is the pituitary gland located?
9. IDENTIFY: Which glands are found in pairs in the body?
10. INFER: The prefix *para-* means "by the side of." Based on this information, where do you think the parathyroid gland is located?

Real-Life Science

EMERGENCY GLAND

Adrenaline is a chemical that is released by the adrenal glands. In times of stress or excitement, the hypothalamus sends a message that triggers the adrenal glands. This releases adrenaline. This surge of adrenaline enables a person to "fight" or "flee" in high-stress times. Scientists believe this response helped early humans to survive in the wild.

An example of adrenaline at work is when a person rescues someone. At that time, the body's heartbeat speeds up, breathing increases, muscles contract, the digestive system shuts down, and blood clots faster. After the emergency has passed, the body returns to normal operations.

The adrenal glands can also be activated by long-term stress, such as pressure from school or a job. This stress can cause artery blockages, which can lead to a heart attack. Long-term stress can cause nervous system disorders, such as headaches and high blood pressure.

Thinking Critically How can the endocrine system affect the other systems in your body?

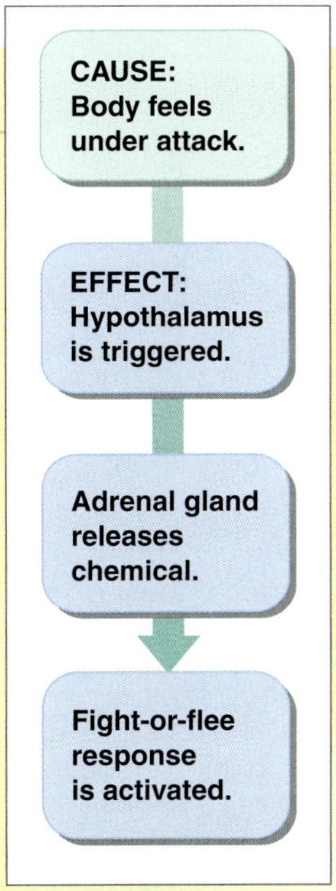

CAUSE: Body feels under attack.

EFFECT: Hypothalamus is triggered.

Adrenal gland releases chemical.

Fight-or-flee response is activated.

▲ **Figure 6-20** The fight or flee response

6-8 What are hormones?

Objectives

Define hormones. Explain some of the jobs of hormones.

Key Terms

hormone (HAWR-mohn)**:** chemical substance that regulates body functions

target cell: cell that responds to a hormone's chemical structure

Hormones The chemical substances made by the endocrine glands are called **hormones.** Hormones affect many of your body's functions. For example, growth hormone, which is made by the pituitary gland, controls how fast and how much you grow.

What activates hormones? When the hypothalamus senses the need for a specific hormone in the body, it stimulates the pituitary gland. The pituitary gland then releases its hormones. These hormones activate other endocrine glands. These glands, in turn, release their own hormones into the bloodstream. Because hormones are carried in the bloodstream, they can control tissues and organs far from the glands that produced them.

Not all hormones affect all tissues and organs. Instead, hormones only affect tissues and organs with specific target cells. **Target cells** respond to a hormone's chemical structure. Hormones travel throughout the body until they find the target cell that responds to them.

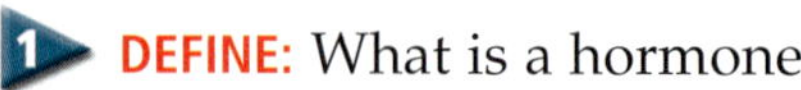

1 DEFINE: What is a hormone?

Jobs of Hormones Growth hormone is only one of many hormones made by your body. Hormones may speed up a body function or slow it down. Other hormones do other jobs. Insulin (IHN-suh-lihn) is a hormone made by the pancreas. Insulin is needed to keep a balanced amount of sugar in the blood. Still other hormones regulate other glands. Figure 6-21 shows some of the different endocrine glands, the hormones they produce, and what each hormone does.

2 INFER: What do you think would happen if a person had too much growth hormone?

HORMONES AND WHAT THEY DO		
Gland	**Hormone**	**Job of Hormone**
Adrenal	Adrenaline	Controls muscle reaction and raises heart rate and blood pressure
Ovaries	Estrogen and Progesterone	Controls physical and reproductive development in women
Pancreas	Insulin	Controls blood sugar levels
Parathyroid	Parathyroid hormone	Controls the amount of calcium and phosphorus in the blood
Pineal	Melatonin	Helps regulate pituitary gland
Pituitary	ACTH	Controls the release of hormones from the adrenal glands
Pituitary	Growth hormone	Controls the growth of bones; controls metabolism
Testes	Testosterone	Controls physical and reproductive development in men
Thymus	Thymosin	Controls the growth of certain white blood cells
Thyroid	Thyroxine	Controls rate of body growth

◀ **Figure 6-21** Different glands produce different hormones.

Reproductive Hormones Some hormones control the development of reproductive organs. The glands that control reproductive organs are different in men and women. Men have glands called testes (TEHS-teez). The testes produce a hormone called testosterone (tehs-TAHS-tuhr-ohn). Females have glands called ovaries (OH-vuh-reez). Ovaries produce hormones called estrogen (EHS-truh-juhn) and progesterone (proh-JEHS-tuhr-ohn).

 STATE: What hormone do the testes produce?

CHECKING CONCEPTS

1. A chemical substance that regulates body functions is called a __________.
2. Insulin is made by the __________.
3. The two endocrine glands that produce substances that develop reproductive organs are testes and __________.
4. Testes are glands found only in __________.
5. Ovaries are glands found only in __________.

THINKING CRITICALLY

6. EXPLAIN: How are insulin and blood sugar level related?
7. APPLY: What is the job of growth hormone?
8. CLASSIFY: Which hormones are found in both males and females? Which are found in only one gender or the other?
9. INFER: What health problems might someone have if the pituitary gland produced too much or too little growth hormone?
10. ANALYZE: What hormone is needed to release adrenal hormones?
11. ANALYZE: What gland produces thymosin?

BUILDING LANGUAGE ARTS SKILLS

Using Prefixes The pancreas is part of the digestive system. It is also an endocrine gland that secretes the hormone insulin. It is the only part of the human body that can be considered an endocrine and exocrine gland. Use a dictionary to discover the meaning of the prefixes *endo-* and *exo-*. Then, find out why the pancreas is considered both an endocrine and an exocrine gland.

How Do They Know That?

TREATING DIABETES WITH INSULIN

If too little insulin is produced by the pancreas, an excess of sugar builds up in the blood. This condition is called diabetes mellitus. Without proper treatment, this can lead to blindness, poor circulation, and even death. Until 1921, however, scientists did not know how to increase the amount of insulin in diabetics.

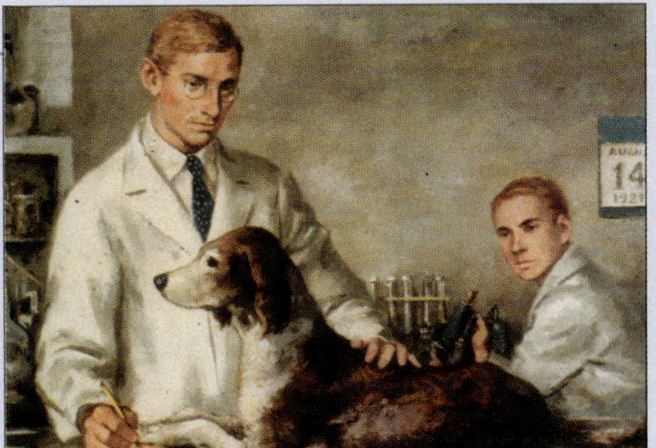

▲ **Figure 6-22** Banting and Best experimented with dogs that were diabetic.

In 1921, Canadian scientist Frederick Banting and medical student Charles Best isolated the part of the pancreas that produces insulin. They extracted insulin from the pancreas of a dog. They then tested it on dogs whose pancreases had been removed. These dogs were diabetics. When the dogs received injections of insulin, they recovered from their diabetes. Banting and Best's discovery led to a treatment for millions of people living with diabetes.

In 1923, Banting received a Nobel Prize in physiology and medicine for his work. Upset that Best was not honored for his contribution, Banting shared his award equally with Best.

Thinking Critically How did Banting and Best's work improve life for diabetics?

THE Big IDEA

How do we respond to artistic expression?

Is music just sound, created by vibration? Are poems just words that we read or hear? Are paintings just strokes of color on a canvas? Or are they much more?

We experience art and we react to it. This ability is possible because of our nervous system. Our sense organs take in the messages. Different parts of the brain process these messages. However, the brain does not process all sensory stimuli the same way. Imaging technology shows different levels of activity in the brain when a person hears music as compared to other sounds. The brain treats music without words differently than music with lyrics.

An experiment published in 1993 seemed to show that listening to classical music could improve memory. The idea became very popular. One state gave out classical music CDs to every new mother. The research was later found to be flawed.

Scientists have learned which parts, or lobes, of the brain are involved in each of the senses. Brain research has come far, but it does not answer key questions about art. How does art create strong emotions? Why do we like one work, but not another? Many artists and art lovers are in no hurry to learn these answers. Enjoying art is enough.

Look at the boxes of text that appear on this page and the next. They point out some art forms and how we sense them. Follow the directions in the Science Log to learn more about "the big idea."✦

Crafts and Touch

Pottery, textiles, and furniture can be beautiful to look at. These art forms are also tempting to touch. To appreciate them, we want to feel the shape and the texture of the pot, the smoothness of the wood, the softness of a silk kimono. The parietal lobe interprets touch.

Figure 6-23 ▶ The brain is divided into sections called lobes. The lobes involved in each form of art are labeled.

Frontal

Floral Arranging and Smell

For many years the art of flower arranging has dealt primarily with color. A new trend has developed in recent years, however. Florists and home gardeners are now paying a lot more attention to smell when creating arrangements. Florists can build arrangements that use flowers with specific types of smell, such as sweet, spicy, and fruity smells. They can also create arrangements that relate to the smells of the season. Examples of flowers with very distinct smells are lilac, hyacinth, sweet pea, and peony. The temporal lobe interprets smell.

Culinary Arts and Taste

Culinary art is the art and science of good eating. Many chefs are creative artists. The kitchen is their art studio. Of course, they want to create food that tastes good. But they pay attention to other things, too: how it looks, how it smells, and how it feels inside your mouth. The parietal lobe interprets tastes.

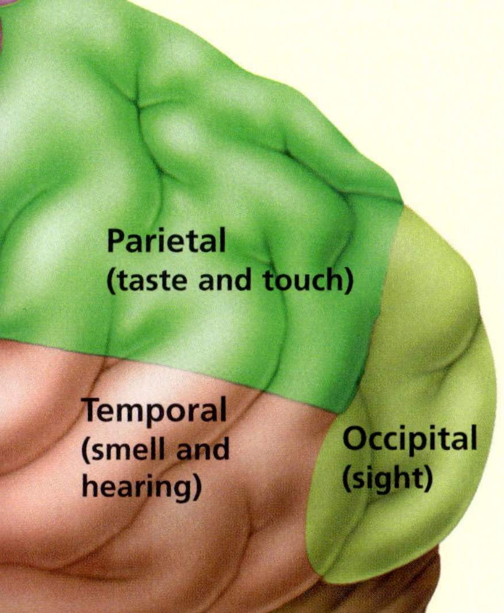

Painting and Sight

The artist George Seurat used a technique called pointillism. He painted dots of different colors next to each other. The color the brain sees is different from the dots. For example, when a red dot is next to a green dot, the brain sees yellow. This is called optical mixing. Scientists understand how our eyes and brains work together to see art. The occipital lobe interprets sights. It is harder to know how we decide what paintings we like and don't like.

Music and Hearing

Have you ever heard a song over and over in your head? Do some songs or types of music make you feel a certain way? Music affects many parts of our brain. When we hear a song in our mind, we are creating an image of it. Even without the sound, the temporal lobe reacts. The emotional power of music is not yet fully understood.

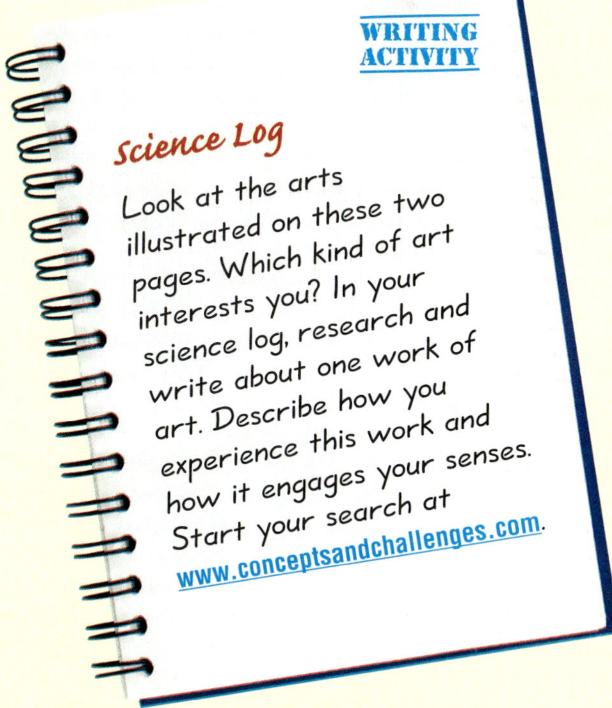

6-9 How do some drugs affect the body?

Objective

Describe the effects of some drugs on the body.

Key Terms

drug: a chemical substance that causes a change in the body

depressant (dee-PREHS-uhnt)**:** drug that slows down the central nervous system

addiction: uncontrollable dependence on a drug

stimulant (STIHM-yuh-luhnt)**:** drug that speeds up the central nervous system

hallucinogen (huh-LOO-sih-nuh-juhn)**:** drug that causes a person to see, hear, smell, taste, and feel things in an altered way

inhalant: everyday product that is inhaled and used as a drug

Drugs A **drug** is a chemical substance that causes a change in the body. Some drugs cause a physical change in the body. Some drugs cause changes in behavior. Drugs can be injected into the body or they can be inhaled, swallowed, or placed on the skin. Many drugs produce abnormal changes that stress the body.

 DEFINE: What is a drug?

Drugs for Medical Use There are two types of drugs for medical use. Drugs that can be bought only with a doctor's written permission are called prescription drugs. Antibiotics are an example of prescription drugs. Before writing a prescription, your doctor considers your illness, age, medical history, and your body frame. A prescription should be used only in the way your doctor prescribes it.

Some medical drugs, such as aspirin and antacids, can be bought without a doctor's prescription. These are called over-the-counter drugs.

 EXPLAIN: Why shouldn't you use a drug prescribed for someone else?

Misuse of Drugs The improper use of a drug is called drug abuse. There are many ways that drugs can be abused. For example, using too much of a drug or using a drug for the wrong reasons are forms of drug abuse. The use of illegal drugs is also drug abuse. The consequences of drug abuse are listed in Figure 6-24 on page 149. Many times prolonged drug abuse leads to death. Sometimes death can occur after only one use of a drug.

 INFER: Why do you think some people abuse drugs?

Depressants **Depressants** are drugs that slow down the central nervous system. They slow down the heartbeat and breathing rate. Large amounts and abuse of depressants can cause a person to go into a coma or even die.

The most widely abused depressant is alcohol. Barbiturates (bahr-BIHCH-uhr-ihts) are depressants commonly used in sleeping pills and sedatives. Narcotics (nahr-KAHT-ihks) are depressants used as painkillers. If barbiturates or narcotics are used over a period of time, the user may develop an **addiction** to the drug. An addiction is an uncontrollable dependence on a drug. People can develop both physical and mental addictions to drugs. The addicted person cannot stop using the drug without going through a period of sickness.

4 DESCRIBE: What effect do barbiturates have on the body?

Stimulants Some drugs speed up the action of the central nervous system. These drugs are called **stimulants.** In many ways, the effects of stimulants are the opposite of those of depressants. Stimulants speed up a person's heartbeat and rate of breathing. Cocaine is a commonly abused stimulant. Crack is a purified form of cocaine that is extremely dangerous. You may be surprised to learn that caffeine also is a stimulant. Caffeine is found in coffee, tea, cola, and chocolate.

POSSIBLE SIDE EFFECTS OF ILLEGAL DRUGS	
Depressants	**Hallucinogens**
Sleepiness Respiratory problems Inability to concentrate Coma Death	Increased heart rate and blood pressure Difficulty sleeping Loss of muscle coordination Seizures Heart and lung failure Violent behavior
Stimulants	**Inhalants**
Increased heart rate and blood pressure Difficulty sleeping Respiratory problems Stroke Violent behavior Heart attack Death	Stomach pains Nosebleeds Damage to liver, lungs, and kidneys Brain damage Involuntary urination Irregular heartbeat Death

▲ **Figure 6-24** Dangers of drug use

Amphetamines (am-FET-uh-meens) also are known as "uppers" or pep pills. Sometimes, doctors prescribe amphetamines to treat some nervous-system disorders. Other times, amphetamines are used to prevent drowsiness. When amphetamines are abused, they can cause violent reactions, convulsions, and even death.

CONTRAST: How does the effect of a stimulant differ from the effect of a depressant?

Hallucinogens Some drugs change the way a person receives information through the senses. For example, they cause a person to see, hear, touch, smell, feel, and taste things in an altered way. These drugs are called **hallucinogens.** Hallucinogens often make a person feel panicky or threatened. For this reason, people who take hallucinogens often are dangerous to themselves and others. LSD and PCP are two commonly abused hallucinogens.

Marijuana is the most widely abused illegal drug in the United States. It comes from a plant and is usually smoked. Marijuana has mind-altering effects. It also slows down the activity of the central nervous system. For this reason, sometimes marijuana is also classified as a depressant.

EXPLAIN: What effect do hallucinogens have on the body?

Abusing Poisons Some drugs are products people use every day, such as hair spray, spray paint, glue, or gasoline. Some people inhale these products because of their strong vapors, or smells. Everyday products that someone inhales and uses as a drug are called **inhalants.** Inhalants are often stimulants. Some of the vapors in inhalants stay in the body for a long time. Inhalants can break down myelin, the protective covering of some nerve cells. This can cause immediate damage to the brain. Inhalants also cause serious damage to the liver and kidneys. Inhalants are poisons and can cause death.

DEFINE: What are inhalants?

CHECKING CONCEPTS

1. What are two types of drugs with medical uses that you can buy over the counter?
2. What effect do depressants have on the body?
3. What group of depressants often are used as painkillers?
4. What effect do stimulants have on the body?

THINKING CRITICALLY

5. **INFER:** What effect does coffee have on the central nervous system?
6. **RELATE:** Which drug, a barbiturate or cocaine, would most likely make a person feel wide awake? Explain your answer.

Web InfoSearch

DARE Many communities have drug abuse prevention programs, such as DARE (Drug Abuse Resistance Education). In these programs, police officers visit classrooms and inform students of the dangers of drug abuse.

SEARCH: Use the Internet to find out about drug abuse prevention programs in your community. Then, make a poster encouraging students to stay off drugs. Start your search at www.conceptsandchallenges.com. Some key search words are **DARE, drug prevention,** and **drug abuse prevention.**

6-10 How does alcohol affect the body?

Objective

Describe the effects alcohol has on the body.

Key Terms

cirrhosis (suh-ROH-sihs)**:** liver disorder that may be caused by the excessive use of alcohol

alcoholic (al-kuh-HAWL-ihk)**:** person who is dependent on alcohol

Ethyl Alcohol One of the most commonly abused drugs is ethyl (ETH-uhl) alcohol. Ethyl alcohol is the alcohol that is in beverages such as beer, wine, and whiskey. Alcohol is a very dangerous drug. Most people think that alcohol is a stimulant. However, alcohol is a depressant. It slows down the action of the central nervous system.

 **EXPLAIN:** What effect does alcohol have on the body?

Alcohol and the Brain The amount of alcohol present in the bloodstream is called Blood Alcohol Concentration (BAC). The effect of alcohol on the body increases as the Blood Alcohol Concentration increases.

When people drink alcohol, their body systems slow down. They think and react more slowly. Their movements become clumsy.

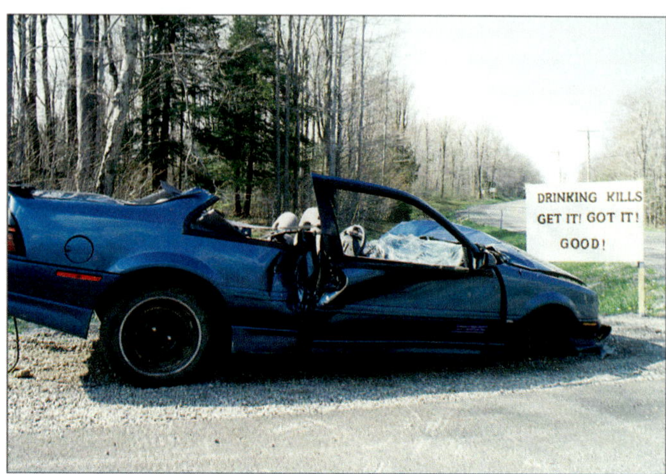

▲ **Figure 6-26** Drinking impairs driving skills.

 **INFER:** Why do you think it is dangerous for a person who has been drinking to drive a car?

Alcohol and the Body Alcohol affects many organs of the body. If a person does not drink very much, or very often, the effects of alcohol wear off after a period of time. However, if the drinking continues over a period of time, the body can be harmed. The liver can be greatly affected by

BLOOD ALCOHOL CONCENTRATION (BAC) AND ITS EFFECTS		
Drinks per Hour*	**BAC (Present)**	**Effects**
1	0.02 – 0.003	Feeling of relaxation
2	0.05 – 0.006	Slight loss of coordination
3	0.08 – 0.09	Loss of coordination; trouble talking and thinking; legal intoxication in most states
4	0.11 – 0.12	Slower reaction time; lack of judgment
7	0.20	Difficulty thinking; loss of motor skills
14	0.40	Unconsciousness; possible vomiting
17	0.50	Deep coma; possible death

*Based on a male weighing 120 lbs

◀ **Figure 6-25**

alcohol. Large amounts of alcohol taken over a long period of time can destroy the liver tissues. The liver then loses its ability to carry out its functions. This condition is called **cirrhosis.** Cirrhosis of the liver often leads to death.

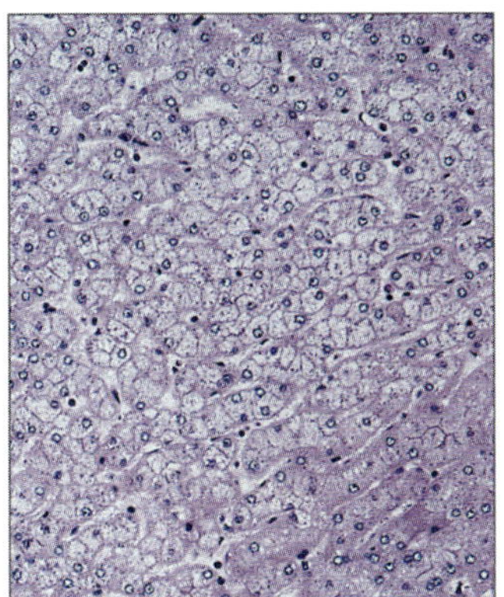
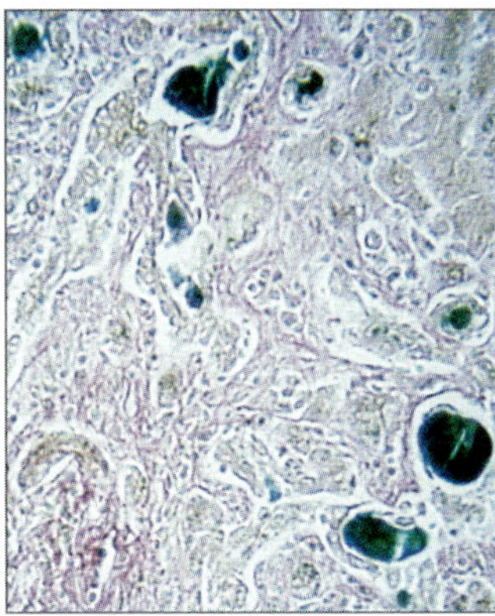

▲ **Figure 6-27** The liver on the left is healthy. The liver on the right has cirrhosis.

 IDENTIFY: What is cirrhosis of the liver?

Alcoholics Alcohol is addictive for some people. These people drink more and more alcohol as time goes by. They become dependent on alcohol. A person who cannot control his or her drinking of alcohol is called an **alcoholic.** Alcoholism is a disease because it causes harmful changes in body organs. Many alcoholics get help from groups such as Alcoholics Anonymous or AL-ATEEN. There are also support groups for family members of alcoholics.

 DESCRIBE: What is an alcoholic?

CHECKING CONCEPTS

1. What kind of alcohol is in alcoholic drinks?
2. What effect does alcohol have on body systems?
3. How does a person act after drinking alcohol?
4. What effect does drinking over a long period of time have on the body?
5. What is a person who is dependent on alcohol called?

THINKING CRITICALLY

6. RELATE: A person drinks a glass of wine every night before dinner. Is this person an alcoholic? Explain your answer.

Real-Life Science

BREATHALYZERS

Drinking alcohol seriously impairs a person's ability to drive. So, it is very important for law enforcement officials to be able to give drivers a test to determine if they have been drinking alcohol and how high their BAC is. It would be impossible for law enforcement officials to take a blood sample from every driver they suspect of being drunk. Instead, they use a device called a breathalyzer to measure the amount of alcohol in a driver's breath.

▲ **Figure 6-28** Breathalyzers measure the amount of alcohol in a person's blood.

How do breathalyzers work? Alcohol is not digested. Instead, it is absorbed into the bloodstream. As blood flows through the lungs, some of the alcohol leaves with the air that is exhaled. Since the amount of alcohol in the breath depends on the amount of alcohol in the blood, a breathalyzer can be used to find the BAC amount in a person's blood.

Thinking Critically How do breathalyzers help keep people safe?

Chapter 6 Challenges

Chapter Summary

Lesson 6-1

- The nervous system controls all of the body's activities. It is made up of the brain, the spinal cord, and nerves.

Lesson 6-2

- The main job of the brain is to receive, interpret, and react to messages from inside and outside the body.

Lesson 6-3

- Any action that causes a response is a stimulus.
- An automatic response to a stimulus is called a **reflex.** The path of a message in a reflex is called a **reflex arc.**

Lesson 6-4

- The **sense organs** are the eyes, nose, skin, ears, and tongue. Sense organs are used to receive stimuli from the environment.

Lesson 6-5

- Different parts of the eye work together to help you see. The main parts of the eye are the **cornea, iris, pupil, lens, retina,** and optic nerve.

Lesson 6-6

- The ears are the sense organs of hearing. The main parts of the ear are the outer ear, the ear bones, and the **cochlea.**

Lesson 6-7

- A **gland** is an organ that makes substances used or released by the body.
- The job of the endocrine system is to help control body functions.

Lesson 6-8

- **Hormones,** produced in **endocrine glands,** control many of the body's activities.

Lesson 6-9

- A **drug** is a chemical substance that causes a change in the body. People who use drugs can become addicted to them.

Lesson 6-10

- Alcohol slows down body systems.

Key Term Challenges

addiction (p. 148)
alcoholic (p. 150)
axon (p. 128)
brainstem (p. 130)
cerebellum (p. 130)
cerebrum (p. 130)
cirrhosis (p. 150)
cochlea (p. 140)
cornea (p. 138)
dendrite (p. 128)
depressant (p. 148)
drug (p. 148)
eardrum (p. 140)
endocrine gland (p. 142)
exocrine gland (p. 142)
gland (p. 142)
hallucinogen (p. 148)
hormone (p. 144)
hypothalamus (p. 142)
inhalant (p. 148)
iris (p. 138)
lens (p. 138)
medulla (p. 130)
neuron (p. 128)
pupil (p. 138)
receptor (p. 132)
reflex (p. 132)
reflex arc (p. 132)
retina (p. 138)
sense organ (p. 134)
stimulant (p. 148)
synapse (p. 128)
target cell (p. 144)

MATCHING **Write the Key Term from above that best matches each description.**

1. clear covering at the front of the eye
2. changes vibrations into nerve signals
3. receives stimuli from the environment
4. controls heartbeat and breathing rate
5. makes chemical substances used or released by the body
6. carries messages away from a nerve cell

IDENTIFYING WORD RELATIONSHIPS **Explain how the words in each pair are related. Write your answers in complete sentences.**

7. endocrine gland, hormone
8. axon, dendrite
9. cerebellum, cerebrum
10. reflex, reflex arc
11. response, stimulus
12. alcoholic, cirrhosis

Content Challenges TEST PREP

MULTIPLE CHOICE Write the letter of the term or phrase that best completes each statement.

1. The lens of the eye focuses images on the
   a. cornea.
   b. pupil.
   c. iris.
   d. retina.
2. Insulin is made by the
   a. pituitary gland.
   b. pancreas.
   c. ovaries.
   d. thyroid.
3. The smallest part of the brain is the
   a. medulla.
   b. cerebrum.
   c. cerebellum.
   d. skull.
4. Adrenaline controls
   a. muscle reaction.
   b. growth.
   c. the amount of calcium in the blood.
   d. blood sugar levels.
5. The cochlea is found in the
   a. outer ear.
   b. middle ear.
   c. inner ear.
   d. eardrum.
6. The "thermostat" of the body is the
   a. cerebrum.
   b. hypothalamus.
   c. pituitary gland.
   d. cerebellum.
7. The nervous system is made up of the brain, the spinal cord, and
   a. muscles.
   b. glands.
   c. nerves.
   d. the skull.
8. The largest cells in the body are
   a. axons.
   b. dendrites.
   c. hormones.
   d. neurons.
9. Drugs that cause people to see things that do not exist are
   a. sleeping pills.
   b. barbiturates.
   c. depressants.
   d. hallucinogens.
10. Cirrhosis of the liver can be caused by
    a. inhalants.
    b. alcohol.
    c. hallucinogens.
    d. stimulants.

TRUE/FALSE Write *true* if the statement is true. If the statement is false, change the underlined term to make the statement true.

11. Estrogen and progesterone are produced by the <u>ovaries</u>.
12. The amount of light entering the eye is controlled by the <u>cornea</u>.
13. The ear responds to <u>light</u> waves.
14. The brain is connected to the spinal cord by the <u>medulla</u>.
15. The path of a message in a reflex is called a <u>synapse</u>.
16. Reflexes are controlled by the <u>brain</u>.
17. Growth hormone is made by the <u>pituitary</u> gland.
18. Alcohol is classified as a <u>depressant</u> drug.

Concept Challenges TEST PREP

WRITTEN RESPONSE **Answer each of the following questions in complete sentences.**

1. **APPLY:** How do reflexes help an organism survive?
2. **COMPARE:** How is the eye like a camera?
3. **COMPARE:** How is the spinal cord like a tree trunk?
4. **EXPLAIN:** How do the nervous system and the endocrine system work together?
5. **INFER:** How do you think a drug addiction affects a person's life?

INTERPRETING A DIAGRAM **Use Figure 6-29 to answer the following questions.**

6. What does thyroxine control?
7. What are two pituitary hormones?
8. What hormone is needed to regulate the pituitary gland?
9. What gland produces insulin?
10. What minerals are affected by parathyroid hormone?
11. What health problems might a person have if that person's thymus gland produced too little thymosin?
12. What three things does adrenaline control?

HORMONES AND WHAT THEY DO		
Gland	**Hormone**	**Job of Hormone**
Adrenal	Adrenaline	Controls muscle reaction and raises heart rate and blood pressure
Ovaries	Estrogen and Progesterone	Controls physical and reproductive development in women
Pancreas	Insulin	Controls blood sugar levels
Parathyroid	Parathyroid hormone	Controls the amount of calcium and phosphorus in the blood
Pineal	Melatonin	Helps regulate pituitary gland
Pituitary	ACTH	Controls the release of hormones from the adrenal glands
Pituitary	Growth hormone	Controls the growth of bones; controls metabolism
Testes	Testosterone	Controls physical and reproductive development in men
Thymus	Thymosin	Controls the growth of certain white blood cells
Thyroid	Thyroxine	Controls rate of body growth

◄ **Figure 6-29**

Chapter 7 Reproduction & Development

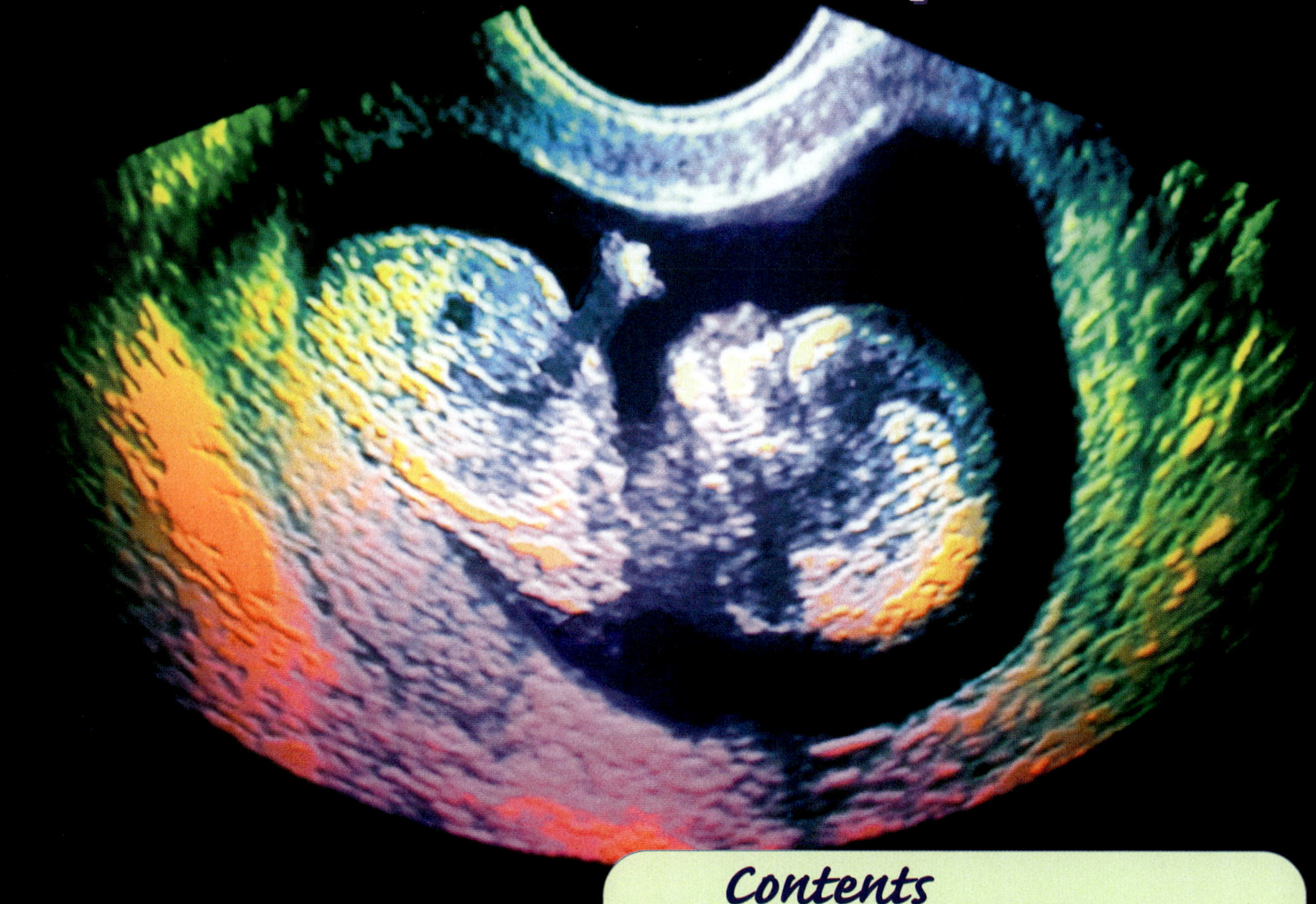

▲ **Figure 7-1** This is an ultrasound picture of a fetus in its sixth month of development.

In what ways have you changed since you were an infant? You can probably think of many. You changed in even more ways during the time before you were born. A human fetus develops inside its mother over a nine month period. During this time, a complex series of changes takes place. From one cell comes a whole new organism, made up of about a trillion cells, each with different functions.

▶ What do you think are some of the changes a newborn baby goes through?

Contents

7-1 What are the parts of the female reproductive system?

7-2 What are the parts of the male reproductive system?

7-3 What is the menstrual cycle?

7-4 How does fertilization take place?

7-5 How does a human embryo develop?

■ **Lab Activity:** Graphing Changes in Fetal Development

7-6 What are the stages of human development?

■ **The Big Idea:** How has technology improved life at various stages?

7-1 What are the parts of the female reproductive system?

Objective

Describe the female reproductive system.

Key Terms

ovary: organ of the female reproductive system that produces hormones and eggs

progesterone: hormone that prepares the uterus for pregnancy

estrogen: hormone that helps regulate the menstrual cycle

oviduct (OH-vih-dukt)**:** long tube between the ovary and the uterus

uterus (YOOT-uhr-uhs)**:** organ in which an embryo develops

cervix (SUHR-vihks)**:** narrow end of the uterus

vagina (vuh-JY-nuh)**:** birth canal

Reproductive Systems Most systems of the body are the same in males and females. This is not true of reproductive systems. The male and female reproductive systems are different. All the organs of the female reproductive system are located inside the body. In the male reproductive system, some organs are inside the body, while others are located in a pouch on the outside of the body. The main job of both the male and female reproductive systems is to produce offspring.

1 COMPARE: How is the reproductive system different from other body systems?

Ovaries The **ovaries** are the main organs of the female reproductive system. Ovaries are egg-shaped structures. Females are born with two ovaries. One ovary lies on each side of the female's body.

The ovaries contain two different kinds of cells. One kind produces the hormones **progesterone** and **estrogen.** Progesterone helps prepare the uterus for pregnancy. Estrogen helps regulate a woman's menstrual cycle. The other kind of cell produces eggs. Eggs are female reproductive cells.

2 DESCRIBE: What do the ovaries produce?

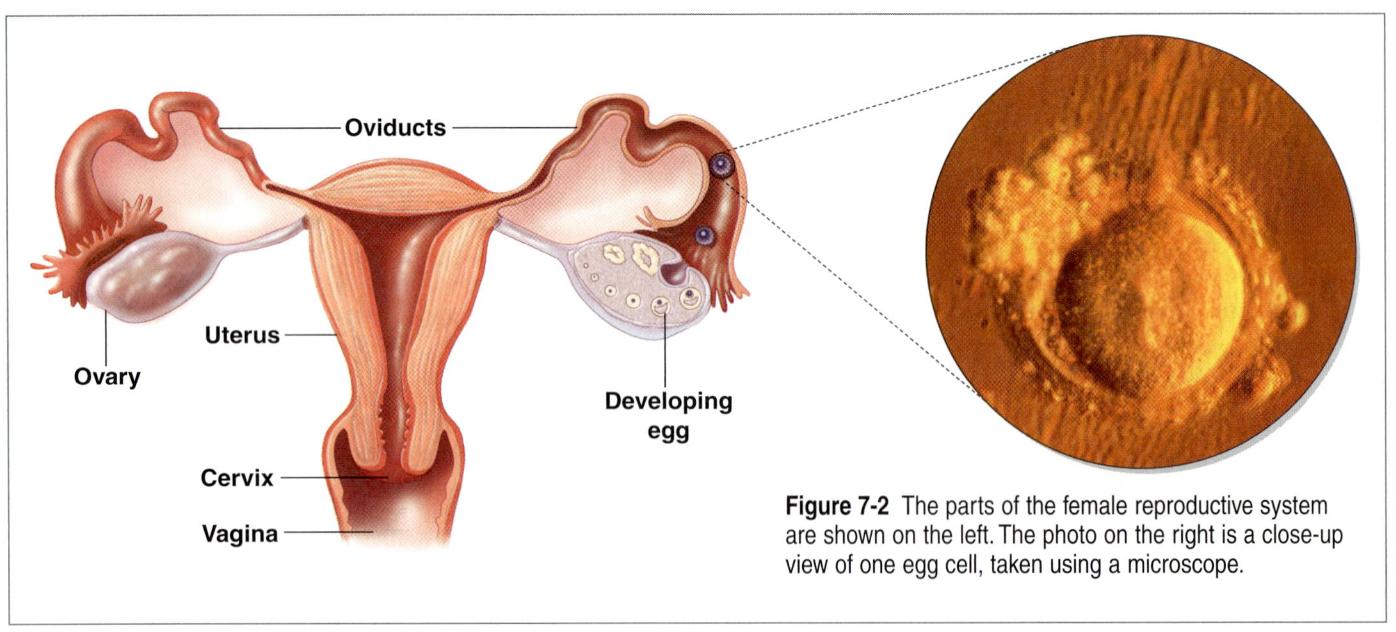

Figure 7-2 The parts of the female reproductive system are shown on the left. The photo on the right is a close-up view of one egg cell, taken using a microscope.

Pathway of Eggs Study the female reproductive system shown in Figure 7-2. A long tube called an **oviduct** lies near each ovary. The oviduct carries eggs to the uterus. The **uterus** is a hollow organ with thick, muscular walls. This is where an embryo develops.

The lower end of the uterus is narrower. This part of the uterus is called the **cervix.** The cervix connects the uterus to the **vagina.** The vagina is the opening through which a baby passes during birth. The vagina is also called the birth canal.

3 EXPLAIN: What is the function of the oviduct?

CHECKING CONCEPTS

1. Which organs of the female reproductive system produce hormones?
2. What are female sex cells called?
3. What is the long tube that carries an egg from the ovary to the uterus?
4. What is the narrow end of the uterus?
5. What is another name for the vagina?

THINKING CRITICALLY

6. **RELATE:** Through which structures of the female reproductive system does a baby pass?
7. **INFER:** The walls of the uterus are flexible and can expand and contract. How does this help a developing embryo?
8. **INFER:** Why is the vagina also called the birth canal?

BUILDING LANGUAGE ARTS SKILLS

Applying Definitions Look up the meaning of the prefix *ovi*. Then look up the meaning of the word *duct*. Relate these definitions to the function of the oviduct. List and define several other terms that contain these word parts.

Science and Technology

TREATMENT OF OVARIAN CYSTS

An ovarian cyst is a fluid-filled sac or a round, baglike membrane in the ovary. Some ovarian cysts form quite normally every month. They contain an egg that is ripening, or getting ready to be released to travel through an oviduct to the uterus. After the egg is released, the cyst normally shrinks and disappears within one to three months.

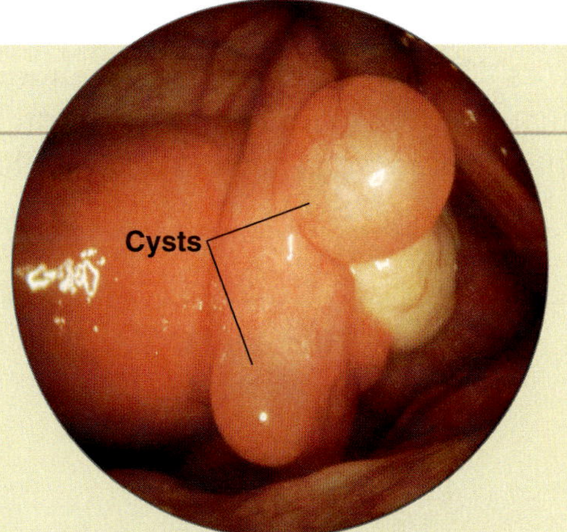

▲ **Figure 7-3** Ovarian cysts can be removed by laparoscopy.

Sometimes the cyst releases the ripening egg but does not shrink. Instead, it may grow as large as a baseball. A sonogram, or a picture made by using sound waves, can be used to determine whether a cyst is a fluid-filled sac, an infection, or a tumor. Perhaps the growth may even be a cancerous tumor. Most ovarian cysts are not cancerous.

Cysts can be removed by surgery. Often this procedure is done by laparoscopy, an operation in which a very small incision is made and a laparoscope is inserted. A laparoscope is a lighted viewing tube that is like a flexible telescope. If tests show that the cyst is cancerous, both ovaries and the uterus may have to be removed.

Thinking Critically If ovarian cysts form normally every month, why might a doctor want to follow up with another examination or a sonogram when one is found?

7-2 What are the parts of the male reproductive system?

Objective

Describe the male reproductive system.

Key Terms

testis, ***pl.*** **testes:** organ of the male reproductive system that produces hormones and sperm

scrotum (SKROHT-uhm)**:** pocket of skin that protects and holds the testes

testosterone (tehs-TAHS-tuhr-ohn)**:** hormone produced in the testes

epididymis (ep-uh-DID-i-mihs)**:** coiled tube that stores sperm

urethra (yoo-REE-thruh)**:** tube that carries urine and sperm to the outside of the male's body

The Testes The organ of the male reproductive system that produce hormones and sperm is the **testes**. The testes are egg-shaped structures located outside the body cavity. The testes rest in a pocket of skin called the **scrotum**. The organs of the male reproductive system are shown in Figure 7-4.

1 IDENTIFY: What are the organs that produce hormones and sperm?

Testosterone Two kinds of cells are located in the testes. One type produces **testosterone**, a hormone that controls the development of secondary sex characteristics. In a male, these characteristics include a deeper voice and the growth of body hair.

Testosterone also causes male sex cells to develop inside the testes. Male sex cells are called sperm. Sperm are stored in a coiled tube called the **epididymis.** One end of the epididymis connects to the testes. The other end connects to a longer tube that extends upward into the body cavity from the testes.

2 DESCRIBE: What substances are produced inside the testes?

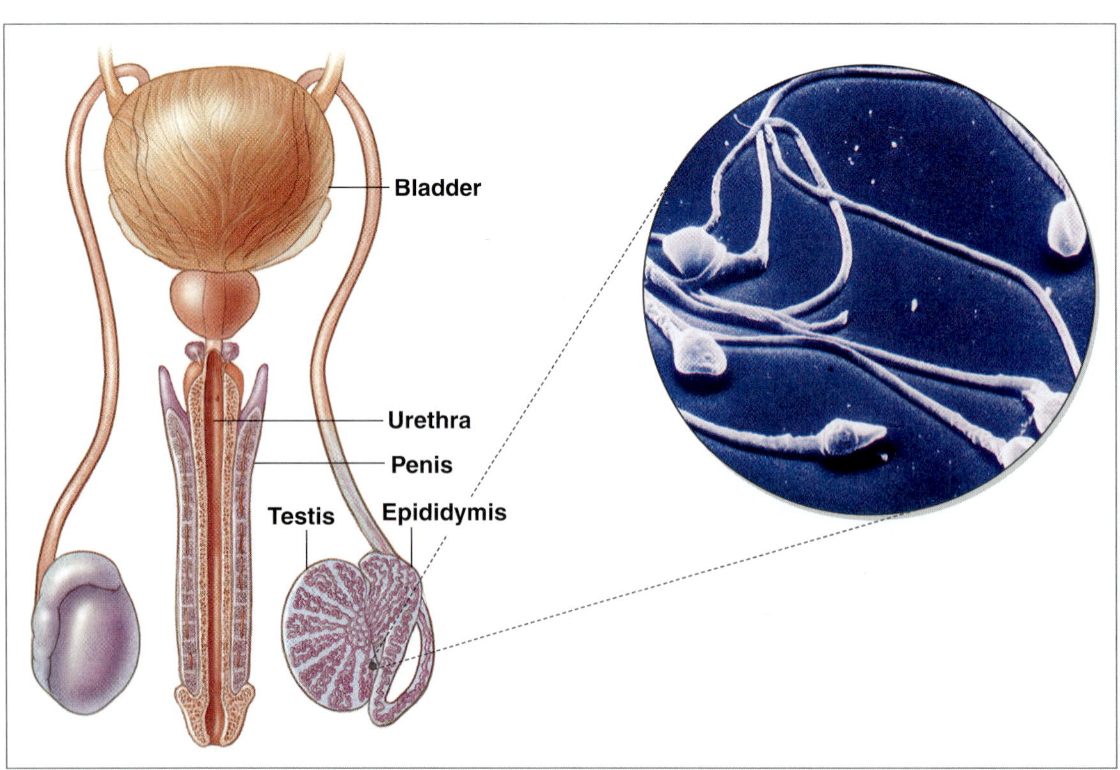

◀ **Figure 7-4** The male reproductive system is shown on the left. The photo on the right shows several sperm cells.

The Urethra The **urethra** is part of the excretory system. Urine made in the kidneys travels from the bladder to the outside of the body through the urethra. The urethra is surrounded and protected by the penis.

In males, the urethra performs another job. It is the passageway through which sperm leave a male's body. For this reason, the urethra is considered to be a part of the male reproductive system as well.

3 **EXPLAIN:** Why is the urethra part of two different body systems in males?

CHECKING CONCEPTS

1. The organs of the male reproductive system that produce hormones and sperm are the __________.
2. The testes are suspended within a pocket of skin called the __________.
3. One kind of cell in the testes produces the hormone __________.
4. Male sex cells are called __________.
5. In males, both sperm and urine leave the body through the __________.
6. The testes produce both testosterone and __________.

THINKING CRITICALLY

7. **COMPARE:** How is the shape of the testes similar to the shape of the ovaries?
8. **RELATE:** To what two male body systems does the urethra belong?

BUILDING SCIENCE SKILLS

Organizing Information When you organize information, you put the information in some kind of order. A table is one way to organize information. Make a table that describes the parts of the male reproductive system. Include a description of the function of each part in the table.

Real-Life Science

SEXUALLY TRANSMITTED DISEASES

A disease that can be passed from one person to another is called a contagious disease. Some contagious diseases are spread by pathogens. Pathogens are harmful microscopic organisms such as bacteria and viruses.

A few contagious diseases are spread through sexual contact with an infected person. These diseases are called sexually transmitted diseases. The pathogens that cause sexually transmitted diseases can live only inside a human body. Outside the body, these pathogens die. Sexually transmitted diseases are not spread by casual contact.

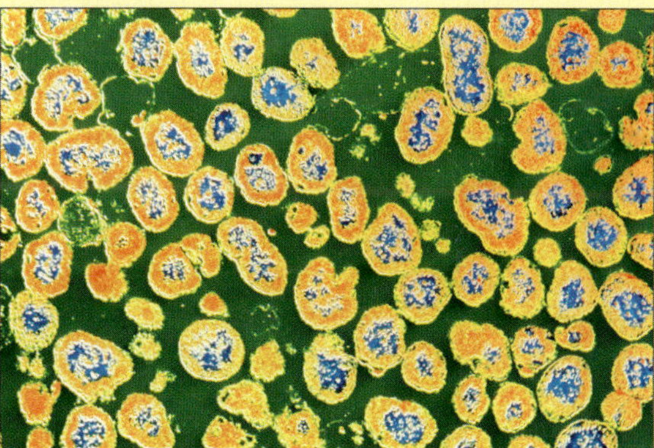

▲ **Figure 7-5** Many sexually transmitted diseases are caused by bacteria such as these Gonorrhea.

Gonorrhea (gahn-uh-REE-uh) and syphilis (SIHF-uh-lihs) are two sexually transmitted diseases. These diseases usually are treated with penicillin or other antibiotics. Many cases of gonorrhea and syphilis are cured through early diagnosis and treatment.

AIDS is also a sexually transmitted disease. HIV, the virus that causes AIDS, attacks an infected person's immune system, so the person cannot fight the disease. There is no known cure for AIDS.

Thinking Critically How can a person avoid getting a sexually transmitted disease?

7-3 What is the menstrual cycle?

Objective

Describe the menstrual cycle.

Key Terms

puberty (PYOO-burh-tee)**:** time at which a person becomes sexually mature

menstrual (MEHN-struhl) **cycle:** monthly cycle of change that occurs in the female reproductive system

ovulation (ahv-yuh-LAY-shuhn)**:** release of a mature egg from the ovary

menstruation (mehn-stroo-AY-shuhn)**:** process by which blood and tissue from the lining of the uterus break apart and leave the body

Menstrual Cycle When a female is born, her body contains all the egg cells she will ever have. However, the eggs are not mature, or fully developed. The eggs do not begin to mature until the female reaches puberty. **Puberty** is the time at which a person becomes sexually mature. Puberty generally begins between the ages of 10 and 14. In females, puberty is often marked by the beginning of the **menstrual cycle.** The menstrual cycle is a monthly cycle of change that occurs in the female reproductive system. Look at Figure 7-6 as you read about the cycle.

1 IDENTIFY: What is the menstrual cycle?

Ovulation The menstrual cycle occurs every 28 to 32 days. It is triggered by the release of hormones in the female reproductive system. These hormones come from both the reproductive system and several glands of the endocrine system. They work together to regulate the menstrual cycle.

One hormone causes an egg to mature in an ovary. Another hormone causes the walls of the uterus to thicken and the supply of blood to the uterus to increase. This happens so that if an egg cell becomes an embryo, the uterus will be ready to support the growth and development of the embryo.

Yet another hormone triggers ovulation. **Ovulation** occurs when a mature egg leaves an ovary and travels into an oviduct.

2 EXPLAIN: What triggers ovulation?

Menstruation After an egg is released from the ovary, it travels through an oviduct. If the egg does not meet sperm in the oviduct, it begins to break apart. The amount of hormones in the reproductive system decreases. This causes the thickened walls of the uterus to also break apart. About 14 days after ovulation, **menstruation** occurs. Menstruation is the process by which blood and tissue from the uterus break apart and leave the body.

Soon after menstruation, a new egg begins to mature in the ovary. The menstrual cycle is repeated. The cycle is continuously repeated well into adulthood. For most females, the menstrual cycle continues until about age 50.

3 IDENTIFY: At about what age does the menstrual cycle stop occurring?

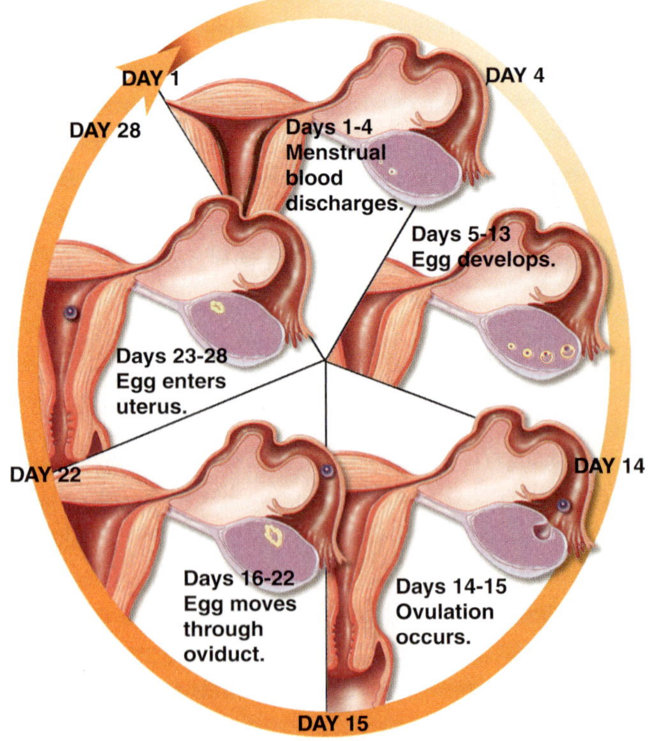

▲ **Figure 7-6** The menstrual cycle takes about 28 days to complete.

CHECKING CONCEPTS

1. A person becomes sexually mature during ___________.
2. A female is born with all the ___________ cells she will have in her lifetime.
3. The series of monthly changes in a female's reproductive system is called the ___________.
4. Ovulation is triggered by the release of ___________ into parts of the reproductive system.
5. During ___________ , blood and tissue from the uterus are released from the body.
6. A mature egg moves from an ovary into an oviduct during ___________.

THINKING CRITICALLY

7. **COMPARE:** What effect do hormones have on the development of sex cells in the female reproductive system?
8. **INFER:** Why is the thickening of the uterus important to reproduction?

INTERPRETING VISUALS

Use Figure 7-6 to answer the following questions.

9. On what day of the menstrual cycle does ovulation take place?
10. On what day does menstruation take place?
11. At what stage is the lining of the uterus the thickest?
12. If it is day 20 of the cycle, what might be happening?

How Do They Know That?

GRAAFIAN FOLLICLES

Reinier de Graaf (1641–1673) was a Dutch physician who lived during the same time as Anton van Leeuwenhoek (1632–1723), the inventor of a powerful, yet simple microscope. Using this microscope, de Graaf observed the large, liquid-filled chambers on the ovary and proposed that their growth was tied to the menstrual cycle. Each of these follicles contained an egg. The follicles were later named after de Graaf and are known today as Graafian follicles.

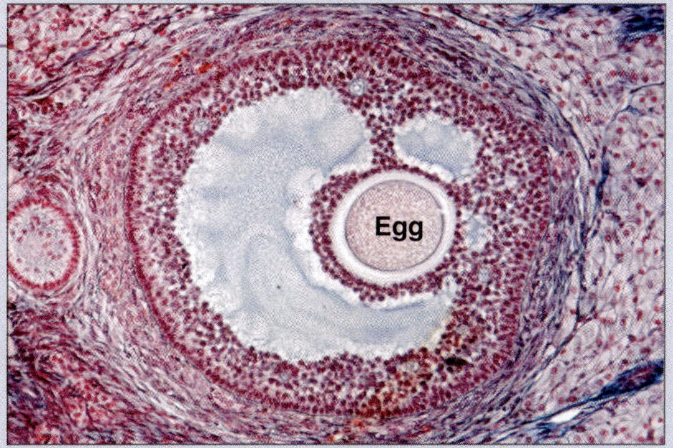

▲ **Figure 7-7** This is a Graafian follicle shown through a microscope.

The Graafian follicle is like a pimple that breaks open on the surface of the ovary. This action releases the egg within a protective layer of cells that surrounds it. The egg breaks free from the Graafian follicle on the ovary about the fourteenth day of the menstrual cycle. This is called ovulation.

The development of the egg and its Graafian follicle is controlled by hormones from the pituitary gland. The month-long cycle of the Graafian follicle and its functions were important discoveries in human biology.

Thinking Critically How do you think the invention of the simple microscope affected studies made by de Graaf and other scientists?

7-4 How does fertilization take place?

Objective

Describe how a sperm cell and an egg cell join to form a zygote.

Key Terms

gamete: reproductive cell

fertilization (fuhrt-uhl-ih-ZAY-shuhn)**:** joining of one sperm cell and one egg cell

zygote (ZY-goht)**:** fertilized egg

Gamete Formation Before reproduction can take place, special cells called gametes must be formed. **Gametes** are reproductive cells. The male reproductive cells are called sperm. The female reproductive cells are called eggs. Gametes are formed through the process of cell division called meiosis. During the formation of gametes, the number of chromosomes in the cells must be reduced to half of the number of chromosomes in normal body cells. This must occur so that the offspring will receive the same number of chromosomes from each parent. This is an important part of sexual reproduction.

1 IDENTIFY: Through which type of cell division are gametes produced?

Sperm Cells Sperm cells are microscopic. The largest part of a sperm cell is the round head. The head contains the cell nucleus. A sperm cell also has a long tail. The motion of the tail helps the sperm cell move. This helps the sperm cell to reach the egg.

2 DESCRIBE: How does a sperm cell move?

Mature Egg During ovulation, a mature egg is released from an ovary. The egg passes into the oviduct. Tiny hairs that move line the walls of the oviduct. The motion of these hairs moves the egg through the oviduct. Muscles lining the oviduct also help move the egg along.

3 EXPLAIN: What causes an egg to move through the oviduct?

Fertilization Sperm cells enter the female reproductive system through the vagina. They move across the uterus and into the oviduct. Of the millions of sperm cells that enter the uterus, only a few may reach the oviduct.

During ovulation, an egg leaves an ovary and enters the oviduct. If a sperm cell meets an egg cell in the oviduct, **fertilization** can occur. Fertilization is the joining of one sperm and one egg. An egg can be fertilized only after ovulation and only by one sperm.

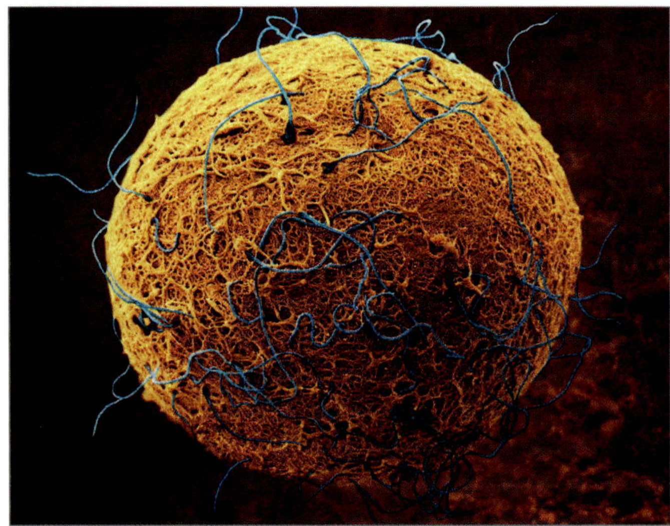

▲ **Figure 7-8** The egg (in yellow) is much larger than the surrounding sperm (in blue).

4 IDENTIFY: What is fertilization?

Zygote During fertilization, the nuclei of a sperm cell and an egg cell join together. The new cell that results from fertilization is called a **zygote.** A zygote is a fertilized egg. Because the nuclei of the two gametes join, they combine their chromosomes. Human gametes each have 23 chromosomes. This means that after fertilization, the zygote will have 46 chromosomes in its nucleus. The zygote travels down the oviduct and enters the uterus. As it travels, it goes through several cell divisions. See Figure 7-9 on the next page.

1 Zygote

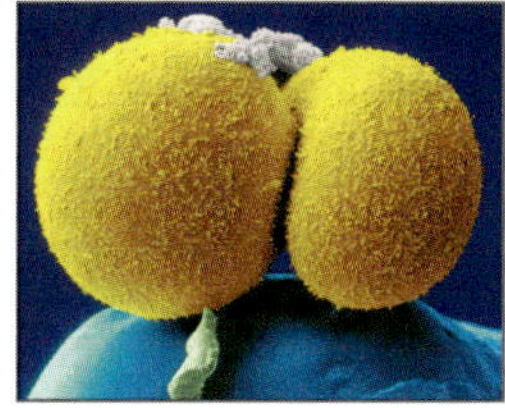

2 Two cells

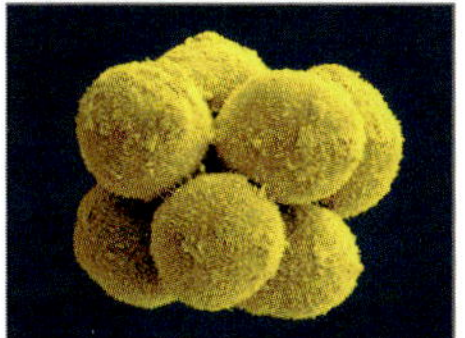

3 Eight cells

4 Many cells

▲ **Figure 7-9** A zygote goes through several cell divisions as it travels down the oviduct.

EXPLAIN: What causes a zygote to form?

CHECKING CONCEPTS

1. A sperm cell moves due to the motion of its ___________.
2. During ___________, a mature egg leaves an ovary and travels into the oviduct.
3. The joining of a sperm cell and an egg cell is called ___________.
4. The new cell produced by fertilization is called a ___________.

THINKING CRITICALLY

5. **RELATE:** During which stage of a female's menstrual cycle can fertilization occur? Why?
6. **CONTRAST:** How is the motion of sperm cells and egg cells different?

BUILDING MATH SKILLS

Calculating Approximately 24 hours after fertilization, the zygote divides into two cells. If the cell divides every 12 hours, how many cells will it have at each of the following time intervals:

a. 36 hours
b. 2 days
c. 3 days
d. 4 days

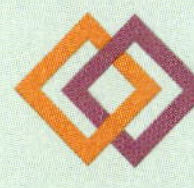

Integrating Physical Science

TOPIC: chemistry

CHEMICALS INVOLVED IN FERTILIZATION

In order for fertilization to occur, sperm must successfully reach the egg cell. Several hundred million sperm can be deposited in the vagina, but only a small fraction of those actually reach the egg. The challenge does not end there. Sperm cells must also get through the egg cell membrane in order to fertilize it.

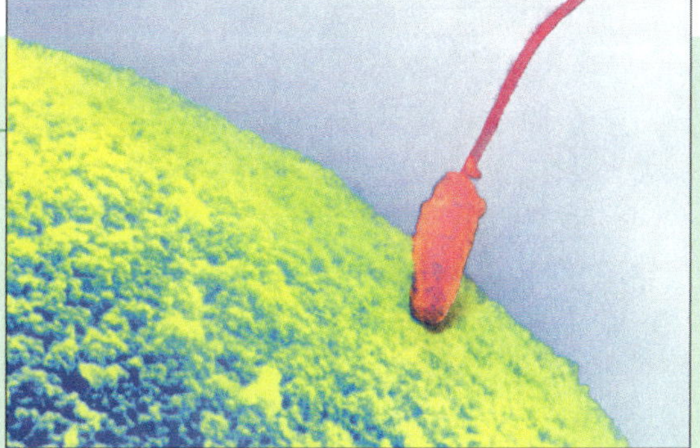

▲ **Figure 7-10** Only one sperm is able to get through the egg's cell membrane.

During this time, the female reproductive organs secrete several chemicals that change the membrane of the sperm cells. This makes the sperm capable of fertilizing the egg. Although many sperm reach the egg, usually only one will be able to get through the cell membrane of the egg. The sperm that successfully reaches the egg and comes in contact with the egg's membrane will release an enzyme. This enzyme disrupts a section of the egg's protective membrane. The sperm cell is then able to enter the egg cell, and fertilization can take place.

After the first sperm enters the cell, other chemical activities take place. These chemical activities prevent other sperm cells from also entering the egg. These chemicals assure that only one sperm cell fertilizes the egg.

Thinking Critically What might the result be if more than one cell were able to fertilize the egg?

7-5 How does a human embryo develop?

Objective

Describe the process by which an embryo develops into a fetus.

Key Terms

embryo (EHM-bree-oh)**:** developing human organism up until eight weeks of pregnancy

fetus (FEET-uhs)**:** term used to describe an embryo eight weeks after fertilization

placenta (pluh-SEHN-tuh)**:** organ through which an embryo receives nourishment and gets rid of wastes

umbilical (um-BIHL-ih-kuhl) **cord:** structure that connects the embryo to the placenta

amnion (AM-nee-uhn)**:** fluid-filled sac that surrounds an embryo

Implantation After fertilization, the zygote divides by mitosis. Two cells are formed. These cells are attached to each other. Both of these cells divide to form four attached cells. This cell division continues until a hollow ball of cells is formed. The hollow ball of cells attaches itself to the lining of the uterus. This is called implantation.

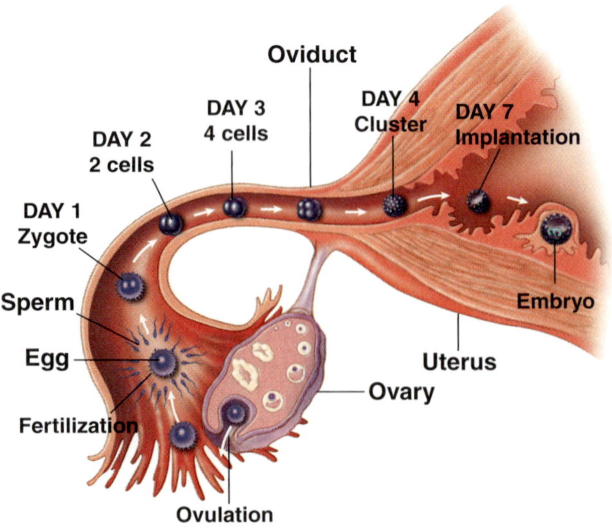

▲ **Figure 7-11** After fertilization, the zygote continues growing before it attaches to the lining of the uterus.

The mass of cells is called an **embryo** until the eighth week of pregnancy. The cells of the embryo will multiply to form tissues and organs.

 IDENTIFY: What is an embryo?

Development After about eight weeks, the embryo has developed a heart, brain, and spinal cord. Eyes and ears also are formed. At about nine weeks, bones form in the skeleton. It is now called a **fetus.** The fetus continues to grow and develop inside the uterus. Between the sixth and the ninth month, the fetus grows very quickly.

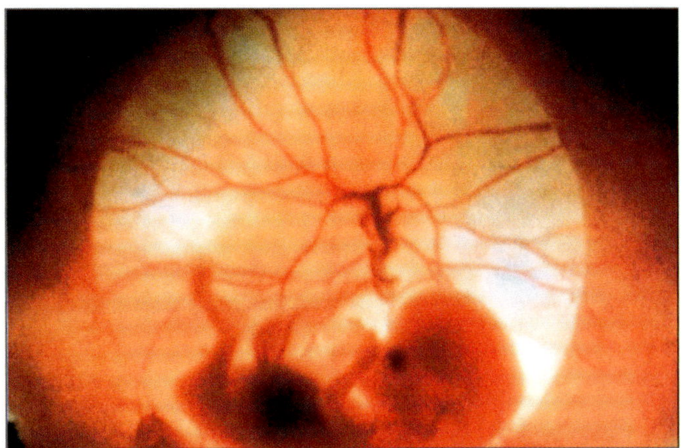

▲ **Figure 7-12** A developing fetus

 DESCRIBE: When is a developing organism called a fetus?

Special Structures During pregnancy, special structures in the mother's body protect and support the embryo as it develops into a fetus. Tissues of the uterus that surround the fetus develop into a thick flat structure called the **placenta.** The placenta is an organ through which the fetus receives nourishment. The fetus also gets rid of wastes through the placenta.

The fetus is attached to the placenta by the **umbilical cord.** The umbilical cord is a thick, ropelike structure. One kind of blood vessel in the umbilical cord carries nourishment from the placenta to the fetus. A different kind of blood vessel carries wastes from the fetus to the placenta. The fetus is surrounded by a clear, fluid-filled sac called the **amnion.** The fluid inside the sac cushions and protects the developing fetus.

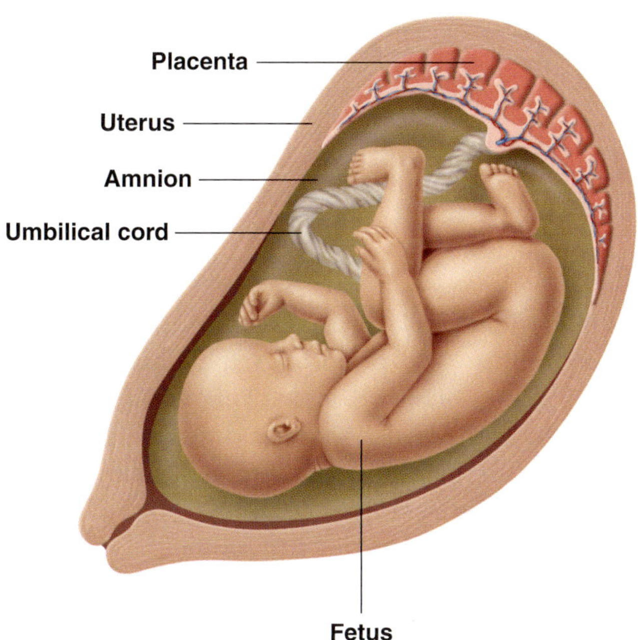

▲ **Figure 7-13** The placenta provides nourishment to the fetus and carries away wastes.

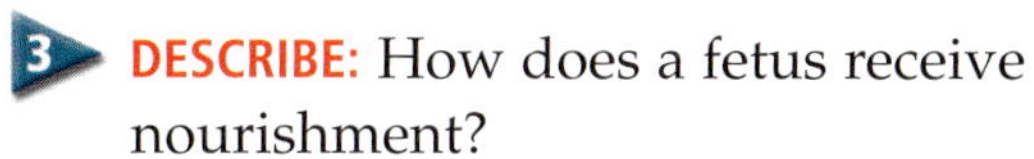

3 **DESCRIBE:** How does a fetus receive nourishment?

Pregnancy The period of development of an organism inside its mother's body is called pregnancy. Pregnancy brings about many changes in a woman's body. Most women gain between 10 and 15 kg during their pregnancy. Some women develop back pain and swollen feet as a result of this extra weight. The most common problem associated with pregnancy is a feeling of exhaustion. A woman's body must work harder to meet her own needs as well as those of her baby.

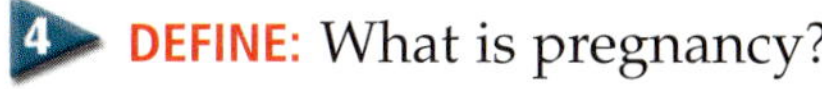

4 **DEFINE:** What is pregnancy?

Birth After about nine months, the fetus is ready to be born. The birth takes place in three stages—labor, delivery, and afterbirth. Hormones in the body of both the mother and the fetus trigger the birth process to begin. The muscles of the uterus begin to contract, or squeeze together. This process is called labor. As labor continues, the muscle contractions become stronger and happen more often. Labor may take only a few hours, or may last up to 20 hours or more.

During delivery, the contractions force the fetus out of the uterus and into the vagina. Eventually, the fetus is pushed out of the mother. The fetus usually comes out head first and is still attached to the placenta by the umbilical cord. The umbilical cord is then cut.

A few seconds after birth, the infant begins to cry. Crying helps the infant's lungs to expand so that it can begin to breathe on its own. The location where the umbilical cord attaches to the infant eventually shrinks and becomes the navel, or belly button. After about 10 to 15 minutes, the placenta is pushed out of the mother. This is called the afterbirth.

5 **IDENTIFY:** What are the three stages of childbirth?

CHECKING CONCEPTS

1. After fertilization, a zygote divides by __________.
2. The umbilical cord connects the embryo to the __________.
3. When the skeleton of an embryo has formed bones, the embryo is called a __________.
4. The embryo receives nourishment and gets rid of wastes through the __________.
5. During labor, muscles in the __________ begin to contract.
6. The place the umbilical cord attaches to eventually becomes the __________.

THINKING CRITICALLY

7. **INFER:** Why does one type of blood vessel bring nutrients to the embryo while another removes its waste products?
8. **INFER:** Why do you think it is dangerous for a pregnant mother to drink alcohol or smoke?

INTERPRETING VISUALS

Use Figure 7-11 to answer the following questions.

9. At what day is the zygote made up of four cells?
10. On what day does implantation occur?
11. Through which part of the female reproductive system does the zygote travel?
12. To which part of the female reproductive system does the embryo attach?

LAB ACTIVITY

Graphing Changes in Fetal Development

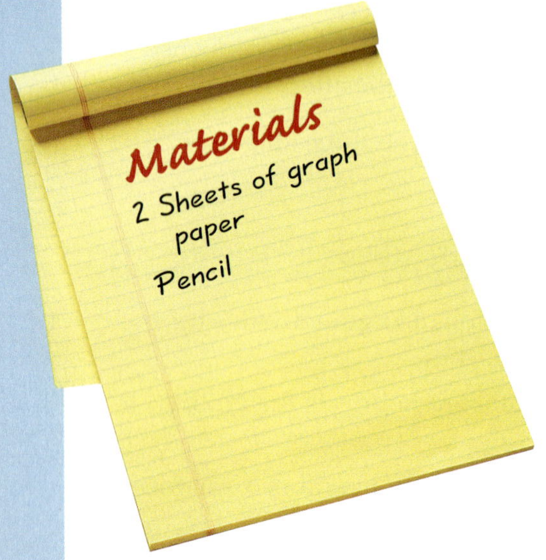

BACKGROUND

After fertilization takes place, an embryo forms from one cell, called the zygote. Eventually the embryo develops into a fetus. This process is very complex. During pregnancy, the fetus increases dramatically in size. It must also develop all of the organ systems it will need to survive on its own after birth.

PURPOSE

In this activity, you will use the information in a data table to create two bar graphs representing the stages of fetal development.

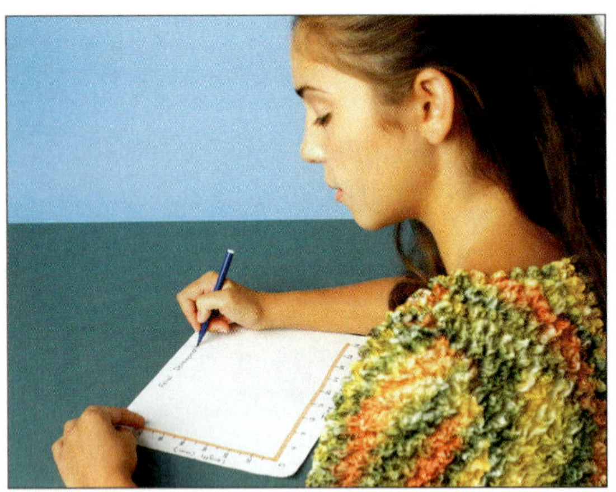

▲ **STEP 2** Create a bar graph.

PROCEDURE

1. Study the information in the data table shown in Figure 7-14.
2. Make a bar graph that shows how the length of a fetus changes as it develops.
3. Find the difference between the shortest and longest lengths in the data table. The difference is the total length that is to be represented on the vertical axis. Use this information to determine the length that one box on the axis represents.
4. Label each column along the horizontal axis with the time it represents.
5. Fill in the column above each time label with a bar whose top ends at the appropriate length line.
6. Repeat Steps 1 to 5 on a separate sheet of graph paper to make a second bar graph showing the increase in mass of a developing fetus.

Average Length and Mass During Fetal Development		
Time (weeks)	Length (millimeters)	Mass (grams)
4	2.5	1
6	9.0	2.5
8	30	5
10	61	14
12	87	45
14	120	110
16	140	200
18	160	320
20	190	460
22	210	630
24	230	820
26	250	1,000
28	270	1,300
30	280	1,700
32	300	2,100
34	335	2,700
36	340	2,900
38	360	3,400

▲ **Figure 7-14** Use this table of average length and mass to make your bar graph.

CONCLUSIONS

1. **OBSERVE:** How long is the embryo at the end of 8 weeks of development?
2. **OBSERVE:** Between which weeks does the developing fetus have the greatest increase in length?
3. **ANALYZE:** Does the length of a developing fetus increase in a set pattern? Explain.
4. **RELATE:** Is there a similar pattern between the increase in mass and the increase in length? Explain.

7-6 What are the stages of human development?

Objective

Identify the stages of the human life cycle.

Key Terms

adolescence: stage of development in which children experience rapid physical growth

menopause: time at which women stop ovulating

Life Cycle A developing fetus goes through a series of stages before birth. Some of these changes are listed in Figure 7-15. After birth, a human also goes through a series of stages. The stages of development are called a life cycle. There are five stages in the human life cycle. Certain events take place at each stage of development that make that stage unique.

FETAL DEVELOPMENT	
Time from Fertilization	**Major Developmental Changes**
1 week	Cluster of cells have implanted into the lining of the uterus.
4 weeks	Spinal cord and brain begin to form. Eyes and ears form. Limb buds appear.
8 weeks	Muscles and bones develop. Blood vessels move to permanent locations.
16 weeks	Face begins to look "human." The brain develops further.
32 weeks	Nervous system develops further. Fetus greatly increases in size.

▲ **Figure 7-15**

1 IDENTIFY: What is a life cycle?

Infancy The earliest stage of human life is called infancy. Infancy begins at birth and ends at age 2. Infants show several innate behaviors such as crying, sucking, and grasping. This stage of life is marked by a rapid increase in size. The muscles and nerves of the infant also develop quickly. Mental skills develop and the infant begins to interact with its surroundings. At about 7 months, infants can usually hold their heads up, roll over, or even crawl.

By age 1, most infants are able to walk and speak a few words. Between the ages of 1 and 2, children become much more aware of their surroundings. They become curious about their environment. They also learn that certain behaviors cause a reaction from their parents.

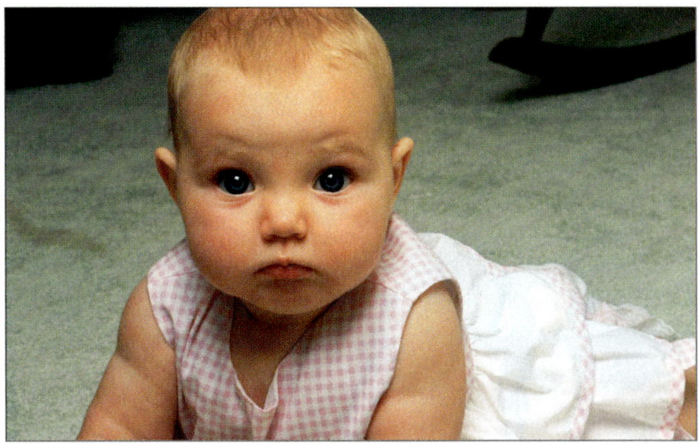

▲ **Figure 7-16** At about 7 months, infants are crawling and holding up their heads.

2 EXPLAIN: What are some of the developmental changes that take place during infancy?

Childhood Childhood usually is defined as the period between ages 2 and 12. During childhood, muscle development allows more complex activities. Children become more independent and are able to feed and dress themselves. Children also develop better coordination. This allows them to participate in activities such as sports or playing an instrument. Mental abilities also increase. Children become much better at expressing themselves verbally at this stage. Most children learn to read and write during this stage of development.

3 DESCRIBE: What are some of the changes a person goes through during childhood?

Adolescence Between the ages of 11 and 14, most young people go through a period of rapid physical change. This state is called **adolescence**. The beginning of adolescence is called puberty. During puberty, the reproductive organs develop. These organs release hormones that cause growth spurts. Adolescents grow taller and gain weight during this period. Males may experience a change in their voices. They may also develop a more muscular build and facial hair. Females usually develop breasts and larger hips during this stage. Adolescents of both sexes develop the ability to reproduce.

4 **EXPLAIN:** What causes rapid growth spurts during puberty?

Adulthood Adulthood is the stage at which the physical growth of the human body is complete. The growth process usually stops between the ages of 18 and 21. Muscle development and coordination reach their peak during early adulthood. Between the ages of 30 and 50, muscle tone and agility may decrease. As a result people in this stage may have to work harder to "stay in shape."

Women between the ages of 45 and 55 experience a developmental change called **menopause.** During this time, ovulation stops and menstruation occurs less often. Usually by age 55, menstruation stops completely.

5 **IDENTIFY:** What is menopause?

Later Years Later years, or the beginning of the aging process, occur at different times in different people. People who have exercised regularly and eaten a balanced diet all of their lives may not show signs of aging until their late 70s or early 80s.

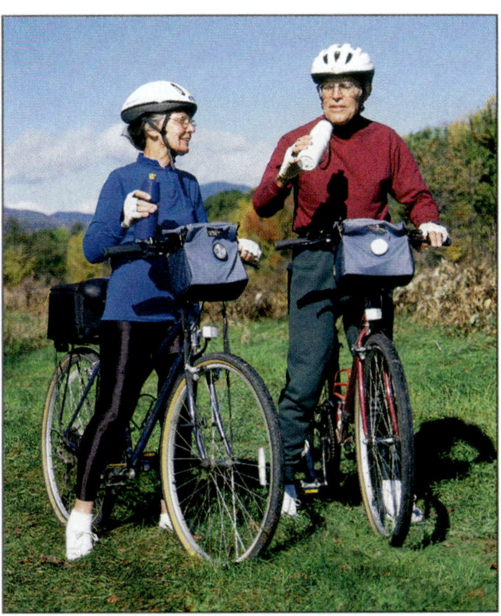

◀ **Figure 7-17** People who exercise may not show signs of aging until their late 70s.

The later years of a person's life are usually marked by a decline in muscle strength. People may move more slowly than before or may need help moving. Sense organs such as the eyes and ears may not work as well. The bones of older adults may become brittle and can break more easily. Despite these developmental changes, people are living longer today than ever before. This is probably due to a greater awareness of exercise and nutrition, and also to advances in medicine.

6 **DESCRIBE:** What effects do diet and exercise have on the aging process?

CHECKING CONCEPTS

1. The earliest stage of human development is called __________.
2. The period between ages 2 and 12 is generally called __________.
3. A person develops the ability to reproduce during the stage called __________.
4. The stage during which the physical growth of the human body is complete is __________.

THINKING CRITICALLY

5. **COMPARE:** Compare muscle development during infancy and the later years.
6. **RELATE:** At what stage is a person most likely to first put together a jigsaw puzzle?

Web InfoSearch

Speech Development Between the ages of 4 and 6 months, infants begin to babble or repeat sounds like "mamama" and "papapa." Infants from all over the world, even deaf infants, sound very much the same. Babbling infants even make sounds that are not part of their native languages.

SEARCH: Use the Internet to find out more about speech development in humans. Make a chart that describes the stages in language development. Start your search at www.conceptsandchallenges.com. Some key search words are **language development, speech development,** and **babbling.**

THE Big IDEA

How has technology improved life at various stages?

Americans are living longer, healthier lives. The average person born in 1900 lived about 47 years. A century later, the average lifespan is almost 77 years.

Medical technology helps improve health at every stage of life. Diagnostic tests, such as ultrasound, help monitor the progress of babies in the womb. Surgeons operate on babies in the first days of life. Vaccines have all but erased many fatal childhood diseases.

Drugs and devices help us prevent, detect, and fight disease. Many cancers can be treated if found early. Screening tests, such as mammograms, help find it. Many types of surgery now require only tiny slits in the skin. This reduces the risk of infection and speeds recovery.

About 35 million people are over age 65. By 2050, that figure will double to 70 million. Much research today is focused on staying healthy in old age. Imaging technology is helping scientists study brain activity. Eventually, they hope to develop drugs that will delay the onset of Alzheimer's disease.

Look at the boxes of text that appear on this page and the next. They point out ways in which technology improves health at every stage of life. Follow the directions in the Science Log to learn more about "the big idea." ✦

Prenatal Ultrasound

Ultrasound technology uses sound waves to create images. During pregnancy, it shows the size and position of the baby. Some doctors use ultrasound to diagnose a serious heart defect before birth. The defect requires three surgeries. The first operation occurs in the first week of life. A study found that babies diagnosed in the womb had a better chance of surviving the first surgery.

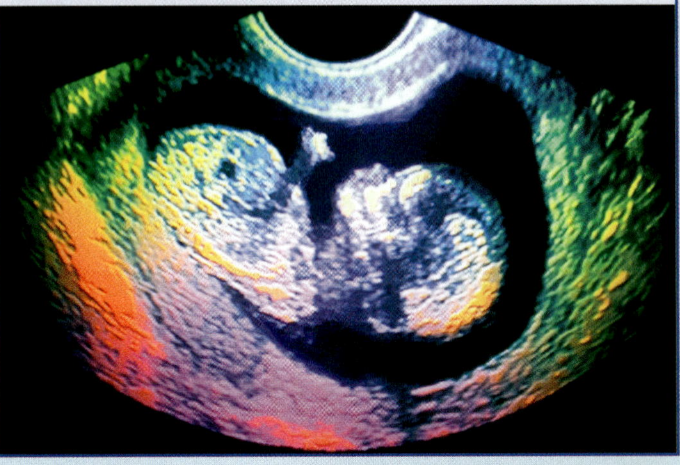

Childhood Vaccinations

Until vaccines were widely available, many children died from common childhood diseases. Others became blind, deaf, or brain damaged. After vaccines were developed, death rates from polio, measles, and whooping cough fell dramatically. Children today are vaccinated against 11 diseases.

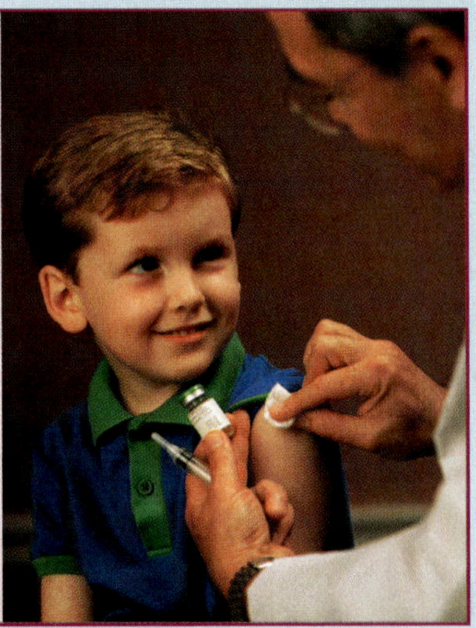

Laser Eye Surgery

Lasers have become an important tool in the field of eye surgery. Doctors can now dramatically improve a patient's vision using lasers, with few negative side effects. Lasers are used to reshape the cornea and focus images on the retina correctly. They can also be used to treat patients with cataracts, a disease of the eye common in middle-aged people.

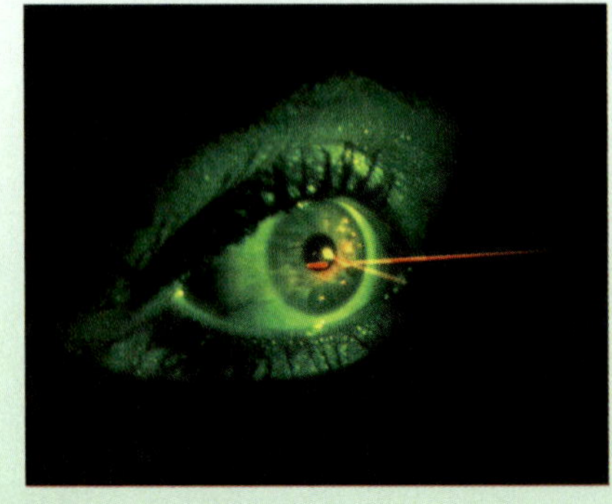

Infant Monitoring

Premature birth is the leading cause of infant death. Special hospital units that treat premature babies have saved many lives. These units are equipped with technology designed for the tiniest humans. They include special machines to monitor heart rate, breathing, and other body functions.

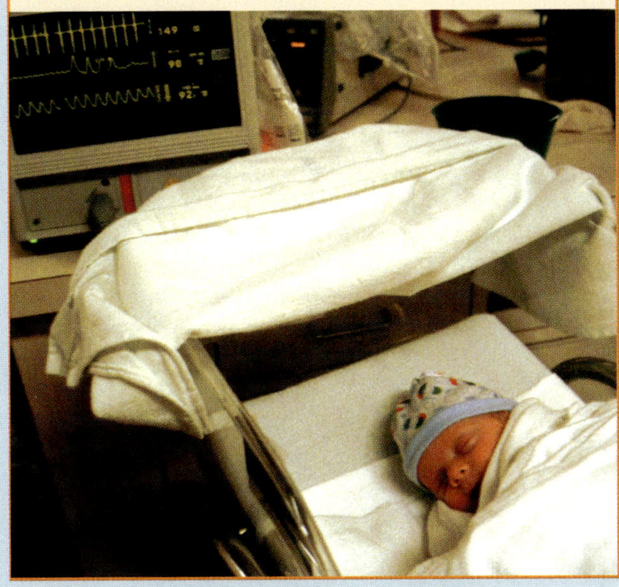

Safety Equipment

Injuries kill more adolescents than all diseases combined. The technologies most important for adolescent health are often not used in the doctor's office. They are things like seat belts and helmets. These are simple solutions that can save lives, but too often they don't. Why? Adolescents are far less likely than any other age group to wear seat belts, and many don't wear helmets during dangerous activities.

Hip Replacement Surgery

Problems with the hip joint are common occurrences for people over the age of 65. An artificial hip replaces the ball and socket joint that connects the leg bone to the hip bone. The new hips are made of materials that provide an easy, gliding motion. Researchers continue to develop better surgical techniques and new materials that will help increase the success rate of hip replacement surgery.

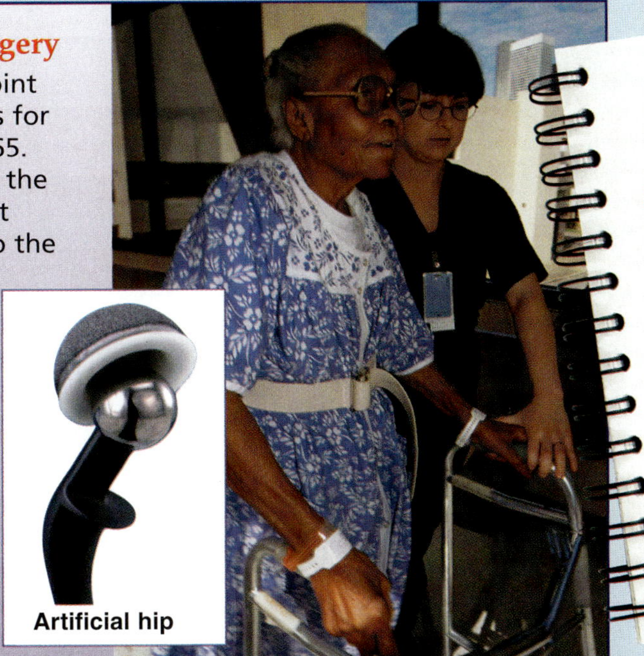

Artificial hip

WRITING ACTIVITY

Science Log

In your science log, research and write about one lifesaving technology. Describe why it is important at a particular stage of life. Start your search at www.conceptsandchallenges.com.

Chapter 7 Challenges

Chapter Summary

Lesson 7-1

- The **ovaries** of the female reproductive system produce hormones and eggs.
- An **embryo** develops inside the **uterus.** The **vagina** is the passageway through which a baby moves during birth.

Lesson 7-2

- The **testes** are the organs of the male reproductive system that produce hormones and sperm.
- In males, both urine and sperm leave the body through the **urethra.**

Lesson 7-3

- **Puberty** is the time when a person becomes sexually mature. The **menstrual cycle** is a series of changes in the female reproductive system that occurs about once a month.
- During **ovulation,** a mature egg leaves an ovary and travels to the **oviduct.**
- The process by which blood and tissue leave the uterus is called **menstruation.**

Lesson 7-4

- **Fertilization** occurs when a sperm cell and an egg cell meet. The new cell produced by fertilization is called a **zygote.**

Lesson 7-5

- An embryo is a hollow ball of cells attached to a wall of the uterus.
- An embryo receives nourishment and rids itself of wastes through the **placenta.** The **umbilical cord** connects an embryo to the placenta. The **amnion** cushions and protects the developing embryo.
- Birth takes place in three stages—labor, delivery, and afterbirth. Birth usually occurs after nine months of development.

Lesson 7-6

- The stages of development in humans are called the human life cycle.
- During **adolescence,** a person goes through a period of rapid physical change.
- Adulthood is the stage at which the physical growth of the body is complete.

Key Term Challenges

adolescence (p. 168)
amnion (p. 164)
cervix (p. 156)
embryo (p. 164)
epididymis (p. 158)
estrogen (p. 156)
fertilization (p. 162)
fetus (p. 164)
gamete (p. 162)
menopause (p. 168)
menstrual cycle (p. 160)
menstruation (p. 160)
ovary (p. 156)
oviduct (p. 156)
ovulation (p. 160)
placenta (p. 164)
progesterone (p. 156)
puberty (p.160)
scrotum (p. 158)
testis (p. 158)
testosterone (p. 158)
umbilical cord (p. 164)
urethra (p. 158)
uterus (p. 156)
vagina (p. 156)
zygote (p. 162)

MATCHING Write the Key Term from above that best matches each description.

1. hollow organ in which an embryo develops
2. process by which blood and tissue from the uterine lining breaks apart and leaves the body
3. clear, fluid-filled sac that protects the developing embryo
4. developing human organism up until eight weeks of pregnancy
5. organ of the male reproductive system that produces hormones and sperm
6. long tube between an ovary and the uterus

FILL IN Write the Key Term from above that best completes each statement.

7. The organs of the female reproductive system that produce eggs are the ___________.
8. Sperm is carried to the outside of the body through the ___________.
9. The release of a mature egg from the ovary is called ___________.
10. The hormone that controls the development of male characteristics is ___________.
11. The ___________ often is called the birth canal.
12. The ___________ connects the uterus to the vagina.

Content Challenges TEST PREP

MULTIPLE CHOICE **Write the letter of the term or phrase that best completes each statement.**

1. In females, puberty begins with the start of
   - **a.** diffusion.
   - **b.** fertilization.
   - **c.** menstruation.
   - **d.** pregnancy.
2. Muscular strength begins to decrease during
   - **a.** infancy.
   - **b.** adolescence.
   - **c.** adulthood.
   - **d.** old age.
3. The release of an egg is called
   - **a.** fertilization.
   - **b.** ovulation.
   - **c.** menstruation.
   - **d.** pregnancy.
4. The structure through which the developing fetus receives nourishment is the
   - **a.** amnion.
   - **b.** uterus.
   - **c.** birth canal.
   - **d.** placenta.
5. Fertilization in humans takes place in the
   - **a.** vagina.
   - **b.** uterus.
   - **c.** ovary.
   - **d.** oviduct.
6. Sperm and testosterone are produced in the
   - **a.** ovaries.
   - **b.** scrotum.
   - **c.** testes.
   - **d.** urethra.
7. The ovaries produce all of the following except
   - **a.** eggs.
   - **b.** progesterone.
   - **c.** estrogen.
   - **d.** testosterone.
8. The most rapid physical changes take place in humans during
   - **a.** childhood.
   - **b.** adolescence.
   - **c.** adulthood.
   - **d.** old age.
9. The narrow end of the uterus is called the
   - **a.** vagina.
   - **b.** cervix.
   - **c.** oviduct.
   - **d.** ovary.

TRUE/FALSE **Write *true* if the statement is true. If the statement is false, change the underlined term to make the statement true.**

10. Once bones form in the skeleton, the embryo is called a <u>fetus</u>.
11. The <u>urethra</u> carries waste between the embryo and the placenta.
12. The process by which blood and tissue leave the uterus is called <u>fertilization</u>.
13. The growth process in humans ends at <u>adolescence</u>.
14. <u>Eggs</u> are female sex cells.
15. An egg can be fertilized by <u>many</u> sperm.
16. The clear fluid-filled sac surrounding the embryo is called the <u>placenta</u>.
17. A <u>zygote</u> undergoes cell division until a hollow ball of cells forms.
18. People develop the ability to reproduce during <u>adulthood</u>.

Concept Challenges TEST PREP

WRITTEN RESPONSE Answer each of the following questions in complete sentences.

1. **COMPARE:** How are the functions of the testes and ovaries similar?
2. **INFER:** Why do you think it is important for a pregnant woman to avoid alcohol, tobacco, and drugs?
3. **IDENTIFY:** How do you think you can slow down the effects of aging?
4. **HYPOTHESIZE:** What would happen if the placenta became detached from the fetus?
5. **INFER:** Why do you think the regular monthly changes in females is called a cycle?

INTERPRETING A DIAGRAM Use Figure 7-18 to answer the following questions.

6. **IDENTIFY:** What organ is represented by letter *A*?
7. **NAME:** Which event is taking place at letter *B*?
8. **IDENTIFY:** What structure is represented by the letter *D*?
9. **IDENTIFY:** Which letter represents the point at which the zygote becomes an embryo?
10. **EXPLAIN:** What is the role of the organ labeled *F* in the female reproductive system?

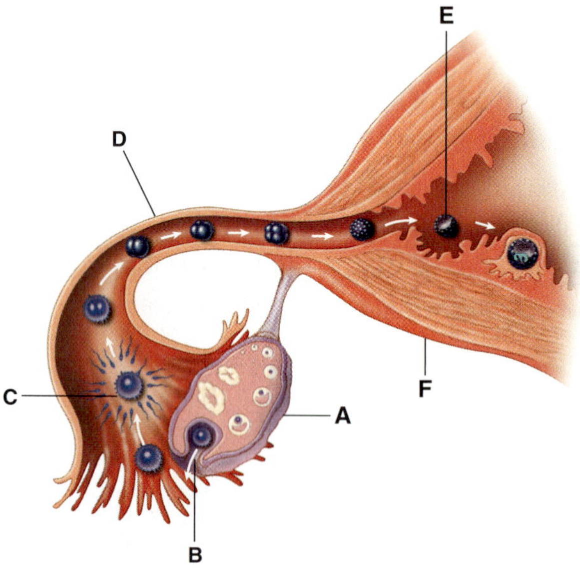

▲ Figure 7-18

Appendix A Metric System

The Metric System and SI Units

The metric system is an international system of measurement based on units of ten. More than 90% of the nations of the world use the metric system. In the United States, both the English system and the metric system are used.

The *Système International*, or SI, has been used as the international measurement system since 1960. The SI is a modernized version of the metric system. Like the metric system, the SI is a decimal system based on units of ten. When you want to change from one unit in the metric system to another unit, you multiply or divide by a multiple of ten.

- When you change from a smaller unit to a larger unit, you divide.
- When you change from a larger unit to a smaller unit, you multiply.

METRIC UNITS		
LENGTH	SYMBOL	RELATIONSHIP
kilometer	km	1 km = 1,000 m
meter	m	1 m = 100 cm
centimeter	cm	1 cm = 10 mm
millimeter	mm	1 mm = 0.1 cm
AREA	SYMBOL	
square kilometer	km^2	1 km^2 = 1,000,000 m^2
square meter	m^2	1 m^2 = 1,000,000 mm^2
square centimeter	cm^2	1 cm^2 = 0.0001 m^2
square millimeter	mm^2	1 mm^2 = 0.000001 m^2
VOLUME	SYMBOL	
cubic meter	m^3	1 m^3 = 1,000,000 cm^3
cubic centimeter	cm^3	1 cm^3 = 0.000001 m^3
liter	L	1 L = 1,000 mL
milliliter	mL	1 mL = 0.001 L
MASS	SYMBOL	
metric ton	t	1 t = 1,000 kg
kilogram	kg	1 kg = 1,000 g
gram	g	1 g = 1,000 mg
centigram	cg	1 cg = 10 mg
milligram	mg	1 mg = 0.001 g
TEMPERATURE	SYMBOL	
Kelvin	K	
degree Celsius	°C	

▲ Figure 1

COMMON METRIC PREFIXES			
micro-	0.000001 or 1/1,000,000	deka-	10
milli-	0.001 or 1/1,000	hecto-	100
centi-	0.01 or 1/100	kilo-	1,000
deci-	0.1 or 1/10	mega-	1,000,000

▲ Figure 2

METRIC-STANDARD EQUIVALENTS	
SI to English	English to SI
LENGTH	
1 kilometer = 0.621 mile (mi)	1 mi = 1.61 km
1 meter = 1.094 yards (yd)	1 yd = 0.914 m
1 meter = 3.28 feet (ft)	1 ft = 0.305 m
1 centimeter = 0.394 inch (in.)	1 in. = 2.54 cm
1 millimeter = 0.039 inch	1 in. = 25.4 mm
AREA	
1 square kilometer = 0.3861 square mile	1 mi^2 = 2.590 km^2
1 square meter = 1.1960 square yards	1 yd^2 = 0.8361 m^2
1 square meter = 10.763 square feet	1 ft^2 = 0.0929 m^2
1 square centimeter = 0.155 square inch	1 $in.^2$ = 6.452 cm^2
VOLUME	
1 cubic meter = 1.3080 cubic yards	1 yd^3 = 0.7646 m^3
1 cubic meter = 35.315 cubic feet	1 ft^3 = 0.0283 m^3
1 cubic centimeter = 0.0610 cubic inch	1 $in.^3$ = 16.39 cm^3
1 liter = 0.2642 gallon (gal)	1 gal = 3.79 L
1 liter = 1.06 quarts (qt)	1 qt = 0.946 L
1 liter = 2.11 pints (pt)	1 pt = 0.47 L
1 milliliter = 0.034 fluid ounce (fl oz)	1 fl oz = 29.57 mL
MASS	
1 metric ton = 0.984 ton	1 ton = 1.016 t
1 kilogram = 2.205 pounds (lb)	1 lb = 0.4536 kg
1 gram = 0.0353 ounce (oz)	1 oz = 28.35 g
TEMPERATURE	
Celsius = 5/9(°F – 32)	Fahrenheit = 9/5°C + 32
0°C = 32°F (Freezing point of water)	72°F = 22°C (Room temperature)
100°C = 212°F (Boiling point of water)	98.6°F = 37°C (Human body temperature)
Kelvin = (°F + 459.67)/1.8	Fahrenheit = (K × 1.8) – 459.67

▲ Figure 3

Appendix B Science Terms

Analyzing Science Terms

You can often unlock the meaning of an unfamiliar science term by analyzing its word parts. Prefixes and suffixes, for example, each carry a meaning that comes from a word root. This word root usually comes from the Latin or Greek language. The following list of prefixes and suffixes provides clues to the meaning of many science terms.

WORD PART	MEANING	EXAMPLE
a-	not, without	abiotic
aero-	air	aerobic
anti-	against	antibodies
bi-	two	biceps, binary fission
bio-	life	biotechnology, biology
carn-	meat, flesh	carnivore
chemo-	of, with, or by chemicals	chemosynthesis
chlor-	green	chloroplasts
cyt-	cell	cytoplasm
-derm	skin, covering	echinoderm, dermatology
di-	twice, double	dicot, disaccharide
eco-	environment, habitat	ecosystem, ecology
ecto-	outer	ectoderm, ectotherm
endo-	inside	endospore, endoskeleton
epi-	on, on the outside	epidermis, epiphyte
exo-	outside	exocrine, exoskeleton
-gen	produce, generate	pathogen, antigen
geo-	earth	geologic, geographic
hemo-	blood	hemoglobin
hydro-	water	hydroponics, hydrophilic
-itis	disease of	appendicitis, dermititis
leuko-	white	leukocyte
-logy	study of, science of	biology, zoology
mono-	one	monocot, monosaccharide
-ose	carbohydrate	glucose, cellulose
photo-	light	photosynthesis, phototropism
-phyll	leaf	mesophyll
-phyte	a plant	bryophyte, anthophyte
-scope	instrument for viewing	microscope
syn-	to put together, with	synthetic, photosynthesis
thigmo-	touch	thigmotropism
trans-	across	transpiration
trop-	turn, respond to	tropism
uni-	one	unicellular

▲ Figure 4

Glossary

Pronunciation and syllabication have been derived from *Webster's New World Dictionary*, Second College Edition, Revised School Printing (Prentice Hall, 1985). Syllables printed in capital letters are given primary stress. (Numbers in parentheses indicate the page number, or page numbers, on which the term is defined.)

PRONUNCIATION KEY					
Symbol	**Example**	**Respelling**	**Symbol**	**Example**	**Respelling**
a	transpiration	(tran-spuh-RAY-shuhn)	oh	biome	(BY-ohm)
ah	composite	(kuhm-PAHZ-iht)	oi	asteroid	(AS-tuhr-oid)
aw	atoll	(A-tawl)	oo	altitude	(AL-tuh-tood)
ay	abrasion	(uh-BRAY-zhuhn)	ow	compound	(KAHM-pownd)
ch	leaching	(LEECH-ing)	s	satellite	(SAT-uhl-yt)
eh	chemical	(KEHM-i-kuhl)	sh	specialization	(spehsh-uhl-ih-ZAY-shuhn)
ee	equinox	(EE-kwih-nahks)	th	thermocline	(THUR-muh-klyn)
f	hemisphere	(HEHM-ih-sfeer)	th	weathering	(WEHTH-uhr-ing)
g	galaxy	(GAL-uhk-see)	uh	volcanism	(VAHL-kuh-nihzm)
ih	anticline	(AN-tih-klyn)	y, eye	anticline, isobar	(AN-tih-klyn), (EYE-soh-bahr)
j	geologic	(jee-uh-LAHJ-ihk)	yoo	cumulus	(KYOOM-yuh-luhs)
k	current	(KUR-uhnt)	z	deposition	(dehp-uh-ZIHSH-uhn)
ks	axis	(AK-sihs)	zh	erosion	(e-ROH-zhuhn)

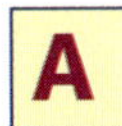

absorption (ab-SAWRP-shuhn)**:** movement of food molecules from the digestive system to the blood (p. 56)

addiction (uh-DIHK-shuhn)**:** uncontrollable dependence on a drug (p. 148)

adolescence: stage of development in which children experience rapid physical growth (p. 168)

AIDS: viral disease that attacks a person's immune system (p. 118)

alcoholic (al-kuh-HAWL-ihk)**:** person who is dependent on alcohol (p. 150)

alveolus (al-VEE-uh-luhs), *pl.* **alveoli:** microscopic air sac in the lungs (p. 86)

amino acid: building block of proteins (p. 40)

amnion (AM-nee-uhn)**:** fluid-filled sac that surrounds an embryo (p. 164)

antibiotic (an-tih-by-AHT-ihk)**:** chemical made by a living organism that kills bacteria (p. 114)

antibody (AN-tih-bahd-ee)**:** molecule the body makes to protect itself from disease (p. 110)

antigen: signal molecule that produces an immune response (p. 110)

aorta (ay-AWR-tuh)**:** largest artery in the body (p. 70)

artery (AHRT-uhr-ee)**:** blood vessel that carries blood away from the heart (p. 70)

atherosclerosis (ath-uhr-oh-skluh-ROH-sis)**:** buildup of fat deposits on artery walls (p. 78)

atrium (AY-tree-uhm), *pl.* **atria:** upper chamber of the heart (p. 68)

axon: fiber that carries messages away from a nerve cell body (p. 128)

B cell: special white blood cell that produces antibodies (p. 112)

benign (bih-NYN) **tumor:** mass of cells that is usually harmless (p. 120)

bile: green liquid that breaks down large droplets of fat into smaller droplets of fat (p. 56)

bladder: excretory organ that stores liquid wastes (p. 98)

brainstem: bundle of nerves at the base of the brain (p. 130)

bronchus (BRAHN-kuhs)**:** tube leading to the lungs (p. 86)

Calorie (KAL-uh-ree)**:** unit used to measure energy from foods (p. 60)

capillary (KAP-uh-ler-ee)**:** tiny blood vessel that connects arteries to veins (p. 70)

carbohydrate (kahr-boh-HY-drayt)**:** nutrient that supplies energy (p. 38)

cardiac (KAHR-dee-ak) **muscle:** type of muscle found only in the heart and major blood vessels (p. 30)

cartilage (KAHRT-uhl-ihj)**:** tough, flexible connective tissue (p. 20)

cerebellum (ser-uh-BEHL-uhm)**:** part of the brain that controls balance and body motion (p. 130)

cerebrum (suh-REE-bruhm)**:** part of the brain that controls the senses and thinking (p. 130)

cervix (SUR-vihks)**:** narrow end of the uterus (p. 156)

chemical digestion: process by which large food molecules are broken down into smaller food molecules (p. 52)

chyme (KYM)**:** thick liquid form in which food leaves the stomach (p. 54)

cilia (SIHL-ee-uh)**:** tiny, hairlike structures (p. 92)

circulation (sur-kyoo-LAY-shuhn)**:** movement of blood through the body (p. 66)

cirrhosis (suh-ROH-sihs)**:** liver disorder that can be caused by the excessive use of alcohol (p. 150)

closed circulatory system: organ system in which blood moves through vessels (p. 66)

cochlea (KAHK-lee-uh)**:** part of the ear that changes vibrations into nerve signals (p. 140)

communication: sharing information (p. 8)

compact bone: mostly solid, dense part of a bone (p. 22)

connective tissue: tissue that holds parts of the body together (p. 16)

constant: something that does not change (p. 11)

contagious: can be spread from one person to another (p. 114)

controlled experiment: experiment in which all the conditions except one are kept constant (p. 11)

cornea (KAWR-nee-uh)**:** clear covering at the front of the eye (p. 138)

coronary (KAWR-uh-ner-ee) **artery:** artery that carries blood and oxygen to the tissues of the heart (p. 78)

data: information you collect when you observe something (p. 3)

deficiency (dee-FIHSH-uhn-see) **disease:** disease caused by the lack of a certain nutrient (p. 42)

dendrite (DEHN-dryt)**:** fiber that carries messages to the nerve cell body (p. 128)

dentin: spongy substance below the enamel of the tooth (p. 52)

depressant (dee-PREHS-uhnt)**:** drug that slows down the central nervous system (p. 148)

dermis: inner layer of skin (p. 102)

diaphragm (DY-uh-fram)**:** sheet of muscle below the lungs (p. 88)

digestion (dih-JEHS-chuhn)**:** process of breaking down food so that it can be used by living things (p. 50)

drug: a chemical substance that causes a change in the body (p. 148)

eardrum: sheet of tissue that vibrates when sounds strike it (p. 140)

embryo (EHM-bree-oh)**:** developing human organism up until eight weeks of pregnancy (p. 164)

emulsification (ee-mul-suh-fih-KAY-shuhn)**:** process of breaking down large droplets of fat into smaller droplets of fat (p. 56)

enamel: hard, outer covering of a tooth (p. 52)

endocrine (EHN-doh-krihn) **gland:** gland that does not have ducts (p. 142)

endocrine (EHN-doh-krihn) **system:** organ system that includes all the glands of the body (p. 18)

enzyme (EHN-zym)**:** protein that controls chemical reactions in the body (p. 52)

epidermis (ehp-uh-DUR-mihs)**:** outer layer of skin (p. 102)

epididymis (ehp-uh-DID-ih-mihs)**:** coiled tube that stores sperm (p. 158)

epiglottis (ehp-uh-GLAHT-ihs): flap of tissue that prevents food from entering the windpipe (p. 50)

epithelial (ehp-ih-THEE-lee-uhl) **tissue:** tissue that covers and protects parts of the body (p. 16)

esophagus (ih-SAHF-uh-guhs): tube that connects the mouth to the stomach (p. 50)

estrogen: hormone that helps regulate the menstrual cycle (p. 156)

evaporation (ee-vap-uh-RAY-shuhn): changing of a liquid to a gas (p. 102)

excretion (ehks-KREE-shuhn): process of removing waste products from the body (p. 98)

exhale: to breathe out (p. 88)

exocrine (ehks-oh-krihn) **gland:** gland that has ducts (p. 142)

extensor (ehk-STEHN-suhr): muscle that straightens a joint (p. 26)

fertilization (fuhrt-uhl-ih-ZAY-shuhn): joining of one sperm cell and one egg cell (p. 162)

fetus (FEET-uhs): term used to describe an embryo eight weeks after fertilization (p. 164)

flexor (FLEHKS-uhr): muscle that bends a joint (p. 26)

fracture: crack or break in a bone (p. 22)

gamete (GAM-eet): reproductive cell (p. 162)

gastric juice: juice produced in the stomach that contains mucus, pepsin, and hydrochloric acid (p. 54)

gland: organ or group of cells that produces and secretes substances used by the body (pp. 18, 142)

gram: basic unit of mass (p. 4)

hallucinogen (huh-LOO-sih-nuh-juhn): drug that causes a person to see, hear, smell, and taste things in an altered way (p. 148)

heart attack: failure of a part of the heart due to a lack of blood and oxygen (p. 78)

hemoglobin (HEE-muh-gloh-bihn): protein found in red blood cells that carries oxygen (p. 72)

hormone (HAWR-mohn): chemical substance that regulates body functions (pp. 66, 144)

hypothalamus (hy-poh-THAL-uh-muhs): part of the brain that tells the pituitary gland to release certain chemicals (p. 142)

hypothesis: suggested answer to a question or problem (p. 10)

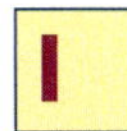

immunity (ih-MYOON-uh-tee): resistance to a specific disease (p. 112)

inhalant: everyday product that is inhaled and used as a drug (p. 148)

inhale: to breathe in (p. 88)

iris (EYE-ris): colored part of the eye that controls the amount of light entering the eye (p. 138)

joint: place where two or more bones meet (p. 24)

kidney: excretory organ that removes waste products from the blood (p. 98)

larynx (LAR-inks): organ located on the top of the trachea that contains the vocal cords (p. 86)

lens (LENZ): part of the eye that focuses an image on the retina (p. 138)

ligament (LIHG-uh-muhnt): type of tissue that connects bones (p. 16)

lipase (LY-pays): enzyme that digests fats and oils (p. 56)

liter: basic unit of liquid volume (p. 4)

malignant (muh-LIHG-nuhnt) **tumor:** harmful mass of cells that can spread throughout the body (p. 120)

malnutrition (mal-noo-TRIHSH-uhn): poor nutrition caused by an unbalanced diet (p. 48)

marrow: soft tissue inside bones that produces blood cells (p. 22)

mass: amount of matter in something (p. 4)

mechanical digestion: process by which large pieces of food are cut and crushed into smaller pieces (p. 52)

medulla (mih-DUL-uh): part of the brain that controls heartbeat and breathing rate (p. 130)

meniscus: curve at the surface of a liquid in a thin tube (p. 4)

menopause: time at which women stop ovulating (p. 168)

menstrual (MEHN-struhl) **cycle:** monthly cycle of change that occurs in the female reproductive system (p. 160)

menstruation (mehn-stroo-AY-shuhn): process by which blood and tissue from the lining of the uterus break apart and leave the body (p. 160)

meter: basic unit of length or distance (p. 4)

mineral: nutrient needed by the body to develop and function properly (p. 44)

model: tool scientists use to represent an object or process (p. 3)

molecule (MAHL-ih-kyool): smallest part of a substance that has all the properties of that substance (p. 40)

mucus (MYOO-kuhs): sticky liquid (p. 92)

nephron (NEHF-rahn): filtering structure of the kidneys (p. 100)

neuron (NOOR-ahn): nerve cell (p. 128)

nicotine (NIHK-uh-teen): stimulant found in tobacco (p. 96)

nutrient (NOO-tree-uhnt): chemical substance that is needed to carry out life processes (p. 38)

organ (AWR-guhn): group of tissues that work together to do a special job (p. 18)

organ system: group of organs that work together (p. 18)

ovary (OH-vuh-ree): organ of the female reproductive system that produces hormones and eggs (p. 156)

oviduct (OH-vih-dukt): long tube between the ovary and the uterus (p. 156)

ovulation (ahv-yuh-LAY-shuhn): release of a mature egg from the ovary (p. 160)

pathogen: any agent that causes disease (p. 110)

pepsin (PEHP-sihn): enzyme that digests proteins (p. 54)

periosteum (per-ee-AHS-tee-uhm): thin membrane that covers a bone (p. 22)

peristalsis (per-uh-STAL-sihs): wavelike movement that moves food through the digestive tract (p. 50)

perspiration (pur-spuh-RAY-shuhn): waste water and salts that leave the body through the skin (p. 102)

pharynx (FAR-inks): tube connecting the mouth to the esophagus (p. 50)

placenta (pluh-SEHN-tuh): organ through which an embryo receives nourishment and gets rid of wastes (p. 164)

plasma (PLAZ-muh): liquid part of blood (p. 72)

platelet (PLAYT-liht): piece of a cell that is involved in blood clotting (p. 72)

pore: tiny opening in the skin (p. 102)

progesterone: hormone that prepares the uterus for pregnancy (p. 156)

protein (PROH-teen): nutrient needed to build and repair cells (p. 38)

puberty (PYOO-burh-tee): time at which a person becomes sexually mature (p. 160)

pulmonary (PUL-muh-ner-ee) **artery:** artery that carries blood from the heart to the lungs (p. 76)

pupil (PYOO-puhl): opening in the center of the iris (p. 138)

receptor: part of a nerve cell that receives stimuli from the environment (p. 132)

reflex: automatic response to a stimulus (p. 132)

reflex arc: path of a message in a reflex (p. 132)

relative age: age of something compared with the age of something else (p. 94)

respiration (rehs-puh-RAY-shuhn): process of carrying oxygen to cells, getting rid of carbon dioxide, and releasing energy (p. 88)

retina (REHT-uhn-uh): part of the eye that receives images from the lens and transmits them to the brain (p. 138)

saliva: liquid in the mouth that helps in digestion (p. 50)

scrotum (SKROHT-uhm): pocket of skin that protects and holds the testes (p. 158)

sense organ: special organ that receives and processes stimuli from the environment (p. 134)

septum: thick tissue wall that separates the left and right sides of the heart (p. 68)

simulation: computer model that usually shows a process (p. 3)

skeletal muscle: muscle attached to the skeleton that makes movement possible (p. 30)

skeletal system: system of bones and cartilage that helps to support and protect the body (p. 20)

smooth muscle: muscle that causes movements (p. 20)

spongy bone: part of a bone with many small pores or spaces (p. 22)

stimulant (STIHM-yuh-luhnt): drug that speeds up the central nervous system (p. 148)

striated (STRY-ayt-uhd) **muscle:** muscle tissue with stripes or dark bands (p. 30)

synapse (SIHN-aps): gap between the axon of one cell and the dendrite of another (p. 128)

target cell: cell that responds to a hormone's chemical structure (p. 144)

T cell: special type of white blood cell that attacks antigens (p. 112)

temperature: measurement of the amount of heat energy something contains (p. 4)

tendon (TEHN-duhn): type of tissue that connects muscle to bone (p. 16)

testis (TEHS-tihs), *pl.* **testes:** organs of the male reproductive system that produce hormones and sperm (p. 158)

testosterone (tes-TAHS-tuhr-ohn): hormone produced in the testes (p. 158)

theory: set of hypotheses that have been supported by testing over and over again (p. 10)

tissue: group of cells that look alike and work together (p. 16)

trachea (TRAY-kee-uh): windpipe (p. 86)

transfusion: transfer of blood from one person into the body of another person (p. 72)

tumor (TOO-muhr): mass or lump of cells (p. 120)

umbilical (uhm-BIHL-ih-kuhl) **cord:** structure that connects the embryo to the placenta (p. 164)

unit: amount used to measure something (p. 4)

urea (yoo-REE-uh): nitrogen compound formed as a waste product (p. 100)

ureter (yoo-REET-uhr): tube that carries liquid waste from the kidneys to the bladder (p. 98)

urethra (yoo-REE-thruh): tube that carries urine and sperm to the outside of the male's body (p. 158)

urine (YOOR-ihn): liquid waste formed in the kidneys (p. 100)

uterus (YOOT-uh-ruhs): organ in which an embryo develops (p. 156)

vagina (vuh-JY-nuh): birth canal (p. 156)

valve: thin flap of tissue that acts like a one-way door (p. 68)

variable: anything that can affect the outcome of an experiment (p. 11)

vein (VAYN): blood vessel that carries blood back to the heart (p. 70)

ventricle (VEHN-trih-kuhl): lower chamber of the heart (p. 68)

vertebra, *pl.* **vertebrae:** bone that makes up the backbone (p. 20)

villus, *pl.* **villi:** fingerlike projection on the lining of the small intestine (p. 56)

vitamin (VYT-uh-mihn): nutrient found in foods that is required by the body and is made by other organisms (p. 42)

volume: amount of space an object takes up (p. 4)

white blood cell: blood cell that protects the body against disease (p. 110)

zygote (ZY-goht): fertilized egg (p. 162)

Index

A

absorption, in small intestine, 56, 57
acetone, 96
acquired immunity, 112
acquired immunodeficiency syndrome (AIDS), 118, 123, 159. *See also* human immunodeficiency virus (HIV), transmission of, 118–119
treatment for, 119
ACTH, 144
active acquired immunity, 112
active transport, 58
addiction, 96, 148
adolescence, 168–169
adrenal gland, 143–144
adrenaline, 143–144
adulthood, 169
aerobic activities, 27
afterbirth, 165
AIDS (*See also* acquired immunodeficiency syndrome)
air pollution, 93
air sacs, 86
AL-ATEEN, 151
alcohol
effect on body, 150–151
ethyl, 150
alcoholic, 150, 151
Alcoholics Anonymous (AA), 151
alcoholism, 151
allergic reactions to penicillin, 115
alveoli, 86–87, 94, 96
Alzheimer's disease, 120, 170
amino acids, 40–41, 58
amnion, 164–165
amoeba, 111
amphetamines, 149
amplitude of vibration, 141
anabolic steroids, 27
anemia, 42, 44
angioplasty, 80
animals
hearing in, 141
sound and, 141
warm-blooded, 66
anorexia, 49
antacids, 148
antibiotics, 148, 159
discovery of, 114–115
antibodies, 110–113
antigens, 110, 111, 112
antiseptics, effectiveness of, 116–117
anus, 99
aorta, 70, 76
appendicitis, 57
appendix, 57
argon, 94
arsenic, 96
arteries, 49, 66, 70, 76, 143
arteriogram, 81
arthritis, 25
arthroscope, 32–33
artificial blood, 73
artificial hearts, 67, 80–81
artistic expression, responding to, 146–147
asbestos, 93
asthma, 87–93
astigmatism, 139
atherosclerosis, 78
atrium, 68, 76–77
autism, 31
axon, 128–129

B

backbone, 20
bacteria, 72, 104, 110–111, 113–115, 116, 159
bacterial diseases, spread of, 114
balance, maintaining, 130
balanced diet, 48–49, 169
ball-and-socket joints, 24
Banting, Frederick, 145
barbiturates, 148
Barnard, Christiaan, 123
B cells, 111–112
Beaumont, William, 55
benign tumors, 120
beriberi, 42
Best, Charles, 145
bicarbonate, 58
biceps, 26, 28
bicuspids, 52
bile, 56, 58
biochemists, 43
biomedical engineering, 101
bionics, treating spinal injuries with, 133
birth, 165, 168
defects, 42
premature, 171
bladder, 98, 159
blood, 16, 66, 72–75, 100
artificial, 73
cells, 20, 44, 74–75, 94, 112
circulation of, 76–77
clotting, 42–43, 143
elements in, 77
flow of, 68
flow of, in heart, 68
blood alcohol concentration (BAC), 150–151
blood plasma, 94
blood pressure, high, 71
bloodstream, 58, 60, 111, 144
blood transfusions, 67, 73
blood types, 73
blood vessels, 18, 66, 70–71, 78, 94
Blum, Mark, 79
bone marrow transplants, 23
bones, 16, 20, 22, 24, 25, 28, 42, 97, 168
compact, 22
formation of, 21
spongy, 22
structure and function of, 20, 22
Bowman's capsule, 100
brachial artery, 77
Braille, Louis, 135
Braille system, 135
brain, 127, 128, 130, 132, 140, 149, 164, 168
diagnosing tumors of, 131
effect of alcohol on, 150
injury of, 131
parts of, 130–131
research on, 146
brainstem, 130–131
breastbone, 68
breathalyzers, 151
breathing, 85, 88, 131, 148
comparing, 88
modeling, 90–91
rapid, 105, 143, 148
breathing machines, 87
bronchus, 86
bronchial artery, 77
bulimia, 49
byproducts, 41, 60, 98

C

caffeine, 148
calcium, 20, 22, 44–45
calcium carbonate, 45
calories, 48, 60
cancer, 96, 109, 123, 157
causes of, 120
lung, 97, 120
preventing, 121
skin, 121
canines, 52
capillaries, 66, 70–71, 76, 77, 94, 100, 103
carbohydrates, 38, 42, 46, 58, 60
carbon, 40–41
carbon dioxide, 60, 66, 88, 98, 105
in circulation, 76
in respiratory system, 86, 94–95, 96
carbon monoxide, 96
cardiac muscle, 30
cardiologist, 79
cardiovascular disease, technology in treating, 80–81
careers
biochemists, 43
biomedical engineers, 101
cardiologist, 79
dental hygienist, 53
doctors, 19, 32, 69
nutritionists, 45
physical therapists, 31
respiratory therapist, 87
surgeons, 69
carotid artery, 77
cartilage, 20–21, 25, 86
catheter, 81
cavities, 53
cells, 65, 98
B, 112
blood, 20, 74–77, 94
egg, 160, 162
membranes, 194
nerve, 128–129, 132
red blood cells, 74, 77, 94
sperm, 162
stem, 121
T, 111–112, 119
target, 144
cellular respiration, 60, 85, 88
byproducts of, 98
waste products of, 60
central nervous system, 127, 148
centrifuge, 72
cerebellum, 130
cerebrum, 130–131
cervix, 156, 157
chemical digestion, 52–53, 54, 56, 58
chemical reaction, 58
chemistry, 58
chickenpox, 112, 118, 126
childhood, 168
chlorine, 44
choking, 51
cholera, 114
cholesterol, 49, 78
chromosomes, 162
chyme, 54, 55, 58
cigarettes
and cancer, 120
cilia, 92, 96, 110
circulation, 66
circulation of blood, 76–77
circulatory system, 18, 36, 66–67, 78, 104
closed, 66
in fighting disease, 110–111

jobs of, 66
cirrhosis, 150, 151
clavicle, 20
closed circulatory system, 66
closed fractures, 22
clotting, 42, 72–73
cocaine, 148
cochlea, 140
coma, 148
common cold, 118
compact bone, 22
complex carbohydrates, 38
compounds, 45
concussion, 131
cones, 138
connective tissue, 16, 21
contagious, 114
contagious disease, 159
cornea, 138
coronary arteries, 77–78
cowpox, 113, 122
crack, 148
cranium, 20
crown, 52
Curie, Marie, 122
cyst, 157

D

Dam, Henrik, 43
deafness, 141
decibel, 141
decomposition reaction, 58
deep brain stimulation, 121
defibrillator, 81
deficiency disease, 42–44
de Graaf, Reinier, 161
dehydration, 104–105
delivery, 165
dendrites, 128–129
dental hygienist, 53
dentin, 52
dentist, 53
deoxyhemoglobin, 77
deoxyribonucleic acid (DNA), testing mummy, 17
depressants, 148–149, 150
dermis, 102, 103
diabetes, 121
insulin for, 145
dialysis, 101
diaphragm, 88, 90
diet, balanced, 48–49, 169
diffusion, 58
digestion, 37, 40, 44, 50–53, 55, 131
chemical, 52, 54, 56, 58
mechanical, 52, 54
process of, 52–53
in small intestine, 56
in stomach, 54
digestive juices, 56
digestive system, 18, 36–37, 50–51, 57, 59, 143
in fighting disease, 110
parts of, 50
digestive tract, 50, 51
diseases, 72, 113, 119
bacterial, 114
cardiovascular, 80
contagious, 159
defense systems for, 110–111
deficiency, 42, 44
impact on society, 122–123
noninfectious, 120–121
resisting, 112
sexually transmitted, 159
viral, 118–119, 126
doctors , 19, 32, 69
Doisy, Edward, 43
Down syndrome, 31
Drew, Charles, 67
Drug Abuse Resistance Education (DARE), 149
drugs, 148
misuse of, 148
ducts, 142

E

eardrum, 140
ears, 130, 134, 140–141, 168
eating disorders, 49
Ebola Fever, 109
eggs, 156, 157, 163
cells, 160, 162
mature, 162
electrocardiogram, 80
electron microscope, 118
elements, 45
Elion, Gertrude Belle, 123
embryo, 164, 166
emphysema, 96
emulsification, 56
enamel, 52
endocrine glands, 142, 144
endocrine system, 18–19, 36, 104, 142–143
job of, 143
endoplasmic reticulum, 40
endoskeleton, 20
energy, 38, 58, 60, 98
turning nutrients into, 60
enzymes, 40–41, 52, 56, 58, 163
epidermis, 102
epididymis, 158
epiglottis, 50, 86
epithelial tissue, 16
esophagus, 50–51, 54
estrogen, 144, 145, 156
ethyl alcohol, 150
evaporation, 102, 103
excretion, 85, 98
of urine, 101
excretory system, 18, 36, 98–99, 104, 159
exercise, 27
exhale, 88
exhaled air, 95
exhaling, 88–89
exocrine glands, 142
exoskeleton, 20
extensors, 26
external respiration, 88
extracorporeal shock wave therapy, 32
eyelashes, 139
eyelids, 139
eyes, 130, 134, 138, 168
parts of, 138
protecting, 139

F

fats, 38, 42–43, 49, 56, 58
fat-soluble vitamins, 42
female reproductive system, 156–157
femoral artery, 77
femur, 22
fertilization, 162–163, 164, 166
chemicals involved in, 163
fetal development, 166–167
fetus, 164, 165, 166, 168
fever, 104
fight or flee response, 143
fixed joints, 24
Fleming, Alexander, 114, 123
flexors, 26
flu, 118, 126
folk medicine, 122
Food Guide Pyramid, 48–49
food labels, reading, 48
foods, 76, 98
contaminated, 116
measuring energy, 60–61
transport of, 66
undigested, 99
formaldehyde, 96
fractures, 22
frequency, 141
functional electrical stimulation, 133

G

gallbladder, 50, 56, 58
gametes, 162
gas exchange, 94–95
gastric juices, 54, 55, 58
germs, identifying, 111, 114
germ theory, 114, 122
glands, 18, 19, 128, 142, 144
endocrine, 142
exocrine, 142
pituitary, 143–144
gliding joints, 24
glucose, 60, 131
goiter, 44
gonorrhea, 159
Graafian follicles, 161
growth hormone, 144

H

hair follicles, 103
hairline fracture, 22
hallucinogens, 148, 149
hearing, 140–141
hearing aids, 141
heart, 18, 27, 66, 76, 101, 164
artificial, 67, 80–81
blood flow in, 68
lung circulation and, 76
parts of, 68–69
transplant, 123
heart attack, 78, 143
heartbeat, 18, 68–69, 80, 131, 148
heart disease, 49, 78–79, 80–81, 87, 96–97
heart valves, 68–69
heat exhaustion, 104
heat illness, 104
heat stroke, 104–105
hemoglobin, 66, 72
iron in, 77
hepatitis, 118, 126
hertz, 141
high blood pressure, 71
high-density lipoproteins (HDLs), 49
hinge joints, 24
histinine acid, 40
hormones, 66, 72, 144–145, 158, 160, 161, 165
and cancer, 120
jobs of, 144
reproductive, 145, 169
human development, stages of, 168–169
human embryo, development of, 164–165
human gametes, 162
Human Genome Project, 123
human immunodeficiency virus (HIV), 118, 119, 159. *See also* acquired immunodeficiency syndrome (AIDS).
hydrochloric acid, 44, 54, 58, 110
hydrogen, 40, 41
hypothalamus, 142, 143, 144

I

imaging technology, 146
immune system, 18, 36, 111, 112, 120, 159
immunity, 112–113, 119
acquired, 112
active acquired, 112
natural, 112
passive acquired, 112–113

implantation, 164
incisors, 52
infancy, 168
influenza (flu), 118, 126
inhalants, 148, 149
inhale, 88
inhaling, 88
innate behaviors, 168
inorganic compounds, 45
insulation, 38
insulin, 144
treating diabetes with, 121, 145
internal respiration, 88
intravenous drugs, transmission of acquired immunodeficiency syndrome by, 118–119
involuntary muscle, 30
iodine, 44
iris, 138
iron, 44
in hemoglobin, 77
isoleucine acid, 40

J

Jenner, Edward, 113, 122
joints, 15, 24–25, 32
kinds of, 24

K

Kelly, Joelle, 31
kidneys, 72, 98–101, 104, 149
response, 104
kidney stones, using sound to break apart, 99
knee, 17, 21
Koch, Robert, 114

L

labor, 165
laparoscopy, 157
large intestine, 50, 57, 98–99
larynx, 86, 97
lasers, 32
and eye surgery, 170
later years, 169
laxatives, 49
Leeuwenhoek, Anton van, 161
lens, 138
leucine acid, 40
leukemia, 23, 97
leukemia drug, 123
life cycle, 168
technology and, 170–171
life processes, 98
ligaments, 16–17, 24
lipase, 58
lithotripsy, 99
liver, 50, 56, 100, 149
low-density lipoproteins (LDLs), 49
lung cancer, 97, 120
lungs, 72, 76–77, 86, 87, 92–93, 96, 98, 110
diseases, 97
Lyme disease, 114
lymphatic system, 111–112
in fighting disease, 111
lymph nodes, 111
lymphocytes, 111
lymph vessels, 111
lysergic acid diethylamide (LSD), 149
lysine acid, 40

M

magnesium, 44
magnetic resonance imaging (MRI), 33, 131
male reproductive system, 158–159
malignant tumors, 120
malnutrition, 48, 49
mammograms, 170
marijuana, 149
marrow, 22
matter, 58
measles, 113, 118, 126
mechanical digestion, 52, 54
mechanical heart, 60
medical technology, 32
medicines, 148
medulla, 130, 131
meiosis, 162
melatonin, 144
memory loss, 120
menopause, 168, 169
menstrual cycle, 156, 160–161
menstruation, 160, 169
methanol, 96
methionine acid, 40
microorganisms, 66, 72, 116
microscope, 161
minerals, 44–46, 72, 99
uses of, 44
miner's asthma, 93
mitochondria, 60
mitosis, 164
molars, 52
molecules, 40, 57–58, 60, 135
protein, 40
mouth, 52, 56, 110
mouthwash, 116
movable joints, 24
mucus, 51, 58, 92, 110
mumps, 113, 118, 126
muscles, 15–16, 26–27, 38, 42, 45, 128, 130, 133, 168
actions of, 26
cardiac, 30
involuntary, 30
movement, 28–29
skeletal, 30
smooth, 30
striated, 30
tissue of, 16
muscular system, 18, 26–27, 36
myelin, 149
myopia, 139

N

narcotics, 148
natural immunity, 112
nephrons, 100–101
nerve cells, 128–129, 132
nerves, 42, 45, 128
nerve tissue, 17
nervous system, 18, 36, 128–129, 168
central, 128, 148
neural stem cells, 121
neurons, 128
nicotine, 96
night blindness, 42
Nightingale, Florence, 122
nitrogen, 40–41
nitrogen compounds, 98
Nixon, Richard, 98
noninfectious diseases, 120–121
nose, 86, 92–93, 110, 130, 135
nutrients, 37–39, 48, 69, 72
testing foods for, 46–47
turning, into energy, 60
nutrition, 37
nutritionists, 45

O

odor receptors, 135
oils, 38, 49, 56
open fractures, 22
open-heart surgery, 80
optical illusions, 139
optic nerve, 138
oral surgery, 53
organic compounds, 45
organs, 18, 144
donated, 123
plant, 19
transplants of, 19, 123
organ systems, 18, 36
organ transplants, 19, 123
osteoporosis, 45
ovarian cysts, treatment of, 157
ovaries, 144–145, 156, 157, 160, 162
over-the-counter drugs, 148
oviduct, 156, 157, 160, 162
ovulation, 160–162, 169
oxidation, 44, 77
oxygen, 40, 41, 69, 72, 74, 76–79, 88, 98
in the air, 94
monitors, 87
in respiratory system, 86, 94–95
transport of, 66
oxyhemoglobin, 77

P

pacemakers, 79
painkillers, 148
pain receptors, 135
pancreas, 50, 56, 58, 121, 144–145
pancreatic amylase, 58
pancreatic duct, 56
pancreatic juices, 58
paralysis, 133
parathyroid gland, 144
parathyroid hormone, 144
Parkinson's disease (PD), research on, 121
partial deafness, 141
partly movable joints, 24
passive acquired immunity, 112–113
Pasteur, Louis, 114, 122–123
pathogens, 110–111, 112–113, 159
PCP, 149
pellagra, 42
penicillin, 114–115, 122–123, 159
penis, 159
pepsin, 54, 58
peptide bonds, 41
periosteum, 22
peristalsis, 50, 51, 56
perspiration, 102, 103, 142
phagocyte, 110–111, 112
pharynx, 50
phenylalanine acid, 40
phosphorus, 44
physical therapists, 31
pineal gland, 144
pitch, 141
pituitary gland, 143–144, 161
pivotal joints, 24
placenta, 164, 165
plant organs, 19
plaque, 49, 53, 80
plasma, 67, 72, 74, 104
platelets, 72–74
poisoning, 149
Salmonella, 114
polio, 113
vaccine for, 123
pores, 102, 103
positron emission tomography (PET), 131
potassium, 44
pregnancy, 165–166
premature birth, 170
prenatal ultrasound, 170
prescription drugs, 148
pressure receptors, 135
progesterone, 144–145, 156
protection, 66
protein molecules, 40

proteins, 38, 46, 52, 56, 58, 100, 160
importance of, 40–41
protein synthesis, 40
puberty, 160, 169
pulmonary artery, 76
pulmonary veins, 76–77
pulse, 70–71
pupils, 138

Q

quartz dust, 93

R

radiation treatments, 23
rapid breathing, 105, 143, 148
reactions, observing, 132
receptors, 132
pain, 135
pressure, 135
touch, 135
rectum, 50, 57, 99
red blood cells, 22, 72–73, 74, 77, 94
red bone marrow, 22
reflex arc, 132–133
reflexes, 132–133
relative age, 94
renal artery, 77
reproductive hormones, 145
reproductive organs, 169
reproductive system, 18, 36
female, 156–157, 160
male, 158–159, 160
resistance, 115
respiration, 85, 88
respiratory system, 18, 36, 86–87, 92–93, 108
in fighting disease, 110
protecting, 93
respiratory therapist, 87
responses, 132
retina, 138, 170
rickets, 42
RNA virus, 119
robotics, 81
rocks, 45
rods, 138
rotator cuff, 33

S

St. Martin, Alexis, 55
saliva, 50, 52
Salk, Jonas, 122–123
Salmonella poisoning, 114
salts, 98, 100, 104
screening tests, 170
scrotum, 158
scurvy, 42
secondhand smoke, 97
sense organs, 127, 130, 134–135, 169
septum, 68
serving size, 48
serum, 114
sexually transmitted diseases, 159
simple carbohydrates, 38
Sittig, Steven, 87
skeletal muscle, 30
skeletal system, 18, 20, 36
skeletons, 15, 20
skin, 16, 98, 102–103, 104, 130, 134–135, 142
disorders of, 42
in fighting disease, 110
skin cancer, 121
skull, 20
small intestine, 50, 56–58, 98
absorption in, 57
digestion in, 56
smallpox, 113
vaccine for, 122
smell, 135
smoking, 96–97
and cancer, 120
smooth muscle, 30
sneeze, 92
sodium, 44–45
sodium chloride, 44–45
sonogram, 157
sound
animals and, 141
frequency of, 141
pitch of, 141
sound waves, 140–141
speech development, 169
sperm, 158, 159, 163
sperm cells, 162
spinal cord, 20, 128, 131–133, 164, 168
spinal injuries, treating, with bionics, 133
spongy bone, 22
sports injuries, treating, 32–33
starches, 38, 46, 56, 58
testing for, 39
stem cells, neural, 121
sternum, 20, 68
stethoscope, 68
stimulants, 96, 148–150
stimulus, 132
stomach, 50, 54–55, 56, 58
chemical digestion in, 54
strep throat, 114
stress, 143
striated muscles, 30
strokes, diagnosing, 131
sugars, 38, 46, 52, 60, 144
sunlight
and cancer, 120
surgeons, 69
sweat, 105
sweat glands, 103
synapses, 128, 129
synthesis reaction, 58
syphilis, 159

T

target cells, 144
tars, 96
taste buds, 134, 136
taste receptors, identifying, 136–137
T cells, 111–112, 119
technology
life cycle and, 170–171
in treating cardiovascular disease, 80–81
teeth, 42, 52
temperature
regulation of, 66
tendons, 16, 26
testes, 144–145, 158
testosterone, 144–145, 158
tetanus, 114
threonine acid, 40
throat, 86, 92
thymosin, 144
thymus gland, 144
thyroid gland, 144
thyroxine, 144
tissues, 16, 118, 144
connective, 16
fluid, 72
epithelial, 16
muscle, 16
nerve, 17
testing mummy, 17
tobacco, 96–97
tongue, 52, 130, 134
tooth decay, 53
touch, 135
touch receptors, 129, 135
trachea, 86, 92–93
transfusions, 67, 72, 73, 118
transplants
bone marrow, 23
heart, 123
organ, 19, 123
trauma, 32
triceps, 26, 29
trytophane acid, 40
tuberculosis, 114
tumors, 120, 151
benign, 120
diagnosing, 131
malignant, 120

U

ulcer, 55
ultrasound, 32, 80, 99, 170
prenatal, 170
umbilical cord, 164, 165
urea, 100
ureters, 98
urethra, 98, 158, 159
urine, 100
excretion of, 101, 159
uterus, 156, 157, 160, 164–165

V

vaccines, 113, 119, 170
polio, 122–123
smallpox, 122
vagina, 156, 157, 162, 163, 165
valine acid, 40
valves
in heart, 68–69
veins, 66, 70, 77
ventricles, 68, 76–77
vertebrae, 20
vibration, 141, 146
villi, 56, 57, 99
viral diseases, 118–119, 126
viruses, 104, 110, 115, 118, 159
and cancer, 120
mutations, 119
vision, 138–139
vitamin A, 42
vitamin B_1 (thiamin), 42
vitamin B_2 (riboflavin), 42
vitamin B_3 (niacin), 42
vitamin C, 42
vitamin D, 42
vitamin E, 42
vitamin K, 42–43
vitamins, 38, 42–43, 46
classifying, 42
fat-soluble, 42
importance of, 42
water-soluble, 42
vocal cords, 86

W

warm-blooded animals, 66
warts, 118
waste products, 65, 72, 98, 103–104
of cellular respiration, 60
forming, 98
transport of, 66
water, 39, 41, 57, 58, 86, 98–99, 100
water-soluble vitamins, 42
white blood cells, 66, 72–74, 110–111, 112–113, 118
windpipe, 50, 86, 92

X

X-ray machines, 32
X-rays, 22, 32, 37, 53, 55, 81, 99, 131
and cancer, 120

Y

yellow fever, 118
yellow bone marrow, 22

Z

zinc, 44
zygote, 162–164, 166

Photo Credits

Photography Credits: All photographs are by the Pearson Learning Group (PLG), John Serafin for PLG, and David Mager for PLG, except as noted below.

Cover: *bkgd.* Bernardo Bucci/Corbis; *inset* Mehau Kulyk/Science Photo Library/Photo Researchers, Inc.

Table of Contents: iii: t G. W. Willis/Animals Animals/Earth Scenes; iii: b Prof. P. Motta/Dept. of Anatomy/University La Sapienza, Rome/Science Photo Library/Photo Researchers, Inc.; iv: b Dr. Linda Stannard/Science Photo Library/Photo Researchers, Inc.; v: ISM/Phototake

Frontmatter: P001 l Susan Leavines/Science Source/Photo Researchers, Inc.; P001 r William Lampas/Omni-Photo Communications; P001 t David Julian/Phototake; P002 l John Pontier/Animals Animals/Earth Scenes; P002 r Michael Bisceglie/Animals Animals/Earth Scenes; P003 Ventura Educational Systems; P003 Siede Preis/Getty Images; P005 r Siede Preis/Getty Images; P007 r Siede Preis/Getty Images; P009 bl American Museum of Natural History/Dorling Kindersley Limited; P009 br Dr. Michael Howell; P009 tk Phil Degginger/Color-Pic, Inc.; P009 r Siede Preis/Getty Images; P010 Jim Zipp/Photo Researchers, Inc.; P011 r Siede Preis/Getty Images; P013 r Siede Preis/Getty Images

Chapter 1: P15 Bohemian Nomad Picturemakers/Corbis; P16 l W. H. Fahrenbach/Visuals Unlimited, Inc.; P16 m Carolina Biological/Visuals Unlimited, Inc.; P16 r Dr. Michael Klein/Peter Arnold, Inc.; P17 Tom & Therisa Stack/Tom Stack & Associates; P19 Custom Medical Stock Photo; P21 l CNRI/Science Photo Library/Photo Researchers, Inc.; P21 r CNRI/Science Photo Library/Photo Researchers, Inc.; P22 A. & F. Michler/Peter Arnold, Inc.; P23 Manfred Kage/Peter Arnold, Inc.; P24 Agence France Presse/Corbis; P30 br Manfred Kage/Peter Arnold, Inc.; P30 l G. W. Willis/Visuals Unlimited, Inc.; P30 tr G. W. Willis/Animals Animals/Earth Scenes; P31 Joelle Kelly; P32 b Chris Trotman/Duomo /Corbis; P32 b inset Photo Researchers, Inc.; P32 t Jean Marc Barey/Angence Vandystadt/Photo Researchers, Inc.; P32 t inset Thor International, Ltd.; P33 b Bob Daemmrich/Stock, Boston, Inc.; P33 b inset Courtesy of Bayshore Health Group Clinical Division, Canada; P33 t Bohemian Nomad Picturemakers/Corbis; P33 t inset SIU Biomend Comm./Custom Medical Stock Photo; P34 Bohemian Nomad Picturemakers/Corbis; P35 Bohemian Nomad Picturemakers/Corbis; P36 Bohemian Nomad Picturemakers/Corbis

Chapter 2: P37 Susan Leavines/Science Source/Photo Researchers, Inc.; P38 l Charles D. Winters/Photo Researchers, Inc.; P38 r E. R. Degginger/Animals Animals/Earth Scenes; P39 Ken Karp/Omni-Photo Communications; P43 Michael Newman/PhotoEdit; P45 Pascal Goetgheluck/Science Photo Library/Photo Researchers, Inc.; P49 Professor P. M. Motta, G. Macchiarelli, S. A. Nottola/Science Photo Library/Photo Researchers, Inc.; P53 Steve Jay Crise/Corbis; P55 Bettmann Archive/Corbis; P57 Prof. P. Motta/Dept. of Anatomy/University La Sapienza, Rome/Science Photo Library/Photo Researchers, Inc.; P60 Martha Cooper/Peter Arnold, Inc.; P62 Susan Leavines/Science Source/Photo Researchers, Inc.; P63 Susan Leavines/Science Source/Photo Researchers, Inc.; P64 Susan Leavines/Science Source/Photo Researchers, Inc.

Chapter 3: P65 Steve Lissau/Rainbow; P67 Charles Drew Papers/Moorland-Spingarn Research Center Howard University; P69 Layne Kennedy/Corbis; P70 l Carolina Biological/Visuals Unlimited, Inc.; P70 r Carolina Biological/Visuals Unlimited, Inc.; P71 Ed Reschke/Peter Arnold, Inc.; P72 l Dorling Kindersley Limited; P72 r Manfred Kage/Peter Arnold, Inc.; P74 b Manfred Kage/Peter Arnold, Inc.; P74 t G. W. Willis, MD/Visuals Unlimited, Inc.; P75 Carolina Biological Supply Co./Phototake; P77 Leonard Lessin/Peter Arnold, Inc.; P78 b Biodisc/Visuals Unlimited, Inc.; P78 t Carolina Biological/Visuals Unlimited, Inc.; P79 Mark Blum, M.D.; P80 b Doug Martin/Photo Researchers, Inc.; P80 t John Sommers/Timepix; P81 bl Mehau Kulyk/Science Photo Library/Photo Researchers, Inc.; P81 r Michal Heron/Pearson Education/PH College; P81 tl Simon Fraser/Science Photo Library/Photo Researchers, Inc.; P82 Steve Lissau/Rainbow; P83 Steve Lissau/Rainbow; P84 Steve Lissau/Rainbow

Chapter 4: P85 John Beatty/Getty Images; P87 Steven Sittig/Mayo Clinic; P92 Prof. P. Motta/Dept. of Anatomy/University "La Sapienza," Rome/Science Photo Library/Photo Researchers, Inc.; P93 David Burnett/Contact Press Images/Picturequest; P96 l James Stevenson/Science Photo Library/Photo Researchers, Inc.; P96 r James Stevenson/Science Photo Library/Photo Researchers, Inc.; P99 Susan Leavines/Photo Researchers, Inc.; P100 Alfred Pasieka/Science Photo Library/Photo Researchers, Inc.; P101 Richard T. Nowitz/Science Source/Photo Researchers, Inc.; P102 Lester V. Bergman/Corbis; P103 b Veronika Burmeister/Visuals Unlimited, Inc.; P103 t Bob Daemmrich/The Image Works; P104 Bob Daemmrich/The Image Works; P105 tr Corbis Digital Stock; P105 bl Alfred Pasieka/Science Photo Library/Photo Researchers, Inc.; P106 John Beatty/Getty Images; P107 John Beatty/Getty Images; P108 John Beatty/Getty Images

Chapter 5: P109 Barry Dowsett/Science Photo Library/Photo Researchers, Inc.; P110 l David M. Phillips/Photo Researchers, Inc.; P110 r Dr. Dennis Kunkel/Phototake; P113 Dr. Stanley Burns/Peter Arnold, Inc.; P115 American Museum of Natural History/Dorling Kindersley Limited; P118 l Dr. Linda Stannard/Science Photo Library/Photo Researchers, Inc.; P118 r NIBSC/Science Photo Library/Photo Researchers, Inc.; P119 Will & Deni McIntyre/Photo Researchers, Inc.; P120 l Jean Claude Revy/Phototake; P120 r NIH/Science Source/Photo Researchers, Inc.; P121 David Leah/Science Photo Library/Photo Researchers, Inc.; P122 bl Dr. Stanley Burns/Peter Arnold, Inc. P122 br American Museum of Natural History/Dorling Kindersley Limited; P122 tl Archive Photos; P122 tm Bridgeman Art Library; P123 tl Will & Deni McIntyre/Photo Researchers, Inc.; P123 bl American Museum of Natural History/Dorling Kindersley Limited; P123 br NIBSC/Science Photo Library/Photo Researchers, Inc.; P124 Barry Dowsett/Science Photo Library/Photo Researchers, Inc.; P125 Barry Dowsett/Science Photo Library/Photo Researchers, Inc.; P126 Barry Dowsett/Science Photo Library/Photo Researchers, Inc.

Chapter 6: P127 Richard Hamilton Smith/Corbis; P130 Corbis Digital Stock; P131 Roger Ressmeyer/Corbis; P132 Damien Lovegrove/Science Photo Library/Photo Researchers, Inc.; P133 PhotoDisc, Inc.; P134 John D. Cunningham/Visuals Unlimited, Inc.; P135 b Royalty Free/Corbis; P135 t Peter Holden/Visuals Unlimited, Inc.; P145 National Library of Medicine; P146 b Jules Frazier/PhotoDisc, Inc.; P146 t Jack Parsons/Omni-Photo Communications; P147 b Richard Hamilton Smith/Corbis; P147 m The Granger Collection New York/The Granger Collection; P147 t John Rizzo Studio, Inc./Foodpix; P150 Bill Beatty/Visuals Unlimited, Inc.; P151 l E. R. Degginger/Animals Animals/Earth Scenes; P151 m O.J. Staats, M.D./Custom Medical Stock Photo; P151 r Custom Medical Stock Photo; P152 Richard Hamilton Smith/Corbis; P153 Richard Hamilton Smith/Corbis; P154 Richard Hamilton Smith/Corbis

Chapter 7: P155 ISM/Phototake; P156 D. Bromhall OSF/Animals Animals/Earth Scenes; P157 Biomedical Communications/Peter Arnold, Inc.; P158 David M. Phillips/Visuals Unlimited, Inc.; P159 Science Photo Library/Custom Medical Stock Photo; P161 Carolina Biological Supply Company/Phototake; P162 Yorgas Nikas/Getty Images; P163 br David M. Phillips/Photo Researchers, Inc.; P163 ml Dr. Yorgos Nikas/Phototake; P163 mr Dr. Nikas/Jason Burns/Phototake; P163 tl Dr. Yorgos Nikas/Science Photo Library/Photo Researchers, Inc.; P163 tr Dr. Yorgos Nikas/Phototake; P164 Petit Format/Nestle/Science Source/Photo Researchers, Inc.; P168 Elizabeth Holmes/Omni-Photo Communications; P169 George & Judy Manna/Photo Researchers, Inc.; P170 b Alexander Tsiaras/Science Course/Photo Researchers, Inc.; P170 m Bob Krist/Corbis; P170 t Sovereign/Phototake; P171 b ER Productions/Corbis; P171 inset SIU BIOMED/Custom Medical Stock Photography; P171 tl Popshots/Omni-Photo Communications; P171 tr Neal Graham/Omni-Photo Communications; P172 ISM/Phototake; P173 ISM/Phototake; P174 ISM/Phototake